HARVARD HISTORICAL STUDIES • 184

Published under the auspices of the
Department of History

from the income of the
Paul Revere Frothingham Bequest
Robert Louis Stroock Fund
Henry Warren Torrey Fund

NATIVE TONGUES

*Colonialism and Race
from Encounter to the Reservation*

SEAN P. HARVEY

Harvard University Press

Cambridge, Massachusetts & London, England

2015

Copyright © 2015 by the President and Fellows of Harvard College
All rights reserved
Printed in the United States of America

First Printing

Cataloging-in-Publication Data available from the Library of Congress

ISBN: 978-0-674-28993-2 (alk. paper)

Contents

Introduction   1

1   Language Encounters and the "Mind of Man,   19
    while in the Savage State"

2   Descent and Relations   49

3   Much More Fertile Than Commonly Supposed   80

4   Four Clicks, Two Gutturals, and a Nasal   113

5   The Unchangeable Character of the "Indian Mind"   145

6   Of Blood and Language   182

    Epilogue   220

    Abbreviations   227
    Notes   235
    Acknowledgments   319
    Index   321

Native Tongues

Introduction

Language was a crucial line of difference in the eighteenth and nineteenth centuries, and it played an important role in colonialism. Some heard race itself in the words and ways of speech of others. After hearing Eastern Abenaki while traveling through what he called Maine, Henry David Thoreau remarked, "There can be no more startling evidence of their being a distinct and comparatively aboriginal race, than to hear this unaltered Indian language, which the white man cannot speak nor understand." He was attentive to the physical features of Native speakers, who included Joe Aitteon and Tahmunt Swasen, and he collected a number of archaeological artifacts; but audible experience was immediate and more significant. Thoreau knew, of course, that languages could be learned. A few years later, perusing an Abenaki dictionary—compiled by a missionary in the early eighteenth century and published by a philologist more than a century later—Thoreau admitted that it allowed him to see Abenakis "from a new point of view." That vantage allowed him to glimpse a path, "as it were threading the woods between our towns still, and yet we can never tread its trail." Encounters with Native languages, in speech and through philology, prompted deep consideration of the significance of human diversity.[1]

While people today might distinguish a biological category of race from spoken language, others would still insist that they can hear "race." Speech in some ways defies the distinction between nature and nurture: an immaterial production of physical organs, a faculty shared by all human beings in forms that differentiate one community from another, an acquired cultural trait usually passed on from parents to children. These problems have long been observed, and whether to define language as a social, political, or racial category (among others) has long been debated. Theorization about language, like the examination of human beings' physical features or ways of life, has occurred within a constant tension of recognizing marks of common humanity and signs of human difference. With respect to Native languages, this occurred in a process inextricable from colonization. By the mid-nineteenth century, philology—the study of sounds, words, and grammatical organization— suggested that real, maybe natural, distinctions separated Indians from whites in what sounds their mouths could form and what their minds could think. Such notions were instrumental in justifying and administering colonialism, but they also resonated with some Native people.[2]

Linguistic evidence was central to variegated "inquiries into the origin, progress, and characteristics of the various races of man." In the nineteenth century those inquiries became known as ethnology, though the field emerged from older traditions and practices. The Judeo-Christian tradition fostered an association of nations and tongues that supported the assumption, affirmed by early modern philosophy, that the relatedness of two languages indicated the shared ancestry of their speakers. In the words of Thomas Jefferson, a gentleman scholar who, as president, extended federal efforts to gather linguistic information on Indians, "knowledge of their several languages would be the most certain evidence of their derivation which could be produced." That speech expressed thought was a commonplace, and since knowledge of linguistic difference went hand in hand with European exploration and imperialism, speculation that linguistic difference might indicate intellectual difference was powerful. As the philosophically minded trader Joseph Howse put it, the "mind and moral character . . . can be attained only through the medium of their Language." Indians themselves could also attribute deep significance to speech. His own "Algic race," according to the mid-nineteenth-century Ojibwe historian William W. Warren, "cannot differ more widely than they do in language," from their "mortal enemies," the "Dakota race." The convergence of shifting modes of U.S. colonialism and changing ideas about how human speech contained evidence of genealogies and psychologies, produced a conception of language by the 1820s that became central to an understanding of race that transcended the body and which lasted for most of the century.[3]

Even as some Indians participated in philological and ethnological debates, language study offered a means for diverse U.S. citizens to conceive of and establish control over Native peoples and resources in the late eighteenth and nineteenth centuries. Benjamin S. Barton, an early national scholar, likened himself "to the new settler in the wilderness of our country" because no one before him had attempted a comprehensive study of the "American languages."

The connections between philology and colonialism were more than metaphorical, however, and diverse social groups contributed to, and challenged, knowledge about Native languages. Traders worked toward linguistic facility because it made for good business. The occasional settler or official hoped that intelligibility would provide a means to resolve disputes without violence. Missionaries sought to communicate difficult religious meanings. These and others, both private citizens and those carrying out federally sponsored work (such as military officers or surveyors), provided linguistic materials, while government officials facilitated this work and sought to apply its results in ever more systematic ways. A variety of figures who did no real work on Native languages themselves, moreover, offered extensive commentary, criticisms, and conjectures on philology and its significance as the broader public encountered philology in diverse aspects of the era's expanding print culture. While the methods of linguistic study were abstruse, the questions about Native people that philology engaged were not. Precisely because philologists explained the ways in which language indicated ancestry and mental traits, a combination that some equated to race, language promised the key to answering, in the words of the missionary H. F. Buckner, *"whence came you, and whither are you bound?"*[4]

Diverse motives propelled philology and responses to it, but their trajectories continuously intersected. Scholars, missionaries, and officials pursued goals that were "independent, but not at variance," according to the Indian agent and ethnologist Henry R. Schoolcraft: "Attainments in the one may, interchangeably, precede or follow attainments in the other." The director of the Indian office (the unofficial precursor to the Bureau of Indian Affairs), Thomas L. McKenney, stressed that conducting Indian affairs effectively "requires an intimate knowledge both of the character of the Indian themselves, of their relations with each other, and to the Government and Laws of the United States." Linguistic knowledge best suited those divergent purposes. Though its prestige would later fade, the study of Native languages was an important part of American intellectual life, crucial to understandings of human descent and difference, and an important means of establishing control over Native communities.[5]

One might understand philology in a variety of ways. Bookish scholars, such as Peter S. Du Ponceau, claimed to pursue the "innocent pleasures" of disinterested knowledge. Conversely, Native people occasionally suspected that language study was part of a "wicked design upon their country," as some Mandans did of Lewis and Clark's clumsy efforts to obtain a vocabulary. Neither stark description, however, does full justice to what one finds in learned essays and popular periodicals, traders' and missionaries' journals, official and private correspondence, Native traditions and writings, or the frequently rich front matter and explanatory notes of Native-language texts. The writings of many collectors and philologists convey an unmistakable curiosity, and their efforts to come to a fuller understanding of Native languages than that which their predecessors had achieved was sincere. Several scholars and missionaries also articulated positions on U.S. Indian affairs characterized then as philanthropic, though we must recognize that they benefited from Native dispossession and that the "philanthropy" they advocated amounted to a program of cultural eradication that sought the extinction of Native languages based on ideas that philologists promoted. In addition, the process of translation, the conversion of something Native into terms more useful to Euro-Americans, was fundamental to colonization writ large, and while the need to gather linguistic information admitted the incompleteness of colonialist control, linguistic mastery offered the prospect of deeper knowledge of peoples over whom the United States asserted power. In this respect, it is significant that the federal government continuously collected linguistic material as it tried to extend its influence across the continent, sought land cessions, forced removal, and confined Native peoples to reservations. A spirit of curiosity and an advance in knowledge was perfectly compatible with broader colonialist assumptions and processes.[6]

Philology in many ways resulted from the collision of Euro-American linguistic colonialism and Native consultants' efforts to maintain linguistic sovereignty. Native people, simply curious or seeking useful relationships, repeated words that travelers and traders scratched into word lists. Others explained sounds and grammatical principles to missionaries engaged in evangelistic and educational projects and to secular scholars theorizing about descent and difference. Such participation allowed Native people to shape how Christian concepts would be conveyed to their people and, at least potentially, to influence how Euro-Americans viewed their communities and their way of life. Such actions, moreover, heightened Euro-American knowledge of Native languages' capacity to convey concepts that Euro-Americans associated with "civilization" and bolstered the continuing use of Native languages until the compulsory boarding schools of the late nineteenth century. Just as language was crucial for practical and ideological aspects of colonialism, so too was language central to the maintenance of peoplehood.[7]

The work of Peter S. Du Ponceau (1760–1844), who is both emblematic of nineteenth-century U.S. philology and a pivotal figure for understanding how a racialized conception of Native languages emerged in the 1820s, provides an example of how scholarship that aimed for objectivity (even if it usually fell far short) and depended upon Native people, supported colonialism. He had worked alongside one of the most prominent language philosophers of the eighteenth century as a young man in France, and upon immigrating to the United States, "Patriotick Zeal" pushed this native French speaker to "convince the world that the true, full and correct knowledge of America and all that belongs to it, can only be obtained in and from America." For guidance in his linguistic work, he read widely in colonial narratives and turned to John Heckewelder, a retired missionary active in the American Philosophical Society, for his experience with the Lenni Lenape (Delaware) and for manuscripts that his colleagues had compiled. In Du Ponceau's mind, French moral philosophy and Moravian missionary work had reached the same conclusion. Just as Pierre-Louis Moreau de Maupertuis had proposed that different languages' grammatical organizations represented different "plans of ideas" that channeled thought in particular ways, the German and English speaking David Zeisberger believed that "Whoever will speak Indian must learn to think in Indian." Du Ponceau's philology stressed the difference of the "American languages," but also their beauty, power, and order.[8]

This work had important implications for U.S. colonialism. The new philology inspired a surge in missionary work focused on Native-language evangelization, education, and publishing, partially supported through federal funding, which lasted several decades. While Du Ponceau advocated benevolence, he urged the officials administering U.S. Indian affairs to recognize the importance of linguistic knowledge, and the federal government requested and received his advice regarding the aims and methods of philological collection. At the same time, his work inspired opposition. Lewis Cass, governor and superintendent of Indian affairs in Michigan Territory, directed Indian agents to collect information that would sway legislators and the public during the removal debates that Native languages and Native minds were as "savage" as popularly imagined.

Native knowledge was central to this process. Besides the Native tutors who taught Zeisberger, Heckewelder, and Cass's informants, Du Ponceau relied upon conversations with Native people to test the reliability of old books and aged teachers. Using a seventeenth-century dictionary, he "ventured to ask" two Huron interpreters, Isaac Waler and Robert Armstrong, several philological questions early in his studies. "Amidst its numerous errors and mistakes, which they easily discovered and pointed out, they gladly recognized the language of their own nation," thereby demolishing assertions that the language was in constant flux because it lacked rules. They also gave Du Ponceau "several examples" of verb conjugations, which "fully satisfied" him that "Huron is constructed on the same plan with the other North American languages, and is equally rich and copious." A similar conversation with two

Chickasaws, Martin Colbert (Ibbaryou Klittubbey) and Killpatrick Carter, "convinced" him that the same was true for their language and Choctaw. Du Ponceau's insistence, following early nineteenth-century European trends, that grammatical information was the most certain form of linguistic knowledge, opened a space for Indians to influence scientific debates.[9]

As much as they shaped what Euro-Americans knew of Native languages, however, Native consultants could not control the uses to which that knowledge was put. Their information provided the basis for Du Ponceau's refutation of European philosophers and for his theory that even unrelated American languages possessed common grammatical forms. The surprising (to the minds of Du Ponceau and his readers) beauty and complexity disproved facile notions that the languages of "savage" or "barbarous" people must reflect that condition (which was, basically, taken for granted). Disproving prevailing eighteenth-century developmentalism, however, rested upon the argument that such a grammatical organization did not change over time. The philological participation of native speakers of Iroquoian and Muskogean languages affirmed the positive aesthetic attributes of Native languages that he had found in Algonquian languages; it also lent support to the notion that all Indians shared a single, fixed "plan of ideas" that was radically different from that of any other known peoples. This genealogical and psychological characterization of Native languages earned literary-scientific praise in Europe and set the agenda for Indian philology in the United States.

Previous scholars have touched upon important aspects of this story. Scholarship on early America has shown that even as Euro-Americans and Natives established the means to facilitate exchange and alliance, improved understanding deepened lines of difference amid increasing settlement and its attendant tensions and violence. In countless face-to-face interactions, speech alongside other physical and cultural traits offered a means to perform one's own identity and exaggerate the perceived differences of others.[10] Intellectual histories of early America, moreover, have noted the place of linguistic ideas in broader religious, philosophical, and nationalist frameworks, while studies of Europe and its empires have focused specifically on the relationship of philology within broader debates about human difference.[11] While we have long recognized how certain attitudes about "savagery" and "the Indian" were pervasive among citizens and officials, a wave of more recent scholarship has traced the centrality of knowledge production to colonialism.[12] Just as Native people shaped the terms of economic exchange and diplomatic alliance in most of North America until the mid-nineteenth century, they played crucial roles in the production of Euro-American philosophical and scientific knowledge.[13] That included knowledge of "race," a legal category imposed from without and at times an identity embraced by people who recognized shared traits, experiences, and goals. Discarding the assumption that "race" must always have rested upon biological features, since that is how scientists came to define it, scholars have shown that from the seventeenth century through the nineteenth century the term denoted a genealogical line and an ill-defined bundle of cultural as well as physical traits.[14] Building on this work, this book explores how theories of linguistic difference intersected with ideas about race, attentive both to Native roles in supplying linguistic information and to the role of the U.S. state in seeking and using it. It is a cultural history that demonstrates how genealogical, psychological, and physiological ideas about language not only produced racial notions about Indians but also shaped the administration and experience of colonialism.

Understanding the study of Native languages and its broader significance in the eighteenth and nineteenth centuries, requires following discrete but intersecting trajectories of ideas about language and race in Europe and the United States, broader changes in U.S. social and cultural life, and processes of colonization and resistance in North America.

Native people and Europeans each possess rich traditions that explain and give meaning to linguistic difference. In some Native traditions, migration plays an important role, either because tongues diverged as people separated from one another, as Onondagas tell, or because the arrival and intermixture of one people among others led to a new speech, as Navajos recall. In a Lakota story, when *"Ikce Oyate, the Real People"* emerged from beneath the earth, they discovered that "they had forgotten the language which they spoke before coming through the cave, and they had to invent a new language that no other creature could understand." Where some people imagined language as a human invention, others believed it to be endowed from another. Old Man Coyote's creation of linguistic diversity, for instance, bound Crows closer together and provided a way to gain the honors of war fighting against those one could not understand. While linguistic difference could produce social conflict, it might also be overcome, as in cases of individual adoption or group integration. The Crawfish people, for instance, lived underground without language, until Choctaws captured and incorporated them and taught them to speak. Such stories explain the past, make sense of the present, and prepare those who know them for future encounters.[15]

Europeans have their own traditions, which at the beginning of colonization were mainly classical and scriptural. The ability to communicate reason effectively was the basis for the political life that distinguished human beings from beasts, according to ancient Greeks, and the unmeaning sounds of barbarians, to some, were not truly language at all. Ancient philosophers debated whether language expressed the essences of things or were merely conventional labels, and some even suggested that different peoples, influenced by varying places and climes, created divergent languages. In contrast, in the book of Genesis, human beings were bestowed with speech, but when they endeavored to build a tower that would reach the heavens, God punished their arrogance by confusing the world's tongues and dispersing its nations. Thereafter, even if one learned the language of another people, his mother tongue could betray him (if he tried pronouncing "shibboleth," for example). For Christians, the New Testament miracle of Pentecost represented a temporary, divine dispensation from these divisions and an authorization for preaching the Word in diverse tongues. Early modern Europeans inherited both the classical association of linguistic difference with a lack of civility and the scriptural gloss that it both indicated humanity's moral failings and provided a way to understand human history. The particular uses to which these stories were put were as varied as those who invoked them, but they provided overarching frameworks through which Europeans made sense of linguistic difference, even as scholars studied unfamiliar languages more closely and attempted to refine theories about peoples.[16]

Europeans colonized the Americas in an era that devoted considerable attention to language, rising out of the centralization of kingdoms, the Protestant Reformation, and the Scientific Revolution. Vernacular tongues gained literary and administrative legitimacy at the expense of Latin, while biblical scholars and natural and moral philosophers, bewailed and attempted to neutralize problems of clarity and sincerity seemingly inherent to human communication, inspiring both efforts to restore the unity lost at Babel through the invention or recovery of a universal language and frequent lionization of the attributes of one's own or a distant tongue. Such trends shaped how colonizers experienced non-European languages, and linguistic descriptions from the Americas and elsewhere shaped the learned's understanding of the range of linguistic possibilities. Among the most important philosophical currents to flow from these concerns was John Locke's theory, articulated in the late seventeenth century, that a person's words shape his very thought. This theory, considerably elaborated by Etienne Bonnot de Condillac, gave rise to a variety of philosophical and ethnological projects in the eighteenth century. Some posited universal stages of social development; others theorized about the intellectual and moral character of national lineages. Such views acquired new relevance for notions of race after Sir William Jones discovered the striking resemblance of Sanskrit and Persian to most European languages, and their utter dissimilarity to Semitic languages and Chinese, by demonstrating how the languages of even widely separated peoples might retain evidence of relationships unrecorded by history. Many philologists also fused genealogical and psychological understandings of language, none more influentially in the nineteenth century than Wilhelm von Humboldt, whose study of diverse non-Indo-European languages underlay a comprehensive, but ambiguous, theory about the influence of languages on their speakers' worldviews that was cited in arguments for the different races' separate creations at midcentury and in support of evolutionary views toward century's end.[17]

In the eighteenth century, theories about descent and difference were rarely essentialist. The learned believed that bodies and minds were largely the products of the natural and social environments in which people lived. Human "tongues"—individuals' vocal organs and the languages they articulated—were every bit as malleable as the rest of human beings' physical and mental lives. This produced some anxiety in the minds of those who felt themselves linguistically transformed as a result of their experiences. Peter Fidler, a Hudson's Bay Company trader on an immersive winter hunt, expressed this view after having "dreamed in the Chipewyan Language the first time." As he reflected, "custom is second nature." Environmentalism in natural history and developmentalist theories in moral philosophy, which put forth a stadial progression of human subsistence, institutions, and modes of thought, were two sides of a coin. While there was considerable debate about whether human beings were originally savage and subsequently ascended to civility or whether humanity was created in a civilized state from which it had degenerated over time, most educated Euro-Americans shared the belief that a people's language would reflect their state of society. By the late eighteenth century, however, hazy notions about "savage" or "barbarous" social conditions among the Native peoples of the Americas converged with efforts, following those of Carl Linnaeus and Johann Friedrich Blumenbach, to group diverse populations into continental "races." Physical features provided the primary basis for these classifications, though races were ascribed differing temperaments and abilities as well.[18]

Ideas of "race" grew out of older notions of lineage (a royal line, for instance, or a breed of domesticated animal) and rested upon the notion that physical, intellectual, and moral traits could be inherited. The emphasis upon inheritance rather than environmentalism, which surfaced in notions of the "hereditary heathenism" of Indians and Africans in the seventeenth century and occasionally appeared alongside stadial assumptions in late eighteenth- and early nineteenth-century works, gained prominence in the 1830s to 1850s, with the rise of essentialist understandings of human difference. Many writers, especially but not exclusively physical ethnologists, stressed the fixity of human races, and an influential few even asserted that different races shared no common ancestor with one another. Although few philologists articulated the latter polygenist position, others drew that conclusion from philologists' description of the fundamental difference between the American languages and other known tongues, and many philologists leaned toward an essentialist understanding of particular languages, if not of minds or bodies. Theories of separate creations were undercut in the 1850s by an archaeological "revolution in human time" that extended understandings of human existence thousands of years beyond the scriptural chronology and by the theory of the origin of species through natural selection, which Charles Darwin articulated at the decade's end. Each provided evolutionary assumptions with scientific legitimacy, but the evolutionism that resulted incorporated the polygenists' pessimism regarding social change. All human beings might have shared a common ancestor and way of life in the distant past, but that made human difference seem more historically cemented in light of the continuing assumption that one generation passed on physical, intellectual, and moral traits to its children. The possibility that social evolution required an almost incomprehensibly vast timespan reinforced colonialist ideologies regarding the inevitability of "savage" or "barbarous" peoples "vanishing" in the face of "civilized" settlers and the need to coerce social transformation. Before and after the Darwinian revolution, the cultural and legal power of "race" rested upon its conflation of ancestry and the physical, intellectual, and moral characteristics that supposedly defined all members of a given type.[19]

The development of these ideas was thoroughly intertwined with the history of European imperialism. Philosophers drew from the diverse accounts of explorers, travelers, traders, officials, and missionaries for evidence of how other languages might have been in the past or proof of inherent racial difference. Theories of linguistic relationship could translate to notions of distant kinship to smooth the edges of empire or to descriptions of the migrations and conquests of "savage" hordes that provided colonizers useful ways to depict indigenous history before colonization. Assumptions about how language reflected and shaped thought and about how language indicated descent intertwined with the projects of missionaries and officials who sought means to exercise power through indigenous languages and concerted campaigns to impose European languages on the colonized. The effects of these latter efforts are felt today, as the world's linguistic diversity declines precipitously.[20]

Colonial Americans and U.S. citizens, as well as Native consultants, were central to this intellectual history. Providing linguistic material that would shed light on Indian origins or "savage" or "barbarous" thought provided colonists the means to participate in the literary and scientific currents of the Atlantic world and to win occasional metropolitan recognition. After independence, U.S. scholars undertook "Indian" studies in a complex tangle of cultural nationalism, colonialism vis-à-vis Native people, postcolonialism vis-à-vis Britain, and provinciality vis-à-vis Europe. Defying old power relationships that attempted to confine their role to collecting specimens rather than interpreting their significance, U.S. etymologists and philologists engaged in their own research and theorizing, creating networks of missionaries, Indian agents, and others, with themselves at the center rather than on the margins. In their publications, U.S. scholars asserted unique expertise on Native people. Claims to equal participation in the transatlantic republic of letters, in other words, depended upon the appropriation of Native languages, persons, and cultures.[21]

Despite the interconnection of the United States with Europe and its empires, colonial and U.S. linguistic study differed in important ways. Much of European philology idealized local dialects or distant relatives as expressions of a *volk* intimately rooted in the land. Although claims to a common "American" identity sometimes competed with facile depictions of "savage" enemies in the United States, Native languages did not represent ancestral speech for settlers and their descendants. Instead, U.S. studies of the "American languages" tended toward investigating useful understandings of Native relationships that addressed lines of alliance and hostility, or of "Indian" difference and its implications for Christian conversion or national citizenship. American philologists were in the European mainstream on the question of language and race until the mid-nineteenth century, though without an extended literary record showing how Native languages changed over time, the methods of U.S. philologists necessarily departed from their Continental counterparts. That divergence, combined with a lack of private patronage, also meant that the study of Native languages did not become institutionalized in universities until the end of the nineteenth century, long after chairs in "Oriental" languages had been established in Europe. Before then, there were no "professional" Native-language philologists. Those who successfully claimed the mantle of expertise in Native languages in the United States found institutional bases in learned societies, missionary organizations, and the federal government.[22]

Broader social and cultural themes also shaped U.S. philology. Languages offered means to construct identities in a diverse country, while dreams of spelling reform, a universal character, an "American" language, or a country (even a continent) united in English assuaged U.S. citizens who feared for national cohesion. Literary, religious, and political writers bestowed considerable attention on the nature of language and problems of meaning. By the same token, representations of foreign speech or defective English provided invidious depictions of ethnicity and race. A crucial precondition for the circulation and dissemination of language study and linguistic debates, moreover, was an exploding print culture that provided the varied venues through which scholars pursued and the public encountered philology, which included learned societies' transactions, religious periodicals, literary reviews, addresses before lyceums and mechanics' associations, popular histories and travel accounts, the odd epic poem or captivity narrative, and increasingly, by the mid-nineteenth century, federal publications. Just as elites worked to preserve other aspects of cultural prestige and political influence through extensive voluntary association, linguistic scholars worked to consolidate their philosophical and scientific authority through learned societies. Missionaries' extensive contributions to philology emerged from the outpouring of evangelical energy and donations sparked by the Second Great Awakening. After midcentury, federal patronage became an increasingly important source of support. Throughout the nineteenth century, philologists, like other would-be experts, often found themselves at odds with a democratic populace that asserted its own knowledge.[23]

The American Revolution let loose a torrent of thinking about race, flowing from theories of natural history and moral philosophy as well as popular prejudices, which lasted throughout the nineteenth century. New republican citizens justified Native dispossession and defined membership in the polity through appeals to nature or ongoing natural processes. Besides assigning different racial stereotypes to Indians and African Americans, U.S. citizens defined "race" itself in different ways with respect to those groups. While notions of skin color were most important for defining slavery and citizenship in black and white, U.S. denial of Native sovereignty and claims to control Native peoples, land, and resources rested upon assertions about the deficiency of Native societies. Even a physiologist, such as Charles Caldwell, considered an asserted absence of "civilization" to be a "distinction as characteristic and strong, and much more important, than the differences in the form of their features, and the colour of their skins." A flawed form of language as well as gender norms that transgressed the ostensibly natural roles of Euro-Americans, a supposed lack of agriculture (by men), and spiritual beliefs consistently dismissed as superstition figured prominently in notions of "savagery" or "barbarism." Scholars debated whether such traits were passing or permanent, and philology competed for influence with archaeology, ethnographic attention to customs and beliefs, and studies of skin color, hair, crania, and sexual reproduction. Disputes over methods and conclusions merged with debates over

Indian removal and the federal reservation program as well as debates over abolition and immigration and over the boundaries of citizenship more broadly, as Americans experienced the changes in nature and society that accompanied the market revolution and early industrialization. Those contests, in turn, produced new waves of theorization about evolution, ancestry, and intermixture that often blurred social state and inheritance and in which language remained prominent. As such, "American Ethnology" attracted the attention of policymakers and those wishing to inform popular sentiments. In a popular journal at midcentury Ephraim G. Squier explained, the "study of man physiologically and psychically" offered the "practical solution" to questions about the "capabilities, impulses and ambitions" of "different races and families" and how their "relations may be adjusted to the greatest attainable advantage of both."[24]

The independence and increasing power of the United States rested upon colonialism. Popular government excluded Native people from the polity and opened land through a combination of military force and diplomacy, while squatters who were trying to stay a step ahead of speculators continually pushed the line of settlement beyond what had been negotiated in successive treaties. When Native people retaliated against white provocations or launched preemptive attacks against trespasses, citizens demanded protection against "savage" violence. Decentralized federalism, which allowed the continual expansion of the "empire for liberty," facilitated this process. Settlement led to new territories and states in which ever more white voters in "frontier" regions pushed legislators and officials to respond to their interests, creating popular pressure for land cession treaties (in which U.S. officials exploited Native linguistic differences), removal of eastern Indians across the Mississippi (justified by notions of savagery in which language occupied a prominent place), and increasing confinement on reservations (which, for a time, many officials hoped to create along linguistic lines). By the 1820s, U.S. citizens and courts and legislatures increasingly dismissed Native groups once understood to be "nations," with whom the United States negotiated and broke treaties, as mere "tribes," with which Congress discontinued the treaty process in 1871.[25]

U.S. democratic colonialism, premised upon race, was committed not only to pushing aside Native people and opening resources to whites but also to transforming Native societies through a "civilization" program. Under the Washington administration, the United States sought to encourage Native acculturation in the hopes that land cessions would follow. By the Jefferson administration, officials demanded land cessions that would leave Native "hunters" with no alternative for subsistence but European-style agriculture. In 1819, Congress began annual appropriations, dispensed mainly to religious organizations, for Native education in plow agriculture, domestic arts, Christianity, and literacy. Though English was always the ultimate goal, the U.S. government began supporting Native-language education after philologists had debunked eighteenth-century misperceptions, and it did so for much of the nineteenth century. Support for "civilization" and racial separation grew side-by-side, and most advocates of the Indian Removal Act (1830) insisted that it extended "philanthropic" goals. Similar justifications accompanied the creation of a federal reservation system in the 1840s and the allotment of reservation lands in the 1880s. Racialized evolutionary frameworks, which legitimated power through assertions about "savagery" yielding to "civilization," obscured the cultural and physical violence of these processes.[26]

Casting colonialism in terms of U.S. policies and intentions, or even focusing strictly on the denial of Native sovereignty, does little to convey how diverse Indians experienced colonization, or the cultural innovation, often in pursuit of traditional values and aims, that it produced. At different times and in countless discrete ways, increasing Native reliance on European trade, combined with the effects of epidemic diseases, prompted many to seek beneficial relationships with colonists and adapt white ways selectively. Seeking material means to prosper, Native communities incorporated traders into kinship systems. Some Native people also sought new alliances or new forms of spiritual power through affiliation with missionaries, and these experiences occasionally produced new religious ideas or new tribal or racial identities. These trends, linked as they often were to the increasing presence of settlers, and related cultural, economic, and territorial pressures, produced numerous nativist movements that sought cultural purification and occasionally a pan-Indian identity or militant resistance to expanding settlements ranging from the mid-eighteenth-century Northeast to the late nineteenth-century West.[27]

This history had varied linguistic facets and effects. Indians learned European tongues, Euro-Americans learned Native languages, and multilingual children of traders and captives played prominent roles as unofficial and official interpreters. Colonization resulted in a remarkable degree of linguistic intermixture that provides evidence of close relationships, and in one dramatic instance, a community of individuals with Cree and French ancestry created a "mixed language" called Michif. Missions produced remarkable linguistic projects; it was the most important field for Euro-Americans developing linguistic knowledge. Native tutors (often misleadingly labeled "assistants") provided services that allowed language learning and language transformation, as they and missionaries imported scriptural terms, coined new words, and worked to alter the meaning of old ones in an extensive translation effort. Those Native linguists, seeking spiritual or temporal advantages from missionaries or ethnologists, produced a growing and varied number of Native-language manuscript materials and books designed for Native readers. Importantly, these texts fixed and extended the reach of certain dialects, which diminished dialectical diversity over time. Although nativists often spoke in an idiom of "red" and "white," they also downplayed linguistic difference among Indians, stressed linguistic difference between Indians and Euro-Americans, and occasionally sought to destroy Native-language missionary texts that symbolized a degree of adaptation that they opposed. At the same time, Natives worked to realize the benefits of their own literacies. Sequoyah, who invented a syllabic system for Cherokee around 1820, was only the most striking such example. In addition, Native intellectuals, such as John Summerfield (Ojibwe) and J. N. B. Hewitt (Tuscarora) published their own grammars and philological essays. As one astonished writer observed, "Indians themselves are becoming philologists and grammarians."[28]

By the end of the nineteenth century, the greatest pressures on Native people and their languages came in the form of compulsory boarding schools, the culmination of colonialist intentions to eliminate whatever cultural elements distinguished Native people from whites. Over the opposition of some missionaries, the Bureau of Indian Affairs mandated English-only instruction in 1886. Thereafter, federal teachers prohibited the speaking of Native languages altogether at boarding schools, a rule "rigidly enforced with a hickory rod." The Omaha ethnologist Francis La Flesche, who suffered the violence of linguistic colonialism and co-produced racial knowledge for the Bureau of Ethnology (established 1879), blamed such policies on whites' "ignorance of the Indian's language, of his mode of thought, his beliefs, his ideals, and his native institutions." Yet that does not quite account for it. The vast majority of whites were ignorant of Native languages, but U.S. officials based their efforts to extinguish Native languages on a century of increasing philological knowledge that blended notions of descent and intellectual difference. While La Flesche stressed that it was "all but impossible" to express the "beauty and picturesqueness, and euphonious playfulness, or the gravity of diction" of Native languages, analogous notions of incommensurability suggested that Native languages could not convey the "civilized" content of English or other European languages. Over the course of the century, numerous philologists, missionaries, and officials, aided often inadvertently by Native consultants, constructed a theory of Native languages as genealogically transmitted and unchanging in their psychological traits.[29]

Native Tongues reveals the varied contexts that produced knowledge of Native languages and its social and political repercussions, as Euro-American philosophical and scientific currents changed over time and diverse Native peoples faced territorial and cultural dispossession. The long view and broad sweep of this study is a product of the sources in two ways. First, searchable digital databases have dramatically augmented our access to a range of elite and popular texts, allowing scholars tremendous opportunities to read the words of past writers and the voices they record. Second, these sources reveal scholars, missionary boards, and the federal government endeavoring to extend the reach of their linguistic knowledge. Expanding our field of view allows us to see connections between processes of intellectual debate and shifting forms of colonialism, while close attention to particularly rich episodes provides a more fine-grained texture to language learning, methods of scholarly collection and study, the tenor of public debates, and various attempts to use philology for administrative ends. Aside from the first chapter, which is more thematic than chronological in its sketch of different realms of intercultural communication and divergent misrepresentations of Native languages, each chapter examines a distinct mode of studying Native languages at a specific historical moment and its relevance for a particular aspect of colonialism and changing notions of descent, psychology, and race, while highlighting scholarly exchanges, popular responses, Native roles, and federal efforts to obtain and implement linguistic knowledge.

Eighteenth-century theories that Native languages reflected a particular stage of social and intellectual development replaced older ideas that humanity shared a single universal grammar. Those theories emerged from more than a century of linguistic encounters that accompanied exploration and colonization. Native communication strategies in trade, Native tutoring in missionary work, and Native oratory in treaty councils prompted distinct Euro-American misrepresentations of Native languages, disparate notions that philosophers thereafter molded into a powerful justification for the intellectual and linguistic superiority of "civilized" Europeans and colonists. Early national citizens continued to employ this view of "savage" languages and minds in the early nineteenth century, which reinforced a long tradition of Euro-American commentary on Native linguistic diversity (a diversity that did not correspond to what colonists and later citizens believed to be cultural and physical similarity among Native people). They turned to language, supplemented by Native tradition, to answer questions of Native origins and Native relationships, convinced that a properly designed tool for collection (a vocabulary) could ensure that shared words resulted from common ancestry and not from subsequent interaction. It was a form of inquiry that both demonstrated U.S. citizens' participation in European learning and provided information useful for U.S. expansion. Federal officials were cognizant of linguistic similarities as they sought Native intermediaries to speak on behalf of the United States, and they tried to exploit linguistic difference as they played one Native nation against another in land cession treaties.

Before the philology of the nineteenth century, genealogical and psychological understandings of language existed, but they did not correspond to "race." Refutation of the dominant psychological understanding of "savage" language and thought within a genealogical framework, however, cast the "American languages" as a racial category (whereas, previously, "American languages" had been a geographic or nationalist term), though the precise nature of this racialization was in flux throughout the remainder of the nineteenth century. Du Ponceau's and Heckewelder's work, which first appeared in 1819, coinciding with a Congressional commitment to annual appropriations for Native "civilization" and with the growing use of Sequoyah's syllabary among Cherokees, meant that the new philology inspired a widespread missionary and official commitment to Native-language education that produced significant cross-fertilization among scholarly, missionary, and administrative philology. Euro-Americans experienced consistent frustration at forming Native sounds and finding adequate means of recording them alphabetically, which fostered notions of the distinctness of Native vocal organs at the same time that difficulties in religious translation and participation in European ethnological debates fostered theories of the uniformity, uniqueness, and occasionally the fixity of a Native plan of thought. Language, in other words, evinced racially distinct bodies and minds. Such theories fused with long-held assumptions about language providing a means to trace descent. The philologist-official Henry R. Schoolcraft summed up, "No people take up or lay down a language at will. It descends with their blood." The presence of essays and debates that frequently engaged simultaneous disputes about assimilation, sovereignty, and removal in streams of print extended the circulation of these ideas far beyond the learned, and some philologists deliberately sought to expand the audience for their work. Adding ostensible evidence to these views, a number of federal projects gathered ever more linguistic information from ever more Native peoples as the United States expanded westward.[30]

The expanding knowledge of Native languages, in light of assumptions about the correlation of language and descent, undermined the notion of a homogenous Indian race. As philologists established clearer relationships among certain Native languages, and thus clearer lines of demarcation among others, philology suggested multiple Native races rather than one "Indian" race. According to the federal explorer and philologist Horatio Hale, "distinct families of languages, or independent races" were one and the same. In the aftermath of Indian removal, a number of federal officials hoped to use linguistic classification as the basis for consolidating Native people into convenient administrative units. Native resistance ensured that those plans came to little, and advances in linguistic knowledge, ironically, undermined the administrative usefulness of philology. From midcentury onward, scholars became increasingly aware of grammatical differences among Native languages (though notions of an underlying intellectual similarity persisted). West of the Mississippi, philologists discovered surprising evidence of linguistic affinity, especially among peoples of remarkably varied subsistence, customs, and ostensible levels of advancement. The divergence of language from way of life—amid heated ethnological debates about the possibility of evolution, the shared descent of all human beings, and the most authoritative way to study race (with philology aggressively challenged by physical ethnologists in the 1830s–1850s)—fragmented the conflation of cultural and biological inheritance that had made "race" such a powerful concept. This destabilization of linguistic "race" as a concept was crucial for the emergence of a truly biological understanding of race in the twentieth century.[31]

Native Tongues does more than explain a linguistic facet of the well-known story of how racial ideas hardened over the course of the eighteenth and nineteenth centuries. Communication gave rise to ideas about language. For those who reacted viscerally to unfamiliar sounds and cadences in Indian country and for those who studied words and grammatical forms at a desk, language indicated ancestry and revealed the intellectual and moral characteristics of peoples. At times philological theories reinforced and at other times they undermined notions of race based on the body. In its mingling of cultural and physical traits, language was even more salient than notions of race rooted in the body alone for a settler population asserting power over Native societies. Understanding how these ideas emerged through countless interactions among scholars and missionaries, Native consultants, and U.S. officials deepens our understanding of the complexity of race in the eighteenth and nineteenth centuries and demonstrates the importance of philology and ethnology for the ideological construction and practical administration of colonialism. It also sharpens our awareness of how pernicious even non-biological measures of difference can be today.

1

Language Encounters and the "Mind of Man, while in the Savage State"

Encounters between Indians and Europeans were frequently language encounters. Some Native people thought the languages of the newcomers sounded more bestial than human. To Mi'kmaqs, the Frenchmen's tendency to interrupt and speak over one another sounded like nothing so much as "ducks and geese, which cry out . . . all together." The Iroquois scorned the way Europeans (and Algonquians) formed sounds like *b* and *p*. Reasonably enough, they thought it was "ridiculous that they must shut their Lips to speak." Native people were also sensitive to the different ways the strangers pronounced words, and what Europeans recognized as merely dialectical differences among themselves could seem deeper to Native listeners. In an anecdote from a later writer, but for which it is easy to imagine earlier analogies, Native persons chided diverse English speakers for their inconsistency in naming an increasingly familiar form of livestock. Was it "cow" or "caow"? Native people drew lines that distanced themselves from the strange sounds of Europeans' tongues and chaotic speech practices.[1]

From the moment of initial encounter, Europeans recorded negative impressions of the sounds of Native languages. The earliest Englishmen in Virginia, such as Thomas Harriot and George Percy, heard "chattering strange words" and a cacophony of "noises like so many Wolves or Devils." After more than a century of language learning, Jesuits in New France could be more precise. According to Pierre Francois Xavier de Charlevoix, the "Sioux Indian hisses rather than speaks. The Huron . . . speaks thro' the throat . . . the Algonquin pronounces with a softer tone, and speaks more naturally." In an era when dozens of vernaculars competed in Europe, and when exploration and imperialism led Europeans to encounter a "language of birds" in China and one ostensibly nearer to "Apes, than men" in Africa, Europeans were prepared for diverse languages. Like indigenous North Americans, Europeans were long accustomed to encountering linguistic difference and making invidious comparisons. While language could be but one aspect of a more broadly felt cultural difference, Europeans and Indians often experienced linguistic difference viscerally and occasionally confronted it as an intellectual problem. Articulating the kind of sentiment that grew more common over the course of the eighteenth century, the trader Edward Umfreville alleged that Sarcee, spoken on the western Great Plains, "rather resembles the confused cackling of hens, than the expression of human ideas." Over the course of the eighteenth century, impressions of Native sounds merged with negative views of the developmental progress of Native minds.[2]

Europeans also expressed astonishment at the variety of Indian languages. North America north of Mexico was filled with "an infinity" of languages, in the words of the widely read French officer Baron Lahontan, and numerous commentators echoed Roger Williams in observing the extent to which "their Dialects doe exceedingly differ." Diversity alone was not what Europeans found most disturbing. For one thing, unlike the commercial peoples of the Mediterranean who had adopted the lingua franca, or even in the empires of Mexico or Peru where Nahuatl and Quechua were widely used, North American Indians had "no universal Language amongst them," according to the French priest Louis Hennepin. Linguistic diversity also bore little correlation to what Europeans perceived as considerable similarity in customs among Indians. In the words of Dutch chronicler Johan de Laet, "barbarians being divided into many nations and people, differ much from one another in language though very little in manners." Over time, some commentators stressed the potential for even greater fragmentation. William Stith, for instance, asserted the "Unstableness and vast Mutability of the *Indian* Tongues." Some suspected linguistic diversity of being part of a diabolical plot to foil evangelization, and others considered it to be merely another manifestation of the land's tremendous fecundity, but, by the eighteenth century most interpreted it as a sign of social disorder.[3]

Although Native people and Europeans alike recognized the advantages of intercultural communication, that impulse existed in tension with the perceived importance of maintaining linguistic boundaries. According to an early New England colonist, William Wood, Indians "love any man that can utter his mind in their words." Yet some feared the results of crossing the language line. Despite the importance of the fur trade to his colony and his own dependence upon interpreters for conducting official business, Richard Ingoldesby worried nonetheless about colonists who had "addicted their minds to the Indian language" in late seventeenth-century New York. Language learning could seem a transgression, even a transformation. Titus King, captured by Western Abenakis during the Seven Years' War, recalled that in a mere six months, captive children "Refuess to Speak there own toungue and Seeminly be Holley Swollowed up with the Indians." These were not merely European qualms. After the Moravian missionary David Zeisberger left an Oneida village, where he had been living and learning the language, for an Onondaga village, angry Oneidas reprimanded him for mixing their tongues and having "thus become half an Onondago and half an Oneida." Not only had the languages become mixed, so too had he. Language learning was useful and common, but it demonstrated a permeability of categories that could unsettle Europeans and Natives alike. Language frequently formed an aspect of identity and, amid broader cultural exchange, adaptation, and rivalries, it seemed to possess a power to shape people.[4]

Numerous individuals learned at least bits and pieces of Native languages, many more heard them spoken, and the learned in Europe sought specimens. Besides offering practical advantages, knowledge of Native languages also offered something more to Europeans: deeper knowledge of Native people. As Roger Williams put it in 1643, in the earliest linguistic publication to emerge from English colonization of North America, *A Key into the Language of America,* "happily may unlocke some *Rarities* concerning the *Natives* themselves, not yet discovered." Despite important differences regarding the use of Indian languages, the motives for employing them, and the success at doing so, a wide survey of North American encounters reveals the common challenges facing those who wished to bridge the communication divide and how Native strategies in different forms of interaction shaped Europeans' linguistic knowledge. Focusing on seventeenth- and eighteenth-century trade, missions, and treaties as particular "contact zones" allows us to view the emergence of distinct kinds of ideas about Indian languages and, thus, the social bases for the concept of savagery. Although European philosophers drew upon literature from across the Americas, and from elsewhere in the world, as they theorized models of social development, the British and French scholars who were most important to the formulation of these ideas were particularly attentive to material from their nations' empires. Eventually, U.S. citizens came to inherit both the consequences of these commercial, religious, and diplomatic interactions as well as the theories that undergirded Euro-Americans' claim to the land. Intercultural communication widened a sense of difference regarding language and ways of thinking.[5]

Encountering Native languages in trade, missionary work, and treaties produced different kinds of linguistic ideas. Enterprising Indians, attempting to communicate their commercial wants without compromising their ability to maintain secrecy, often employed lexically limited pidgins, though Europeans were frequently oblivious to this fact. If attracted to the religious ideas of the newcomers, some Indians volunteered their services not only as interpreters but also as tutors to missionaries, conveying the dramatic difference in the organizations of Native and European languages. Powerful Native groups established the terms for diplomacy, which was conducted in highly formal and ritualized modes of discourse that shaped listeners' ideas of the languages' sounds and cadence, beauty and gravitas, regardless of whether they understood the meaning of what was said.

Such encounters produced nearly two centuries of contradictory representations of startlingly diverse "American languages" that ranged from the Amazon to the Arctic. Bits and pieces of Native languages and speechways were part of a tide of information from exploration and colonization that flowed into Europe, prompting a reconsideration of the meaning of human difference. By the mid-eighteenth century, philosophers, enjoying the benefits of empire, pulled promiscuously from these sources and synthesized influential models of the progress of languages and societies through stages. They explained eloquence as a result of linguistic poverty, each manifestating incomplete intellectual development. All rude or uncultivated, "barbarous" or "savage" peoples shared these traits. This set of theories did not paint Indians as possessing inherent and unchanging characteristics, but it provided a framework for understanding a supposedly "savage" mind, based in language, that would be mobilized in support of an essentialist view of "race" in the nineteenth century.[6]

Trade, Pidgins, and Linguistic Poverty

Trade was among the earliest and most important modes of Native–European interaction, with Native people eager to exchange worn furs and newly trapped and processed pelts for the bright, sharp, durable, and lightweight items the newcomers brought with them. Nonverbal behavior, such as gesturing, might make one's meaning known, and it had its place, but the benefits of speech promised fuller intelligibility. Because trade possessed different values for Native and white participants, with one side seeing it in terms of relationship-building gift giving (which brought useful or pleasing items) and the other in terms of sheer economic exchange, being able to express desires and expectations was crucial in an environment in which, according to the writings and word lists of European observers, limited comprehension increased tensions. In southern New England in the early seventeenth century, Roger Williams recorded that trade required "Wisedome, Patience, and Faithfulnesse in dealing: for they frequently say *Cuppánawem*, you lye, *Cuttassokakómme*, you deceive me." Several decades later in New Sweden, John Campanius noted among common phrases, "*Paeaeta, aetticke nijr apitzi bakànta.* Give it to me back again, or else you shall get cut"; "*Ætticke chijr chalebacks chaetti.* I think you are a parasite; you have nothing to live on." Fuller understanding of requests, suggestions, or demands allowed greater precision in exchange and could prevent embers of suspicion or frustration from flaring into violence. Moreover, linguistic skill simply made for good business. Like many before and after him, the mid-eighteenth-century trader James Kenny set about "making a dictionary" for himself as one of his initial tasks. It took some time, but Delawares were "mightly pleas'd" when he demonstrated his commitment to them by having "preferr'd their Tongue in learning most of it." Being able to "converse a little with them" built good will and eventually even trust in a tense environment. Traders needed to under-stand Native people not only as customers for manufactured goods but also as suppliers for beaver furs, and later deerskins and sea otter pelts, and they needed to be able to convey things reliably themselves.[7]

Learning a language, however, was more easily said than done. With luck, one could pick up words here and there by staying close to a ship, fort, or trading post. This was the approach of many of those who engaged in ad hoc exchange as part of their travels. Native curiosity could benefit Europeans in this regard. James Rosier, a gentleman on an English expedition to North America in the early seventeenth century, for instance, picked up the "names of divers things" after trade had concluded for the day, and "when they per-ceived me to note them downe, they would of themselves, fetch fishes, and fruit bushes, and stand by me to see me write their names." Gifts could also grease the wheels of communication. The French missionary Louis Hennepin, nearly a century later, hoped to "gain them by Presents to learn their Language." Others' efforts were foiled. Across the continent at the end of the eighteenth century, William Beresford found the inhabitants "very close and uncommu-nicative." Repeated attempts to learn words earned him only "a sarcastic laugh" or "silent contempt."[8]

Immersion was the most reliable strategy for language learning, but it required Native people to accept and often provide for a stranger. Recognizing potential advantages to such an arrangement, sometimes they agreed. Known to be linguistic sponges, children were occasionally sent to live in Native villages so that they might be useful when they grew older. Fathers sent away sons: Conrad Weiser, an influential trader and interpreter in the Iroquoian–Algonquian–European borderlands in the mid-eighteenth century, acquired his knowledge of Mohawk in this way. And trading firms sent young employees to pick up linguistic skills, as John Long did Mohawk and Ojibwe. Men from Canada to Carolina frequently sought to form close relationships with women who would live with them, dress pelts and skins, provide valuable kinship connections, and teach them Native words and ways. The surveyor John Lawson rarely found British traders "without an *Indian* Female for his Bedfellow," archly reporting that this "correspondence makes them learn the *Indian* Tongue much the sooner." Intimacy could fortify patience and overcome Native reticence to teach their languages to Europeans.[9]

Without immersion or intimacy, language learning was often only partial. Linguistically open-minded and studious traders frequently committed errors, and matters other than simple exchange often stumped them. According to John White, a gentleman traveler on the first English attempt to establish a "Virginia" in what is today North Carolina, "the Natives and English understand so much of one anothers language, as may enable them to trade one with another, and fit them for conference about things that are subject to outward sense" but nothing beyond that. A century later, in the far north, James Isham experienced similar frustration in his attempts to learn Chipewyan, succeeding in "little more than the Names of goods they traffick in," and even these words seemed to have "many meanings." White was a curious and sensitive ethnographic observer, and Isham had already learned the unrelated Cree language from his wife. Limited interactions, however, produced limited learning for each.[10]

Throughout North America, even before European contact, Native people employed pidgins (languages deliberately limited in vocabulary and shorn of most grammatical inflections) and jargons (even simpler modes of speech, often composed of two or more tongues) to facilitate trade. Forms of Pidgin Algonquian that stretched in varying forms from what the newcomers called Virginia to New England and the use of Mobilian Jargon throughout the southeast are the most well-known examples. Those who learned something of actual languages recognized these forms of speech for what they were. The Jesuit missionary Paul Le Jeune, for instance, noticed a "jargon . . . which is neither French nor Savage; and yet when the French use it, they think they are speaking the Savage Tongue, and the Savages, in using it, think they are speaking good French." Another Jesuit, Joseph François Lafitau, described the peoples in this process being "forced, equally on both sides, to approach each other in their own language." This linguistic middle ground allowed some communication, but the result, a form of "speech without rhyme or reason," according to Lafitau, illuminated little besides the "needs of trade or for their common defence." These simplified idioms, which coexisted with and were later supplanted by pidginized European languages, were the most important means of communication available to Indians and Europeans in the early stages of trade and interaction.[11]

Trade and other forms of limited interaction frequently led to learning not a language but a pidgin. Hearing Native people speaking a pidgin or jargon with Europeans, and later speaking their native tongue with their own people, some newcomers speculated that Indians frequently changed their language. In a manner, they did. Other colonists had a surer hold on the linguistic terrain. In his journey to Acadia at the beginning of the seventeenth century, Marc Lescarbot distinguished between a jargon that Mi'kmaqs used to promote "traffic" and another "language of their own, known only to themselves." Mohicans spoke to the Dutch "only in half sentences, shortened words . . . and all things which have only a rude resemblance to each other, they frequently call by the same name." Even those colonists who learned this "made-up childish language . . . and get along well in trade, are nevertheless wholly in the dark and bewildered when they hear the savages talking among themselves." This was not an accident, according to the minister Jonas Michaëlius, for "they rather design to conceal their language from us than to properly communicate it, except in things which happen in daily trade; saying that it is sufficient for us to understand them in that." Perhaps northeastern Natives shared the concerns of counterparts in the Caribbean. The French writer Charles de Rochefort, drawing on the knowledge of a local missionary, suggested that Caribs, seeking "commerce," but "very shie in communicating" their language, "fram'd another bastard-speech" to use with "Christians" because they feared that "to reveal the grounds of their Language . . . might prejudice their Nation." Colonization increased the importance of pidgins and jargons. In addition to providing convenience that could quicken the exchange of furs and skins for goods that promised practical utility and increased power, pidgins and jargons provided what linguists call a "sociolinguistic buffer" against the surveillance and interference of the newcomers. Indians had good reason to share only limited linguistic knowledge, but this strategy had significant ramifications.[12]

Despite the sporadic recognition of seventeenth-century writers that pidgins and jargons were not Native peoples' actual languages, and although the use of pidgins declined in places of long-established and highly concentrated European presence, notions about Indian linguistic poverty persisted throughout the eighteenth century. Antoine-Simone Le Page du Pratz, a literary-minded military officer, noted a "corrupted *Chicasaw* language" in use among Native people near French settlements in Louisiana. Jonathan Carver similarly recognized the prevalence of the closely related Ojibwe and Cree as a lingua franca in the northern fur trade, stretching from the Great Lakes to Hudson's Bay, but he believed that it had words only for the "necessaries or conveniences of life, and to express their wants, which in a state of nature can be but few." On the Pacific coast, Alexander Walker found Nootka Jargon in use and dismissed it as "deficient" and "wanting" in grammatical precision. "A Savage is a Man in a state of infancy," Walker declared, and like children, "these People are at a loss for words to explain their sentiments, particularly on subjects, that were not immediately before their senses." Notions of linguistic poverty owed some of their persistence to widely read ethnographic accounts that focused on those with whom Europeans had only recently made contact through expanding channels of trade. Such trade continued to be the primary site of Native–white interaction west of the Appalachians until the 1780s and for most of the continent west of the Mississippi until the mid-nineteenth century.[13]

Travelers, traders, and others did not always realize that they were taking down or learning languages that had been dumbed down, both for their own benefit and to allow Indians to preserve a desirable cultural distance. This led to dismissive appraisals of a given language's worth, and by the mid-eighteenth century, the learned reinforced such views. Notions of linguistic, and perhaps intellectual, poverty were further elaborated in missions, where other ideas about Indian languages, based on deeper linguistic knowledge, also took shape. Indeed, no zone of contact produced more linguistic knowledge than missions.[14]

Missions, Translation, and Intellectual Difference

Certain kinds of Indians and Europeans—mainly missionaries and those who sought to form relationships with them—deliberately sought to communicate with one another without an interpreter to achieve linguistic understanding deeper than that which a pidgin provided. Colonization produced tremendous change in Native America, from the devastation wrought by the newcomers' diseases to increased violence as Native groups waged war on one another to take captives to bolster declining populations, secure plentiful hunting grounds, and position themselves advantageously vis-à-vis European trade. While missionaries sought conversion, an absolute spiritual transformation, those whom they viewed as potential or actual "converts" sought new forms of spiritual power or expedient alliances with Christians. Many Indians committed themselves sincerely to new faiths and fully grasped their theological complexities, but they also incorporated what they learned into traditional frameworks of belief and practice. Native languages provided a crucial means to convey and shape new religious knowledge.[15]

Learning Native languages united theologically, geographically, and chronologically disparate missionary efforts in North America. The initial missionaries in New France were mainly Franciscan Recollects, but Jesuits came to predominate for more than a century after 1625, eventually scattered from Acadia, across the Great Lakes, and southward to the Illinois country and Louisiana. Puritans established a series of "praying towns" in New England between 1650 and 1675, with some Native Christian communities flourishing. Congregationalists, Presbyterians, and Anglicans all began new efforts in and on the fringes of British colonies in the eighteenth century; however, their success paled next to that of Pietist Moravians in the mid- to late eighteenth century, whose mission villages stretched from western Connecticut to the Ohio country. These sects differed in beliefs and methods, including over the importance of neophytes reading the Bible for themselves, and they often viewed missionaries of other denominations as religious rivals. For all of them, however, success in language learning demonstrated commitment, motives that differentiated them from other Europeans, and, perhaps, spiritual power. Unlike traders, who were often content with scattered words, many missionaries undertook to learn Native languages well enough to preach and convert (they hoped) and perhaps to translate portions of liturgies, scripture, or other books. "Attack[ing] the enemy upon their own ground, with their own weapons,—that is to say, by a knowledge of the Montagnais, Algonquin, and Huron tongues" provided seventeenth-century Jesuits in New France the best means to combat "superstition, error, barbarism, and consequently, sin." Pietist Moravians in the eighteenth-century mid-Atlantic might put it more mildly, conceiving that speaking might open hearts to God's grace, which alone would "translate him out of Death and into Life." For this message, missionaries and interested Natives only reluctantly relied on interpreters, who might "on Purpose give things a different and wrong Turn." Catholic and Protestant (Calvinist and Pietist) missionaries faced common challenges as they worked with Native tutors, reached for an understanding of sounds and syntax, and labored to translate these in ways compatible with Christian faith, however defined, into oral preaching and writings. Often drawing similar conclusions, missionary knowledge created a basis for speculation on Indians' different ways of thinking.[16]

Many Native people seem to have experienced linguistic difference and the Christian message as intertwined challenges. John Eliot's account of Native conversion narratives, descriptions of personal struggles with faith and the eventual experience of grace that Puritans considered necessary evidence of conversion, which were meant to show the progress of the gospel to potential benefactors in England, provide evidence of Native reactions to missionary preaching. Upon hearing the story of Adam and Eve, Monotunkquanit's "heart said, It may be God made English men, but not us poore naked men, as we are of a strange language." Despite missionaries' reassurances, this issue resurfaced repeatedly. An opponent of the missions taunted his countrymen that they "prayed in vaine, because Jesus Christ" was a "stranger" to "*Indian* language," and Waban, a Nipmuck Christian leader, "feared . . . if I prayed to God in our Language, whether could God understand my prayers." Native people attracted to other varieties of Christianity may have felt similar misgivings and hopes.[17]

Whether they found the message or messengers compelling for spiritual or temporal reasons, some Native people became willing teachers in a rigorous education project. Because Jesuit efforts were centralized to a considerable degree, with missionaries in the field sending detailed reports to France, we have an extraordinarily rich record that describes their experiences in trying to learn Native languages. Scattered observations from a variety of other missionary texts also provide evidence of this process. It began with finding a suitable tutor, which was not easy. Traders, for instance, were seldom helpful. Even if they desired to contribute to missionary efforts, and not all did, they tended to be unsuited to the role of instructor. According to Pierre Biard, one of the first Jesuits to attempt to learn Native languages in New France, their knowledge was limited and, lacking classical educations, they "could not impart by rules" what they knew. Indians, for their part, often avoided playing such a role. After spending an afternoon "playing the clown" in his attempts to learn the language, he found himself "deceived, and mocked anew." The "Savages either could not, or would not explain" what was needed. There was not always ambiguity. One Montagnais man repeatedly fed "vile words" to the unwitting Paul Le Jeune, ridiculing a missionary who seemed "haughty" and a "parasite." During a winter's lodging he heard, "at every turn . . . *eca titou, eca titou nama khitirinisin,* 'Shut up, shut up, thou hast no sense.'" At times, according to Jean-Pierre Aulneau, a missionary among the Crees in the early eighteenth century, "what little" missionaries learned "has been picked up in spite of them." Conditions, talent, pride, and occasionally overt opposition conspired against even those clerics who wanted to learn Native languages.[18]

Language learning was difficult work that proceeded in discrete but overlapping phases, all of which required talented and willing teachers. Gesture and

wunnamukkuteyeue wauwacheg   I. John.   Chrift uoonohteaeneunq

wonk womonogkut neemattin Paule, neyane
waantamóonk aninnumauut,kœfukkuhhum-
unkou.
16 Neyane wonk ut wame œfukkuh-
whonganit yeufh naut nœwadt, nifh neádt
nawhutch fiohkog wohtamunat , nifh nag
matta nehtuhtauogig, & nœchumwefitcheg
uppannenehéouh, neyanteauhettit onkatog-
anafh wufiukwhonganafh , en nehenwoache
uppaguanuonganuout.

17 Newutche kenaau womonogig , yeufh
negonne wahteauog , kuhkinneafek ifhkone
monchaaitteaóg nafhpe uppanneunnantam-
œonganœo matchefecheg , woh kupenufh-
aumwœ, wutch nehenwonche kunmenetik-
ompauonganuout.
18 Qut nafhpekegk kitteamonteanittuonk,
& wahneonat nul-Lordumun & nœwadcha-
nuwacneumtn Jefus Chrift noh fohiumwœ-
naj naneefwe yeuyeu kah micheme. Amen.

Negonne nanwe wut-Epiftleum JOHN.

CHAP. I.

Ne ohtagkup wutch wefke kutchifik
ne nœtamogkup, ne naumogkup ,
wutch kuhkelukquonónut, ne moni-
ne.mugkup, kah mamufinnumagkup ut ke-
nutcheganunonut , papaume pomantamoe
wut.innowaonk.
2 Newutche pomantamóonk mo wahteau-
wahuwon, kah nunnaumunnaonup, kah nœ-
wauwomun,kah kenahtinnnnunan, ne micheme pomantamóonk ne weetomukup wutœofhimau, kah mo kœwahteauwahetteanan.
3 Ne naumagkup kah nœotamagkuup kœ-
wanteauwahenunan, onk kenaau wonk woh
kœweeche moappumimun, kah wunnamufh-
kut nœweeche moapputuonganun weeche
wutœofhin , kah wunnaumonuh Jefus
Chrift.
4 Kah yeufh kœfukkuhhumauununáno-
nafh kœwekontamœonganœo woh numwoh-
taut.
5 Neit yeu nehtamóonk, ne nœotamauog-
kut, kah kœwahteauwahununan , noh God
wequai, kah ut nagum wanne pohkenano.
6 Tohneit nœowaog noh nœoweechemoa-
yeumoun, kah pomufhaog pohkenaiyeuut ,
nuppannœowonan , kah matta nutufumun
wunnamuhkuteyeuœuk.
7 Qut pomufhaog wequaiyeuut, neyane
noh appit wequaiyeuut, nœoweeche moayeu-
zimun, kah œfqheonk Jefus Chrit wunnaumonuh, kuppahkhikquuan wutch wame mat-
chefconganit.
8 Nœowaog matta nœomatchefeonganéu-
mun, nutafœokekomómun nuhhogkanonog ,
kah wunnamuhkuteyeuœuk matta nutappeh-
tunkœomun.
9 Sampœaog nummatchefeonganunonafh,
noh pabuhtanumukqufu, kah fampweufu
kutahquoantamunkqunnanónut   kummat-
chefeonganunonafh , kah kuppahkhukqun-
nanonut wutch wame pannefconganit.
10 Nœowaog matta nummatchefeumun ,
kuppannœowaeneuhéoun, kah wuttinnœwa-
onk matta kutapehtunkœounan.

CHAP. II.

Nummukkiéiu nog , yeufh kœfukkuh-
au nauunun.œfifij matta kummatche-
icunnaout, kah howan matchefeit, nukke-
nœotamwanihitteamun weeche wutœofhimau
Jefus Chrift fampweufeaen.
2 Kah noh wunnohteayeuaenin wutch
kummatchefeong anunonah,kah matta webe
kuttaihénonafh, qut wonk wutch unmat-
chefeongafh mamuife muttaok.
3 Kah ne nafhpe nœowahteomun noh nœo-
waheon, nanauwehteauogkut wuttinnœwá-
ongafh.
4 Noh ánœowadt, noh nœonœowáheh , kah
matta nanauwehteauunk wutannœoteámœo-
ongafh, noh pannœowaeniñ, kah wunnamuh-
kuteyéuœ matta wutappehtauoh.
5 Qut howán nánauwehteauont wuttin-
nœowáonk, ut wuhhogkat wunnamuhkut ,
womonáonk God pannuppeteázuun,ne nafhpe
nœowáhteomun nutappehtauoun.
6 Noh ánœowadt, nutapehtau, noh wok
ne wuttin pomufhon neyane pomufhánit.
7 Neematog wanne nœofukkuhhumœoh
wuike naumatuonk, qut nukkone naunátu-
onk, ne ahtunkup wutch kutchifiik. nukkó-
ne ánœoteámœonk, ne wuttinnœwáonk ne
nœotamóg waj kutchifiik.
8 Wonk, wuike naumátuonk kœfukkuh-
humáuonumwœ , ne wunnumuhkutéyeuuk
ut wuhhogkát kah ut kuhhogkáout, newutche pohkenai paumfheau , kah wunnamuhkut wequai yeuyeu wohfumœomœo
9 Noh ánœowadt, nen nutap wequáiyeuut,
kah fekeneauont wematoh, noh appu pohkenahtu nô pajeh yeuyeu
10 Noh womonont weematoh, appu wequáiyeuut, kah matta wunuhkomóonk tog-
kuliittafununat ut wuhhogkát.
11 Qut noh fekeneáuont weematoh, appu
pohkenahtu, kah pomufhau pohkenahtu , &
matta wáhteauou uttoh áont , newutche
pohkenni pogkennumwehteomœo wuikefuk-
quafh.
12 Kœfukkuhhumauonumwœ mukkie-
fog, newutche kummatchefeongánoafh kut-
ahquo-

The Gospel of John declared, "In the beginning was the Word." For missionaries, success depended upon learning Native languages. The *Holy Bible containing Old Testament and the New, Translated into the Indian Language* (1663) is attributed to John Eliot, but the missionary relied on Native tutors to teach him the Massachusett language and to help translate Christian concepts. (Courtesy of the American Antiquarian Society, Worcester, MA) pantomime usually initiated the process. Hurons explained things to the Recollect Gabriel Sagard "by figures, similitudes, and external demonstrations," either by "tracing the object on the ground" with a stick or by "making very unseemly movements" with their bodies. Missionaries did their share of gesturing, too, but they considered this method undignified, unreliable, and insufficient for the intangible. At the same time, learning to distinguish between unfamiliar sounds and accustoming one's mouth to unfamiliar positions to pronounce them loomed as further hurdles. To Josiah Cotton, who penned an eighteenth-century English-Massachusett dialogue, the best way to "learn Indian" was "by talking with Indians, and minding their words, and manner of pronouncing." The Jesuit Francesco Bressani bewailed the variety of "accents, breathings, and changes of tone, without which . . . speech would be altogether unintelligible." Conversation and repetition might allow a missionary to clear these hurdles and begin collecting, according to François Le Mercier, "words from the mouths of savages as so many precious stones." The need for patient teachers was especially important because coherent speech required more than simply stringing together the names of things. After one filled his "memory with all the words that stand for each particular thing," Le Jeune related, one still had to "learn the knot or Syntax that joins them together."[19]

As European philosophers debated whether a universal grammar underlay all languages, the most successful missionaries, in extensive consultation with Native tutors, came to understand just how dramatically Native languages diverged from other known languages. The difference that most struck European observers was the degree to which single words in Algonquian and Iroquoian languages could incorporate several distinct roots, and lexical elements that marked what Europeans identified as pronouns and adverbs, into a single verbal phrase. The "key to the secret," according to Jean de Brebeuf, perhaps the most talented seventeenth-century Jesuit linguist in North America, was forming "compound words." Educated clergymen, familiar with the classical languages, had some experience with memorizing declensions and conjugations and parsing grammatical forms, and they often tried to force Native forms into familiar categories. Jerome Lalemant believed that Jesuits had "arranged" a variety of languages "according to . . . [the principles] of Greek and Latin." Others were more wary. Francesco Bressani stressed that Huron possessed "inflections altogether unknown to the most learned of Europe." These languages, "very different . . . but most beautiful," proved (to him) that language was a divine gift, "it being impossible that so excellent a System, which surpasses that of all European languages that we know, is the product of minds rude and unversed in every science." Sebastien Rasles, a Jesuit among Abenakis in the early eighteenth century, praised the "form of expression and the spirit of the language" for its "real beauties" and "indescribable force." He stressed, how-ever, that it was "entirely different from the spirit and form of our European languages." Even more than other stages of their linguistic tutelage, therefore, learning the "turn and arrangement" of words required "familiar and frequent intercourse with these tribes." A missionary was "fortunate," Rasle believed, if he could "express himself elegantly . . . after ten years of constant study."[20]

Some missionaries despaired at their difficulties and at the process itself. Gabriel Sagard simply gave up, concluding that Huron was "a savage language almost without rule." The frustrated Paul Le Jeune approached a deeper insight. Struggling with a variety of Montagnais words that conveyed related concepts but that seemed to share "neither relation, nor alliance, nor any affinity" with the ostensibly related term, Le Jeune realized that he depended upon his Native teachers. Missionaries "could not understand them if they did not have suffi-cient intelligence to vary and choose more common words." Language learning demanded diligence and talent, but it also required Indian instructors cogni-zant of and sympathetic toward European students' shortcomings.[21]

The imbalanced relationship of Native teacher and European student upended the assumed colonial hierarchy, an inversion some missionaries handled better than others. Numerous Jesuits, for their considerable linguistic success, recorded an acute sense of discomfort. Pierre Biard bemoaned the need "to learn" the language "from the stupid natives." Brebeuf claimed to feel "pleasure" in his tutelage, but he warned those who might follow him to resign themselves to being a "humble Scholar, and then, good God! with what masters!—women, children, and all the Savages,—and exposed to their laughter" merely to "begin to stammer a little." His young assistant, Pierre Joseph Marie Chaumonot, so "feared" Huron "mockeries" that his instruction felt like "torture." Experiencing doubts and humiliations, many missionaries attempted to reclaim the role of teacher. The Jesuit missionary-historian Joseph François Lafitau insisted that Native consultants "appear quite surprised" when missionaries explained the grammatical principles of Native languages, "which they had never perceived." The Puritan John Eliot acknowledged the help of "a pregnant witted young man" named Cockenoe, but he titled an early linguistic work *The Indian Grammar Begun: or, an Essay to Bring the Indian Language into Rules* (1666), sug-gesting that such rules had not existed previously.[22]

Missionaries compiled lexicons and grammatical observations not only to facilitate language learning but also to relieve the agonizing dependency that they felt as students of Native teachers. As Le Jeune shared, "if we could learn the language, and reduce it to rules, there would be no more need of following these barbarians." One incident especially illustrates the importance that mis-sionaries assigned to these linguistic materials. Anticipating execution at the hands of Hurons who were determined to defend themselves against disease and cultural assault, Brebeuf considered his most important preparation to be placing "our Dictionary, and all that we have of the language, in a place of safety." Although Brebeuf avoided the expected fate on that occasion, he was later put to death. Other missionaries suspected that books could only take one so far. Although he compiled an extensive Abenaki dictionary—stolen by New Englanders in a raid with Mohawks that took his life—Sebastien Rasles considered books to be, ultimately, "quite useless." To his mind, "practice is the only master that is able to teach us." Missionaries valued linguistic texts highly, but texts could not, despite some missionaries' hopes, replace frequent interactions with Native speakers.[23]

As missionaries turned to translation, Native translators played a crucial role in making the ostensibly universal truths of Christianity intelligible to Indians by shaping them in ways that resonated with traditional beliefs and values. Brebeuf spoke the sentiments of all missionaries when he admitted, "we say not what we wish, but what we can." Fortunately for him, a Huron speaker "dilated upon . . . and amplified" his message "and in better terms." Missionaries, moreover, complained repeatedly about Native languages lacking terms for concepts central to Christianity. In many instances, missionaries and translators sought to appropriate Native terms for new ends or even create new terms using Native elements. David Brainerd, an eighteenth-century Presbyterian missionary, relied upon Moses Tunda Tatemy to engage fellow Delawares in repeated conversations to "fix the precise Meaning" of new terms or old ones with new Christian significance. Around the same time, at the Moravian mission of Pachgatgoch in what is today western Connecticut, Native interpreters pushed missionaries simply to introduce European terms, since they were "lacking suitable words in their language to express" words such as *"grace, blessing,* and *redemption."*[24]

While some missionaries may have embarked upon their work interested in the possibility of a universal language and eager to repair the damage of Babel, grappling with practical difficulties of translation prompted a torrent of commentary upon the divergence of Native languages from European languages. Although they were "fairly gorged with richness" in things from the natural world, there were countless words, according to Le Jeune "never found in the thoughts or upon the lips of the Savages" because they had "no true religion nor knowledge of the virtues, neither public authority nor government, neither Kingdom nor Republic, nor sciences." Revealing the perceived limits of conversion and education more broadly, missionaries doubted whether they could convey to Indians anything that they did not already know. Biard worried about how Montagnais seemed to lack terms for things that were "abstract, internal, spiritual, or distinct," or which expressed any "universal and generic ideas," specifically because he was "certain that these miserable people, continually weakened by hardships . . . will always remain in a perpetual infancy as to language and reason." After all, "where words, the messengers and dispensers of thought and speech, remain totally rude, poor and confused, it is impossible that the mind and reason can be greatly refined, rich and disciplined." These flaws seemed inherent to "the very nature of the language." Separated by confession, considerable distance, and nearly a century, the Presbyterian David Brainerd similarly complained of the *"Defectiveness"* of the Delaware language in the mid-eighteenth century. He too suspected that the problem went deeper. Meeting disappointment in evangelization, he asserted that Delawares themselves possessed *"no Foundation in their Minds to begin upon."* Echoing, extending, and elevating the authority of views of Native linguistic poverty that early travelers had voiced, many missionaries convinced themselves that Native languages, and perhaps minds, were deeply deficient, as part of a broader view of tenacious "savagery" that both magnified successes and excused failures.[25]

Where some fretted over what Native languages lacked, others stressed differences in what Native languages contained, especially their grammatical structure. In the mid-seventeenth century, John Eliot offered an explanation for Massachusett speakers' "delight in *Compounding of* words." He suggested, *"It seems their desires are* slow, *but* strong; / *Because they be utter'd* double-breath't, *and* long." Frustrated at the uneven success of his evangelization project, which demanded outward Native submission to European ways, John Eliot suggested that Native grammatical difference invited sin. New terms that missionaries coined, especially when they contained definitions of new concepts, highlighted this problem. Citing *Nummatchekodtantamoonganunnonash* (our lusts), Cotton Mather made the derogatory quip that Indian words had "been growing ever since Babel." In addition to the perceived danger of Native words carrying old (ostensibly heathenish or superstitious) associations after they were applied to Christian concepts, the perceived moral implications of Native grammatical forms offered another reason, Mather and others feared, Indians could "scarce retain their Language without a Tincture of other Salvage Inclinations." This was considerably darker than, though not unrelated to, the Moravian David Zeisberger's observation on the connection between thinking and speaking in Delaware.[26]

In the eighteenth century these kinds of observations converged with missionaries' increasing understanding of seeming grammatical similarities across Native languages and the impulse to think of language as a reflection of ancestry as well as thought, as new philosophical currents from Europe stressed the conventionality of language. While examples of language learning ran against potentially essentialist explanations of linguistic difference, others noted a seeming paradox. "Language is, in a sense, an arbitrary thing, and the words of which it is composed are only signs adopted to represent the things to which they have been attached," Lafitau suggested in 1724. "But on the other hand . . . language was instituted to express our thoughts and has an essential connection to the operations of the soul and the objects on which our thoughts turn." Languages must share certain fundamental traits, he believed, but nearly a century of Jesuit language learning in Canada called this philosophical axiom into question in a practical sense. The admission is all the more striking because Lafitau, reacting against currents of religious skepticism in Europe, sought to explain the unity of the human mind and its development over time, and because he believed Native societies descended from and still resembled ancient Greeks. The Native languages that he knew seemed to share among themselves "almost the same distinctive character, the same way of thinking and tricks of expression." This "totally different structure," Lafitau suspected, accounted for Europeans' difficulty in learning Native languages. In the mid-eighteenth century, Jonathan Edwards, Jr., grew up as a native speaker of Mohican while his father ministered to the Congregationalist mission community at Stockbridge. In his boyhood, he remembered, his "thoughts ran in Indian." He discarded the language as he grew older, using it only to record sins in his diary, continuing a New England tradition of linking Native languages with illicit urges. Later in life, he subjected the language to philosophical investigation, recognizing the degree to which seemingly unrelated languages like Mohican and Mohawk resembled one another in structure, and speculating on how grammatical differences in Native languages shaped Indians' deficient English. For Edwards, and for many more, speculating upon linguistic deficiency and connections between speech and thought could be easily merged. [27]

Experiences in colonial missions, attempts to justify cultural transformation and explain sometimes limited success, and increasing linguistic knowledge all prodded Europeans to wonder about the ways in which language shaped Indians' moral and intellectual lives in ways that distinguished them from Europeans. The knowledge of missionaries, like that of traders, also made its way to other philosophically minded colonists. The military officer Le Page du Pratz, for instance, asserted that Indians (excepting the Natchez, the last of the Mississippian chiefdoms, which a French–Choctaw alliance destroyed in the 1730s), possessed "barren" languages and the "same way of speaking and thinking." Officers and officials also derived linguistic ideas from another, diplomatically crucial form of interaction.[28]

Treaties, Oratory, and Indian Eloquence

Just as Native–European interactions through trade and missions produced ideas of linguistic difference, so too did their political interactions, which rested upon speech-giving in council. Throughout the eighteenth century, European empires attempted to assert control over North America by competing to extend commercial and diplomatic relations with Native people, as the latter worked to take advantage of those relations to maintain economic, political, and cultural autonomy. Gaining allies in war, accepting a missionary, reinforcing amicable ties after incidents of tension or violence, or negotiating use of (or, Europeans insisted, title to) land required a treaty council, which had originated among the Haudenosaunee (League Iroquois), spread widely across North America, and which Native people imposed on Europeans seeking accord from the early days of colonization.

Treaty councils were formal and ritualized events that proceeded in well-defined phases where only a few spoke publicly, and speakers tolerated neither interruption nor hasty reply. These assemblies, in the opinion of the Moravian missionary David Zeisberger, were "as quiet and orderly as if they were acts of devotion." On such occasions, Indians gathered to watch and verbally affirm, from the dozens to the hundreds, and colonists gathered too, mainly for the spectacle. Impatient officials tended to focus on the expected end result, a written agreement to certain terms; but for Native people, the purpose of these events was to speak and listen, each party reminding the other of the benefits of a mutually respectful and advantageous relationship. Oratory was central to these practices. Although early travelers who encountered Indians outside formal diplomatic settings usually believed, like John Lawson, that reports of Native "Flights of Stile" in speeches were unbelievable precisely because they were convinced that Native languages were "deficient," a number of well-placed Europeans knew otherwise. Colonial or imperial officials rarely learned Native languages in any degree of detail, but observations stemming from their official duties indicate the distinct impression of Native languages that Native oratory left upon them.[29]

Appropriately for occasions for intercultural communication, language frequently emerged as an issue at treaty councils. As numerous scholars have demonstrated, many Native people and Europeans pointed to an absence of writing as among the most important features of Native languages, and this characterization surfaced repeatedly in colonial accounts of treaties. Europeans assigned ideological importance to alphabetic literacy, and they found Native unfamiliarity with it useful in treaties, particularly when scribes deliberately falsified words spoken in council. When two groups disputed what had been agreed to at an earlier meeting, some Native people refused to acknowledge the authority of a written document, precisely because of its taint by association with Europeans. Having no need for writing, and relying instead upon wampum belts as records, Lauurance Sagourrab (Penobscot) considered it their "Indian distinction." Spoken language, however, also drew attention, fueled by a mid-eighteenth-century wave of prophecy in the Iroquois–Algonquian–colonial borderlands that was inflected to varying degrees with calls for cultural purification, physical separation of Indians and Europeans, and militant resistance to colonial expansion. Addressing Sir William Johnson, a British superintendent of Indian affairs who possessed Mohawk kinship connections, on the related issues of encroaching white settlement and British–French war over competing claims to North America in 1762, an Onondaga speaker related, "One of our people lately, in a vision, was told by the Great Spirit above, that when He first made the World, He gave this large Island to the Indians for their Use; at the same time He gave other Parts of the World beyond the great Waters to the rest of his creating, and gave them different languages." Treaties were occasions for demonstrating respectful autonomy and enacting social identities, which made them politically meaningful performances of cultural differences in which language often figured prominently.[30]

Indeed, Native people demanded not only that their voices but that their languages be heard. After observing a council between Saponis and the Virginia governor, the eighteenth-century traveler John Fontaine remarked, "Notwithstanding some of them could speak good English, yet when they treat of any thing that concerns their nation, they will not treat but in their own language, and that by an interpreter, nor will not answer to any question made to them without it be in their own tongue." Trustworthy interpreters, therefore, were crucial for empires attempting to assert control over events and peoples. In 1758, amid the reversal of fortunes that would lead eventually to his nation ceding its North American claims to Britain, the French officer Louis Antoine de Bougainville blamed the "vile souls" employed as interpreters for weakening France's influence over Abenakis. The strict protocol for what constituted proper speech elevated interpreters' importance since the ability to grasp what was said and garble a reply was simply insufficient. Native people expected to be "spoke to in their own Way." As witnesses to these events and readers of Benjamin Franklin's popular collection of mid-eighteenth-century treaty accounts learned, a successful council required "skill in the *Indian* Languages and Methods of Business."[31]

The kind of speech suitable for the council fire was a far cry from what was appropriate in a longhouse or trading post. While European speakers tended to be governors or other colonial leaders, Native speakers were not "chiefs" with special political authority but rather trained orators who spoke in a way distinctive to the setting. Lafitau considered the "council style . . . so noble and obscure that often they themselves do not understand what is being said." Indeed, among Indians, only those being raised to speak on behalf of their people at treaty councils received training in memory, elocution, performance, and the fictive kinship titles by which one nation referred to another in formal address. This training so distinguished an orator from his countrymen, in the opinion of Brebeuf, that he thought "some seem to be born orators." Few colonists harbored any realistic hopes of understanding what was said without the aid of an interpreter. Full interpretation for a colonial audience, moreover, might require more than an approximate rendering of the words that the orator had used. Zeisberger, for instance, noted that "when a belt [of wampum] is given few words are spoken, and they must be words of great importance, frequently requiring an explanation."[32]

Even as it surpassed most Europeans' comprehension, some individuals recognized distinct features of this "council style." Besides the use of wampum, many noted particular gestures and other aspects of physical performance. Distinct spoken elements were also crucial to this register of speech. Europeans repeatedly noted that orators seemed to address their audience with considerable gravity. In New France, Brebeuf recorded that Huron orators "raise and quaver the voice . . . slowly, decidedly, distinctly" in a way of speaking called *acwentonch*. This style was calm and measured. Speaking of southeastern councils, James Adair, a trader with a Chickasaw wife, stressed that orators "never speak above their natural key." Some Europeans, like the New York lieutenant governor Cadwallader Colden, found Native oratory "sonorous and bold"; others, such as Zeisberger, cringed at its "very pompous and boastful tone," though even the latter confessed to being "profoundly impressed." Verbal performance did not end there. Colden, who admitted to being "ignorant of their Language," was dimly aware that "their best Speakers" employed "some Kind of Elegancy in varying and compounding their Words." While "common Ears are ever sensible" to it, few attained the "Art." Pierre Maillard, a missionary to Mi'kmaqs in Acadia, offered a clearer explanation. Speakers "treating of solemn, or weighty matters" employed distinctive grammatical forms, choosing to "terminate the verb and the noun by another inflexion, than what is used for

This engraving of an Iroquois council from Joseph François Lafitau's *Moeurs des sauvages américaquains* (1724) depicts the central role of the orator. The use of wampum was distinctive to eastern North America, though the garb and poses evoke classical antiquity, illustrating Europeans' association of Indian eloquence with a past age. (Courtesy of the Library Company of Philadelphia)

trivial or common conversation." Gesture, cadence, diction, tone, and specific grammatical constructions contributed to a formal oratorical performance.[33]

These linguistic and performative elements, combined with widespread commentary on the figures of speech orators used to convey their meanings, fostered considerable interest in Indian eloquence. Throughout eastern North America, whether they were among the small few who could understand them as they were being spoken or were among the greater part who heard them rendered through interpreters, Europeans became acutely aware of what Brebeuf called the "infinity of Metaphors" that Native orators used. Occasionally recognized in the mid-seventeenth century, these "circumlocutions, and other rhetorical methods" became an object of considerable attention in the eighteenth century. According to Alexander Henry, who traveled among Ojibwes in the mid-eighteenth century, the "Indian manner of speech is so extravagantly figurative, that it is only for a perfect master to follow it entirely." Diplomatic forms, therefore, had consequences for intelligibility.[34]

Delegates of the British Empire, the colonies, the Six Nations, and diverse western Indians, mutually distrustful and sometimes hostile to one another, repeatedly confronted the intertwined issues of eloquence and interpretation in the second half of the eighteenth century, as each side groped "to find true Sense and Meaning" in others' words and deeds. Because of the occasional difficulty of determining what a particular speaker meant, Benjamin Franklin stressed in his treaty accounts that meetings between colonial and imperial officials and their Native counterparts presented risks that those who sought conflict could "take Advantage of any Misunderstandings" that arose. Avoiding such moments was among the only reasons an orator might accept interruption, as occurred at the Treaty of Easton in 1756, a crucial moment in the Seven Years' War. When the Delaware orator Teedyuscung used a particularly loaded word "with great Earnestness, and in a very pathetic Tone," Conrad Weiser, the most trusted interpreter in the northern colonies, "knew the Word to have a very extensive and forcible Sense," but he had to ask what was "meant by *Whish-shickly* on this particular Occasion." Clarifying its significance, Teedyuscung stressed that insufficient effort could frustrate a desired end, and he demanded that the colonies "perform every promise you have made to us." Referring to the violence then ravaging what colonists considered the fringe of settlement in Pennsylvania and Virginia, he warned, the "Times are dangerous." The British superintendent of Indian affairs, the man responsible for maintaining Britain's Covenant Chain alliance with the Six Nations—the legal basis for much of the eighteenth-century expansion of New York, Pennsylvania, and Virginia—came to recognize oratory itself as a political problem. Despite his own fluency in Mohawk, William Johnson, after his considerable diplomatic experiences during the Seven Years' War, suspected that orators' "mode of Expression . . . in matters of much moment" made their speeches "liable to misconstruction."[35]

Others who shared similar experiences in the U.S. revolutionary era came to similar conclusions. David Zeisberger had experience among several different Iroquoian and Algonquian groups and could speak Onondaga and Delaware. He recognized that the "formal language" used in councils differed "as much from the common language as does the language used by the whites in legal procedure, from the language of ordinary intercourse," but he did not claim to understand everything. Zeisberger directed his comments to a Moravian author in Britain then compiling a history of Moravian missions, with considerable ethnographic information, for a learned audience. During the American War for Independence, in which he supported the patriot cause and worked alongside Moravian Delawares in an attempt to keep their countrymen from warring against the rebellious and expansionist colonies, Zeisberger noted that Native orators sometimes "intend to speak in an obscure and reserved manner" by using "allusions" that listeners had to "puzzle out" for themselves.

Those on the opposite side of the imperial rift agreed. Guy Johnson, nephew and successor of the superintendent, put it succinctly to the Scottish philosopher William Robertson in the late eighteenth century. The Native "stile in public Transactions," Johnson admitted, was "hardly intelligible to our Interpreters."[36]

Even beyond its diplomatic implications, Europeans and colonists had become convinced that there was deep significance to this manner of expression by the mid-eighteenth century. Indeed, some believed that oratory conveyed some eloquence that characterized the languages themselves. In an account that the Royal Society published in its *Philosophical Transactions*, William Johnson described "extremely emphatical" Iroquois speeches, "adorned with noble images, strong metaphors, and . . . allegory." These traits, he believed, indicated Indians' "eastern" origin. In a book that argued that the Indians were the Lost Tribes of Israel, James Adair likewise stressed southeastern Indians' "bold metaphors and allegories," which seemed to echo those found in the Old Testament. Colden noted this "Eastern" trait as well, but he also suggested an important alternative significance for it. "Speech-making," and the "*Urbanitas*, or Atticism" in the language itself, was the "natural Consequence of a perfect Republican Government: When no single Person has a power to compel, the Arts of Persuasion alone must prevail." While some viewed Native eloquence as indicative of Indian origins, others viewed it as a product of Native social organization. The political importance of treaty councils amid the pressures of settlement, imperial rivalry, and divergent struggles for independence, combined with the philosophical significance of Native eloquence as a representation of Native speech seemingly at odds with linguistic or intellectual poverty, made each objects of considerable attention in the eighteenth century.[37]

"Savage" Enlightenment

Some writers in Europe sought to reconcile the divergent, and at times contradictory, "facts" about Native languages' poverty, organization, and eloquence that colonial language encounters had produced. While Spanish chroniclers had used Native languages to establish hierarchy in the sixteenth and seventeenth centuries, and some, such as José de Acosta, emphasized the importance of empirical description, they neither tied diverse linguistic features together into a single theory nor argued that one form of language or its mode of physical preservation and transmission might develop into another. Gradually, in an intellectual climate in which the learned increasingly accepted the universality of natural laws and rejected static conceptions of nature and society, vague assertions of similarity between ancient peoples and contemporary "savages" morphed into the assumption that the latter represented an early condition of humanity. By the eighteenth century, French and British writers drew upon divergent notions of Native languages to piece together a coherent account of the conditions and capacities of peoples. Philosophers and other scholars stressed the necessity of empirical evidence, for which they relied on centuries of colonial reports and travel narratives, as well as ongoing exchange networks that Atlantic commerce made possible, but they also insisted that their own distance from the Americas made them disinterested writers who could extract truth from the biased accounts of explorers, missionaries, travelers, and colonists. The resulting theories were far from monolithic, but most insisted upon human unity by forcing Indians and their languages into ostensibly universal categories in a way that validated the assumed superiority of Europeans. While similar questions and practices united these authors, their descriptions of Native speech varied at times, though they also tended to share common features. Together, Enlightenment philosophers provided a way to understand human psychology and intellectual development as well as a powerful justification for their nation's empires by using language to define what William Robertson called, the "mind of man, while in the savage state."[38]

By establishing language to be a human convention, John Locke's *Essay Concerning Human Understanding* (1690) transformed what meaning could be found in colonial accounts. Locke described how ideas originated in the body's sense perceptions and how human beings arbitrarily attached sounds to ideas to communicate them with others. Even the most complex ideas, he said, were nothing more than simple ideas, originating in the senses, grouped together and labeled with sounds. That words were conventions with no inherent link to what they represented was an old idea, expressed by Aristotle (against Plato) and suffusing seventeenth-century philosophy. The radicalism of Locke's theory lay in its assertion that no ideas were innate, a claim that rested upon what he knew of "languages of remote Countries or Ages." A people, such as "ancient savage *Americans*," who had not experienced a given thing would possess no idea of it and have no word for it. More radically, Locke suggested that even if two peoples had experienced similar things, if separated by space or time, they would group and name the resulting ideas in their own ways. That one language could express in one word what another language could express only in several proved that these were "voluntary Collection[s] of *Ideas* put together in the mind, independent from any original Patterns in Nature." Although many disputed its materialist focus by denying the mind's dependence upon the body, and many others rejected that language could be truly arbitrary since observant and reasoning individuals must discern something in a thing that impels them to denote it by a particular sound, Locke's focus on language's role in thinking made the *Essay* revolutionary.[39]

On this foundation, Etienne Bonnot de Condillac constructed a theory of linguistic origin and development that dominated the second half of the eighteenth century. While Locke was concerned with how individuals reasoned in the present, Condillac's *Essay on the Origin of Human Knowledge* (1746) focused on how the natural expression of feelings and emotions, appetites and desires by naturally sociable human beings developed into spoken and written language over time. Avoiding the appearance of challenging scripture, he cautiously framed his speculations by imagining two children lost in a desert "sometime after the Deluge," but he turned to accounts of "American Indians" for evidence. "Barbarian nations," he suggested, revealed the "seeds of the arts which have developed among the civilized nations." All animals expressed urges, but people living in societies began to associate cries and movements with specific referents. Attaching artificial, though not arbitrary, signs to the world's phenomena allowed gradually increasing control over the chaos of individual sense perceptions. Manipulating signs in one's mind and sharing ideas with others transformed the passive reception of sensory stimuli into an active process, creating a collective accretion of knowledge. Initially, signs were few and imprecise; but decomposing perceptions into discrete components and imposing logical order on the disassembled parts sharpened reasoning. Imagination, memory, and reflection furthered this process over time, since "organs develop slowly, our reason even more slowly." Discovering new objects, experiencing new things, and encountering new peoples each expanded the intellects of individuals and nations. New and improved signs allowed clearer understanding and increasing mastery over nature. In its spoken and written forms—Condillac's work was crucial for the process by which philosophers exalted the visual above the auditory as a reliable source of knowledge—the progress of language brought precision at the price of imagery. Great writers would bring a language to its greatest precision and refinement, but only through successive stages, which corresponded to the rude pictures drawn by the "savages of Canada," the "hieroglyphs" of ancient Egypt and Mexico, contemporary Chinese characters (erroneously thought to represent pure ideas), and finally alphabetic literacy. Different languages, Condillac wrote in his subsequent *Logic* (1780), were "as many analytical methods." Each created intellectual "habits" and established "the rules of our judgments, and constitute our knowledge, our opinions, our prejudices."[40]

In language philosophy, scholars from Britain to France to Germany to Italy engaged in the same debates about the interconnectedness and seeming interdependence of language, the mind, and society, building upon and frequently challenging Condillac's description of linguistic-intellectual-social development. French and Scottish authors, in particular, joined that question with those of seventeenth-century writers on natural law, Charles-Louis de Secondat, baron de Montesquieu's emphasis on environment and modes of subsistence, and colonial accounts that hinted at the resemblance of Native people in present to other societies in earlier ages. Language, like other aspects of Native life, resulted from the state of society of its speakers in this theory, which most eighteenth-century writers upon moral philosophy, epistemology, rhetoric, natural history, and travel adopted and glossed.[41]

While all human beings drew knowledge from the senses, for "savages" the senses were practically the only source. Passions ruled, experiences were few, and intercourse was limited. Since progress in the development of signs had been minimal, a savage could not yet combine ideas into general classes, abstract qualities from things, or analyze his own mental processes. Where Jean-Jacques Rousseau suggested that without abstraction, the names of things would accumulate quickly, with persons giving each new tree, for example, a different name, Adam Smith believed that since rudimentary abstraction must occur at the earliest stages, persons would simply name each "the tree." Philosophers disagreed on the details, but there was consensus that Indians could express only what was "material or corporeal." In the words of Charles Marie La Condamine, who traveled to South America on an expedition to measure the earth at the equator, all the diverse languages he encountered in Brazil were "missing terms to express abstract or universal ideas," both "metaphysical" and "moral." Outdoing La Condamine by generalizing further to encompass all Native Americans, William Robertson stressed that "*Time, space, substance,* and a thousand other terms which represent abstract and universal ideas, are altogether unknown to them." While some writers focused on the individual or collective reflection that could improve signs, Smith and several others stressed the linguistic effects of war, commerce, and the intermixture of peoples. Much of the commentary on "savage" or "barbarous" languages or peoples did not address the possibility of change at all.[42]

Philosophers reconciled this intellectual-linguistic poverty with assertions of Indian eloquence. Hugh Blair, whose *Lectures on Rhetoric and Belles Lettres* (1783) went through more than three dozen American editions before the mid-nineteenth century, illustrated this through references to the Old Testament, the epic poems of Homer and the fraudulent Celtic bard Ossian, and Colden's history of the Iroquois. Having achieved only minimal reflection, supposedly savage speakers privileged the tangible. Orators supplemented their speech with "belts and strings of wampum," and their words were "full of strong allusions to sensible qualities," which made the "American and Indian languages," like all other savage languages, poetic, yet imprecise. Savages were "governed by imagination and passion, more than by reason," and "their speech must be deeply tinctured by their genius." More specifically, "the want of proper names for every object, obliged them to use one name for many; and of course, to express themselves by comparisons, metaphors, allusions, and all those substituted forms of Speech which render language figurative." To civilized listeners, whose own languages had transcended this figurative stage and become analytical, imagery was ornamental; but savages supposedly could reason only ineffectively with the few words they possessed. Comparison, and thus striking but obscuring metaphor, was inevitable.[43]

The defectively rational aspects of Indian speech, according to this theory, went deeper than words and the images they invoked: they pervaded the organization of the languages themselves. Colonial missionaries had established the similar grammatical structure of several different Native languages, noting how they merged into single words what were separately expressed parts of speech in European languages. In Rousseau's words, early languages "gave each word the meaning of a sentence." Others found that hard to accept. James Beattie, for instance, thought it "very improbable, that long words should be found among barbarians." Believing complexity must result from cultivation, he could not "imagine, that they, whose garments are but a rag, and whose lodgings a hole, should affect superfluities in their language." Reconciling a theory of Native deficiency with increasing knowledge of Native languages, however, pushed philosophers toward the former view, and James Burnet, Lord Monboddo, offered an explanation. Synthesizing diverse accounts, both from those who understood a Native language (such as Sebastien Rasles) and those who did not (like Gabriel Sagard), Monboddo asserted that "all the barbarous languages have . . . words of remarkable length" precisely because languages developed, in intellectual and physical processes, over time. Indians' little "progress . . . in the art of thinking" produced grammatical forms that expressed "things as they are conceived by savages . . . mixed together as they are in nature." Speakers ostensibly failed to distinguish substances from qualities and conflated agents, actions, objects, and relations because they had not yet learned to decompose their sense perceptions. Seizing upon depictions of Native languages as "full of vowels, with very few consonants," Monboddo claimed that Indians expressed ideas through barely articulated sounds, "little better than animal cries produced from the throat, of different tones, a little broken and divided by some guttural consonants." Worsening the situation, because there were no true rules, these languages were "constantly changing and fluctuating," which hindered social cohesion and political development. Monboddo and others believed that Native tongues were strikingly different from those of Europeans because Native minds and bodies remained mired in savagery.[44]

There was widespread interest in the anatomy, physiology, and mechanics of speech in the eighteenth century. It was crucial to a "natural history of speech," as the title of a beautifully illustrated book by Antoine Court de Gébelin made plain. According to Charles de Brosses, who used Lafitau's account, humanity possessed a "construction of the vocal organs" that could "render only certain sounds," and he insisted, following Condillac and contra Locke, that human beings must recognize some quality of a thing that leads them to name it in a certain way. Yet, his influential *Traité de la formation méchanique des langues et des principes physiques de l'étymologie* (1765) stressed that cultivation produced a change in pronunciation, with uncultivated peoples using "a harsh inflection & not a gentle inflection." La Condamine, an explorer turned philosopher, described the strange pronunciation of a Huron girl, supposedly found in the forests of Champagne. It "was all spoken from the throat, with very little use of the tongue, and none at all of the lips." Even her laughter was little more than "drawing her breath inwards." Indian languages ostensibly demonstrated that articulation—using the various parts of the mouth to differentiate sound produced through the flow of air through the throat and vibrations of the vocal chords—was difficult and developed only over time.[45]

Precisely because of the way language seemed so speak to the mind and the body, the implications of such theories reached to the heart of eighteenth-century philosophical and natural-historical debates about materialism, environmentalism, and evolution. To support his theory that America was literally a "new world," with its nature unhealthy and its people incompletely formed, George-Louis Leclerc, comte de Buffon, concisely asserted, "Their arts were emerging as was their society . . . their ideas undeveloped, their organs rude and their language barbarous." Buffon's perspective was degenerationist, positing deviation from an earlier condition, but linguistic theories led others in more radical, evolutionary directions. Having heard Huron sounds and finding insufficient abstract terms in Brazilian languages, La Condamine pondered, "by what slow and insensible degrees we have past from the mere animal to the savage, and from the savage to the civilized man." Mute "wild men" and orangutans—Carl Linnaeus dubbed the former a distinct variety of humanity, and Monboddo considered the latter "a barbarous nation, that has not yet learned the use of speech"—may have blurred the boundaries between human beings and other animals, but most writers clung to language as a distinguishing feature of humanity. Even those who attempted to link Africans

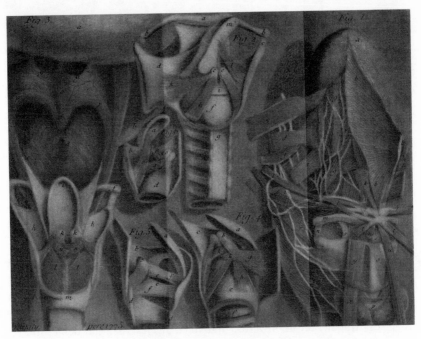

Interest in the anatomy and physiology of speech grew more pronounced in the
eighteenth century, as this striking plate from Antoine Court de Gébelin's *Histoire
naturelle de la parole* (1776) illustrates. A "natural history of speech" was a part of a
broader Enlightenment project that defined in starker terms differences in sound,
words, and speech among the world's peoples. (Courtesy of the Library Company of
Philadelphia)

and their descendants with apes, such as Charles White, admitted that a
"chasm" separated them in speech. The anatomist Peter Camper validated this
learned inclination by demonstrating the difference between simian vocal
organs and those of human beings. For all the denigration of the languages of
"Indian Americans," the trader-historian James Adair stressed, "not one of
them expresses himself by the natural cries of brute animals."[46]

Conviction in such a dividing line between humanity and beasts, however,
endowed linguistic differences within the human species with even greater
significance. In Rousseau's maxim, "Speech distinguishes man among the
animals; language distinguishes nations from each other." Eighteenth-century
emphases upon social condition and national affiliation could work against
the logic of "race" in the limited—and still contested—sense of biological,
continental groups of humanity, as put forward by Linnaeus and Johann
Friedrich Blumenbach, but such distinctions were often confused. The works
of Cornelius de Pauw, Guillaume Thomas François Raynal, and William

Robertson spoke in terms of savagery and barbarism, but they applied that social condition to all the Native peoples of the Americas. A "tribe of savages on the banks of the Danube must nearly resemble one upon the plains washed by the Missisippi [sic]" because "the disposition and manners of men . . . arise from the state of society in which they live," Robertson asserted, but certain "features" and "qualities" were "common to the whole race" of people indigenous to the Americas.[47]

By the late eighteenth century, moreover, scholars stressed the importance of heredity alongside natural and social environments to explain human languages and human beings themselves. Johann Gottfried Herder, for instance, engaged stadial ideas even as explained language as an individual creative act, rather than as the product of sociability, and emphasized the fact that languages were the inheritance of national communities that followed distinct paths of development. He argued that the "analysis of all savage languages," such as Huron, Quechua, and Carib, among others, revealed that they were "prodigal and needy . . . each in its own manner" because each was "interconnected with the custom, character, and origin of the people." Even those firmly embedded in the Scottish stadial tradition, who resisted the starkest materialist implications of Lockean psychology, could see language in similar terms. For James Dunbar, "language may be accounted in part *natural,* in part *artificial:* in one view it is the work of providence, in another it is the work of man." He acknowledged that there was an "obvious" link between habit and expression, but he explicitly denied that social condition determined speech, stressing that "language, from various causes, may arrive at a pitch of refinement, unauthorized by the tone of public manners." Near the end of his *Essay on the History of Mankind in Rude and Cultivated Ages* (1780), he clarified, "there is often an invisible preparation of natural causes, which concurs with the civil order of things in prolonging the honours or even the infamy of a *race;* and hereditary characteristics are interwoven into the genius and essence of the mind." Social state offered a powerful, synthesizing explanation—varied yet largely coherent and ideologically useful for those who claimed the mantle of "civilization" to justify claims to the North American land—of the features of Native languages. It was one that would last, in countless idiosyncratic iterations, for much of the nineteenth century, when it increasingly merged with ideas of ancestry to describe "savagery" and language alike as an inheritance.[48]

Philosophers took scattered, conflicting raw material of travel accounts and transformed it into a set of assumptions, widely disputed in details, which provided a foundation to the science of humanity and supported European imperialism. Separate pieces emerged from various sites of linguistic interaction. Ideas of linguistic poverty emerged from trade, where Indians willingly formed pidgins from their languages in their attempts to acquire new goods but balked at providing Europeans with linguistic information that could compromise desirable social distance; these ideas also sprang from missionary frustration that Christian concepts could not be easily rendered into Indian languages. The missionary context was also crucial for elaborating linguistically based notions of Indians' intellectual differences rooted in their extended tutelage under Native teachers, who explained how Indian languages were constructed. Those missionaries learned that the organization was considerably different from the organization of any other known languages. In treaties, Europeans witnessed the formal, ritualized, and metaphor-rich mode of speech suitable for statecraft. Only in the mid-eighteenth century did philosophers synthesize these divergent linguistic notions into descriptions of the traits that all "savage languages" must possess. Despite varied conjectures, there was broad agreement that the speech of uncultivated peoples must be basically alike in certain features (being unwritten and possessing harsh sounds, few words, and a grammar fundamentally unlike "civilized" European tongues) and that these traits reflected underlying intellectual difference. Language was one facet of a broader definition of savagery as a stage of society—a concept, importantly, that did not exclude attention to ancestry and inheritance—that justified dispossession; but for some, the perceived connections between language and mind imbued it with primary importance. This theory did not posit innate intellectual difference. Later writers, however, would incorporate understandings of "savage" languages, as products of "Indian" vocal organs and minds, transmitted in ways not entirely clear from one generation to another, in their racial theories.

Even as philosophers elaborated this stadial view of language, which purported to explain how the intellectual foundation and physical articulation of a language corresponded to its speakers' level of social development, other writers turned to language to trace the descent and history of peoples. Theories of savagery and civilization, in their linguistic and other aspects, were of paramount importance to citizens of the new U.S. nation as a framework for understanding Native characteristics and capabilities, but they offered a guide neither for answering the question of Indian origins nor for classifying Native peoples in useful ways. To do these things, Europeans and Americans alike turned to language for genealogical information.

2

Descent and Relations

In 1809–1810, John Norton (Teyoninhokarawen, or "The Open Door") journeyed from upper Canada to Cherokee country, noting that Indians and Euro-Americans had intermingled and intermarried in the borderlands of their habitations, coming to share a common "complexion" and ways of life, which combined with histories of trade and captivity to make discerning a person's background difficult. Norton, an adopted Mohawk who claimed Cherokee in addition to Scot descent, even found his own identity questioned after uttering some broken Cherokee, overhearing companions say, *"Yeawiyoukeklisko* (I think he is a native)." As imperfect an indicator as it was—after all, the languages learned by traders and captives did not indicate their ancestry—his hosts turned to language not only to pin down affiliation but also to answer questions of descent and past relations.[1]

"Some old Cherokees," for instance, preserved a tradition that their ancestors and those of "the Nottowegui or Five Nations" formerly had been one. In the past, they "spoke a similar language; but, separating, it gradually varied until it finally became unintelligible to each other." Although "ancient wars" had deepened the differences over time, Cherokees alerted Norton, "a few words, and the idioms, of the two languages, resemble each other" still. Indeed, those wars had produced substantial numbers of captives who were adopted and married in their new communities, which may have encouraged recognition of shared ancestry. Euro-American commentators had disagreed about Cherokee in the eighteenth century, debating whether it was related to other southeastern languages, entirely unrelated to any other, or perhaps the product of linguistic intermixture. According to this tradition, the Iroquois

and Cherokees comprised a single "Nottowegui race," most easily distinguished from the neighboring "Algonquin race" by the sounds of their speech:
the former's utterances were strewn with "gutturals and aspirations" and
lacked the "labial" sounds that the latter used frequently. That narrow conception of "race" was at odds with prominent European naturalists such as
Linnaeus and Blumenbach, who used the term to encompass all of the Native
peoples of the Americas, and with the Shawnee brothers Tenskwatawa and
Tecumseh, who sought to create a pan-Indian racial identity. Mindful of those
efforts, Norton came to believe that all Indians east of the Mississippi, "however different their language and degree of improvement . . . look upon each
other as brethren of the same family." Despite clearly recognizing linguistic
similarity and difference, Norton also noted that these lines did not define
Native allegiances. [2]

European philosophical and literary practice also relied on language to
trace the relations of people. Toward this end, Norton desired a vocabulary
from visiting Creeks, thinking that Muskogee sounded somewhat like
Algonquian languages. His hosts were skeptical. Rather, they assured him
that southern Indians recognized that the language "bears some resemblance"
to and might "be of the same root" as Choctaw. Besides indicating kinship
among peoples of eastern North America, Norton hoped, further, that comparing Native languages with those of Asia would solve the puzzle of Indian
origins, though he worried that the "fluctuating state of languages" and the
fact that so many were "buried in oblivion together with the independence of
those who spoke them" made success "very improbable." Norton had access to
Native traditions and he was attuned to contemporary European letters,
translating the gospel of John and, reportedly, Sir Walter Scott's *The Lady of
the Lake* into Mohawk. His journey through Cherokee country offers just one
example of how Native and European understandings of the relationship
between languages and peoples collided and at times reinforced one another
in the context of U.S. colonialism and nativist efforts to convince Indians of
their shared racial ancestry as a means to resist further dispossession. [3]

Language possessed seductive explanatory power in the late eighteenth and
early nineteenth centuries precisely because it seemed to straddle "natural" and
conventional categories at a moment when those boundaries were particularly undefined, with Euro-Americans frequently disregarding Native social-
political units in favor of uncertain and unsettled categories of "tribe," "nation,"
and "race." Throughout the eighteenth century, Indian languages were a salient
marker of difference, a means to communicate among various Native and
Euro-American peoples, and a subject of philosophical investigation. In the

early American republic, these varied uses remained. U.S. citizens, like Thomas Jefferson and Benjamin Smith Barton, took up etymology—the study of the derivation and affinities of words, which, in the absence of written records, were expected to reveal historical information—in their efforts to determine Indian origins. In the administration of colonialism, U.S. officials attended to linguistic similarities when they sought diplomacy and capitalized upon linguistic difference in land cession treaties. As president, Jefferson urged federal explorers, Indian agents, and military men to collect linguistic information that could illuminate American antiquity and contemporary Native relationships. Jeffersonian taxonomy, which defined Native peoples as linguistically fragmented and insisted that linguistic change consisted of continual divergence of one people from another, confronted an Indian intellectual revolution, at once inclusive and divisive, that called for cultural reform, militant resistance to U.S. expansion, and Indian unity. Only after this movement's military defeat did U.S. officials and scholars turn to an ambitiously simplifying taxonomy.

Etymology and Affinities

Even amid the learned's gradual definition of savagery as a stage of society through which all peoples at some point passed, many Europeans and Americans attempted to understand Native languages in terms of descent. The historical relationships among languages became a subject of learned study in the early modern era, as scholars traced the shared descent of the Romance languages from Latin, of the Germanic languages from some Teutonic ancestor, and, some postulated, a kinship of each group with Greek. Colonists applied a similar framework to Native languages. Such efforts provided a means to comprehend Native diversity and to fit Indians into some account of the ancestry and migrations of the world's peoples. Some learned colonists, such as Thomas Morton, thought they heard traces of Greek and Latin, while many more joined Roger Williams in finding some "affinitie" between Hebrew and Native words or forms of speech (as in the ostensibly "Eastern" cast of Indian eloquence). If true, such evidence would support the prominent view that American Indians descended from the Lost Tribes of Israel or that all languages descended from Hebrew. Some scholars even joined such theories of particular Native languages' analogies with Hebrew to assertions of all Native languages' shared descent. Writing to a fellow of the Royal Society, for instance, Experience Mayhew, who grew up a native speaker of Wampanoag as his father ministered on Martha's Vineyard, asserted, on the basis of their similar "compounding and declineing of words," that all Indians "betwixt Canada and New Spain . . . speak what was Originally one and ye same Language." Throughout the eighteenth century, colonials continued to seek evidence that would connect Indians to old-world peoples. To take representative examples, the military officer Antoine Simon Le Page du Pratz, the missionary Charles Beatty, and the explorer Jonathan Carver alerted readers to ostensible traces of Phoenician, Welsh, and Chinese in Native languages. Orthodox theories of humanity demanded shared descent from Adam and Eve, and scholars exerted themselves to find proof in the American languages.[4]

Yet, similarities were not always apparent. In 1708, the Dutch scholar Adrian Reland drew upon linguistic materials from throughout the Americas, including from the publications of John Eliot and Baron Lahontan, to compare American languages to those of Europe, Africa, and Asia. Reland found no compelling similarities. Scholars had long known that languages changed over time, and many suspected that Indian languages were especially prone to change. Morton, leader of the notorious Indian-English community of "Merrymount" in early Massachusetts, blamed Native "covetous desire" to trade for leading to linguistic intermixture, for instance, while Reland speculated, drawing upon colonial observers who did not understand that they knew only a pidgin, that Indians frequently changed their speech. By the mid-eighteenth century, conjectural notions of a savagery as a stage of society characterized by its nomadism, fragmentation, and lack of the writing that could give a language greater permanence, had gained broad acceptance and provided a new way to understand Native linguistic diversity. In addition, the theory of Epicurus and Lucretius that varying environments affected the languages of nations found new life as early-modern scholars attempted to trace all of the world's languages not to a single original tongue, but rather to a small number of principal languages. In this view, one could trace the descent of a daughter tongue to its mother and kinship among sister languages, but no relationships could be detected across families. For the orthodox, Babel provided convincing explanation for linguistic diversity; for those convinced of the conventionality of language, the tower's rubble was unnecessary. The learned of each persuasion tended to conflate languages and nations, and so studied tongues to trace the genealogies of peoples.[5]

Over the course of the eighteenth century, etymology, or the derivation and comparison of words, acquired even greater authority as the key to tracing the descent and migrations of peoples as philosophers articulated why languages, in the words of Gottfried Wilhelm Leibniz, were both the "best mirrors of the human mind" and the "oldest monuments of peoples." Those who believed that languages retained traces of divine inspiration accepted this premise, as did those who followed John Locke in believing that languages were nothing but an accretion of arbitrary words agreed upon by a community to designate things, and those who advocated the intermediate position ascendant in the latter half of the eighteenth century. Leibniz, the most prestigious of the last group, argued that some quality in a thing struck human minds in such a way to prompt naming it with a particular sound. Language did not give voice to the essences of things but rather expressed human knowledge (modified, according to some, by stage of development or particular national histories). "Etymologie" (1756), a condensed version of Charles de Brosses's long-circulating manuscript on the "mechanical formation of languages, and on the physical principles of etymology" in Diderot's and d'Alembert's *Encyclopédie* articulated this view. An influential account of New France, by Pierre François Xavier de Charlevoix, offered a similar theory that directly addressed the American languages and Indian origins. The Jesuit historian suggested that there were "three mother-tongues from which all the rest are derived" in the portions of eastern and central North America familiar to the Jesuits: "the Sioux, Algonquin, and Huron languages." Believing the Americas to have received multiple groups of emigrants following the Deluge, he argued that each of these mother tongues were "formed from nature" and, as such, each possessed "their peculiar geniuses." Rather than compare misleading similarities in distant peoples' manners and customs, Charlevoix strongly urged the learned to study travelers' word lists and missionaries' dictionaries and grammars because mother tongues were less susceptible to change over time and distance than were their daughters. Comparison of the "principal Languages of *America*" with those of the old world provided the "Way of ascending to the Original of Nations, which is the least equivocal."[6]

Etymology allowed an investigator to discover "affinity" between words. "Affinity" was a protean concept in the eighteenth century. In moral philosophy, it described the feeling that drew one naturally sociable person to another; in chemistry, the force of attraction, analogous to gravity, that bound certain substances together in compounds; and in botany and zoology, the resemblance, and perhaps relation, between organisms' parts that provided a basis for classification. The concept resonated in language study for all of these varied connotations. Languages were themselves products of human sociability, particular vocalizations of the universal human urge to join with others in society. Etymology analyzed words of similar meaning in different languages and separated their component parts (letters, syllables) to uncover persisting correspondence. Those similarities, the result of either descent or relations, allowed classification of languages into groups of nearer or further resemblance. In its precise legal sense, two people shared "alliance or affinity" if they were each related to the same person without being related to one another, and etymologists admitted that resemblances between words might indicate merely "ancient intercourse"; but those motivated to solve the puzzle of Indian origins frequently succumbed to the temptation to interpret "affinities, or analogies" as evidence of "absolute derivation" from a common source. While many scholars used etymology to search for long-forgotten physical origins of abstract concepts in labels for sense perceptions, it also lent itself to genealogy.[7]

Leibniz established the most important intellectual framework for undertaking such studies. He urged that recording "every language in the universe," according to a specialized vocabulary, would provide the most conclusive proof of the "origins, kinships, and migrations" of peoples. Unlike the miscellaneous word lists that travelers had included in their accounts since the mid-fourteenth century, a philosophical vocabulary only contained words—such as those for family relations, body parts, numbers, things in nature, and common actions—that represented ideas that would have been, by necessity, among the first that any people would name. If one group, through travel or trade, subsequently encountered another group that possessed unfamiliar but desirable skills or things, the first people might adopt the name along with whatever new idea or item they were incorporating into their lives. There would be no impulse, however, for people to adopt new words for things they had named long ago. Far from being random selections of words, philosophical vocabularies could ostensibly ensure that linguistic affinities resulted from shared descent because they supposedly excluded linguistic evidence of human exchange. They also had the benefit, in an enlightened era that held ocular observation as the most reliable form of empiricism, of making visual what was auditory. By the mid-eighteenth century, curious readers encountered these ideas outside philosophical texts. Several decades before Leibniz's linguistic writings appeared in English, for instance, Philip John von Strahlenberg cited the philosopher's "Advice" that the "Languages of North-Asia" were the key to the "nice and ticklish Point" of the "Transmigration of Nations." He even suggested, without evidence, that similarities existed between Native languages in Pennsylvania and those of "nations descended from the *Tartar-* and *Hunno-Scythians*." Strahlenberg, thus, indicated his support for a prominent theory of Indian origins that dated to the sixteenth-century Spanish Jesuit José de Acosta and provided an unlikely set of relations to European languages, which Leibniz and others suspected were descended from some unknown Central Asian mother tongue. While Leibniz himself was struck by the utter difference of the languages of the Americas from those of other parts of the globe, several others used his ideas to investigate Indian languages.[8]

Although it was broadly assumed that Indians shared a common descent with the rest of humanity, the orthodox idea of monogenesis required defense against polygenist theories that posited multiple creations. In the seventeenth century, Isaac La Peyère had offered a biblically based theory, echoing an earlier Islamic tradition, that God had created other human beings before Adam, and in the eighteenth century Voltaire and others offered naturalistic analogues that explained human difference through separate creations. These theories occasionally prophesied the future as they imagined the ancient past. Subordinating the importance of Native linguistic diversity to what he viewed as Indians' physical and cultural similarity, the colonial surveyor Bernard Romans asserted that there were "as many *Adams* and *Eves* . . . as we find species of the human genus." That fundamental difference could explain why, Romans argued, Indians were "incapable of civilization." The trader James Adair, the most thorough eighteenth-century expositor of the Lost Tribes theory, pointed to a stream of supposed similarities between Native languages and Hebrew explicitly to refute the "wild notion of Indians as Pre-Adamites." His labored comparisons, however, convinced few.[9]

The increase in linguistic information that accompanied, and facilitated, the growth of European empires provided conclusive evidence, in the minds of some, that Native languages and peoples possessed different lineages than Europeans. No eighteenth-century theory regarding Native origins and development was more explosive than that offered by Henry Homes, Lord Kames, in *Sketches of the History of Man* (1774), which attempted to reconcile revelation, moral philosophy, and linguistic difference. The most plausible explanation for human diversity was that "God created many pairs of the human race," each of whom, with their offspring, would "gather knowledge from experience, and . . . form a language." This polygenist theory might seem to contradict revelation, but Babel could "reconcile sacred and profane history." While human beings' natural sociability should have prevented social, and with it linguistic, separation, the dispersal of nations that followed the tower's fall "deprived them of society." Reduced to a state of savagery, different nations formed tongues and ascended to civilization at different times. Most readers believed that Kames invoked scripture disingenuously, only to cloak an argument for separate creations. The philosopher's interests in language were genealogical as well as stadial. Pointing to the "general embarrassment American origins has caused the learned," Kames argued that since no American languages resembled those of Asia or elsewhere, "the original inhabitants of America are a race distinct from all others." To understand human similarities and differences in the eighteenth century, the learned relied upon a natural history that accepted the transformative power of the environment and a moral philosophy that posited peoples' uneven passage through stages of social development. Language remained the most authoritative means to establish, or debunk, the shared kinship of peoples. [10]

Against this backdrop, two European savants attempted to collect American specimens that might establish etymological links between the languages of the Americas and Asia in the 1770s–1780s. Antoine Court de Gébelin sought materials that he could incorporate into *Monde Primitif* (1773–1782), an ambitious work of thousands of pages that attempted to explain the physiological and psychological bases of universal grammar, recover the primordial language, detail the ways in which barbarous religions allegorically represented divine truth, and demonstrate the primary importance of agriculture to intellect, civility, and prosperity. Responding to his request for assistance while minister to France, Benjamin Franklin passed along John Eliot's Massachusett grammar, David Zeisberger's Delaware spelling book and a sketch of the pictographs carved into Dighton Rock from Stephen Sewall, professor of Hebrew at Harvard College. The "numerous" similarities between the Native languages of northeastern North America and ancient Phoenician and modern Malay languages convinced Court de Gébelin that their speakers were "of the Oriental race." [11]

Catherine the Great sent out broader calls to European literati in 1773 and again in 1784 to collect specimens of the world's languages. The Russian empress solicited Marie Joseph Paul, Marquis de Lafayette, to obtain North American vocabularies for her "Universal dictionary," a request that the general passed on to Franklin and George Washington. Relying, indirectly, on the knowledge of missionaries, Native consultants, and well-placed American officials, Catherine the Great received extensive materials. These vocabularies, following the ideas of Leibniz—who had first urged the Russian Empire to collect all it could of the languages within its vast dominion early in the century—included words "common to the most barbarous of languages, or which serve to trace the progress of . . . elementary knowledge from one people to another." Those would have been at crossed purposes for those interested in ancestry. Peter S. Pallas published the results in *Linguarum Totius Orbis Vocabularia Comparativa* (1787–1789), commonly known as *Comparative Lexicons*.

The Empress declared it "a matter of little concern" to herself whether others would find "striking facts" in the book, but she was less philosophical about foreigners gathering information in her empire. When John Ledyard attempted—with the support of Thomas Jefferson, then minister to France— to collect ethnographic and geographic information on an attempted overland journey from European Russia, across Asia, to North America, the empress had him arrested and banished.[12]

European savants expected American provincials to provide linguistic raw materials for Continental philosophy, but no-longer colonial Americans rejected this role. "Great question has arisen from whence came those aboriginal inhabitants of America," and Jefferson and others intended to answer it for themselves. Newly independent citizens possessed a country with only a limited history, and many looked to the continent's ancient past to fill the void. There was considerable learned and popular curiosity about the earthen "mounds," which were becoming increasingly known as Anglo-Americans entered the Ohio Valley. Both those, like Jefferson, who suspected that these western reports were exaggerated, and those, like Benjamin Smith Barton, who celebrated the "stupendous eminence" of these structures turned to the study of Native languages because they believed that linguistic similarities provided more reliable evidence of ancestry than mutable beliefs, customs, and building practices, a body molded by its environment, or unwritten traditions. In George Washington's words, languages represented "vestiges" by which "the descent or kindred of nations, whose origens are lost in remote antiquity or illiterate darkness, might be more rationally investigated." Explorers and geographers had established the proximity of North America to Europe and Asia, and physical "resemblance" supported the "conjecture" that Indians and the "red men of Asia" shared an ancestor, but Jefferson and others insisted "the only means we can have of coming at the descent and relations among the Indians, is by a collection and comparative view of their languages."[13]

Words and Descent

U.S. citizens were attentive to Native words. "Indian names" had "indelibly stamped," in the words of the early nineteenth-century poet Lydia H. Sigourney, "our states and territories, bays, lakes and rivers." Americans usually ascribed such names the status of memorial of a vanishing people. They were, in Sigourney's phrasing, "dialects of yore." Most such place names were as much adaptations of Native words as they were simple expropriations of them. Whites simplified difficult pronunciations out of convenience. "Nor ought the harsh guttural sounds of the natives to be retained," the lexicographer Noah Webster insisted in his *American Spelling Book,* since U.S. citizens possessed linguistic liberty. "Where popular practice has softened and abridged words of this kind, the change has been made in conformity to the genius of our language, which is accommodated to a civilized people." The early republic marked increasing interest in the origins of indigenous toponyms, in part because new citizens groped toward an "American" identity as part of a broader colonialist project to claim "native" status for themselves. Others had earthier concerns. "Knowledge of the meaning of Aboriginal names of places," suggested the Maine surveyor Moses Greenleaf, "may lead to valuable discoveries in soils, products, minerals, &c." Confident that the land and its wealth were theirs, U.S. citizens claimed a freedom to use Native words, vestiges of a waning past, as they saw fit.[14]

Desire to create linguistic memorials informed the taking and gathering of Indian vocabularies, but Jefferson and Barton, the new nation's most important collectors, had broader ambitions. Although each operated in a private capacity until 1801, when Jefferson became president, each possessed impressive connections that enabled them to join the energies of private institutions and the federal Indian apparatus to gather linguistic information. While Jefferson served as its president, for example, the American Philosophical Society (APS) turned its attention to the "Customs, Manners, Languages and Character of the Indian nations, ancient and modern, and their migrations." Vocabularies formed part of a comprehensive program for investigating the continent's physical and human history, based on an underlying taxonomic method that sought to impose useful order on geographically disparate plants, rocks, and people. Although numerous individuals complained of the difficulty of collecting a vocabulary, would-be contributors were assured that "the best methods of obtaining information . . . will naturally suggest themselves." Americans insisted that they were competent to observe and record the phenomena of nature and, supposedly not far removed, savage life. Although their motives, premises, and conclusions diverged, Jefferson and Barton each planned to determine whether any similarities existed between Native languages and those of Europe and Asia, in part through comparison with "the great Russian vocabulary," and each aimed to discern "what relations of language existed among our own aborigines." The latter focus distinguished these American projects from their European counterparts.[15]

Jefferson devoted considerable effort to establishing a network for linguistic collection and a method that would facilitate comparison. He recorded only one vocabulary himself, on the back of an envelope, from Unkechaugs on Long Island, as he and James Madison indulged their inclinations for opposition politics and natural history on a journey through New York in 1791. As early as 1783, however, and sporadically in the next two decades, he requested linguistic materials from well-placed men, such as Indian agents, surveyors, missionaries, and gentlemen naturalists. Benjamin Hawkins, for example, promised vocabularies of the unrelated Cherokee and Choctaw, noting that the latter was "radically the same" as Chickasaw. While learning "appellations" was relatively easy, grasping grammatical "agreement and Concord" was not, so he turned to the Creek chief Alexander McGillivray, who had a "taste for natural history with a good library." Hawkins found these efforts "flattering to them, and it amuses me," though he also hoped to put his growing knowledge to use as Indian agent. Within a decade, Jefferson had designed and printed a blank vocabulary of his own design. It listed 280 words for "such objects in nature as must be familiar to every people, savage or civilized," along the lines then common among the learned, though his vocabulary conspicuously lacked words for "God" and "Heaven." Recognizing that linguistic information would be useful for religion as well as philosophy, the New-York Missionary Society instructed evangelists to collect vocabularies using Jefferson's printed form. By the turn of the nineteenth century, Jefferson also sought vocabularies of "such tribes of the Missisipi as are within our reach." Those who sent linguistic materials to Jefferson, and he frequently received unsolicited contributions, hoped for gratitude, beneficial ties to a person of influence, and perhaps prestige among the learned.[16]

Linguistic information on the Americas was far from complete, but as Jefferson argued in *Notes on the State of Virginia* (1787), his book-length response to a French questionnaire on the state's natural and civil history, one "remarkable fact" about the continent's "radical languages" (those which did not evince similarities in words to any other) seemed undeniable. There were, by his count, "twenty in America for one in Asia." Those languages might share a common ancestor, but "if they ever were the same, they have lost all resemblance to one another." Dialects could drift apart in "a few ages only," as had the Germanic languages. For "all vestiges of their common origin" to disappear, however, "must require an immense course of time; perhaps not less than many people give to the age of the earth." The bones of mastodons and giant moose could demonstrate the grandeur of American fauna to disprove Buffon's theory that the continent's only recent emergence from the depths resulted in American immaturity and weakness, but Native languages, Jefferson believed, indicated that America was as old as the other continents. "A greater number

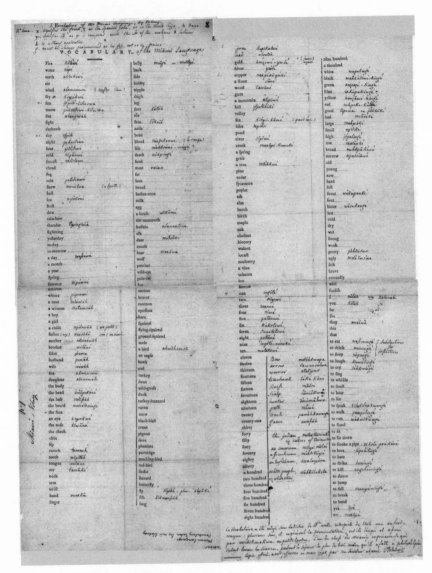

This Miami vocabulary, taken by Constantin-François Volney from the chief Little
Turtle and the U.S. interpreter and former captive William Wells, used Thomas
Jefferson's form. By printing blank copies of a carefully selected list of words,
Jefferson hoped to acquire a standardized means of comparing multiple Native
languages to determine lines of descent. (Courtesy of the American Philosophical
Society, Philadelphia)

of those radical changes of language having taken place among the red men of America," moreover, "proves them of greater antiquity than those of Asia." Although Jefferson admitted that vocabularies could demonstrate only relation, "not decide which is the mother country, and which the colony," he proposed a shocking conclusion of descent nonetheless. In 1786, Jefferson told Yale president and antiquarian Ezra Stiles that the "single fact" of Indian linguistic diversity convinced him that the supposedly "new world" had in fact populated the old. Etymology allowed the author of the Declaration of Independence to reject a colonial past for ancient Americans.[17]

Among the learned, Jefferson received little support for his linguistic theory of Indians' American origins. The Pennsylvania traveler and writer Henry Marie Brackenridge accepted that linguistic diversity, "greater perhaps than all the world besides," might prove American antiquity, but he was silent on Indians' origins. The New York naturalist Samuel L. Mitchell, in contrast, considered it possible that "America was the cradle of the human race," but he did not think that language would decide the question. The European literati also took notice of Jefferson's views. Alexander von Humboldt counted "some hundreds" of dialects of more than twenty languages in Mexico alone. While the celebrated Prussian explorer believed that these proved the "great variety of races and origin" among Indians, he insisted that American Indians had Asian ancestors. The closest affirmation of Jefferson's theories, as related by Constantin-François Volney at the end of the eighteenth century, came from a Miami chief. Besides using Jefferson's form to obtain a vocabulary from Little Turtle and William Wells, an adopted Miami and a U.S. interpreter, the French philosophical traveler sought a Native opinion on the question of Indian origins. After viewing a map that displayed the proximity of Asia and America, Little Turtle accepted the possibility of unknown kinsmen, but he wondered why "should not these Tartars, who are like us, have gone first from the American side? . . . Why should not their fathers and our's been born in our country?" After all, he explained, Miamis were "Metoktheniaka (*born of the soil*)."[18] Support from a heathen tradition, which in its assertion that Indians had always been of and in their land might undermine dispossession, did nothing to convince the learned, devout, or interested to accept Jefferson's theory.

Only one person attempted to refute Jefferson through a comparable project. Benjamin Smith Barton turned to language as part of an effort to reconstruct the continent's ancient history and "the origin of the American nations" from Indian customs and traditions, arts, and bodies, which he began while studying medicine and imbibing the Scottish science of man and society in Edinburgh. After his return, Barton still swam in the intellectual currents of the British

Atlantic. Like other American practitioners of natural history in this era, he strained against old imperial expectations while fearing that political independence would fray ties to centers of learning. He asserted U.S. citizens' "new manhood" and their advantageous situation for obtaining "American" natural-historical and ethnographic materials as he sought to establish a correspondence with prominent naturalists such as Sir Joseph Banks. As early as 1787, Barton recognized that there was "no one circumstance of so much consequence in ascertaining the affinity which different nations bear to each other, than the similarity of their languages." He "met with but little success" in his studies, however, until he returned to Philadelphia, obtained some "very mutilated" vocabularies, and established a network that in many respects mirrored Jefferson's own. Each tried to place himself at the center of a collective enterprise, precisely where a well-situated metropolitan would have sat in the colonial era. Indeed, Barton took the kinds of liberties that colonials had complained of, including claiming others' work as his own. Barton took advantage of the federal apparatus and, in one instance, the Secretary of War authorized him to enter the Cherokee and Creek nations to collect "usefull information relative to the language & natural history of the country." Traveling naturalists, like William Bartram and Constantine S. Rafinesque, provided materials, and Barton also cultivated ties with missionary organizations, particularly the Moravians. Most importantly, Barton assiduously took vocabularies as Native delegations passed through Philadelphia, "the greater part of them as they were pronounced by the Indians themselves." He extracted words from these varied materials and inserted them in a comparative vocabulary. Compared to Jefferson's, Barton's version was considerably shorter, consisting initially of 54 words and later extended to 70. Each corresponded to a word included in Pallas's *Comparative Lexicons*, which Barton had received as a gift from Joseph Priestley in 1796.[19]

New Views on the Origin of the Tribes and Nations of America, originally published in 1797, but with a substantially enlarged edition appearing the following year, explicitly confronted prevailing views about Indian origins and linguistic diversity. Jefferson provided a crucial foil, as did the Jesuit historian Francisco Xavier Clavigero. Barton rejected the former's insistence that there were hundreds of radically distinct Native languages and the latter's assertion that etymology could not prove their descent from old world tongues. The Mexican creole priest doubted that any expanse of time could erase all evidence of linguistic similarity, and the hemisphere's languages were demonstrably different from any others, so Clavigero concluded that the ancient inhabitants of America were "descended from different nations, or from different families, dispersed after the confusion of tongues." Barton, on the other hand, was sure that he found similarities between widely dispersed languages, both among Indians and between them and the peoples of the old world. These affinities, at a stroke, refuted Clavigero's assertions of the present distinctness of the American languages, Jefferson's startling assertion of American origins, and polygenists' contention that "the Americans are in strict language the aborigines of the soil, and not emigrants from other parts of the world." Abstractly, Barton condemned the fact that "religious prejudices . . . obscure the question," but his etymology led him to an account of Indian origins that adhered to the biblical narrative.[20]

Barton insisted that his researches, included as a long comparative vocabulary in *New Views*, "seem to render it certain, that the nations of America and those of Asia have a common origin." "Unequivocal vestiges" of the languages of Asia, spoken by "nations, so celebrated in . . . the revolutions and fortunes of his species, are to be found in the languages both of North and South-America!!" Many of these affinities were "very inconsiderable," but he urged Americans to examine the "sources of these languages in Asia," where they would find languages "from whence are derived considerable portions of the languages of the Delaware-stock, the Six-Nations, the Cheerake, the Creeks, the Chikkasah, Choktah, and many other tribes, in North and South-America." From his earliest musings, Barton had suspected that America had been "peopled from a thousand sources" and, after a decade of studies, he was convinced that it was "folly to suppose, that any American tribe is exclusively descended from any one tribe or nation of the world."[21]

Although, like many others, he believed in Indians' multiple Asian origins, Barton rejected the notion of the Americas' radical linguistic diversity. Against a century of scholarship, for example, he insisted that the languages of the Six Nations and Delawares were "not *radically* different," pointing to similarities such as those between the Narragansett word for "star" *(Anockquus)* and the final syllables of its Onondaga counterpart *(Otschischtenochqua)*. He also pointed out similarities—admittedly, "neither numerous nor very striking"—between Iroquoian, Muskogean, and Siouan languages, which made them "unquestionably the same," and he linked these with languages in Mexico and the isthmus of Panama that linguists today classify as entirely unrelated. Despite the "great chasms, or desiderata," of the vocabularies, Barton convinced himself that he had "NOT DISCOVERED MORE THAN ONE RADICAL LANGUAGE IN THE TWO AMERICAS." While many would disagree, Barton considered himself an authority and, as in other aspects of his natural history, resigned himself to being unable to persuade those with fixed opinions.[22]

Etymology led Barton to seemingly contradictory conclusions—Indians' diverse Asian origins and the radical singularity of the American languages— that he squeezed into scriptural form. If single Indian languages evinced simi- larities to multiple old-world tongues, it was simply because "all the languages of the earth bear some affinity to each other." Indeed, he "discovered some striking affinities between the language of the Yolofs (one of the blackest nations of Africa) and the American tribes" and, in 1803, he attempted to dem- onstrate that "many English words do, unquestionably exist . . . among the Indian nations of America." Linguistic diversity proved not that Asians descended from Indians, as Jefferson contended, but only that "the Americans . . . have been longer separated from each other in America, than the Asiatics . . . have been separated from each other in Asia." Recognizing that language only proved relation, not the direction of descent, he relied on Native tradition, the historical record, and the seemingly greater demographic density in western North America to prove Indians' Asian ancestry. Clavigero and others testified to Indian languages' resistance to change, which made it "probable that many hundred, perhaps three or four thousand, years have been necessary to produce the difference of dialects, which we observe between many American and Asiatic nations." Barton's etymology drew tortured affinities to assert Indians' Asian origin, then claimed that the obvious dissimilarity of words in those scattered languages proved that America was just ancient enough to refute Buffon and support biblical chronology.[23]

Jefferson and Barton pursued common methods and shared similar assump- tions. Both wanted to determine relations among Indians and between them and the inhabitants of Asia, who were commonly believed to resemble one another in body and customs. Each assumed that fragmentation and ever greater divergence produced linguistic diversity, utilizing a tool—the com- parative vocabulary—that was designed to exclude the effects of mingling after some imagined primordial point. This ignored the numerous eighteenth- century writers that had stressed that language change resulted from com- merce, war, and intermarriage, as well as the lexicographers (both those who celebrated a distinct national language and those who denounced it) who rec- ognized that Native words were altering English in the United States. A model that identified discrete stocks and defined linguistic change as one of steady divergence from a shared ancestor dominated the developing European practice of philology, which adapted the genealogical model present in the Old Testament. It also offered a useful way to imagine peoples in the new republic, allowing citizens sensitive about their provinciality and fearing fur- ther degeneration to elide the possibility of intermixture and root themselves in a British stock even as they looked forward to creating something uniquely their own.[24]

Despite similar approaches and frameworks, the two reached dramatically different conclusions. Jefferson believed that Native languages were radically fragmented; Barton believed that each was related to another and to Asian languages. These conclusions stemmed from divergent premises. Jefferson's argument that fragmentation revealed immense duration assumed that unity had once characterized those languages in North America. Barton, on the other hand, assumed a more ancient unity that had already fragmented when diverse old-world peoples came to North America. To describe the results of these processes, each employed unsettled terminology. Usually using "tribe" to refer to Native social-political communities, Jefferson once suggested that a "nation" was a "confederation" of "tribes" that descended from a single "stock" and, elsewhere, he lumped all "tribes" into a single Indian "race." Barton sometimes used "tribe" and "nation" interchangeably, at other times referred to a single "tribe" as a "race" unto themselves, and once drew attention to different "American tribes (speaking the same language) whose complexions are different." Untangling such meanings proved difficult, especially as the settler republic waged war to possess western lands.[25]

Tribes, Nations, and Races in the Ohio Country

Jefferson's view of Indians' extreme linguistic fragmentation and Barton's view of Indians' radical linguistic unity were each outliers. By the beginning of the eighteenth century, missionaries, officials, and others had disseminated the view that the Native languages of northeastern North America were divided into two broad groups. The languages of the Haudenosaunee and Huron were similar, as were several tongues related to Montagnais and Massachusett; but the lexicons of the former were dissimilar to those of the latter. These two groups, occasionally identified then as "nations" or even "races," correspond to what modern linguists identify as the Iroquoian and Algonquian language families. Beyond simply recognizing the relatedness of languages, some noted the regularity with which one language diverged from another within the group, and others noted how John Eliot's translation project, by fixing a continuum of languages in a single textual form, had reduced linguistic diversity. Others still suggested analogous groupings for languages farther south and west by the end of the century.[26]

Familiarity with such similarities and differences held spiritual and temporal significance. It suggested along what lines evangelistic efforts could be easily extended. It also offered insight into lines of alliance and hostility in Native America, or at least that was the prominent assumption, which could be found in colonial accounts from Peru to New France. In the estimation of the early eighteenth-century English surveyor John Lawson, "Difference of Speech causes Jealousies and Fears amongst them, which bring Wars, wherein they destroy one another; otherwise the Christians had not (in all Probability) settled *America* so easily." Informed citizens knew of bloody seventeenth-century wars between Hurons and League Iroquois, that the Creek nation contained several languages, and that the Odawa chief Pontiac had led a linguistically diverse coalition in 1763. Yet there had been a rapprochement between the Iroquois and Wyandots (descendants of the Wendat, or Hurons) in the eighteenth century, some reports suggested that language remained a fault line in Creek society, and pan-Indian unity remained elusive.[27]

American officials sought linguistic information because the political, perhaps ancestral, relations among different Native groups was a pressing matter that confronted the new republic's Indian affairs. After the Treaty of Paris (1783) concluded the War for Independence with Britain, the United States attempted to impose treaties upon the diverse peoples north of the Ohio River, declaring Indians to have been conquered in the war and demanding land cessions in return for peace. These conquest treaties did little to staunch the flow of blood on the borderlands, while the encroachments of settlers and the imperiousness of officials—at one meeting, the commissioner Richard Butler dashed a Shawnee wampum string against a table—inspired what would become a pan-Indian confederation of unprecedented size and unity that included Iroquois, Wyandots, and a number of Algonquian nations.[28]

U.S. responses to Catherine the Great's call for North American vocabularies reflect these issues. In *Observations on the Language of the Muhhekaneew Indians* (1788), an address delivered to the Connecticut Society of Arts and Sciences and sent to George Washington in the hopes that it would be forwarded to the Russian empress, Jonathan Edwards, Jr., argued that the languages of New England, the mid-Atlantic, the Great Lakes, and the Ohio country were "mere dialects of the same original language." According to Edwards—a native Mohican speaker who verified his observations with Yoghum, a "principal man" among the Stockbridges—the lexical difference between these and Mohawk was stark. They seemed to share an "analogous" structure, which tantalized Edwards because it "coincides with that of Hebrew," but Algonquian and Iroquoian words were "totally different" From one another. Richard Butler, a Shawnee-speaking former trader who was a commissioner at each of the three conquest treaties, addressed relations in the

Ohio country more explicitly. The varied materials he sent to Washington included a dialogue contrasting Shawnees' "council or business language" with their "common conversation," several vocabularies (obtained with the help of David Zeisberger and the college-educated chief John Killbuck, or William Henry), and a highly speculative essay. The "great extent westward" that Shawnee was *partly understood* among the "western tribes," combined with the "exceedingly" different language of the Iroquois, revealed a *"certain difference of people."* Like their "Tarter" ancestors, in Butler's opinion, the Iroquois were a "very warlike people," and following the precedent of the Haudenosaunee-British Covenant Chain alliance, Butler viewed them as "Conquerors of all the Indian Nations" between the Ohio River and the Great Lakes. Wars had "depopulated . . . the Western Country of its ancient inhabitants," who migrated to build an empire in Mexico, leaving behind the region's "traces of antiquity" in the earthen mounds. Edwards and Butler each addressed the linguistic difference of Iroquoian and Algonquian languages, and the latter used this knowledge to construct an epic past that denied Algonquian right to contested land in the Ohio Country.[29]

Washington understood the Russian project's relevance to Native–white relations. As the Confederation negotiated its conquest treaties, he reflected, to "know the affinity of tongues, seems to be one step towards promoting the affinity of nations." Considering humanity's "progressive state of improvement and melioration," etymology might "lay the foundation for that assimilation of language, which, producing assimilation of manners and interests, should one day remove many of the causes of hostility from amongst mankind." By 1791, the western confederacy had twice routed U.S. armies, undermining citizens' confidence in the new government's strength and foiling the administration's efforts to stabilize the country's finances by surveying and selling land. The first president sought diplomacy but confronted Ohio Valley Indians who included Delawares and Shawnees who had migrated to the region in a deliberate attempt to distance themselves from white settlement, fraudulent treaties, and decades of violence. Hoping to neutralize distrust and gain time to train a new army, the administration turned to a Native intermediary to promote the country's new, more just, and inexpensive policies, which acknowledged Native rights of possession and offered payment and education in the arts of "civilization" in exchange for voluntary land cessions. Achieving assimilation in English, alongside Christianity and other Euro-American ways, would guide U.S. colonialism, but Washington intended to impose a victor's peace. Philosophy and Indian policy each focused on what Lafayette called the "several idioms of the Nations on the Banks of the Oyho."[30]

Recognizing U.S. needs, hoping to make the federal government an ally against land-hungry New Yorkers, and intending to free his nation from Iroquois influence by renewing relationships with the western nations, a Christian Mohican chief from Stockbridge offered his services. In presenting his qualifications, Hendrick Aupaumut stressed the benefits that Mohicans could provide that other nations, particularly the Iroquois, could not. The Six Nations had made war against the western Indians a century earlier and, more recently, had convinced them to raise the hatchet against American independence. Mohicans, on the other hand, fought as patriots during the revolution and they hoped "to effect an accommodation" between the United States and the western nations, with whom they already possessed ties. Because "the Shawanees are my younger brother—the Miamies my fathers—the Delawares my grandfathers—the Chippawas my grandchildren," Aupaumut told the U.S. commissioner Timothy Pickering, they "always paid great respect to my advice." In this speech, whether intentionally or unintentionally, Aupaumut named only the nations to which Mohicans were linguistically related. In a letter of support to Henry Knox, the Secretary of War, the missionary Samuel Kirkland did the same.[31]

Although Mohicans had formed a close relationship with Christian Iroquois—indeed, they had established New Stockbridge on Oneida land (as had the eastern Algonquians of Brothertown), and Oneidas and Tuscaroras had accompanied Mohicans to the council—Pickering fixated on Mohicans' "remarkable" ability to communicate with distant western nations easily, even as the languages of the neighboring Iroquois were unintelligible to them. Aupaumut pressed home his linguistic advantages, perhaps to the point of exaggeration, once it was clear that U.S. officials valued them so highly. Linguistically ignorant commissioners were concerned that something would be rendered incorrectly, either inadvertently or intentionally to stoke smoldering resentment. He assured Pickering, "As I understand the Delaware Language & shall mix with them, I shall know whether they rightly interpreted the Commissioner's Speeches, and can correct what they mistake." More surprisingly, Pickering "particularly recollect[ed] his telling me, that his language and the languages of the Chippeways and others of the western tribes were so similar, that he could converse with them." Other accounts from the era undermine that claim. His supposed ability to understand and neutralize misrepresentations, however, comforted U.S. officials, who feared that Indians opposed to peace "told many lies" and that linguistically skilled British agents had "whispered in the ear of the Shawanese, not to believe a word" of U.S. appeals or promises. Upon arriving at the western confederacy's council fire,

Aupaumut reported, "we immediately begun to speak together as our fathers & forefathers use to do." Aupaumut convinced Pickering that the Iroquois were linguistically, and perhaps diplomatically, isolated, while Mohicans were fluent in the words and ways of both whites and the western Indians. Aupaumut's value as an intermediary rested not merely on his role as an interpreter or cultural broker, but on the relationships evinced in languages.[32]

Native people recognized extended linguistic relationships. Members of the Iroquois League, for instance, interpreted their linguistic similarities as a product of their common descent. In his *Sketches of Ancient History of the Six Nations* (1828), David Cusick (Tuscarora) recorded a tradition that explained how each group's "language was altered" long ago, and one Onondaga man, perhaps less trusting of tradition, described to Barton how "accidental circumstances" had created "differences of dialect" among League members over time. Algonquians preserved analogous knowledge. The Mohegan missionary Samson Occom, for example, thought that his language was the "mother tongue" for "the Indian nations along the seacoast from New England to Georgia." Of course, acknowledged common descent and recognizable linguistic similarities did not guarantee intelligibility. When Aupaumut and other Mohicans invited Occom to minister to New Stockbridge, considering it a "duty" to install "one of our own Collour," Occom had to preach in English because his Mohegan was so distant from his listeners' Mohican. These were just two of the "tribes" that the "most intelligent and credible Indians of the Lenape stock" knew, according to John Heckewelder, spoke "dialects of their language" and were "offspring the same original stock." Together they "constituted together one people, one family," even "one blood." Farther west, other Algonquians also preserved traditions about shared ancestry and linguistic change.[33]

Contemporary observers recorded divergent traditions concerning whether Algonquian and Iroquoian peoples shared a common origin. John Norton recorded contradictory Iroquois traditions about linguistic diversity. One explained that different peoples emerged speaking distinct tongues; the other recounted that the Delaware and Iroquois "races" had been one people until two groups lost their common speech after allowing Grandmother to fall into the water while arguing over which branch to take at a fork in river. Divergent traditions were in circulation elsewhere, too. Heckewelder, for instance, recorded that Iroquois were "*Strangers & Enemies*" to Mohicans and Delawares, who declared that "their Language has not the least affinity" to that of the "Méngue (or Maquas)." Captain Pipe (Delaware), on the other hand, related that his people sprang from a Wyandot virgin speaking a different language.

While the Moravian missionary Heckewelder had assisted Zeisberger, Killbuck, and White Eyes in preserving Delaware neutrality in the early stages of the War for Independence, Captain Pipe was the most influential chief who pressed for closer alliance with Wyandots and the British. Asserting the relatedness, or not, of Algonquians and Iroquoians could serve political ends.[34]

The true diplomatic issue, however, concerned social and political, not linguistic, relationships. At times, Aupaumut described Mohicans' ties with Ohio Valley Algonquians as the result of "ancient covenant[s]" producing "friendship and connections." In addition, despite Euro-American speculation, language did not determine political alliances in Native America. Mohicans possessed ties, likewise expressed in terms of kinship, to linguistically unrelated nations such as Wyandots. Moreover, Joseph Brant, a Mohawk, encouraged Indian unity under Iroquois direction. Insisting that "We are all Relations," he advised the confederacy's nations to resist claiming particular tracts of the Ohio Country as their own, and warned against any "yanky Indian," like Aupaumut, who would undermine their unity. Although the confederacy's members believed that all "Red People" shared common interests, there was, in fact, some Algonquian distrust of the Iroquois. As Brant complained, "Shawanoes, Delwares and Miamis, held Private Councils many nights, to which none of the Six Nations were invited." Aupaumut, representing Mohicans, traditional rivals of Mohawks, provided a means for U.S. officials to foil what they mistakenly believed to be the Iroquois–British direction of the western confederacy.[35]

In the end, Aupaumut's embassy failed to prevent more bloodshed and dispossession. The United States defeated the western confederacy at Fallen Timbers, offering "civilization" in exchange for land cessions and at the Treaty of Greenville (1795), while Mohicans and their Oneida hosts experienced increasing pressure in New York. Yet the episode highlights U.S. efforts to understand *"relationship,* as the Indians call it." John Heckewelder, a Moravian missionary who served as a U.S. commissioner in these same years, stressed the importance of doing so. The "nations or tribes connected with each other are not always connected by blood," Heckewelder admitted, but he believed that Native peoples' traditions of "lineal descent" could confirm the significance of linguistic affinity. Here and in other instances, administrative and religious uses of language study overlapped. Such knowledge allowed missionaries to prioritize some languages over others, and it could extend U.S. influence, and thus perhaps conversion and "civilization," in the West. Understanding the linguistic ties and divisions that demarcated "tribes" and "nations" facilitated colonialism.[36]

Jeffersonian Taxonomy in Exploration and Dispossession

Jefferson held a view of Native linguistic fragmentation, which became particularly important after his election to the presidency in 1800. At some point in the early nineteenth century, as he conceived a program of federal Indian removal, Jefferson revised his view of American antiquity, finding it "difficult to conceive" that time alone, no matter how "remote," could account for North American linguistic diversity. Colonial and U.S. experience with treaty councils where Indians refused to speak any but their own language pointed to a different explanation in Jefferson's mind. With no coercive authority, supposedly savage societies were prone to schism. When a dispute pushed one group to break away, perhaps they refused to speak the language they had formerly shared. "They have use but for few words and possess but few," Jefferson reasoned. "It would require but a small effort of the mind to invent these and to acquire the habit of using them."[37] This theory provided ideological support for dispossession in its reliance upon defining Indians as savage to undermine Native ties and claims to the North American land. But Jefferson's view of linguistic fragmentation had other applications as well.

In the 1780s–1790s, Jefferson's interest in Native vocabularies centered on the question of Indian origins, but he became more interested in particular linguistic relations among Native people by 1800. Contemporaries had quite fairly criticized him for ignoring the well-known Algonquian and Iroquoian language families. Accordingly, Jefferson revised his estimates of Native diversity downward—slightly. In 1786, he guessed that there were an "infinite" number of radically different languages in North America, but in 1812, he estimated merely a "hundred languages of America, differing fundamentally every one from every other, as much as Greek from Gothic." Those languages were long supposed to have been related, just as he assumed that Indians and their languages descended from a common stock. Believing that languages could be "arbitrarily" grouped into a "useful distribution into genera and species," he thought classifications could stress either the similarities among Native groups or the differences that separated them. Although some sneered at public support for linguistic collection, as president, Jefferson institutionalized it, directing federal officials and military men to collect vocabularies whenever possible and to gather evidence of meaningful linguistic relations within overall Native fragmentation. Knowledge of these relations supported different aspects of Jeffersonian Indian policy.[38]

Continental exploration, as an extension of continental commerce, was crucial to this vision. Even before the Louisiana Purchase was final, Jefferson used the expiration of the Trade and Intercourse Acts, which regulated all commerce between U.S. citizens and Native people, to urge Congress to fund a federal exploratory expedition. These laws attempted to increase U.S. influence in Indian country by establishing a "factory system" in which federally operated trading posts could undersell British affiliated traders, whose influence U.S. officials feared. Although such trade encouraged the very hunting that supposedly inhibited a turn to European-style agriculture, it fostered useful connections between Native people and federal agents, which U.S. exploration could extend. Besides standard queries concerning numbers, territorial claims, and customs, Jefferson directed the Corps of Discovery and subsequent expeditions to record each nation's "language, traditions, monuments." He issued federal explorers copies of his blank vocabularies, and he instructed Meriwether Lewis "to take those of every tribe beyond [the Mississippi], which he possibly could." By providing evidence to the international community that the United States had fulfilled its obligation to expand knowledge, the country demonstrated and justified its commercial and territorial claims. Although some Americans charged preceding empires with having neglected to collect specimens of Native languages, British explorers had published western vocabularies in the previous twenty years. Linguistic knowledge, moreover, would also help Americans allay jealousies, confer on matters of trade (hopefully parrying continuing British influence), and encourage "civilization" and conversion, all of which were crucial components of Indian policy. "There was no part of his instructions," Jefferson affirmed, that Lewis "executed more fully or carefully, never meeting with a single Indian of a new tribe, without making his vocabulary the first object." In all, the captains recorded twenty-three "distinct Indian languages."[39]

At both Fort Mandan and Fort Clatsop, where the Corps of Discovery spent winters and had the most extended opportunities to collect information and to write up more formally what had previously been observed, Lewis and Clark made linguistic observations oriented toward questions of descent. William Clark thought that Sauks and Foxes were "so perfectly consolidated that they may, in fact, be considered as one nation only. They speak the same language." More dramatically, he attempted to reduce the diverse score of "tribes" they found in the Missouri Valley into four "great nations," all of which, by virtue of the "great many words" they shared, must have been the "Same nation" in the not-too-distant past. According to Nicholas Biddle, who penned a narrative of the expedition based on the official journals, the social diversity of the Pacific Northwest was even more difficult to comprehend. "Similarity of dress and manners, and houses and language . . . much more than the feeble restraints of Indian government contribute to make one people." Language offered a strategy to distinguish (or not) between Native groups that, to outsiders, seemed to possess nearly identical manners, customs, and beliefs.[40]

Other explorers and Indian agents engaged these questions as well. "From the similarity of their language," John Johnston, an Indian agent in Ohio, observed that the Three Fires (Ojibwes, Odawas, and Potawatomis) "must have been one nation at no remote period." In contrast to those nations, the "physiognomy, as well as their language, and opinions" of the Lakotas, according to a young Henry R. Schoolcraft, who explored the upper Mississippi under the Indian superintendent Lewis Cass, "mark them as a distinct race." On the Long Expedition to the Rocky Mountains, Thomas Say concluded that Pawnees were a "race distinct" from other Plains groups and, although Loup Pawnees "deny having any natural affinity" to Grand and Republican Pawnees, "their language . . . proves them to be of the same origin." Because the number of distinct Native social groups frequently bewildered U.S. citizens and officials responsible for administering colonialism, inquirers sought elusive evidence of nationhood and indications of shared racial descent.[41]

Linguistic similarity and difference also seemed to offer a clue to alliances and hostilities. Even Jefferson, committed to a view of Native fragmentation, believed that on the eve of colonization, forty "tribes" deriving from "three different stocks" inhabited the Chesapeake, with "amity" and "confederation" encompassing those who shared "the language of the nation." Allied to one another, Monacans and Mannahoacs waged "joint and perpetual war" upon the Powhatans. Jeffersonian explorers, Indian agents, and military men likewise looked to language to explain hostilities in Native America. Jefferson's Secretary of War, Henry Dearborn, suspected that the "Creek nation being a collection of the remnants of several Tribes their local disputes may originate in the difference of descent, of manners or language." An Indian agent, John Sibley, identified more than thirty Indian groups in Louisiana who spoke what he considered almost twenty different languages. Half a dozen of them spoke Caddo, shared a tradition of Caddo descent, and joined Caddos "in all their wars" against Osages and others. Even when language was not explicit, it seems to lurk in the background of reports, as when the army surgeon Edwin James called Winnebagos, Iowas, and "other tribes commonly called Sioux . . . the hereditary enemies of the Algonkin bands." Such simplifications were potentially useful, since knowledge of alliances and hostilities informed processes of extending trade and promoting orderly settlement.[42]

Reality, however, often frustrated predicted alignments of language, nationality, and alliance. Lewis and Clark were surprised at warfare between Lakotas and Assiniboins in the northern Plains and at the mutual autonomy of groups that spoke "the same language" along the Oregon coast. Nowhere was the inadequacy of language as a guide to alliance more glaring than in the Ohio and Illinois countries, where U.S. manipulation of divisions among Native peoples was a longstanding concern to those who opposed further white settlement. The Shawnee orator Painted Pole (Messaquakenoe) exhorted a council of the western confederacy in 1792 that "all the Americans wanted was to divide us," and that same year Brant told Aupaumut, it was "always the way of the White People; to disunite the Indians, and set them to fighting one with another." Indeed, such efforts to divide Native people and clear Indian title became even more important in the Jefferson administration than they had been in previous Federalist administrations because of the higher priority that Jefferson placed on extending landownership among white citizens, which was the key to his vision of U.S. prosperity and independence.[43]

Little more than a decade later, Tenskwatawa, also known as the Shawnee Prophet, and his brother Tecumseh were leading a divisive movement that called for Native people to transcend old loyalties of clan, village, tribe, and language and realize that they, regardless of previous rivalries and wars, were a single people. The brothers were heirs to nearly a century of prophets who had sounded similar notes, but Jeffersonian policies of accelerating land sales by playing Native groups against one another contributed to the formation of a Native audience receptive to their message. Whereas the Washington administration had offered education in the hopes that "civilized" Indians (i.e., male farmers) would voluntarily cede excess land in exchange for money that could be used to improve private holdings, Jefferson sought to impose "civilization" by forcing Native communities to cede hunting grounds and leave them no alternative but European-style farming. Toward this end, his administration negotiated thirty-two treaties with twelve Native groups, totaling 200,000 square miles of ceded territory. To increase their chances of gaining cessions, the administration deliberately invited a variety of nations with tenuous claims to a particular tract of land, hoping that they would be especially eager to gain by its sale. Language offered a means for U.S. officials to insist upon social fragmentation.[44]

Linguistic diversity was real, but not all Native peoples accepted its social-political significance. Shawnees were perhaps especially suited to appreciate forging trans-linguistic relationships. Their homeland had once connected Algonquians east and west of the Appalachians, and for a time Shawnees joined the Creeks. They were among the first to embrace the teachings of Indian unity, separate creations, and cultural purification that emerged as diverse Native groups migrated, coalesced, and created new identities for themselves in the mid-eighteenth century. They formed close relationships with Delawares, Miamis, Mingos (Iroquois who broke away from the League), Wyandots, and Chickamauga Cherokees to resist Euro-American expansion into the Ohio Valley. Although contemporary traditions link the Shawnee language and people to Delawares and Mohicans, Kickapoos, and Tuckebatchee Creeks, Tenskwatawa provided an account of Shawnee origins and history that gave no attention to linguistic similarities or differences. There were those who joined together and others they fought, which implied that alliance and even nationhood were a matter of choice. The Shawnee Prophet admitted that Indian unity was an innovative message, but, he asserted, "Indians were once different people; they are now but one." Among the Creeks, the nativist message found a receptive audience among the "Red Sticks," a group that might have drawn its strength from the multiethnic nation's non-Muskogee minority. Concerned with the "inviolable confusion of languages" among Red Sticks, Hillis Hadjo (or Josiah Francis) told them that the Master of Breath would "teach him the different languages that he would want to use." [45]

The program that Tenskwatawa and Tecumseh offered, however, divided Native communities by deepening fractures over the desirable extent of acculturation, the best strategies for responding to U.S. colonialism, and reluctance to join politically with those who were linguistically different. Consider a tradition of Shawnee origins related by Black Hoof, an opponent of the nativist program who pushed Shawnees to adapt to U.S. political economy in an effort to preserve their Ohio lands. "Each nation of Indians was made by the great spirit, in the skies, and when they were finished he brought them down and gave them a place upon the earth. While he was descending he sang four songs, which were adopted by the Indians. This accounts for the great difference in the manner of singing, among different nations." When the Great Spirit placed the Shawnees "in the centre of the island," "they found none about them who spoke their own language." The Shawnee nation had originated in a confederacy of distinct peoples, which had cohered over time, but, contra Tenskwatawa, there had been limits to this political affiliation. Those "tribes," according to Black Hoof, "all spoke the same language, which greatly facilitated their union." Some Native people attached political significance to linguistic difference. [46]

A confrontation in 1810 at Vincennes, the territorial capital of Indiana, between Tecumseh and Governor and Indian Superintendent William H. Harrison, illustrates the political uses to which U.S. officials could put linguistic difference. Because all Indians were one "nation," sharing a "red" color and holding their land in common, Tecumseh told Harrison that previous land cession treaties were illegitimate. He charged U.S. officials with creating "distinctions of Indian tribes in allotting to each a particular track of land to make them to war with each other." This was merely a means to "prevent the Indians" from "unit[ing] and . . . consider[ing] their land as the common property of the whole." The Shawnee chief informed Harrison that they had united in spite of the governor's efforts to "sow discord" and "excit[e] jealousies." He warned Harrison that refusal to disavow the previous year's Treaty of Fort Wayne (1809), which gouged cessions from remaining Native lands, would mean war. In reply, Harrison attacked Tecumseh's central claim. It was "ridiculous to assert that the red men constituted but one nation," he told the council, "for, if such had been the intention of the Great Spirit, he would not have put different tongues in their heads, but have taught them all to speak the same language." Council protocol underlined the point, since the speech would be translated separately for each attending tribe. It was rendered first into Shawnee and, as the Potawatomi interpreter began, Tecumseh leapt up and, "with great vehemence" and "violent gestures," declared that "all the governor had said was *false*." The meeting adjourned with weapons drawn. Although Tecumseh may have been using a form of sign language to demonstrate the relative insignificance of linguistic difference, Harrison's insistence that linguistic diversity precluded Indian unity provided him with a framework, which resonated with emphasis upon linguistic difference in Native opposition to pan-Indianism and in Jeffersonian taxonomy, to dispute Tecumseh's charges and defend U.S. treaty practice. The United States extended land cessions and worked to deepen Native divisions by waging war against the western confederacy in 1811–1813 and intervening in the Creek Civil War in 1813–1814.[47]

Classification could entail lumping or splitting, but either could be strategically employed as U.S. officials dubbed preexisting Native communities "nations" that possessed land-use rights and the political authority to cede land. Similarity of speech among Miami, Wea, Piankeshaw, and Eel River speakers lent credence to the claim of Little Turtle that the others were merely part of the Miamis. Acknowledging this, and disbursing additional annuity payments to him, substantially increased the influence of one who favored adaptation to white ways. Caleb Swan, an army officer during the Washington administration, had stressed that Muskogean speakers in Spanish Florida were "the original Stock of the Creek nation; but the language had undergone so great a Change" that Creeks "hardly understood it." These people—whom the United States targeted in the First Seminole War (1817–1818)—"were still considered as members" of the Creek confederacy, however, "till the United States treated with them as with an independent nation," according to Albert Gallatin, an ethnologist who had served as Jefferson's Secretary of the Treasury.[48]

Similar patterns emerged in the trans-Mississippi west in the years before coercive federal Indian removal. Determining whether a group spoke a principal language or a derivative one (what Jefferson called the "stock" and the "shoot") provided a means to determine priority among Native groups. Reporting on the region between the Arkansas and Red rivers in 1818, Stephen H. Long informed the War Department that "language, shape and features" proved Quapaws to be a "branch" that had "separated" from the "original stalk" of Osages. Thus, the land claims of the Osages, a powerful group whose friendship the United States valued highly, had a "better foundation, and can probably be more easily substantiated than that of any other tribe or nation of Indians." Gallatin, who had begun compiling incoming linguistic information while in Jefferson's cabinet, pushed the federal government to regularize the process of collection the following decade as philology gained prestige. The War Department instructed its agents that "primitive words . . . afford a strong proof of the common origin, at no very remote period, of the tribes speaking such dialects." These words, moreover, particularly geographic names, "would assist us in finding out the ancient boundaries of certain tribes."[49]

Albert Gallatin's "A Synopsis of the Indian Tribes within the United States East of the Rocky Mountains, and in the British and Russian Possessions in North America" (1836) was the first authoritative linguistic classification and ethnographic map of the region east of the Rocky Mountains and north of Mexico available to the public. By then, according to Gallatin, scholars, missionaries, and officials had "positive knowledge" of the languages of every "existing tribe, east of the Mississippi," excepting only the Alabamas, a nation among the Creeks. Growing out of work that he began in the Jefferson administration and continued during the removal debates, his "Synopsis" superseded previous classifications that mixed often linguistically meaningless geographic groupings, notional links to old-world tongues, and fanciful stories about the western mounds. It enlarged and clarified counterparts to well-understood Algonquian and Iroquoian groupings, including "Athapaska" and "Esquimaux" families in British Canada and Russian Alaska; a "Chahta-Muskhog" family that included each of the large southeastern nations except the Cherokees; and a diverse "Sioux" family in the middle of the continent. The last included Mandans and Lakotas, respectively agricultural villagers who had hosted the Corps of Discovery and migratory bison hunters whom the expedition viewed with hostility. Betraying the Jeffersonian impulse to conflate alliance and linguistic affinity, Gallatin thought it noteworthy that Osages were "perpetually at war with all the other Indians, without excepting the Kansas, who speak the same dialect with themselves," and he mistakenly classified Cheyennes,

Albert Gallatin published the first map of the continent's known Native language
families in the second volume of the American Antiquarian Society's transactions in
1836, under the title, representative in its conflation of peoples and their tongues,
"Map of the Indian Tribes of North America about 1600 A.D. along the Atlantic; &
about 1800 A.D. westwardly." While its colors illustrate knowledge of the Southeast
and the Great Plains, and British and Russian America, its blankness indicates the
limits of philologists' knowledge of the area beyond the Louisiana Purchase.
(Courtesy of the American Antiquarian Society, Worcester, MA)

close allies of Lakotas, as Sioux, though in reality they speak an Algonquian
language. In all, his classification reduced eighty-one tribes to twenty-seven
families, though he also noted a convincing resemblance between Cherokee
and the Iroquoian family, which two missionary-educated Cherokees, John
Ridge and Elias Boudinot, confirmed.[50]

Language promised a way to distinguish a Native "tribe" or "nation," "stock"
or "race"; but a variety of circumstances defeated efforts in this regard. Upon
retiring from the presidency, Jefferson planned to compile the vocabularies that

he and his explorers and agents had collected. As his trunks made their way from Washington to Monticello, Ned, a slave searching for valuables, threw all the vocabularies into the James River, for which his left hand was burned and he received 39 lashes on his bare back. Dispirited, Jefferson sent what was recovered to Barton, who had repeatedly promised a forthcoming work that would provide additional evidence of Indians' origins and relations. The heralded book never appeared, however, and the vocabularies were lost when Barton died in 1815. A few years later, deserters stole the saddle bags containing the numerous vocabularies of western nations that Thomas Say had collected on the Long Expedition. It worsened the "confusion and uncertainty . . . between the frontiers of New Mexico and the United States" confronting federal officials, who were also forced to rely on British traders for information on the Oregon country. Resistance, opportunism, and overwhelming deficiency of knowledge made reliable taxonomy impossible in much of the West before the 1840s.[51]

Compilation of ostensibly vanishing fragments of "American" languages demonstrated U.S. participation in the learned world and provided materials for better understanding the continent's antiquity. But there were other reasons for citizens, explorers, Indian agents, and military men to collect vocabularies and other evidence of Native languages. In the early years of the United States, federal officials sought ways to use language, assuming that it corresponded to the ancestry of peoples, to further colonialism. Although impulses to simplify the complexity of Native America and to exploit its diversity were at odds, the unifying theme was the attention of U.S. officials to lines of similarity and difference, the intention to put such knowledge to practical use, and the reliance, many times, upon Native knowledge of these relationships. The results of white philosophy and science could convince Native peoples of the propriety of consolidation or division only if they resonated with Native traditions or experiences.

Conviction that it provided a marker of ancestry was just one way language both facilitated expansion and provided crucial material for the construction of national and racial lines in the early United States. Although some writers occasionally spoke of linguistically related peoples as races, there was no essentialist understanding of language in this era. The belief that language recorded human descent would later provide a foundation for such a view but only after it merged with widening speculation and debate on what languages, particularly their grammatical forms, revealed of the intellectual and moral attainments of their speakers.

3

Much More Fertile Than Commonly Supposed

John Heckewelder learned the Lenni Lenape (Delaware) language and culture as a Moravian missionary. In station after station, from Greenland to the Caribbean to Asia and Africa, the Unitas Fratrum sought to preach the gospel and restore human unity by creating a global community of faith. Repairing the damage of Babel depended upon learning Native languages and using them successfully in evangelization, but, for a time, the Brethren's linguistic knowledge was controversial. Nativists who called for purification of white influences and for racial separation distrusted the missionaries, as did white settlers, for whom Moravians' relationships with Native people converged with their ethnic difference—as German speakers who possessed a radical faith, unfamiliar religious practices, and an exclusivist communitarian social organization—to foster suspicion. Mid-eighteenth-century judicial proceedings in Connecticut and New York challenged Moravians' linguistic work and the broader public remained suspicious amid settler–Native violence and imperial rivalries of the revolutionary era. Heckewelder experienced it himself when Pennsylvania settlers "politely" interrogated him in 1773. By the end of the eighteenth century, as Moravian faith and practice came more closely to resemble that of other American Protestants, and as men like David Zeisberger and his assistant Heckewelder offered their expertise to U.S. officials, military officers, and men of learning, Moravians shed their earlier aura of frontier intrigue and acquired a reputation for philanthropy.[1]

Heckewelder's experiences as a missionary shaped his views of Lenni Lenape and other Native languages and their significance for what would be called ethnology. Because of his literacy and because of the close relationships he formed with mission-affiliated Delawares and some of their kinsmen,

Heckewelder also served as a "clerk" at the "great Council of the Nation," responsible for recording speeches from the mouths of orators. Hearing the most skilled speakers use the tongue's "purest and most elegant" form, Heckewelder was struck with the language's beauty, gravity, and expressiveness. He knew that ordinary conversation was more prosaic, but its most formal register demonstrated what could be done with the language. As a missionary, he was inclined to view Native people in terms of potential, and his duties in preaching and religious translation reinforced for him how effectively fluent speakers could meaningfully communicate Christian ideas. With Zeisberger, he suspected that Delaware was the "Mother Tongue" to other Algonquian languages, and hearing Delawares consistently addressed as *"grandfather"* by other Native groups in council confirmed the theory that other Algonquians descended from Delawares. Beyond promising insight into Native descent and relations, language was also the "indispensible requisite" for accurately comprehending Native beliefs and institutions. Indians were usually reluctant to answer whites' "pestering" about their *"heathenish customs,"* but they were "proud," Heckewelder found, to teach respectful Euro-Americans their tongue, which offered the possibility of gaining the desired ethnographic information more indirectly. Missionaries alone, because of their linguistic skills and supposed disinterestedness, could provide "authentic accounts" of Native people. If learned men made "proper use" of missionaries' knowledge, they could "correct many gross errors . . . respecting the character and customs of the Indians."[2]

By the 1790s, with few U.S. citizens fearing Native people east of the Ohio River, Heckewelder worked with scholars from the American Philosophical Society (APS) to make Indians objects of curiosity and pity. In doing so, he followed the example of his friend and mentor Zeisberger, who had opened Moravian missionary knowledge to philosophical gaze, despite his worries that Moravians' linguistic work might be misused. He contributed to a fellow Moravian's history of the Brethren's missions and, with the help of the Christian Delaware John Killbuck, he passed along materials to the projects of Court de Gébelin and Catherine the Great, in the hopes that it would cultivate goodwill from influential U.S. officials. More clearly than Zeisberger or other contemporaries, Heckewelder recognized that the dissemination of ethnographic knowledge gained in missions could cultivate public support for "philanthropy." From the Moravian town of Bethlehem, Pennsylvania, Heckewelder formed close relationships with two members of the APS in Philadelphia, the etymologist Benjamin S. Barton and the philologist Peter S. Du Ponceau. Learned societies allowed elites to demonstrate cultural authority, but they also arose for many of the same reasons as did other voluntary associations: they offered venues for sociability among those with similar interests and values and the opportunity to organize individuals to realize shared ends. In the minds of many, the goals of missionaries and scholars were not far removed. Just as Moravians imagined evangelism as the means to purify languages and overcome the confusion of tongues, many supporters of U.S. efforts to offer instruction in white ways imagined that process as a means to restore an ancient cultivation. Through these collaborations, especially with Du Ponceau, Heckewelder's views had a profound effect on ideas about Native languages throughout the nineteenth century and of their place in missionary programs and U.S. policies.[3]

The material that Heckewelder provided, which included the missionary texts that other Moravian missionaries had compiled, revealed the lexical richness and grammatical sophistication of a variety of Native languages that had been dismissed as "savage" in the eighteenth century. Barton, for instance, became convinced that Native grammars, like the similarities in Native vocabularies and the traces of monumental architecture throughout the continent, indicated the previous advancement of Native people. His conclusions collided with increasing skepticism that collecting and comparing words adequately answered genealogical and psychological questions, and with growing criticism of the notion that environments shaped peoples' bodies and speech. While some scholars turned to studying Indians through monuments and traditions and their old-world parallels to discern questions of civilization and descent, others turned to a deeper study of languages that focused on their grammatical organization. Most policymakers continued to believe that people were malleable, an assumption they acted upon in expanding the federal "civilization" program following peace with the northwest confederacy, Red Stick Creeks, and Seminoles in 1813–1818. Because commentary on Native grammatical systems frequently either stated or implied the capacity of Indians for cultivation, advocates of an increasingly aggressive U.S. "civilization" program pointed to linguistic studies for support.

Degeneration, Civilization, and Grammar

Europeans and U.S. citizens in the eighteenth and early nineteenth centuries imagined savagery in broad agreement. In addition to being superstitious and unreflective, cruel in war and imperious toward women, possessed of a hunting subsistence and a schism-prone tribal organization that inhibited the desire for private property and advancement, "savage" peoples were imagined to possess specific linguistic features: unwritten and ever-changing tongues of harsh sounds, few words, and grammatical disorder that expressed a way of thinking different from cultivated peoples. The American Bible Society put it concisely in claiming that Indians were "divided from us by their language, their manners, their ignorance, their degradation,—by every thing which distinguishes savage from civilized man." There was no consensus among the learned, however, on when this social condition emerged. Some suspected, as did Thomas Jefferson, that humanity was in its "rudest state" at the "infancy of creation." Others believed that barbarism or savagery was the result of a historical process of decline from a condition of original civilization. Benjamin S. Barton leaned toward the latter view. While Jefferson's opinions "differed . . . in one or two essential points" from his own, in Barton's words, they agreed that, "civilization has been constantly preceded by barbarity and rudeness."[4]

Theories of nature and scriptural accounts could each support conceptions of degeneration, and these resonated in the social and cultural climate of the early United States. The era's natural history, under the influence of Buffon, stressed the power of the environment to change living things. As human beings and animals moved beyond the site of their creation, they encountered different geographic conditions, and new environments shaped their bodies. Blumenbach, collector of skulls and coiner of the term "Caucasian," understood human racial differences to have emerged in this way. Philosophical understandings of divergence from an original condition fit well with the narrative of decline in the book of Genesis. Cain and Abel, the sons of Adam and Eve, tilled the soil and tended flocks, respectively. Since Europeans considered farming and shepherding to be more advanced modes of subsistence than hunting, and since settlers and officials ignored the degree to which eastern North American Indians cultivated fields and orchards, self-interested observers saw in Native peoples' small, egalitarian, seasonally migratory societies evidence that confirmed revelation. In the early republic, when U.S. society was experiencing its own massive population movement, which outpaced the establishment of religious and social institutions, fears regarding cultural degeneration were widespread.[5]

Those who pondered the significance of the story of the Tower of Babel— itself apparent evidence of political centralization and monumental architecture at an early period—elaborated this interpretive framework in varying ways. Jacob Böhme (or Behmen), a philosophical mystic who was especially influential among eighteenth-century Moravians, believed that God endowed Adam with speech that expressed the essences of things. At Babel, Böhme wrote in *Mysterium Magnum* (1623), God both confused this correspondence between speech and nature and splintered previous unity. Over time and space, as nations dispersed, seventy-two imperfect "Head languages," which corresponded in some way to their speakers and their homeland, degenerated into countless "collateral Affinities." Their connections, however, could be recovered. Naturalistic explanations of human savagery and diversity could support similar historical interpretations, as in Samuel Stanhope Smith's *Essay on the Causes of the Variety of Complexion and Figure in the Human Species* (1787). Although his major focus was to refute Jefferson and others on the permanence and significance of physical difference by stressing the power of climate and social condition to alter the human body, Smith also leveled "Strictures" against Lord Kames's covert polygenism. Since Kames stressed the absence of links between the American languages and those of Asia, Smith sought to demonstrate that linguistic difference would emerge "in *the nature of things*" despite humanity's innate sociability. Although God created people fully possessed of the knowledge necessary for religion and civilization, human laziness and willfulness, combined with the influence of the natural and social environment, caused degeneration from the primitive state. "The habits of solitude and silence incline a savage rarely to speak," Smith asserted, and the abandonment of settled life for hunting—an overpowering temptation in the bountiful American "wilderness"—would further decrease opportunities for intercourse. Small, wandering groups would forget old words and coin new ones as new places and climes produced new wants and introduced them to new things. "Diversity of language," Smith explained, "necessarily springs out of the savage state."[6]

For most citizens of the new nation, the deficiency of Indians, their minds, and their languages were a given, emerging as a common theme among the learned. In a prize-winning address before the APS, William Thornton asserted that "savage nations" possessed little more than the sounds of "beasts . . . a few syllables compose their whole vocabulary, and express all that their appetites crave." Benjamin Lincoln informed the Massachusetts Historical Society that he had found it "impossible to convey . . . the sentiments attempted" in his abortive efforts to negotiate with the western confederacy, since "without ideas, they cannot have language." The following year, Thomas Pierronet explained to the same society that Montagnais was "almost impossible to reduce . . . to the rules of grammar." Indians, moreover, possessed only "vague and imperfect traditions," in Jefferson's words, to substitute for their lack of alphabetic writing, which provided but "feeble" evidence for historical enquiry. Even in an era when celebrating "American" subjects spurred considerable learned endeavor, U.S. citizens echoed Europeans' denigration of the sounds, words, forms, and orality of Native languages, and these estimates formed a crucial part of a broader definition of savagery.[7]

7 ELEGUP.—1770.

—————

Enda hokunk likhechtite quenaga talli enda luwundasik Babel.
1 Mos. 11. &c.

The story of the Tower of Babel, from the book of Genesis, was crucial for Euro-American understandings of the linguistic differentiation of humanity over time. It also played a prominent role in narratives of Indian degeneration into savagery. This chapter, from Abraham Luckenbach's *Forty-Six Select Scripture Narratives from the Old Testament, Embellished with Engravings, for the Use of Indian Youth* (1838) illustrates a Moravian missionary's effort to make the story meaningful for a Delaware audience. (Courtesy of the American Antiquarian Society, Worcester, Massachusetts)

Benjamin S. Barton, however, came to reject these axioms of linguistic savagery. Beyond his interest in the origin, relations, and migrations of people, Barton also studied the *"American monuments"* as part of the "natural and the moral history of the native inhabitants." As in his etymological work, Barton sought information that would shed light on past ages through his network of correspondents and by seeking interviews with Native people passing through Philadelphia. The "knowledge, and liberality" of John Heckewelder proved to be especially important to these researches, reinforcing Barton's opinions on Native traditions and transforming his opinions on Native languages, though in the end Barton made only limited use of the extensive information that Heckewelder provided. Barton presented "Observations and Conjectures" to the APS in 1796, aiming to refute the "invective" and "eloquent puerilities" of European theorists of Native savagery. Toward this end, he linked the peoples of the Mississippi Valley and Mesoamerica, home to soaring stone pyramids that preceded colonization, in their artifacts and astronomical knowledge. More fundamentally, Barton argued that the historical record, Native traditions and, especially, the American languages proved a level of advancement among Native people within territory claimed by the United States that surpassed what was known of their descendants. As he confided to Heckewelder in 1800, Barton hoped to "convince the world whether Christians or Philosophers, that the man of America, possessing intellectual powers of the highest kind, is capable of arriving at, and of enjoying, the blessings of civilized life."[8]

Although some Native traditions recorded that the mounds had been built by a distinct people that preceded their ancestors, Barton seized on a number of Native traditions that described a decline from once greater numbers and knowledge. This confirmed the "*known* declension" that colonial accounts documented, and suggested, to Barton, that former Native advancement explained the monumental architecture. Hendrick Aupaumut, for instance, likely shared with Barton that Mohicans preserved a cultural memory that moral degeneration, following contact with immoral European settlers, accompanied a physical decline from a "more civilized" state. As more recent scholars have demonstrated, the human loss and social deterioration that these traditions describe were rooted in the epidemic diseases of the Columbian exchange, which produced devastating demographic collapse that compromised subsistence and the transmission of traditional skills. Wars over hunting grounds and access to European goods exacerbated this trend. These convulsions placed strain on some forms of social organization and beliefs. In 1803, for instance, former South Carolina governor John Drayton shared with Barton that John Nettles, a Catawba educated at the College of William & Mary, remembered hearing from elders that his people had once worshiped and made sacrifices to the sun. As Heckewelder stated at a later date, Native traditions, particularly those of "the most intelligent and creditable old Indians," shed light on the pre-European American past because they were "transmit[ted] . . . by a regular chain" from one generation to another.[9]

Native accounts from this era describe language change. Samson Occom, for instance, denounced colonization for having "corrupted" Native speech. "Whereas he had a pure and holy language, in his innocency," the Mohegan missionary wrote, "he *now* curses, swears, and profanes the holy name of God, and curses and damns his fellow-creatures." Since Michel de Montaigne's "On Cannibals," Europeans had cataloged the words absent from Native languages to evoke the supposedly natural virtues of peoples free from European vices, and Occom's echo of William Shakespeare's Caliban was deliberate, but not all accounts appear so literary. One U.S. Indian agent claimed to have heard an Ojibwe tradition that "great changes have taken place" in the way Ojibwe was spoken, and "these changes keep pace with the decline of the tribe from their ancient standard of forest morals and their departure from their ancient customs." Henry R. Schoolcraft recounted this tradition with condescension, but it suggests Native commentary regarding a linguistic aspect to social changes resulting from colonization.[10]

When Barton examined Native languages, he believed he recognized evidence of linguistic degeneration that countered philosophical generalizations about savage languages. In this essay, delivered one year before the appearance of *New Views*, Barton introduced his theory that the American languages were not radically diverse. There were many dialects, but these had "receded so little from the parent stock, that we cannot hesitate to conclude that the period is not very remote when the tribes who speak them were one and the same people." This "great consolidation of the Americans, in former ages" held social, in addition to genealogical, significance. Since "extensive associations of men . . . cannot long subsist, in the savage state," Indians they must have been "much more cultivated than we have ever known them." In addition, Barton learned of a variety of Native graphic practices, ranging from ancient petroglyphs to representations of Iroquois clans to paintings in the central plazas of Creek towns. These were "vestiges of . . . hieroglyphicks," in his opinion, that resembled markings found in Asia and revealed earlier Native advancement toward the development of a written language and, thus, civilization.[11]

Attention to grammatical features in the American languages provided further crucial evidence. Such materials and other published records, especially Heckewelder's Moravian materials and the Jesuit histories of Charlevoix and Clavigero, convinced Barton that "many of these languages are much more fertile than has been commonly supposed." For that very reason, against assertions that they were in constant flux, Barton stressed that Native speech "preserve[d] its genius" and that Native people retained their languages over time. Besides references to the special form of speech used at councils, colonial histories and travel accounts also provided evidence that some Native languages possessed "expressions of reverence and courtesy," and even separate forms of speech for "nobles" and "common people," which indicated a degree of social differentiation within Native communities that philosophers had presumed absent in the savage state. Far from evincing evidence of linguistic savagery, the "structure of the languages of many of the American tribes is favourable to the idea, that these people were, formerly, much more improved than they are at present." He had once believed that ancient Europeans had built the mounds, but the cumulative linguistic evidence—not the mounds themselves or anything excavated from them—convinced Barton that the ancestors of still-living Native people were the mound builders.[12]

Barton was not alone in thinking that the American languages revealed that their speakers once possessed greater civilization. After amassing considerable linguistic materials in his travels in Spanish America, Alexander von Humboldt struggled to reconcile ostensibly uncultivated peoples with towering ruins and "languages of which the mechanism proves an ancient civilization." Johann Severin Vater, a German philologist working with Humboldt's material, agreed, finding "modes of expression" that were "the product of a certain civilization, & of a delicate power of abstraction." This idea also found some currency among U.S. missionaries, who communicated it to federal officials. In 1818, the discovery of "as much refinement, as in many polished languages" convinced Cyrus Kingsbury that Cherokees' ancestors must have been "far more improved, than the present race." Since savages spoke savage languages, linguistic richness and stability revealed civilization, if not presently, then previously.[13]

This view of American antiquity had explicit relevance for the American present. In his work's early stages, Barton told the Creek chief Alexander McGillivray that it would "rescue from the prejudices of European writers the character of these nations" and, perhaps, protect them from "the vicious part of our countrymen" who sought their land. While Barton's father, the Anglican minister Thomas Barton, had defended, against the cries of the Philadelphia Quaker elite, the Paxton Boys' murder of peaceful Indians at Conestoga only a few miles from the family home in 1763, the son rejected such views. If Native people had once lived in denser, more complex societies, and still possessed remarkably developed languages, "we learn," as Barton wrote in his dedication of *New Views* to Thomas Jefferson, "that the Americans are susceptible of improvement." He reminded the man then serving as U.S. vice president, "to extend the empire of civility and knowledge" was "peculiarly worthy of the notice of the United States." Yet, Barton believed, as did Jefferson and many others, that Native social advancement required dispossession, thereby supporting white interests. Reflecting on the westward movement of Lenni

Lenapes over the course of the eighteenth century, the Pennsylvanian predicted "an immense change in the geographical situation of our tribes" in the coming years. While he admitted that the "ravages of tyrants" were frequently to blame for such migrations, Barton assured readers that in this case Indians were simply "incapable of prospering in the neighbourhood of the whites, especially the enterprising Anglo-Americans."[14]

As president, Jefferson accelerated the U.S. civilization program, just as his administration accelerated land acquisition, and he combined this with an effort to convince Native groups to exchange claims they held east of the Mississippi for land west of the river. Sauks and Foxes signed the first such treaty in 1804, but Cherokees and the other southern nations were targets from the beginning. Land cessions would leave Native families no alternative but to adapt to U.S. political economy, which the paternalistic Jefferson insisted was best for whites and Native people. Jefferson thought that directed action, in a proper "order of progression," could accelerate the supposed civilizing process. This began with arts of subsistence, teaching the use of domestic animals, agriculture for men, and spinning and weaving for women. The "acquisition of property" would follow, which required literacy and numeracy for recording and calculating transactions. He rejected the usefulness of Native-language translations and ideas of Native linguistic sophistication. Deriding Indian languages and orthodox Christianity at a stroke, he asserted, "Their barren vocabularies cannot be vehicles for ideas of the fall of man, his redemption, the triune composition of the Godhead, and other mystical doctrines considered by most Christians of the present date as essential elements of faith." Besides, Jefferson believed, with many others, that participation in U.S. society required language change. Elevating Indians to "civilization" began with their mode of subsistence, in Jefferson's view, but its completion required English.[15]

"Civilization" entailed the surrender of lands, spiritual transformation, and language loss. Jefferson's program demanded a rejection of traditional social and spiritual roles, which linked the ritual knowledge of women to plants and of men to animals. It also pushed adoption of the pen and book, which some Native people believed the creator intended for whites alone. While some Indians eagerly adapted new ways, many others were understandably reluctant to embrace "improvement" that inverted the natural order as well as their lives. Refusing the choices that the Jefferson administration offered, some followed prophets such as Tenskwatawa, Tecumseh, and Hillis Hadjo, who opposed U.S. demands for land cessions and cultural change. Fearful and resentful of Native resistance, the United States went to war with the western confederacy in 1811–1813 and intervened in the Creek Civil War in 1813–1814, conflicts that merged with the War of 1812. While Barton remained optimistic

about relations with "their brethren of another colour" despite the probability
of future warfare, Jefferson asserted that the war that his policies had provoked left "extermination" or removal as U.S. citizens' only options.[16]

Etymology and Environmentalism Assailed

As they discussed the likely effects of war, Jefferson and Barton were turning
away from their efforts to discover Indians' ancestry and relations by collecting
and comparing words. Jefferson abandoned vocabulary collection and determined that savagery, not the antiquity of Native claims to the land, accounted
for linguistic diversity. Barton, too, came to reject the importance of etymology. As late as 1803, he insisted that "etymology (though it has often been
abused), is susceptible, in innumerable instances, of the greatest certainty" in
revealing the ancient affinities of nations, and he expected that the "most
finished *Anthropologia* . . . will be constructed, in a considerable degree, upon
the affinities of languages." A decade later, however, he disingenuously claimed
that another "polar star" had always guided his study of American antiquity.
All evidence pointed to the fact that America, until European discovery, was
"almost exclusively inhabited by a race of men not essentially different in their
physical features" and mode of life. Bodily remains, artifacts, and monuments
of earth and stone, stretching from the Alleghenies to the Andes, Barton
asserted with confusion, "uniformly represent[ed] one species, I was going to
say one *variety* of men. Every where the American (or rather I would say the
Asiatic) face and features are seen." In the portion of a decade bracketed by the
U.S. assault upon Prophetstown in 1811 and the Indian Civilization Act of
1819, U.S. scholars turned away from etymology and followed European trends
in seeking a deeper means to use language to study ancestry and the mind,
even as the questions of whether Indians were Asian or American in origin, a
variety or a species of humanity, still lingered.[17]

From the 1780s to the 1810s, as the United States sought expansion and
"civilization," and as European scholars refined their approach to studying
languages and peoples, etymology had sparked considerable debate. Barton's
work garnered some praise. William Jenks lauded Barton for collecting new
evidence that led to the "same conclusions" as the prominent British scholars
William Bryant and Sir William Jones. This affirmed, for the New England
minister and antiquarian, that "etymological enquiry, cautiously and diligently
pursued," in combination with broader ethnographic study of beliefs and customs, would "connect . . . our Indian population with the ancient achieve-
ments of the early descendants of Noah." James Cowles Prichard, a young

British physician at the outset of a prominent career in ethnology, similarly thought that Barton's "elaborate comparison" had "proved that the languages of the American tribes are connected with those of the Eastern Asiatics." Many of those friendly to environmentalism and the fundamental accuracy of the scriptural account of human origins and dispersion eagerly grasped Barton's insistence on Asian origins and degeneration.[18]

Others, however, criticized Barton's etymology severely. Volney congratulated him for "opening a mine of valuable and curious knowledge," but he doubted the soundness of Barton's work, especially its purported demonstration of relationships among the American languages. Vater similarly acknowledged Barton's efforts but blasted his methods. He complained to Jefferson, "how little sufficient a collection of words, however extensive, can be" for determining "the affinities of any language." Sound philology compared only neighboring languages and took care not to confuse lexical roots with grammatical inflections, two axioms that Barton ignored. Even with this lack of rigor, Vater found the similarities "trifling," since "the words between which even a distant resemblance is shewn, are very few indeed." In Humboldt's concise evaluation, Barton's studies had reached "no important conclusion." Indeed, to overcome the "feeble evidence" connecting the languages of the two continents, he urged scholars to examine instead "the cosmogonies, the monuments, the hieroglyphics, and institutions of the people of America and Asia." Such a plea, from a man with a towering reputation in Europe and in the United States, would prove central to the construction of an "Oriental" interpretation of pre-Columbian civilizations. Barton's methods and claims provided a target for European savants who intended to preserve their privileged position in evaluating the place of Indians in global histories of humanity.[19]

Even Americans who shared many of Barton's motivations were skeptical of his results. Fellow APS member Nicholas Collin accepted that "languages are the widely scattered and jumbled fragments of a mirror," in which one could still find reflections of humanity's "infant thoughts and lisping accents," and he affirmed that "several languages of North America are more allied with the Asiatic and European than is generally known." Like Barton, therefore, he rejected "false lines of separation" between the ostensibly distinct "general complexions of languages, as oriental and occidental, maternal and filial, ancient and modern, savage and civilized." Barton's etymologies, however, were unconvincing. Besides, Collin comforted himself, "the confusion of tongues . . . gives full permission to seek new origins" for different languages. If he thought of Lord Kames, the Lutheran minister did not record it. John

Heckewelder, Barton's most important source, personally believed that Indians were the descendants of the Lost Tribes, but he concluded that "something more [was] wanting to prove the *Origin* of the Indians of this Country than bare sounds of Words."[20]

Etymology's methods faced trenchant criticism. The British philologist Sir William Jones, for instance, asserted that "no form of reasoning is . . . weaker or more delusive," and he castigated "the licentiousness of etymologists" in rearranging letters or substituting one for another as they strained for affinities. James H. McCulloh, an antiquarian who claimed authority from his service on "the frontiers" as a U.S. army surgeon in the War of 1812, offered a detailed examination of why "etymological inquiry, appears defective." Many of the problems lay in collecting vocabularies. If one pointed to one's hand, would a consultant reply with the word for "hand," "my hand," or "your hand"? If he pointed to a stone, would a "savage" mistakenly offer a word that conveyed that he made hatchets from that stone or that it held some spiritual power? The likelihood that collectors could accurately convey what they sought was slim. Those collectors, moreover, varied widely in their abilities to distinguish sounds precisely and record them accurately. Armchair scholars, finally, too seldom considered the varying pronunciations that different Europeans attached to the same letters: words that might resemble one another on paper could sound nothing alike. Etymologists, including Barton, wandered in an "endless labyrinth of conjecture."[21]

Though Jefferson's collection efforts led to no published opinions after *Notes on the State of Virginia,* his work met opposition nonetheless. Some of those he expected to collect vocabularies doubted the usefulness of the process. John Ledyard realized the "thousand dangers and difficulties" of vocabulary collection on his surreptitious Russian journey. So, instead of relying on the "art" of writing words, he turned to "nature," judging his impressions of "the tone & inflexion of the voice" as sufficient to determine the "analogy of Languages." Also mindful of the "imperfect resemblance of words," William Dunbar, a planter and former trader and surveyor in West Florida, turned to study what linguists now know as Plains Indian Sign Language to trace Indian origins to Asia. To some would-be collectors, words scratched in a list could obscure more than they revealed.[22]

Etymology generally, and Jefferson's in particular, also suffered criticism because of its entanglement with broader debates about atheism and the French Revolution, since in the Anglophone world it was associated with controversial attempts to prove the physical origins of abstract terms and with political radicalism. Suspecting radical materialist implications in ideas about

Indians' American origins, Clement Moore stressed that if "Moses knew no more about the age of the world than a Mohock," then Jefferson must have meant to imply that "man is of the same nature with the rest of the animal creation . . . not rendered distinct from them by an immortal soul, but merely by the superiority of his faculties." Elijah Parrish similarly railed against Jefferson's "wanton denial of revelation," warning Americans of an infidel president, for "When the wicked beareth rule, the people mourn." Jefferson's etymology, in the minds of some New England Federalists at least, was inextricable from a putatively atheist philosophy. In the context of the bloodshed and social leveling of the French Revolution, and fears of similar scenes at home, a biblical framework offered a reassuring way for understanding human difference.[23]

Some scholars, seeking to reinforce scriptural narratives and promote increased "civilization" efforts, turned to grammatical evidence to support the theory that Indians were the descendants of the Lost Tribes of Israel. The era's most influential version of this thesis was Elias Boudinot's *A Star in the West* (1816), which incorporated Jonathan Edwards, Jr.'s earlier observation of the "analogous" grammatical structure of Mohican, Mohawk, and Hebrew. Boudinot argued that "in their roots, idiom, and construction" Indian languages had "the whole genius of the Hebrew." "Blind chance could not have directed so great a number of remote and warring savage nations to fix on, and unite in so nice a . . . grammatical construction of language, where there was no knowledge of letters or syntax." This resemblance was imperfect, but that was because migration had led to intercourse with "the inhabitants of Scythia or Tartary," which "adulterate[d]" the language before Indians' ancestors had crossed the Bering Strait. Other philanthropists and missionaries made similar claims. So too did William Apess (Pequot). Since neither he nor most of the rest of his nation knew any Pequot, he relied on Boudinot to demonstrate the "evident approach" of Hebrew and Native languages. Unlike Apess, who advocated Native sovereignty, most of those who articulated the Lost Tribes theory did so to support a more "benevolent" form of colonialism by bringing increased assimilationist pressure to bear on Native communities. Despite its resonance among the faithful, both white and some Natives, claims of linguistic proof of the "Lost Tribes" thesis convinced few scholars.[24]

This turn to grammar reflected important European trends in the study of language. Despite being maligned, etymology had produced interest in the origin, relations, and development of language, which the revolutionary work of William Jones only intensified. Examining "the roots of verbs, and . . . the forms of grammar" convinced Jones, a jurist in British India who approached the study of Persian and Sanskrit as an aid to his official duties, that those languages must have descended from a common ancestor with Greek, Latin, and most of the modern languages of Europe. This fact, with the utter difference of the Semitic languages and Chinese, led Jones to conclude that there were three "races of men"—corresponding, respectively, to Noah's sons Ham, Shem, and Japhet—"that essentially differ in language, religion, manners, and other known characteristics." The people soon to be dubbed "Indo-European" or "Aryan" (whom Jones idiosyncratically associated with Ham, though usually Ham was associated with Africa and Japhet with Europe), had established colonies and spread "civilization" throughout the world, even in ancient Mexico and Peru, though Jones gave no attention to their languages. The scriptural framework of Jones's work, which appeared in the late 1780s and 1790s, added to its appeal at a time when materialist theories came under philosophical and political attack, but Jones's work also provided an authoritative model for using grammatical evidence from language to trace racial ancestry.[25]

Scholars interested in descent and migrations, however, increasingly confronted mounting evidence from Asia and the Americas that bodies and languages seemed to contradict one another. While Prichard thought that physical and linguistic evidence combined to prove the shared descent of American Indians and Asians, for instance, Humboldt reached the opposite conclusion. Vater, one of the first scholars to attempt a comprehensive comparative view of the American languages, observed an uncomfortable fact that would be widely noted in the succeeding decades. Different classifications were fundamentally incompatible. While Blumenbach divided Europeans and Asians into different races according to their distinct crania, Jones presented linguistic evidence that "Hindoos" were distinct from "Arabs" and "Tartars" but belonged to the same race as Europeans. Ethnologists, thus, had to grapple with "the Entire difference which exists between the languages of those whose skulls are formed on the same mould . . . & the affinity between the languages of those whose skulls are differently formed." The origins and relations of nations were still obscure, Vater cautioned, and "All traces of their origin do not always lead back to the same point." The methodological puzzle would grow rancorous by midcentury.[26]

In addition to throwing doubt on Native descent and relations, increasing knowledge of the sophistication of Native grammatical forms also seemed to warn against any simple correspondence between languages and climate or social condition. Charles Caldwell, a Philadelphia physician, opposed theories that natural or social environments could alter bodies or speech. Language, according to the onetime student of Barton—whom the teacher had "entirely failed to convince" that Indians had built the mounds or that their languages could be traced to Asia—had "no essential dependence on external circumstances . . . once formed, it becomes appended to a people with an adherence almost as firm as that of their existence." Juan Ignacio Molina, a creole Jesuit who penned a history of Chile, admitted that the "influence of climate may undoubtedly affect language so far as to modify it, but can never produce a complete change in its primitive structure." The New England minister Thaddeus Mason Harris was so struck with Molina's remark that he repeated it in an address before the American Antiquarian Society. Deeper consideration of Native languages led Humboldt, known now as a scholar who stressed the overriding importance of natural and social environments for shaping human institutions, to reconsider his earlier view that Native languages suggested previous civilization. Those languages instead seemed to evince "great analogy in the intellectual disposition of the American tribes, from Greenland to the magellanic regions." By 1818, he asserted that the "influence of climate, and of external circumstances vanishes before that which depends on the race, on the hereditary and individual dispositions of men."[27]

Where scholars like Barton and missionaries like Kingsbury had suggested that Native grammatical organization contained proof of earlier civilization, by the second decade of the nineteenth century, scholars suggested that it proved only that language and civilization were unconnected. Although environmentalism remained a prominent aspect of learned theories, explanations of humanity's physical and linguistic differences that focused on heredity and nebulous suggestions of unchanging races grew increasingly common in the 1810s and 1820s.

Plans of Ideas

A new "science of languages" emerged after "the general pacification of 1814." That year marked the end of the Napoleonic Wars in Europe and, in the United States, peace with the western confederacy and the final battles against the Red Stick Creeks and Britain (the Battle of New Orleans excepted). Increasing numbers of linguistic scholars, building on the work of Jones, argued that languages' mechanisms for modifying words to indicate qualities and circumstances (morphology) and for arranging them in such a way to make one's thoughts intelligible (syntax) offered a more certain means than etymology to answer genealogical and developmental questions. In the United States, this philology drew from continuing interest in the history of English,

the ascent of "Indo-European" studies on the Continent, and the earlier poly-
glot collection projects of Peter S. Pallas, Lorenzo Hervás y Panduro, and the
team of Johann Christoph Adelung and Johann Severin Vater, which included
linguistic material from the Americas as well as Europe, Africa, Asia, and the
Pacific Islands. A voracious appetite for new linguistic information among the
learned in Europe presented U.S. scholars with a singular opportunity to participate in a prestigious, cosmopolitan project. Those studies, in turn, held
important implications for the lives of Native people.[28]

The first U.S. scholar to claim a place in the new philology by studying U.S.
colonial subjects was Peter S. Du Ponceau, an active member in the APS and
a prominent lawyer in Philadelphia who used his knowledge of several
European languages to build a thriving practice. On behalf of the APS's new
Historical and Literary Committee (HLC), he opened a correspondence with
John Heckewelder in 1816, the same year Vater released the volume of the "stupendous" *Mithridates* that detailed the grammatical construction of the languages of North America. Du Ponceau was "mortified as well as astonished
that so much knowledge respecting the languages of the Aborigines of our
Country should be possessed at the furthermost end of Europe, while we know
so little." Although he had worked with Court de Gébelin on *Monde Primitif*
as a young man, before accompanying Baron von Steuben to North America
during the War for Independence, Du Ponceau thought that recovering
humanity's original language was "impossible," and he lamented that language
study had "been too long confined to mere 'word hunting.'" The retired missionary was surprised at the attention to "a Language indeed *dead*" to most
U.S. citizens, but Heckewelder forwarded Zeisberger's manuscript grammar
of Lenni Lenape and, later, several other Moravian texts. Although he never
"learnt it by Gramar rules," Heckewelder also provided expertise on how
Delaware was actually spoken, since he had once been "competent to understand *every word* they said, & *yet*, can plainly see the necessity of every syllable
in a word for to explain themselves properly." At the outset, Heckewelder
warned that he would "in some points, differ from what others have said and
written." By accepting and extending what Heckewelder claimed, Du Ponceau
became the most influential philologist in the country.[29]

In January 1819, the Historical and Literary Committee published its initial
volume of *Transactions*. It held Du Ponceau's report on "the General Character
and Forms" of Native languages; an ethnography and history of the Lenni
Lenape by Heckewelder; and Du Ponceau's highly edited and self-consciously
literary version of their linguistic correspondence, which featured Heckewelder
as a learned, patient teacher and himself as a precocious, far-seeing student.

Disavowing that he held preconceived notions regarding Indians' descent and relations, while acknowledging the relevance of philology for uncovering the "all-important history of man," Du Ponceau made clear that his main goal was to understand and explain, more fully than Vater had, the "character & physiognomy of the American languages as far as regards their grammatical forms & construction & the manner in which they *combine ideas together in the form of words.*" More than any of his American predecessors, Du Ponceau merged the study of descent with that of thought.[30]

Based on his first two years of study, Du Ponceau offered three "propositions or rather questions." He admitted that these were not "positive facts," since available knowledge on Native languages was "very limited," but Du Ponceau reported to the learned world:

1. That the American languages in general are rich in words and in grammatical forms, and that in their complicated construction, the greatest order, method, and regularity prevail.
2. That these complicated forms, which I call *polysynthetic*, appear to exist in all those languages, from Greenland to Cape Horn.
3. That these forms appear to differ essentially from those of the ancient and modern languages of the old hemisphere.

Each of the three statements marked a radical departure from prevailing views of the philosophy of language, Indian origins, and the science of society.[31]

Proving these points required a detailed examination of Native lexicons and grammatical organization. Their words were "not, as many suppose, confined to the expression of things relating to their usual occupations and physical existence." In the realms of economic and religious life, their languages easily expressed what was needed. Heckewelder, for instance, pointed to several related expressions, "beautiful" in sound and sentiment, which Delawares applied to God, including *Eluwantowit* ("God above all)." Missionaries' success in using Native languages to preach "abstruse" Christian subjects provided testimony and Native men and women, whenever they were asked, "always and uniformly" reported that "they were never at a loss for words or phrases in which to clothe every idea that occurred to them."[32]

Du Ponceau and Heckewelder also explained how Native languages differed from European languages without being inferior to them. Despite having no terms corresponding to "to have" and "to be," the American languages could convey what those auxiliary verbs entailed. Indeed, "in every language, there are more ideas, perhaps, understood, than are actually expressed." Terms or pronunciation in some Native languages varied according to whether the speaker was male or female. In addition, *"genders,* are not, as with us, descriptive of the *masculine* and *feminine* species, but of the *animate* and *inanimate* kinds" in Delaware. It illustrated the "curious connexion . . . in the mind of an Indian between man and the brute creation," which deserved fuller investigation, but the animate–inanimate distinction was no better or worse than classifications in other languages. The pair also introduced the learned world to the *"particular"* number, later dubbed the "American plural," which distinguished whether "we" included or excluded the listener. Duly impressed, Du Ponceau pronounced this distinction, "founded in nature, and ought to have a place in a system of Universal Grammar."[33]

Far from lacking syntax, as so many had suggested, Du Ponceau found in the American languages a "perfectly regular order and method, and with fewer exceptions or anomalies" than in any other language. Any writers who said otherwise must have been "perfectly bewildered," arrogantly assuming what they "could not comprehend was necessarily barbarous." To demonstrate that Delaware used related words for analogous concepts, Heckewelder counted thirty-four different words, derived from the root *wulit,* which expressed *"happiness* and its derivatives." The pair detailed the intricate means through which the American languages formed these words, which Du Ponceau dubbed "polysynthesis." Native words were long because, by "inter-weaving together the most significant sounds or syllables" of different words, Native speakers formed compound words that expressed subject, verb, object, and accompanying qualities or relations in such a way that allowed individual creativity within set principles. Through "various forms and inflections" a speaker could express "the principal action" and "the moral ideas and physical objects connected with it" in numerous ways. They could even combine mul-tiple verbs with associated ideas, as in *n'schingiwipoma,* "I do not like to eat with him." Far from lacking grammar, Native languages were overflowing with complex but ordered forms.[34]

This description of polysynthesis relied on—yet transformed and provided a grammatical explanation for—longstanding stereotypes of Indian eloquence. Many of the world's languages form compound words from distinct roots, and a single unit of meaning in many Native languages incorporates elements marking what Europeans identify as adverbs and pronouns into a verb. Du Ponceau's understanding of Delaware and other Native languages, however, emerged from Heckewelder's casting of the most formal and elaborate register of the language as the language in its purest form. Whereas eighteenth-century commentators had claimed that an incomplete analysis forced Indians to rely on metaphor, thus lending their words a poetic cast, Du Ponceau and Heckewelder suggested that a distinct grammatical organization produced Indian eloquence. The American languages possessed "beauty . . . force and energy." Because they could "express much in a few words . . . raise at once in the mind by a few magic sounds, whole masses of thoughts which strike by a kind of instantaneous intuition." The American languages were not savage: they approached "perfection." When the power to combine multiple ideas in a single word was found in the supposedly "barbarous dialects of savage nations," philosophers imagined that it illustrated intellectual deficiency, even though in Greek and Sanskrit it was "considered as some of the greatest efforts of the human mind." Du Ponceau rejected such hypocrisy, whether it came from eighteenth-century philosophers like Lord Monboddo or nineteenth-century philologists like Friedrich von Schelegel. While the latter characterized the "apparent richness" of the American languages as being "in truth utter poverty," a mere "agglomeration of atoms" with "no living productive germ," Du Ponceau insisted that the grammatical organization of the American languages was uniquely powerful. For example, instead of five discrete and "tedious" English words, such as "Thou who makest me happy," in the Delaware *Wulamalessohalian*, "the lover, the object beloved, and the delicious sentiment which their mutual passion inspires . . . are fused together." The "mind is awakened to each idea," therefore, by each "component part" of the word. He marveled that it was "in the languages of savages that these beautiful forms are found!" Late in life, Du Ponceau fondly recalled hearing the "supernatural voice" of an Abenaki man singing French opera near Valley Forge during the war—Nia-man (or Colonel Louis) was the first Indian he had ever met. Du Ponceau was prone to romanticism. His enthusiasm for the American languages blended new philology with older philosophical currents.[35]

Study of the American languages convinced Du Ponceau of "how little the world has yet advanced in . . . *Universal Grammar.*" In his opinion, the "epithet *barbarous* is much too soon and too easily applied, when we speak of sounds and of languages that we do not know." Different tongues used different means to modify words and string them together, so parts of speech varied significantly among languages, and they employed different sounds to express them. A "natural logic," an "innate sense of order, regularity and method . . . possessed even by savage nations," could be found in all languages. It demonstrated the "admirable variety of modes of conveying human thoughts by means of the different organs and senses with which the Almighty has provided us." Among Du Ponceau's most important conclusions was that, contra the views of Monboddo and Barton both, there was no "necessary connexion between the greater or lesser degree of civilisation of a people, and the organisation of their language."[36]

Drawing on a blend of missionary work and European philosophy, Du Ponceau understood linguistic difference to represent epistemological difference. The Moravian David Zeisberger, whose missionary texts were crucial for Du Ponceau's developing ideas, recognized that Delaware had "its own fixed rules, to which those must conform who will speak intelligibly." Because these rules bore "no resemblance" to those of European languages, Zeisberger stressed that one had to "think in Indian" to express oneself properly. This characterization was not necessarily invidious, since his grammar was a pedagogical work. Following the model established by Jan Amos Comenius, a seventeenth-century language philosopher and bishop of the Bohemian Brethren, Zeisberger deliberately called attention to what distinguished one language from another. Du Ponceau elaborated on such observations by drawing on the conjectures of an eighteenth-century French philosopher, Pierre-Louis Moreau de Maupertuis, that widely separated languages possessed widely divergent "plans of ideas." All peoples experienced the same "primitive perceptions," Maupertuis believed, but against the prevailing tendency in mid-eighteenth-century philosophy, Maupertuis argued that different peoples applied different arbitrary labels to them. Because these labels cast concepts in ways that permanently influenced that nation's knowledge, Maupertuis argued, studying the "*jargons* of the most savage peoples" could unlock "the history of our mind."[37]

Du Ponceau drew upon, and transformed, these ideas. Befitting one who would succeed Benjamin Franklin in the presidency of the APS, Du Ponceau imagined language as a kind of intellectual "electricity" that imposed order on the chaos of sense perception. Since Du Ponceau assumed that ideas "were conceived as they are expressed," he believed "many combinations of ideas may take place in the human mind." Du Ponceau labeled his "comparative study of the grammatical forms and idiomatic construction of languages" with a term that had been coined by the philosopher Antoine Louis Claude Destutt de Tracy: "ideology." Rather than aim to create a philosophically improved system of signs that could be the basis for social reform, which had been Destutt's ambitious goal, Du Ponceau sought to "analyze and distinguish the different shapes in which ideas combine themselves in order to fix impressions in our minds, and transmit them to those of others." Du Ponceau's sincere curiosity about the American languages suffuses his correspondence, and to one fellow scholar, he confessed that "ideology" allowed him "to muse and dream more than any other," and he found the resulting "inferences . . . highly attractive." This epistemological focus on peoples' "plans of ideas" led him away from the mainstream of European comparative philology, which moved toward finding constant laws of phonetic change to determine shared descent. Du Ponceau, instead, fused missionary observations, eighteenth-century language philosophy, and nineteenth-century philology into a grammar-based ethnology.[38]

On the basis of wide reading and extensive conversations, in person and by letter, Du Ponceau reached conclusions relevant, he thought, for far more than the Delaware language alone. Scattered grammatical information from a variety of texts from Greenland, the Caribbean, Mesoamerica, and South America allowed Du Ponceau to compare what he knew of Delaware with languages spoken in those regions. To obtain information beyond what one could find in books, Du Ponceau established a vast network of correspondents that resembled what Jefferson and Barton had established, but on a more extended scale. Missionaries of multiple persuasions, federal officers and territorial governors, and the occasional "lady" who possessed the necessary "talents," were all pressed into philological service at a moment when Americans were pouring westward. As a result, he received vocabularies from distant nations with whom few Americans had much contact, including Caddos, Pawnees, Crows, Flatheads (Kalispel), and Shoshones. At times he sought to forge close links between the APS and the federal government. His personal research was "in a manner of a public nature for the promotion of national Science," and he advised the War Department on collecting linguistic material as it prepared the Long Expedition to the Rocky Mountains. Because the American languages stretched beyond national boundaries, Du Ponceau also urged officials in Canada and Mexico to contribute what they knew. He anticipated that Latin America would produce a "fruitful Source of information" for the APS, and make it "the *Center* of scientific communication between the *new* world and the old." He obtained vocabularies from the Caribbean and Central and South America. Following settler and missionary interests westward, Du Ponceau counted on colonialism for his philology, and, mirroring the commercial aspirations of U.S. merchants, he hoped Latin American independence would provide new materials and opportunities. Cumulatively, his reading, this correspondence, and consultations with Native people shaped a philology that, for Du Ponceau, was hemispherically "American" in scope.[39]

Consultations with Native people, in person and through letters, provided evidence to refute European philosophers and supported the theory that even unrelated American languages possessed common grammatical forms, but they also qualified Du Ponceau's inference that all of the American languages would contain traits that Delaware possessed. The new attention to grammar promised an even more central role than they had performed in lexical collection. Huron and Chickasaw interpreters, for instance, confirmed that Iroquoian and Muskogean languages shared grammatical traits with the Algonquian languages. In a grammar that he hoped the APS would publish, Eleazer Williams even described Mohawk as illustrating "the Indian syntax." Yet Williams also challenged stereotypes about Native languages. After providing a 16-syllable word, he quipped that use of such potential words would force Indians to "renounc[e] the use of speech, or else incur the danger of losing our breath." Williams, grandson of "the unredeemed captive" of colonial Deerfield and the author of religious translations that had elicited Jefferson's ridicule, also insisted that Mohawk possessed gender in the European sense and not the animate–inanimate classification of Delaware. Other Native philologists made analogous distinctions. Dom Pedro Perez, a "native Peruvian Indian . . . of good education," convinced Du Ponceau that Quechua possessed the verb "to be," which he had claimed that the American languages lacked. David Brown, who worked with another philologist on a Cherokee grammar, corrected the mistaken notion that Cherokee contained an exclusive plural; it possessed a dual number in addition to a plural that marked a group of more than two. Each man denied that their language was part of some undifferentiated "American" mass. As Du Ponceau reflected, "absolute uniformity is not to be found in any of the works of nature; and there is no reason why languages should be excepted from this universal rule." Although he accepted these distinctions on the authority of these Native philologists, and although his portrayal of Native languages was positive, he held to his theory of a relatively uniform Indian "plan of ideas." It added a new facet to old assumptions of Indians' fundamental similarity among themselves and fundamental difference from Europeans, and ascribed those traits to nature.[40]

Du Ponceau also compared what he knew of the American languages with those spoken elsewhere in the world, searching especially for grammatical similarities that would indicate shared descent. His nine volumes of "Notebooks on Philology" reveal his assiduous collection of relevant material. Vater had pointed to similarities between the American languages and Chukchi, Niger-Congo languages, and Basque, but Du Ponceau refuted each hypothesis. The people of Kamchatka he believed merely a "colony" of North American "Eskimaux," and it was too "strange" to think that "the idioms of the black and red races of mankind should be constructed on a similar plan." Most intriguing was Basque, the sole language of Western Europe that philology had excluded from the Indo-European family. At first, he "inclined" toward Vater's theory, since "mountainous countries are known to be the repositories of ancient languages." Indeed, Du Ponceau found a "striking resemblance" between the American languages and a language of the Caucasus, perhaps "the cradle of the human race," as well as a "strong affinity" between the American languages and that of the Berbers, a "white race of men" in the Atlas Mountains of North Africa, who lived, "like our *ultra-Mississippian* Indians . . . in a state of savage independence." None of these similarities, how-ever, convinced him of shared descent. "Essential differences," he concluded, separated the American languages from Basque, and from "Tartar" languages, which invalidated linguistic claims for that theory of Indian origins. Du Ponceau discounted any hypothetical connections to Chinese most force-fully. He became an authority on Chinese—counted among the first western scholars to recognize that Chinese characters represented spoken words rather than pure ideas—but Du Ponceau considered the American languages and Chinese, possessing vastly different organizations, to be "the top and bottom of the idiomatic scale." (Though, late in life, a Mexican philologist, Emmanuele Naxera, swayed Du Ponceau with startling assertions about the similarity between it and the Mesoamerican language Otomi.) As U.S. linguistic knowl-edge expanded with its commerce, Du Ponceau grew "very anxious" to learn if any American languages resembled any of the Malayan languages, already known to stretch from Madagascar to the furthest reaches of Polynesia, but he was "not very sanguine" in his expectations.[41]

A shared "plan of ideas" united the American languages from Greenland to Patagonia, and "essential differences" separated them from other languages. Authors as philosophically opposed as Corneille de Pauw and Thomas Jefferson had once asserted diversity to be the continent's fundamental lin-guistic fact, though some previous writers had suggested that unrelated lan-guages seemed to share a similar grammatical structure, most recently Alexander von Humboldt. Finding that the languages of widely separated, socially different, and etymologically dissimilar Native people "so strikingly similar in their forms, that one would imagine the same mind presided over their original formation," Du Ponceau concluded that "the similarity extends through the whole of the language of this race of men." Just as strikingly, no other races seemed to share them. When correspondents pressed him to acknowledge the implications of his studies, however, Du Ponceau insisted that he kept his "mind perfectly open" on the subject of Indian origins. To explain how the world's languages had come to be so grammatically different,

Du Ponceau advised, "looking up to the GREAT FIRST CAUSE." The appeal to the divine expressed a sentiment prominent among the era's naturalists, who sought to impose order on the overwhelming number of facts that had been collected in the preceding decades, and in so doing, assert their scientific authority, but Du Ponceau also hinted at the deep natural significance of linguistic difference.[42]

Du Ponceau and Heckewelder hoped that their philology would give "a precise, and at the same time an interesting direction to the study of the Indian languages." It accomplished the goal. Indeed, nearly everything written about Native languages, and about "Indian" origins and modes of thinking, in the United States and much that appeared in Europe, for the next three decades either built upon or challenged their work. The results were varied and sometimes unexpected. Piety notwithstanding, his conclusions sat uneasily with religiously orthodox explanations of human diversity. In challenging prevailing theories of savagism, moreover, his philology prepared the ground for theories that asserted more insidious forms of Indian linguistic and intellectual difference. In the short term, however, people viewed philology as relevant for the "civilization" program. The appearance of the pair's work just as the federal government was extending its ostensible benevolence—undoing the political autonomy of Native societies and destroying Native cultures— proved crucial to the immediate reception of the new philology.[43]

Philology, Philanthropy, and Learned Society

Du Ponceau tirelessly, as the HLC's corresponding secretary and driving force, disseminated the new philology at home and abroad in the hopes of amplifying its significance, and he reported on the "great excitement" that it seemed to be producing. His efforts in the latter regard marked an important effort to extricate the United States from currents that continued the old flow toward Britain. To break the country's "colonial spirit," which lingered even after the War of 1812, Du Ponceau thought Americans should seek "foreign alliances" to achieve intellectual independence. Philadelphia philology became an important conduit for German learning in the United States due to its Moravian connections and the correspondence that Du Ponceau opened with Continental specialists in non-Indo-European languages, such as Vater, Julius Klaproth, and Wilhelm von Humboldt (the explorer's brother). Although the last became something of a rival, Du Ponceau did not initially envision competition over what he referred to, sarcastically, as the "barbarous idioms of our Savages." As he shared with Joseph von Hammer, an Austrian Orientalist, "it is best for each country to attend most particularly to those studies which may be properly called *national,* and . . . as we cannot in America be expected to add much to the existing knowledge of the concerns of the old Hemisphere, it is best that we should apply ourselves to those things that are near to us, and respecting which Europe may expect information from our quarter." Nationalism and colonialism intertwined as Du Ponceau and others presented U.S. philology to Europeans, and as they confronted philology's apparent implications for U.S. Indian affairs.[44]

Besides maintaining an extensive private correspondence, Du Ponceau's efforts to spread philology within the United States centered on cultivating relationships between the HLC and similar institutions across the country, in the hopes that "much more may be done by an union of efforts than by a single & Solitary endeavor." To prove the value of such unions, Du Ponceau shared his connections with prestigious European scholars and acted as an intermediary, forwarding U.S. publications and receiving European volumes in return, which he passed along to the appropriate institutions. Besides the APS, which dated to 1743, the nation's other learned societies had all appeared in a wave of voluntary association that accompanied the American Revolution. Centered initially in eastern cities, they sprouted in the trans-Appalachian West by the 1820s. Such institutions acted as venues to hear and present scholarship, but they also provided an intellectual community, amiable company for the learned, and the cultural prestige that went along with exclusive membership, though education and status did not translate into unchallenged philosophical authority since ordinary citizens claimed the ability to observe and understand nature and "savagery" without elite instruction. Institutions also collected funds to publish philology in transactions, collections, and memoirs, publicizing members' erudition and allowing the participation (intellectual and monetary) of distant members who could not attend meetings. These ties resulted in the reciprocal exchange of volumes, thus facilitating the circulation of ideas and inspiring further researches. Publication, in turn, produced review essays in local journals, frequently excerpted farther afield. The appearances of these sparked extended written conversations and more publications. Voluntary organizations, epistolary networks, and a vibrant print culture in an expanding country, among citizens eager to claim literary, philosophical, or scientific reputations, reinforced one another and spread the reach of the new philology, as members of the American Academy of Arts and Sciences, the historical societies of numerous states, and the American Antiquarian Society, joined the APS in what Du Ponceau called "the Indian Republic of Letters."[45]

Du Ponceau and Heckewelder's philology met a varied reception. Some merely scoffed at the esoteric content and seemingly improbable theories of the new philology. It was "so profound and abstruse" that the reviewer for the

London *Quarterly Review* "confess[ed]" his "utter inability to comprehend any part of it." Confusion and satire were common companions. A Philadelphia *Port-Folio* reviewer, skeptical of the pair's work, sarcastically urged his countrymen to adopt an *"American Language!"* that would "destroy every vestige of our ancient colonial dependence" to England. The Philadelphia *Friend* conceded, somewhat, the "interest" in "Indian languages" but concluded, "It is but natural that we should feel a more direct and immediate curiosity, to know the characters and adventures of those by whom they were supplanted and overrun."[46]

Others recognized the importance of Du Ponceau's and Heckewelder's work for answering questions of Indian origins and perhaps civilization. It was "perhaps destined to create a new era in the history of primitive language," predicted the Barton protégé Thomas Nuttall, "a history of morals, of remote connections, of vicissitudes and emigrations . . . more durably impressed than if engraven upon tablets of brass." The Episcopal priest Samuel F. Jarvis turned his attention to the Lost Tribes thesis, deciding that the American languages' "plan of thought" was too different from Hebrew, making them a "separate class in human speech." Although he built on the work of Du Ponceau, Jarvis took shelter beneath the ruins of Babel, suggesting to the New-York Historical Society that at the confusion of tongues, God "planned the systems of speech, as to make similar grammatical forms characterize the great divisions in the human race." John D. Clifford, an antiquarian from Lexington, Kentucky, who articulated an elaborate, Indo-European-inflected theory of the Ohio Valley earthworks, told readers of the *Western Review and Miscellaneous Magazine* that the compound form of Sanscrit and other ancient languages of Asia . . . corresponds in some measure with the form of our Indian languages." The new philology seemed to address issues of ancestry and civilization, but it was not alone in that regard.[47]

In 1820, the initial publication of the American Antiquarian Society (AAS), which had been established in 1812 in Worcester, Massachusetts, criticized the new philology while offering a dramatic explanation of the mounds. This New England institution maintained connections with emigrant archaeologists in the Ohio Valley. Excavating artifacts from local mounds could be profitable, when sold to collectors, and prestigious, if forwarded to institutions like the AAS. *Archaeologia Americana* (1820) was the product of such relationships. In the volume's primary article, Caleb Atwater drew from the work of Humboldt, Jones, and especially Clifford, imagining the ancestors of North American Indians as savage "Tartar" invaders who had destroyed a preexisting "Hindoo" society, forcing the latter people to flee southward, where they built even greater civilizations. Besides providing the most detailed theory of a separate race of Mound Builders yet to appear, the volume's contributors also dismissed the usefulness of language as a mode of evidence. For Atwater, philology was unnecessary because monuments spoke "a language as expressive as the most studied inscriptions of latter times upon brass and marble." Samuel L. Mitchell, a prominent New York naturalist, even more explicitly ridiculed "etymological research and grammatical conjecture." Although some of its members supported philanthropy and linguistic collection and comparison, and in the 1830s it would publish one of the most important pieces of ante-bellum philology, the AAS provided a forum for those who rejected both etymology's dubious results and environmentalist explanations of human difference, undermining notions of Native "civilization" in the past or present.[48]

In varied ways, ethnology seemed relevant to Indian conversion and "civilization" at a pivotal moment. The same year Du Ponceau and Heckewelder published their work, Congress passed the Indian Civilization Act (1819), which established the first annual federal appropriation ($10,000) for Native education in white ways. In an effort to make the "Civilization Fund" stretch further, President James Monroe and Secretary of War John C. Calhoun disbursed it through missionary societies that established schools rather than creating new federal institutions. Philosophers and philanthropists, "searching for the origin, and . . . meliorating the condition, of the aborigines," according to the Rhode-Island Historical Society, were engaged in related pursuits. Increased attention to "civilization" was crucial in shaping how U.S. citizens interpreted the new philology.[49]

In its depiction of Indians, the HLC's *Transactions* stood in marked contrast to *Archaeologia Americana*. The longest item was Heckewelder's history of the Lenni Lenape, which tenaciously argued that dispossession of Delawares and others and their depiction as "savages" were equally unjust. Since Britain had entered the Covenant Chain alliance, colonists and U.S. citizens had valued Iroquois accomplishments and testimony more highly than that of the Delawares. The latter, Heckewelder insisted, were natural republicans who partially adhered to divine law despite degeneration, so civilization would be simple if whites would devote themselves to the task. He explicitly intended his history to give "the public an opportunity of judging" whether "the Indians or the frontier White People . . . were the greatest Savages." Blood and mutual suspicion lay beneath Pennsylvania's idealized past. Given Moravians' and the Philadelphia elite's rancorous and still recent history with inhabitants of the "backcountry," readers concluded, quite reasonably, that the HLC's *Transactions* supported philanthropy. Reviewing the volume, John Pickering affirmed that its "favorable picture" of "Indian character" made him "feel more kindly towards that unfortunate race whom we ourselves have helped to corrupt and degrade." Heckewelder's views influenced the reception of the new philology even after his death in 1823.[50]

Although he claimed to have "never yet reflected seriously" upon the capacity of Indians for civilization even a decade after he began his studies of their languages, Du Ponceau also supported philanthropy. His publications used the idealized myth of William Penn's friendship with Delawares as a mode of social-political criticism, blasted frontier prejudice, expressed hopes that Zeisberger's grammar could improve Native–white relations, and his philological notebooks included clippings of Native orators chastising whites for failing to live up to treaty agreements and to the commands of their common God. Recognizing the value of missionary correspondents, Du Ponceau sought their contributions and praised their efforts, offering that "science must rejoice to be admitted to a participation of . . . so high & so noble an object." Missionaries, in turn, recognized the value of forging links with scholars like Du Ponceau. Daniel Butrick, for example, sent specimens of Cherokee verbs that alluded to the pernicious effects of land pressures on conversion, providing conjugations of "to take" and the negative of "to redeem."[51]

Yet Du Ponceau's philology offered limited support for philanthropists. It lent no support to the scriptural narrative, and he explicitly refuted any link between language and civilization. It also generated striking questions. If a single Lenni Lenape verb "*n'dellauchsi*" meant "'I live, move about,' or 'I so live that I move about,'" Du Ponceau asked, did Indians have "no idea of 'life,' but when connected with 'locomotion?'" If "*nihillatamen* ['I own, I am master of']" shared the same root as "*nihilla* ['I kill, or strike dead'],", with "right, power, and force confounded together, as if there was no difference between them," were Indians unable to recognize authority founded upon anything but strength? The first association supported stereotypical depictions of nomadic Indians, while the latter contradicted assumptions of Native communities' lack of coercive institutions; but together they went to the heart of Native capacity for settled agriculture and republican government. Heckewelder instructed him that Delawares could indeed express "life" independent of movement, and Du Ponceau reflected that all languages revealed questionable etymological associations. That these questions emerged, however, reveals doubts about incorporation and anticipated the similar questions that others would ask.[52]

A number of readers of the HLC's *Transactions* recognized philanthropic allies in the philologists nonetheless and praised the "labours of all such

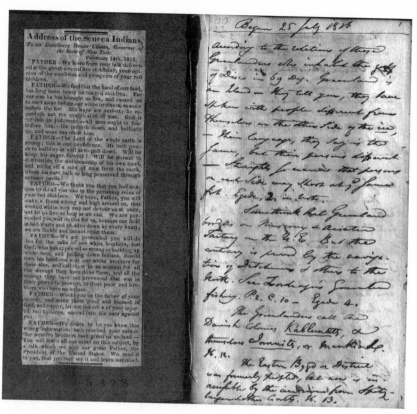

In this newspaper excerpt of a speech, a Seneca orator, possibly Red Jacket, requests "a fence strong and high . . . that wicked white men may not devour us," and warns New York governor Dewitt Clinton and the reading audience that God might "visit our white brothers for their sins." Pasted on the inside flap of the 2nd volume of Peter S. Du Ponceau's "Notebooks on Philology," which contained his notes on American Indian and other of the world's languages, the clipping indicates the connection that that he felt between his philology and what he and many other whites considered a benevolent stance toward Indian affairs. (Courtesy of the American Philosophical Society, Philadelphia)

benevolent men." Some who did so did not quite understand the new philology. John Adams, the former president, admitted that Du Ponceau's "profound researches" had "diminished in some measure certain prejudices I had conceived especially against the Indians of North America." He likened the work to that of Court de Gébelin and suggested that cycles of civilization and degeneration could explain "the mysteries" Du Ponceau had discovered. The New York minister Frederick Christian Schaffer was the most explicit in congratulating Du Ponceau on his "most powerful plea" for Indians' "claim . . . to *humane*, to *respectful treatment,* and to all possible *justice* at the hands of their white countrymen." He had just submitted a petition to Congress pressing for greater support for Indian education and, "Had your book previously appeared, I should have used no other argument than a reference to it." Sharing his ideas about Indians' "Tartar" origins, however, Schaffer insisted upon the importance of "the analogy . . . of *words.*" These commentators recognized no difference between the philology of Du Ponceau and Heckewelder, which debunked notions of savage languages, and eighteenth-century etymologists' attempts to recover the original language or Indians' ancestors, but they appreciated its bearing on the issue of a "benevolent" colonialism.[53]

John Pickering, an established scholar of English and Greek, understood the new philology, and appreciated its potential usefulness. Over the years, he and Du Ponceau would form a close friendship. In Salem and Boston, Pickering was distant from Philadelphia, but they shared interests in philology and the law and possessed, in Du Ponceau's estimation, "kindred mind[s] connected . . . by feelings of pure & disinterested affection." The friendship blossomed as Pickering poured his intellectual energies into philology, to the detriment, he often feared, of his legal career. Lauding Du Ponceau's "extensive views" and Heckewelder's "practical knowledge," Pickering tried to bring their work to a wider audience than the few who read the HLC *Transactions.* In a series of articles in the *North American Review* and in a widely cited essay in *Encylopaedia Americana,* he conveyed the excitement of witnessing "the epoch of a *new science*" and explained its methods and conclusions. Against expected critics who would question the utility of such studies, "when there is no literature to compensate us for our labor," Pickering highlighted its potential for answering questions about Indian origins and human thought. Studying human speech as a science required "ascertaining all the facts or phenomena" before generalization was possible. U.S. scholars, therefore, were instrumental for advancing a prestigious European project. Linguistic knowledge, moreover, would improve "communication with the various tribes on our borders, either with a view to the common concerns of life or the diffusion of our religion among them." To its supporters, philology would aid science and civilization.[54]

Son of the former commissioner and department secretary, Pickering never played a role in the administration of U.S. Indian affairs, but he put his philology in service of philanthropy. Besides serving as a reviewer and would-be popularizer, Pickering created a "uniform orthography" for recording Native languages and collaborated on a Cherokee grammar, each at the behest of the American Board of Commissioners for Foreign Missions. He also undertook a substantial editorial program. With his family's roots in New England, he turned his attention to the region's history of missionary philology. Through the Massachusetts Historical Society and the American Academy of Arts and Sciences, he published a series of editions designed to make more widely accessible "rare and valuable memorials of the Indian languages," such as those of John Eliot, Josiah Cotton, Jonathan Edwards, Jr., and the Jesuit Sebastien Rasles. These centuries-old materials demonstrated that "however extraordinary" the new theories seemed, they were not the result of "philological enthusiasm." The short essays accompanying these new editions elaborated and clarified details, sometimes on the authority of missionary-educated Native consultants like Eleazer Williams and David Brown, and reported new information, such as that received through federal exploration. The publication of these "memorials," in turn, prompted some readers, like the army surgeon Edwin James, to reflect upon how much "more considerable" the missionary work of previous centuries had been compared to the efforts of "the present generation."[55]

The inference that the new philology provided scientific clout for philanthropy gave rise to one of the most important criticisms it faced: that it was misinformation for a social-political goal. James H. McCulloh, a Baltimore antiquarian critical of etymology, admitted that he found the new philology "perplexing and unsatisfactory," but he asserted that the "misapprehended views" of Native languages' "grammatical richness" stemmed from missionaries' eagerness to prove Native "capacity for instruction." The archaeologist Caleb Atwater, who later served as U.S. treaty commissioner, mocked easterners who "venture to pronounce ideas about languages, not even one word of which they ever heard correctly pronounced" and who "manufactured nearly whole languages, upon philosophical principle." He suspected that polysynthesis was nothing more than "half a dozen words" mashed together and "praise[d] . . . for their expressiveness!" While he ridiculed philology, he also expressed skepticism of the "civilization" program and a hostility to voluntary associations typical of democratically minded whites, sarcastically advocating that "Congress give up our Indian affairs" to "the venerable DUPONCEAU," the APS, and the "host of philanthropists" in Philadelphia. In the minds of supporters and critics alike, the new philology was inextricable from questions about Native education and assimilation.[56]

The philology that emerged in the United States in the second decade of the nineteenth century grew out of decades-long convergence of science and colonialism, which had begun in the 1790s. Europeans and Americans criticized the limits of mere etymology for answering the most important questions of Indians' past and future, while the federal government pushed its "civilization" program in an effort to hurry land cessions. Even after such efforts produced war in 1811–1814, Congress increased the amount and fixed the regularity of the program's funding. The numerous scholars who pursued these studies reached varied conclusions regarding Native ancestry, ostensible degeneration since the primitive dispersal of nations, and level of cultivation before European conquerors and colonists had arrived. John Heckewelder was a crucial figure linking questions of philosophy and policy. His experience as a Moravian missionary had convinced him of the value of Native languages and traditions and of the ability of Native people themselves to adopt U.S. civilization. He provided Barton ample reasons for supposing that Indians had once been civilized and could be easily made so again, even as others denied the usefulness of language at all and proposed theories, rooted in skepticism about current Indians' abilities, that a different race had built the pre-Columbian monuments. After Barton's death, Heckewelder collaborated with Du Ponceau to demolish philosophical stereotypes of savage languages through detailed examination of Native languages' grammatical organization. Advocates of philanthropy seized on these studies as evidence that a proper course of education and conversion would raise Native people to civilization and open the door to their social incorporation. They did so despite Du Ponceau's own opinion that language and social condition were unrelated, an opinion that provided the crucial foundation for theories about Indians' uniform, racially unique, and unchanging "plan of ideas."

For the next several decades, Du Ponceau's and Heckewelder's philology inspired a surge in missionary work and established an important agenda for research into questions of just who Indians were and how they thought. The defense, even celebration, of the force, flexibility, and beauty of the American languages, possessed by a distinct race, produced a renewed commitment among missionary organizations, flush with money from the federal "Civilization Fund," to use Native languages as the most effective means of instruction. In their attention to how to record unfamiliar sounds with familiar letters, and to physical processes of pronunciation, these efforts resulted in new understandings of Native languages as inextricable from Native bodies, which were crucial for the emergence of a racialized understanding of Indian languages at midcentury.

4

Four Clicks, Two Gutturals, and a Nasal

In his short life, David Brown (A-wih) labored tirelessly to produce Cherokee texts in multiple writing systems that would provide the means for his countrymen to be "translated from the dominions of darkness unto the glorious kingdom of Christ." While at Brainerd, a school in the Cherokee nation that the American Board of Commissioners for Foreign Missions (ABCFM) operated with federal "civilization" funds, he worked with Daniel S. Butrick to create the first Cherokee spelling book in 1819. Supporters, such as the Baptist missionary Evan Jones, found it "simple and natural," while critics, such as John Heckewelder, were "altogether at a loss to understand any thing of it." Opinion was divided because Butrick and Brown's reasonable goal of having no letter represent "more than one sound" meant that they had to turn some letters backward and upside down, and they had to change the values of others. Continuing his studies at the Foreign Mission School, an ABCFM boarding school in Connecticut, and at Andover Theological Seminary, Brown collaborated with John Pickering on a Cherokee grammar that employed a standardized alphabet of the philologist's design. The board had high hopes for this orthography, but Brown recognized its "defects." When he returned to the Cherokee nation in 1824, Brown learned that Sequoyah, an unschooled opponent of the missions, had been engaged in his own "philosophical researches" and had invented a syllabary for Cherokee. Brown intended to "improve the system," but he recognized that because it had become "universally adopted in the nation," it was already an extraordinary boon for evangelism.[1]

Brown considered his "native language in its philosophy, genius, and symphony . . . inferior to few, if any, in the world," but a speech impediment, combined with years of absence that eroded his fluency in speaking Cherokee, made him an ineffective preacher. Thus, he seized on the work he could do for the mission as a translator and philologist, providing "scriptures—good books and religious tracts" as well as a "dictionary and grammar." In 1826, the Cherokee National Council commissioned him, with George Lowery, to translate the nation's laws, then the New Testament. The latter project passed through multiple stages, as he compared the English and the original Greek versions, translated a Cherokee version in Pickering's alphabet, and finally wrote it in Sequoyah's syllabary. Besides requiring concepts that had, at best, tenuous analogues in his native language, Brown found that even proper names needed to be, as he said, "Cherokeeized" lest they "corrupt . . . the sweet Cherokee, by introducing sounds foreign & disagreeable to the Cherokee ear." The "true name" of the nation, *Tsuh-luh-kee'*, had already suffered "corruption" in English.[2]

Brown denied the "erroneous theory" that Indians "are incapable of civilization," and his translation projects publicized Cherokee advances, as did his many letters that appeared in newspapers and periodicals, but he did not seek assimilation. Before an audience in Pickering's hometown of Salem, Massachusetts, in 1823, Brown stressed his own "Aboriginal blood," and he blamed whites alone for the "hereditary animosity" between themselves and Indians. Denying notions of Indian extinction, he alerted his listeners to the fact that "council fires still burn" in "Tsalagi" and among Creeks, Choctaws, and Chickasaws. With Christianity, "a barbarian . . . easily becomes a civilized man," but it would be as "nations" that these people would "unite with the great commonwealth, and . . . participate in the glory to which our happy America is destined." Brown accepted the syllabary as an effective mode of recording Cherokee sounds and, despite Sequoyah's intent for the syllabary to insulate Cherokee society from white influence, Brown appropriated it to spread the gospel. Consumption killed him in 1829, before he could see his Cherokee New Testament published or his nation forcibly removed. His dissemination of political innovations, his defense of Cherokee nationhood, and his determination to extend the ways in which his language was used, while at the same time preserving its purity against English contamination, reveal that Brown was committed to political and linguistic sovereignty.[3]

The praise of the American languages in the work of John Heckewelder and Peter S. Du Ponceau led mission organizations to apply the new philology to evangelization. The leader in this movement was the ABCFM, the nation's largest missionary organization and the leading recipient of federal "civilization" funds. Considerable orthographic experimentation followed, within the constraints of effectiveness and the demands of Native communities. The sounds that missionaries and their readers tried to pronounce, and in some instances the appearance of the characters themselves, however, increased perceptions that Native people could not be assimilated. While Sequoyah had intended the syllabary to promote Cherokees' improvement and autonomy, the syllabary offered an alternative to missionaries struggling to write down Native languages, one that would aid the work of conversion immediately and could provide an intermediate step toward eventual English literacy and social assimilation. At the same time, amid increasing calls in Georgia and other states to remove the large southern nations, white-educated Cherokees held up the extraordinary invention as proof of Cherokee civilization, in the hopes of swaying public opinion against removal, while downplaying its obvious rejection of English literacy and its implications for preserving Native sovereignty. Different parties used the syllabary for competing ends, and different scholars and officials found the syllabary to represent divergent things: proof of independent "civilization" or its impossibility without white influence. While many recoiled from the syllabary's demonstration that assimilation would not necessarily follow "civilization," missionaries to other Native people considered non-alphabetic writing systems perhaps more suited to Native languages and speakers. U.S. expansion, moreover, introduced Americans to languages seemingly unlike those they had previously encountered. Futile efforts to pronounce sounds and contain them within English alphabetical values fueled speculation about the difference of Native characters and bodies, deepening an expansive view of race as something that could be heard as well as seen.

A Question of Character

Following the conclusion of war in 1815, surging nationalism and millennialism fostered calls to reform society, extend American principles, and take the Word to heathen peoples around the world. There was no consensus, however, on just how this should be accomplished. Despite the known success of missionaries who had used Native languages as vehicles for Christianity, the social appeal of linguistic uniformity had long been attractive in English America. Even at the height of John Eliot's missionary-linguistic work, for instance, Daniel Gookin had noted that "changing . . . the language of a barbarous people, into the speech of a more civil and potent nation that have conquered them, hath been an approved experiment, to reduce such a people unto the civility and religion of the prevailing nation."[4]

At issue was more than efficiency. Few Native-language books escaped King Philip's War (1675–1676), the massive conflict between the New England colonies and an alliance of Wampanoags, Narragansetts, and others that left "Praying Indians" physically and culturally exposed. Some combination of Indians and colonists burned, tore, or submerged a thousand copies of the Massachusett Bible and New Testament. Examples from the early-national era demonstrate that such actions might appeal to whites or Native people in moments of crisis. During the American War for Independence, soldiers in John Sullivan's expedition into Iroquoia "destroyed" all of the Mohawk translations of the Church of England's Book of Common Prayer as they razed Iroquois villages and fields. Similarly, mere months before Choctaws signed a removal treaty in 1830, "Chahta books [were] sentenced to be burned or thrown into the creeks," by nativists as part of a broader program that preached Choctaws' separate creation and need for cultural revitalization. Destroying Native-language texts, designed to facilitate not only communication but also transformation, allowed both whites and Indians to imagine the maintenance of cultural purity.[5]

Linguistic homogeneity was important to many Americans' sense of nationhood in the early republic. Paeans to the English language and confident anticipation of its spread across the continent were routine among northerners, southerners, diverse ethnic backgrounds, and all party persuasions. Noah Webster, a zealous proponent of the new nation's linguistic independence, predicted in 1789 that "within a century and a half, North America will be peopled with a hundred millions of men, *all speaking the same language.*" Such views implied the disappearance of the American languages. Thomas Jefferson, the most outspoken theorist of Indian linguistic diversity, eagerly recorded the death of Native languages, as did his Indian agents, because language represented peoplehood, and where there was no distinct people, Jefferson believed that the United States assumed title to the land. Indian removal offered an accelerated means to "finally consolidate our whole country to one nation only" and transmute whites into "aborigines" in a process similar to the Saxon military and linguistic conquest of Celtic Britons. National linguistic homogeneity was only the first step. While considering the colonization of African Americans in the aftermath of Gabriel's Rebellion, he envisioned North and South America being hemispherically united in language and republican laws, "without blot or mixture." Startlingly, amid the War of 1812, the notoriously Anglophobic Jefferson even imagined the United States and Britain engaged in a shared global project of settler-colonialism that would make English "the organ of the development of the human mind."[6]

Missionaries and the War Department pursued policies in conformity with this language ideology at the beginning of the nineteenth century. Groups once committed to Native-language evangelization, such as the Moravians, sought refuge in English by the early nineteenth century. Even as he produced Native-language texts, David Zeisberger confessed that it was "more proper for . . . Converts, to learn English," according to Heckewelder. The same goal led Jefferson to scale the "wall of separation" between church and state by authorizing several hundred dollars for Gideon Blackburn in 1803 because he approved of the Presbyterian missionary's "laudable plan" for establishing an English school among the Cherokees. Several hundred children learned to read English there in the decade following the school's establishment in 1804. When New England Calvinists established the Congregational-Presbyterian American Board in 1810, they debated how best to evangelize on a global scale. Opinions within the board were divided. While one member recommended establishing an institution, such as existed in British India, to teach the indigenous languages of North America, Lyman Beecher reminded missionaries awaiting their ordination in 1818, "By how few had Eliot's Bible ever been read!" English education promised economy by saving the time of translation and the expense of publication in diverse, unwritten, and seemingly fading languages, so the board adopted "an extended system upon Mr. Blackburn's plan." It hoped that, "assimilated in language, they will more readily become assimilated in habits and manners to their white neighbors."[7]

This emphasis on English dovetailed with the goals of some Native people in the early nineteenth century. Cherokees, for instance, demanded English education as the precondition for any mission. This imperative was not incompatible with maintaining cultural autonomy. Consider the later career of Hendrick Aupaumut, who continued advocating Native adaptation to U.S. society, even as he remained committed to Mohicans' linguistic inheritance. His repeated use of Mohican words in "History of the Muhheakonnuk Indians," which appeared in slightly different forms in the *Collections* of the Massachusetts Historical Society (1804) and the inaugural report of the American Society for Promoting the Civilization and General Improvement of the Indian Tribes in the United States (1824), demonstrated his skepticism that English could fully convey Mohican concepts and his commitment not merely to hold onto his language but also to bring it to a white audience. He advocated English literacy, however, as being central to the survival and prosperity of Native peoples. Adapting a Native idiom on behalf of the Jefferson administration, the New Stockbridge chief presented Delawares with a "white belt of wampum with a piece of paper, sewed on one end, on which was written, A B C. 1 2 3."[8]

Although the American Bible Society, established in 1816, continued to encourage the publication of scriptural translations since increasing knowledge of linguistic similarities among Native groups renewed hopes of their feasibility, an English-language Native educational program had garnered significant support among federal officials, missionaries, and other persons who considered themselves benevolent after the Indian Civilization Act (1819). Advising the War Department in 1820 on how best to use the "civilization fund," Jedidiah Morse stated a commonplace when he urged, "As fast as possible let Indians forget their own languages . . . and learn ours, which will at once open to them the whole field of every kind of useful knowledge." The prevalence of this view provided an opening to those who opposed the "civilization" program. As part of a robust argument for Indian removal and the imminent "extinction of the Indian race" in 1830, Georgia Congressman Richard Wilde mocked would-be philanthropists' talk of "preserving the Indians," when in fact they intended to transform their ways of life and "supersede their imperfect jargon by teaching them your own rich, copious, energetic tongue."[9]

Even as the federal government and private societies pursued this course, however, some white Americans observed the consequences of assimilationist pressures, particularly near highly concentrated Euro-American settlements. Touring the Native Christian community of Brothertown, New York, at the end of the eighteenth century, Benjamin S. Barton observed, "They all speak the English language; very few of them speak the Indian dialects." They lived like whites and possessed "a great deal of white blood. . . . In short, they are no longer Indians, or in that state of society which we call savage." It struck him, however, that they did "not appear . . . to be more respectable for having relinquished the savage state." Two decades later, a missionary from the neighboring community of New Stockbridge elaborated this idea. John Sergeant, who as the son of Stockbridge's first missionary was a native Mohican speaker, argued that if Native people "lose their own language, they will lose with it their national pride and respectability." Such had been the fate of Brothertown Indians, who were now, in Sergeant's opinion, "more corrupt than any Indians in the country." Observations such as these engaged old and insidious stereotypes that denied the ability of Native people to adapt without ceasing to be truly "Indian," but they also primed self-styled philanthropists in the early republic to consider whether alternatives to English education might produce less deleterious social consequences.[10]

The new philology combined with the surprising experiences of missionaries on the ground to galvanize this sentiment, motivating investigation and appreciation of Native languages, just as the federal government established its civilization fund. Daniel S. Butrick, for example, who had been among those Beecher admonished against Native-language education in 1818, became convinced within a year among the Cherokees that their "language exceeds all my former expectations in richness & beauty." Within a few years, an interval that also included the publication of the work of Du Ponceau and Heckewelder, increasing numbers of missionaries experienced similar linguistic conversions. In addition, "philanthropists" came to realize that Native groups that were not enclaves amid dense white settlement would not surrender their language. As the *American Quarterly Review* observed in 1830, "if the suppression of the Indian idioms be indispensable," then Native civilization was "hopeless." As a result, missionary methods underwent an important shift. Among "the most important features in the plan of modern missions," the *Christian Herald and Seaman's Magazine* reported in 1822, was "to seize upon the flitting sound, and reduce it to the rigid rules of grammar."[11]

Native-language education was rarely conceived to be an end in itself. Missionaries and officials hoped all Native-language education would further assimilation. If curiosity about reading their native language could be piqued, this line of thought went, then Native students would "apprehend . . . the nature and benefits of alphabetical writing" more generally. The wealth of available books in English would do the rest. Native-language instruction was, in the words of the Presbyterian missionary Stephen Riggs, a "safe investment towards the acquisition of English." The assimilationist argument for Native-language education underlined the importance of an English-based orthography. After all, since "Indians upon our frontier must eventually learn to speak English," the Methodist missionary Peter King explained, it was best not to "embarrass . . . *children of the forest*" by forcing them to learn different writing systems or even "different sounds to the same character." Eventually, "the English language and English people, shall extinguish, as it is fast doing, the differences of language, customs, and manners, and blend the various European and Aboriginal nations . . . into a Great Family, one an indivisible," at least according to the *Religious Intelligencer.*[12]

Like their predecessors, nineteenth-century missionaries discovered that language learning was no easy task. The dramatically different grammatical organization of Native languages loomed as a daunting obstacle but not the most immediate one. Before they could turn to translation and effective proselytization, missionaries had to hear new sounds and learn how to utter them. As Roger Williams had noted in 1643, "the Life of all Language is the pronuntiation." More than a century later, a Delaware man instructed John Heckewelder that he would have no luck learning the language until he acquired "an Indian *ear*." Nineteenth-century missionaries agreed. It was not enough to be able to memorize the *"principles of language"* from a page: few pedagogical texts existed, especially for non-Algonquian languages. Missions needed those who "have an *ear* that can readily *distinguish sounds*," Henry Perkins instructed the Methodist board, as well as "men *whose organs will readily yield to the pronunciations of foreign tongues.*"[13] Missionary success required diligence, aptitude, physical talents, and willingness to submit—only in part and for a higher cause—to Native speech.

In the 1820s, the American Board directed its missionaries to make learning Native languages their priority and to deliver frequent reports on the progress of their language acquisition. These reports allowed the board to collect information on effective study strategies, which they shared with those who were struggling. The board concluded, for example, that "mingling with the people" was the best method, and it cautioned its missionaries against an "unwillingness to use such words & phrases as you had learned, & waiting for more perfect knowledge." Instead, the board urged them to do as Cyrus Byington had done among the Choctaws: "speak such words, as you can use, every time you have occasion for them." Unsurprisingly, missionaries occasionally resented the assumption that what worked for one student must work for another. The board also urged missionaries to create texts. Dictionaries and grammars aided not only future learners but also the compiler, and religious translations would aid Native conversion and, if printed, publicize the success of "civilization" effort. The board frequently published portions of missionary letters on language learning, translation, and the production of texts in venues like the *Missionary Herald,* to encourage readers' imaginary participation, and perhaps financial investment, in evangelism. Discussions of translating and printing texts even appeared in children's books. These practices disseminated the society's linguistic efforts as well as notions of Native linguistic difference.[14]

To further its missionaries' linguistic success, the American Board also forged mutually beneficial ties with philologists who possessed specialized knowledge and missionary sympathies. To aid the process of recording unfamiliar sounds with visible marks, the board approached John Pickering, a fellow New Englander whose work as a reviewer and editor widened the audience for philology and linked it with public responsibilities for Native education. After working with Thomas Hopoo, a native Hawaiian, and the board missionary Hiram Bingham to create an alphabet for that language, Pickering wrote *An Essay on the Adoption of a Uniform Orthography for the Indian Languages of North America* (1820), which appeared in the *Memoirs* of the American Academy of Arts and Sciences. Such a system had long been a goal in Europe, its colonies, and the United States. An encounter with Carolina Algonquian led Thomas Harriot to devise a phonetic orthography with universal ambitions late in the sixteenth century, which had some influence among seventeenth-century scholars searching for a universal language, and the APS awarded William Thornton's "Universal Alphabet" a prize for most useful invention in 1793. For his part, Pickering imagined the "uniform orthography" as an American contribution to the efforts of William Jones and Volney, who had proposed standardizations for the languages of Asia.[15]

Pickering aimed to create a *"practical"* system that could record the *"fundamental* sounds of the principal Indian languages." This was not as straightforward as it might sound. The English alphabet was an obvious choice, but many were skeptical about whether it could conveniently capture the variety of Native sounds. The previous century had witnessed numerous attempts to rationalize English orthography, with would-be reformers, such as Noah Webster, ridiculing the English alphabet as more "capricious and irregular" than any other. For this reason, some recommended Greek, Armenian, or Hebrew letters, or one of the countless systems of characters strewn through two centuries of philosophy, as better fitted to fix Native speech on the page, though, as one young philologist noted, "new characters . . . from their very strangeness, have an uncouth and somewhat repulsive appearance." Du Ponceau had suggested a roman alphabet with German values, which varied less than their English counterparts and which would harmonize new work with Moravian materials and the best European philology. Pickering agreed that the roman alphabet was best and, like Jones, he considered English pronunciation "disgracefully and almost ridiculously imperfect." He chose, nonetheless, simply to modify the English alphabet by setting fixed values on single letters and letter combinations. Saving souls and the science of languages— mutually supportive enterprises—required a uniform method of recording Native speech.[16]

Because it promised a useful combination of relative precision with the familiarity and accessibility of the roman alphabet, missionaries consulted Pickering's essay almost immediately. Within a decade, the American Board mandated that its missionaries use it as the basis for recording American Indian languages and, eventually, the board also used it in Asia and Africa. It had shortcomings nonetheless. In any system, as Pickering recognized, a vowel did not represent a single sound but rather a continuum, "a *series* of sounds . . . more or less extensive according to the genius of different languages." Consonants presented challenges too. Some "elementary sounds" in a given language "must be learned from a native." Distinguishing these, with

the many "delicate distinctions of fundamental sounds" and assigning characters to each could only be the "long and careful" work of those who "reside
among the different tribes." These circumstances posed problems for accuracy,
uniformity, or both.[17]

Board missionaries adopted Pickering's system with varying degrees of
confidence and satisfaction. Precision was crucial because missionaries sometimes read religious translations aloud to Native listeners before they actually
understood the language, so success required unerring pronunciation. Daniel
Butrick thought the orthography was insufficient for this goal. Because
Cherokee "abounds with vowel sounds," which "must . . . be distinguished
with the greatest accuracy," he thought each should be designated by a "distinct character." At Buffalo Creek, Asher Wright similarly concluded that the
orthography had to be "modified to meet the exigencies of the Seneca language." Pickering's alphabet provided a base, "as far as it could," when Stephen
Riggs confronted Dakota, but some sounds "cannot be exactly represented, by
any *heaping together* of English consonants." He had to assign several letters
new values to accommodate the language's "four *clicks* and two *gutturals* and a
nasal." Cyrus Byington found "such a difference" between Choctaw and other
languages that he resolved simply to write to Pickering for guidance. In short,
Native languages resisted any "uniform orthography."[18]

Whites mistakenly believed that they could determine what marks would
represent Native sounds. As Pickering saw it, Americans had "only to ascertain . . . every elementary sound, and then arrange the letters, by which we
may choose to represent sounds, in the order of our alphabet." Henry R.
Schoolcraft, a U.S. Indian agent and philologist, similarly insisted, "To the
native, it matters little, what system of orthography he is taught to read by." In
reality, however, designing and disseminating an orthography sometimes
entailed competition with those devised in other missionary efforts. More
importantly, missionaries confronted Native readers or potential readers who
possessed clear preferences. Peter Jones, a Methodist Ojibwe, noted that his
literate countrymen "complained" when missionaries or their boards tried to
impose an unfamiliar writing system, which "induced" him "to fall in with
their desires" when he composed an Ojibwe hymnbook. The Catholic missionary Eugene Vetromile similarly recognized the need to "gratify" the "just
requests" of Penobscot readers. To make books "acceptable to the Indians," as
the Baptist missionary chronicler Isaac McCoy recognized, missionaries of all
creeds had to accommodate Native readers on matters of spelling.[19]

The Buffalo Creek mission provides an instructive example. Unlike most
Native groups among whom U.S. missionaries were working, Senecas already

possessed an alphabet, which Jabez Hyde had introduced while working under the auspices of the New-York Missionary Society. Although there were few texts in the nation besides worn hymn books, a considerable number could read according to the old alphabet, and they contested the imposition of an entirely new mode of spelling, which the American Board sought for the convenience of a standardized scheme in its missions. To literate Senecas, whatever books the board printed should benefit those who could already read. The board, however, instructed T. S. Harris to teach the young using the new orthography and to urge older Senecas to adopt it. A decade later, older Senecas still read the old way, and the dispute tangled with divisions between Christians and traditionalists and between pro- and anti-removal parties. A new missionary, Asher Wright, advised that such rifts might be exploited to bring Hyde's alphabet into "disrepute," but he conceded that "reconciling the people to changes" would be difficult. "The abuse of Pickering's system," Wright reported, had "excited such a prejudice against that mode" that it could only "be retained . . . with such additions and corrections as will overcome their objections." The documentation of this controversy is more unique than missionaries' frequent need to negotiate with Native people on matters of orthography.[20]

The most prominent example of Native orthographic demands dictating the policy of missionaries is that of the Cherokees, whose National Council rejected a proposal to replace Sequoyah's syllabary with the uniform orthography. Either "force of national pride" or its "greater convenience" had led Cherokees to adopt the syllabary and, Pickering grumbled, "so strong is their partiality for this national alphabet, that our missionaries have been obliged to yield." He was so frustrated with the rapid and exclusive spread of the syllabary that he discontinued work on the Cherokee grammar. The board, however, at the urging of Samuel A. Worcester, used the syllabary to its advantage. It was his "systematic arrangement" of Sequoyah's syllabary—meaning that the characters were ordered according to English vowel sounds—that became the most widely publicized form of the invention. Worcester recognized the advantages of an orthography standardized for all the board's missions, but the syllabary was simpler for Cherokee, and the ability to read in it could be taught far more quickly. More importantly, the abstract question of superiority was immaterial. Implementing Pickering's alphabet would require the board to "overcome strong feelings of disappointment, to kindle enthusiasm in the place of aversion, and by the assiduous labor of years, to attain, probably at best, what . . . is already attained." If the board printed books in the syllabary, "they will be read," but "if in any other, they will be useless." With pressures mounting in 1827, as Georgia extended discriminatory laws over

Cherokee people and land in an effort to force "voluntary" removal, Worcester judged that Cherokees faced a "crisis." The need to convert as many, as quickly, as possible demanded that the board adopt the syllabary.[21]

Syllabary: Civilization or Sovereignty

Sequoyah, also known as George Guess (or Guest, Guyst, or Gist), invented the syllabary around 1820. Although his father or grandfather was a Scottish trader or captive, his full-blooded, traditionalist mother and her people raised him speaking only Cherokee. Indians in the early nineteenth century were neither mystified with writing nor necessarily resistant to it. Hearing several friends discuss how viewing ink on a page could provide the same information as hearing speech, Sequoyah concluded that the "white man is no magician." Anyone could draw shapes and Sequoyah recognized that he and another could "agree . . . by what name to call those marks and that will be writing and can be understood."[22]

Intrigued by the possibility of a more reliable means to transmit knowledge across distances and generations, Sequoyah devoted considerable thought to how one might convey speech to the eyes. After several unsuccessful attempts, he had the insight that a limited number of sounds composed all Cherokee words. With the help of his wife and daughter, he listened to conversations and speeches to isolate the discrete sounds his people made. Amid ridicule and charges of witchcraft, Sequoyah designated each with its own mark, which he either invented or took from bibles, newspapers, and spelling books scattered through the country. Each character represented a syllable rather than an elementary sound and, if the shape of a mark was that of a roman letter, there was no correspondence between its Cherokee and European sounds. Sequoyah eventually reduced the entire language to eighty-five syllabic characters. In an initial attempt to convince a kinsman, his daughter Ahyokah read from her father's list of characters and rattled off the name of each. Extracted from recognizable words, George Lowery thought the string of syllables sounded as foreign as "Creek" (Muskogee), and he suspected that memory fooled them into thinking that they read what they merely recalled. Sequoyah then summoned more of the nation's prominent men. He sent Ahyokah out of earshot and asked them to name anything they wished, which he recorded and gave to another man to take to his daughter, who read it immediately. The exercise was repeated with roles reversed. His countrymen were surprised but unconvinced. Sequoyah suggested that several promising boys be selected to learn the system. Their examinations several months later proved the syllabary's viability. Most could learn and begin teaching it to others in mere days. Syllabic literacy, according to the American Board missionary William Chamberlain, "spread . . . through the nation like fire among the leaves."[23]

Today linguists identify the syllabary as an example of "diffusion," meaning that a known example of writing inspired the invention of an unrelated system; but that does not begin to capture the significance of Sequoyah's achievement. Travelers found "Cherokee letters painted or cut on the trees by the road side, on fences, houses, and often on pieces of bark or board lying about the houses." Thousands of men and women, "by mutual assistance, without extraneous impulse or aid, acquired the art of reading," using "a character wholly original." Nativist traditions circulating among northern, southern, and western nations around this time articulated the belief that writing marked eternal cultural difference between Indians and whites. Literacy was unsuited to Indians, in this view, because the Great Spirit had not given it to them. In marked contrast, contemporary Cherokee legends—which come to us in versions that posit the separate creations of white and Native people, and in versions that describe their shared descent—illustrate both the propriety of Native literacy and white perfidy. The Creator had originally given Indians the book, but the white man stole it. Sequoyah, who had invented the syllabary so his people could benefit from writing without submitting to the danger of missionaries' indoctrination or manipulation, could have been seen to reclaim writing for Cherokees.[24]

An Indian inventing letters fascinated white Americans, particularly in light of its place within notions of the development of society through discrete stages. According to many eighteenth-century philosophers, written characters enhanced each of the functions that philosophy assigned to language itself: improving intellect, sociability, and, according to some, individual innovation. In *The Origin of Laws, Arts, and Sciences, and Their Progress amongst the Most Ancient Nations* (1761), a cornerstone of eighteenth-century moral philosophy, Antoine Yves Goguet argued, if "ferocious people" acquired "the cultivation of letters, they will be instantly humanized." Edward Gibbon, in the opening volume of *The Decline and Fall of the Roman Empire* (1776), similarly identified the "use of letters" as the "principal circumstance that distinguishes a civilized people from a herd of savages incapable of knowledge or reflection." This was not merely a neoclassical conceit, since romantic poets such as Samuel Taylor Coleridge expressed similar sentiments in the 1820s, asserting that "Civilization and the conditions under which a people have become progressive . . . commences with an alphabet, or with some equivalent discovery imperfectly answering the same purpose." The *Encyclopaedia Americana* provided the

In this portrait, by Charles Bird King circa 1838, Sequoyah points to the tablet containing the syllabic characters that he had invented to write Cherokee. It illustrates the wonder with which whites viewed the invention of writing by an Indian and elides the ways in which the inventor, who was among the first of the "voluntary" Cherokee emigrants across the Mississippi, intended the syllabary to provide the benefits of writing while avoiding further infiltration of white culture. (Courtesy of the American Antiquarian Society, Worcester, MA)

pithiest formulation: "the art of writing—the great source of civilization." The learned expected writing to emerge as society advanced, and they anticipated that it would facilitate progress.[25]

Believing that writing was among the most salient markers of civilization, colonial travelers and missionaries had highlighted the absence of letters among Native societies, and throughout the early nineteenth century, whites struggled to fit other Native graphic practices into what they knew of writing elsewhere. A number of authors, from the seventeenth through the nineteenth centuries, attested to Indian "hieroglyphics" on rocks, trees, sticks, skins, and bark scrolls, which recorded clan affiliations, traveling information, sacred songs, and histories. In some instances, they aided nativists spreading prophecies of separate creations and cultural purification or, in others, Christian messages. It was difficult, however, for Europeans to conceive how representations of things could come to represent sounds. "Savages articulate their mother tongue, without troubling themselves about the analysis of sentences, or the separation of words," the philosopher James Beattie pronounced, "how then should they think of expressing . . . simple sounds by visible and permanent symbols!" "Savages," in this view, merely blurted words without reflection.[26]

Other philosophers, however, suggested a path from hieroglyphics to an alphabet. Noting the practice of "Ethiopians, and some people of India," Goguet pointed to a syllabic stage, in which a character marked a syllable rather than a simple sound, as "the first step men made to express and represent words, otherwise than by painting objects." In their influential books on rhetoric and linguistic development, Hugh Blair and Lord Monboddo agreed, as do some linguists today. The new philology made this transition seem all the more possible since "delicate, indeed, must be the ear, to understand compound ideas, from articulations, which are the compound of fractions extracted from separate words." As Peter S. Chazotte, a refugee language philosopher from St. Domingue, explained, "people unacquainted with letters, and obliged to exercise the sense of hearing to acquire languages, are better analysts of sounds . . . than those who acquire languages by means of letters."[27]

Yet the new philology had also called into question the assumed connection between language and social condition. Although Du Ponceau rejected any connection between civilization and grammatical organization, he believed that social advancement prodded peoples to invent writing, and he recognized that certain forms of writing were better adapted than others for certain kinds of languages. Just as a system of logograms suited a monosyllabic language without inflections, such as Chinese, a *"syllabarium"* suited Cherokee. Sequoyah's "intuitive genius" provided an example of "nature caught in the act of the invention of writing." Regardless, Du Ponceau wrote to Pickering, it would not protect the "poor Cherokees" from being "driven from their ancient seats, to make room for the diggers of gold." Albert Gallatin believed that the "syllabic alphabet" was "perhaps the fact best calculated to give a higher opinion of Indian intelligence" to the public, but he considered the farming of free men to be more important in establishing the existence of civilization. Philologists praised Sequoyah's achievement, but they tended to downplay its social significance.[28]

Those who opposed the civilization program and supported removal, moreover, pointed to Native–white intermarriage to undermine the philosophical and ethnological significance of the syllabary. While the earliest reports made no mention of Sequoyah's lineage, later accounts emphasized his white ancestry. In the most important justification for the pending removal, Lewis Cass claimed that the syllabary and other adaptations of white ways were "confined, in a great measure, to some of the *half-breeds* and their immediate connexions." Cass's criticism was a charged one, since such intermixture sparked violence. When Cherokee students married white women, for instance, riots in Cornwall forced the American Board to close the Foreign Mission School permanently. Charles Caldwell offered the fullest dismissal of the syllabary in *Thoughts on the Original Unity of the Human Race* (1830). He believed in Indians' pending "extinction" because he believed that the southern nations had shown that "intermarriages" alone brought civilization. The "Cherokee alphabet" that the "half breed" Sequoyah had introduced only confirmed, in Caldwell's mind, that "the Caucasian race" was the sole inventors of the world's arts. Whites had "awakened" the "train of thought" that led to the syllabary, so it was "virtually . . . a Caucasian production." Caldwell used this assertion to bolster his deeper argument about polygenesis and fixed racial hierarchy. By midcentury, this line of thought would spread among ethnologists and in the wider press. For these figures, and for the likeminded, the syllabary offered one means among others to "prove" what they were already convinced of, namely the inferiority of Indians, and to press for a more aggressive colonialism.[29]

Those who pushed Cherokees to reject traditional ways as vestiges of a savage past but who supported Cherokees' right to remain on their traditional lands, on the other hand, constructed narratives of Sequoyah's invention that resonated with older philosophical assumptions. This is particularly true of the earliest detailed account, which appeared in *Lectures on American Literature* (1828) by Samuel L. Knapp, and in a letter from the same year by Jeremiah Evarts, the corresponding secretary of the American Board. Promising to reveal the "mental operations" behind Sequoyah's "discovery," Knapp described the train of advances that followed Sequoyah's abandonment of "the excitements of war, and the pleasures of the chase" and adoption of the European trade of silversmithing. He turned to "arbitrary signs" only after he realized that using "pictorial signs, images of birds and beasts" to convey sounds would be "difficult or impossible."[30]

Details such as the progression from pictures to arbitrary characters and from attempting to denote whole words to analyzing component sounds confirmed notions of how alphabets might have been in invented in the past. Sequoyah had initially tried to designate a character for each word, but when the limits of memory prohibited this approach, Evarts explained, Sequoyah "began to analyze the words," noticing that one character could denote the common syllables found in many different words. This insight was especially fitting because—as Sequoyah himself or David Brown, who served as interpreter in Evarts's interview with him, must have explained—in Cherokee each syllable ends in a vowel sound, which dramatically limits the language's total number of syllables. Sequoyah further limited the number of signs by assigning a common *s* sound its own character, arriving at a final number of eighty-five. Sequoyah likened fixing marks on paper to "catching a wild animal and taming it." Domestication of speech promised improvement, just as raising livestock offered many Cherokees a means to enjoy the benefits of participation in the market economy without violating traditional spiritual-gender boundaries. Knapp and Evarts, or interpreters such as Brown, likely embellished certain details and suppressed others in their descriptions, which countless newspapers and journals repeated, to bring Cherokee reality into closer alignment with philosophical conjectures and national expectations.[31]

This strategy required further eliding the inventor's opposition to assimilation. Whereas Knapp noted that Sequoyah had fought against the United States in the Ohio country "when he was quite young," Evarts ignored this fact altogether. Each insisted on Sequoyah's total unfamiliarity with English, but recent scholarship has suggested that he might not have been entirely ignorant of it. If true, that suggests, even more starkly, that he may have deliberately rejected English literacy. Neither account mentioned that Sequoyah's first composition detailed Cherokee boundaries with the states of Georgia and Tennessee, though one taken down by George Lowery and the white writer John Howard Payne noted this fact.[32]

Cherokees who encountered moral philosophy and history in white schooling elaborated the significance of "civilization" narratives and linked them to the fight against removal. John Ridge and Elias Boudinot (Buck Watie), the Cherokee students at the center of the Cornwall riots, were especially prominent in their attempts, in public speeches and essays in abolitionist and other reform periodicals, to announce the syllabary as a powerful illustration of civilization taking root in the Cherokee nation. Boudinot, who adopted the name of the philanthropist author of *A Star in the West*, numbered the "invention of letters" first among several recent events, along with the translation of the New Testament into Cherokee and the "organization of a Government," which provided "a powerful argument in favor of Indian improvement." The syllabary had even "opened a spacious channel for the instruction of adult Cherokees." According to Boudinot, however, the "fabric of Indian civilization" depended upon "the Cherokee Nation" prevailing in "her struggle" with Georgia. Although John Ridge believed that the creation of republican political institutions was the "best criterion" for gauging their improvement, for an audience at Boston's Old South Church, he also stressed that the "Cherokees . . . were once a nation of savages," who became "the only modern nation, who could claim the honor of having invented an Alphabet." Cherokees who wished to publicize the syllabary highlighted the injustice of dispossession in light of Cherokee improvement, but they also hinted at Cherokee autonomy.[33]

Whites who opposed the growing pressure for federal removal seized on the invention to stress Cherokee civilization, but they confronted Cherokee sovereignty. In an influential petition to Congress against Indian removal, Catharine Beecher called attention to the syllabary. Indians were "independent nations and distinct communities," and Cherokees, in particular, possessed a "civilized government" and a "simple and beautiful language . . . with its own peculiar alphabet." As Evarts, who wrote the most influential essays opposing Indian removal under the name "William Penn," told David Brown, publicizing Cherokee civilization would be their "greatest defense as a people . . . the more advances you make the more firmly you will be fixed to your soil."[34]

Philologists were sensitive to the fact that the syllabary implicitly rejected the terms of assimilation. Henry R. Schoolcraft, a federal Indian agent to Ojibwes who supported removal, pronounced the syllabary "very inartificially constructed, and for all practical purposes, about as useful as it would be to convert an almanac into metre." Unless Native students learned to read in the "English alphabet," Anglo-American literature and science, and the King James Bible, would be a "dead letter" to them. John Pickering and the Prussian philologist Wilhelm von Humboldt discussed these issues as well. Humboldt congratulated Boudinot on Cherokees' "noble attempt to preserve in its integrity the language of your ancestors, & to associate it with the progressive march of mind & knowledge." With Pickering, however, he shared how "very remarkable" it was that the American languages could "maintain themselves . . . by an alphabet entirely different from ours" amid Euro-American society. Pickering, who opposed removal, decided that the syllabary was "very unphilosophical." He worried that a distinct writing system would impair "communication between these Indians and the white people." Volumes of strange characters suggested a form of civilization that impeded potential incorporation.[35]

Missionaries and federal officials also believed that the syllabary demonstrated Native development outside of whites' controlling influence. It could spread the gospel, but the American Board warned "intelligent Cherokees" that the "general use of this alphabet, so unlike to every other" would shut out the "respect and sympathy of other nations." Thomas L. McKenney, the director of the Indian office who advocated voluntary removal because he thought it would accelerate Cherokee social transformation, but opposed the coercive removal of Andrew Jackson's administration, dipped into the civilization fund to publish a copy of the syllabary and make "the *public* acquainted with the extraordinary discovery." It, combined with broader material and spiritual change, convinced him, and he hoped it would convince others, that the Cherokees were "a civilized people." However, he stressed that English would allow "intercourse" with white neighbors and the easier defense of Cherokee "rights." English—of itself—could even change Cherokees' "character and destiny." By providing an alternative, McKenney decided, Sequoyah's invention would "prove an evil, rather than a good." In his own account of Sequoyah's life and invention, McKenney offered a version of the civilization narrative (while also noting that Sequoyah possessed white ancestry), but "civilization," as such, was not the issue. The syllabary challenged the long-standing assumptions that civilization would bring assimilation and that religious and civil imperatives were one and the same.[36]

Such concerns arose from the limited spread of English in the Cherokee nation and in most other Native communities. For years, acculturating Cherokees had assured U.S. officials and citizens that the nation's "progressive approach toward Civilized Life" included the spread of English, which further proved that they were "rapidly assimilating to . . . our white Brothers & Sisters." Exaggerating English literacy in an essay for the ethnologist Albert Gallatin during the removal crisis, John Ridge estimated that about one-third of Cherokees were literate in English, while the remaining two-thirds held the syllabary in "high esteem." Modern tallies, however, suggest that only 15 percent of the nation could speak English, and even fewer could read it. The Cherokee National Council was pulled in opposite directions. It printed its records in English to advertise its advances, but it also printed in Sequoyan because it needed the vast majority of non-English readers to accept its legitimacy. The Cherokee government funded the publication of the bilingual *Cherokee Phoenix*, originally under Boudinot's editorship, to diffuse learning and mobilize white public opinion, but its incommensurate columns of Sequoyan and English demonstrated the difficulty of reaching Cherokee and white audiences simultaneously. The syllabary, like Cherokee political innovations, demonstrated social transformation analogous to "civilization," but in forms that made clear Cherokee resistance to assimilation.[37]

Missionaries recognized their poor record in teaching English to Cherokees and to other Native people. They partially blamed the problems that the language and its alphabet posed to Native students. The American Board recognized Cherokees' frustration at "deceitful" English letters, and the philologist Samuel S. Haldeman similarly pointed to Cherokees' "distrust" of the English alphabet, to explain their preference for the syllabary. Evan Jones, a Baptist, explained that the "dark and tedious business of spelling and combining sounds which they cannot articulate, and which convey no ideas to their minds" blocked Native students' paths. Others extended similar views to nations as diverse as Dakotas and Choctaws. Teaching English to children with "painted faces, wearing a blanket and breechcloth," Stephen Riggs assured his readers, was very different from teaching spelling to those who had heard the language since the cradle. This line of thought seeped toward more essentialist views in missionaries' attempt to explain their limited success. As the American Board reported, "those of unmixed origin" possessed an "almost unconquerable propensity to speak . . . in their mother tongue." Cyrus Byington sounded a similar note, advising against "the expectation of changing their national language & making them all speak English—we might as well undertake to change their blood or the color of their skin." In this view, missionaries and others associated white ancestry with a greater interest in, perhaps capacity for, civilization and a willingness to adopt English. They also suggested that language might be less a learned institution than something innate.[38]

Pronouncing and Marking Race

Sequoyah's syllabary sparked wonder and emulation. Other Native people praised the invention as evidence of "the superiority of the Indian mind." A veteran of his own nation's successful struggle against removal, Ga-I-Wah-Go-Wah, or Nicholson H. Parker (Seneca), wondered what might have been if the "invention had been given a fair trial among redmen in a time of peace and prosperity." Sequoyah might have wondered the same thing. A few years after the fraudulent Treaty of New Echota (1835) and the resulting Trail of Tears forcibly reunited eastern and western Cherokees in Indian Territory,

Sequoyah set off after Cherokees who had migrated even farther west to teach them the syllabary. Late in the nineteenth century, an ethnographer recorded testimony that he may have pursued "linguistic investigations among the remote tribes . . . with a view of devising a universal Indian alphabet." Sequoyah never accomplished that feat, so far as we know, but his influence stretched across the continent nonetheless. Recognizing their appeal to Native readers and their practical pedagogical benefits, a number of Native and white missionaries experimented with syllabaries of their own.[39]

Regardless of their deviation from civil goals, syllabaries promised to quicken the pace of conversion. As Loring S. Williams exclaimed, "Who can but admire what the Lord is doing in the Cherokee Nation by means of the Sylabic System!" The American Board teacher lobbied for the mission to abandon its adaptation of Pickering's orthography for his own "Plan for writing the Choctaw Language with Characters denoting Sylabic Sounds." Williams "venture[d]" that he could teach Choctaws to read their language in six weeks, which would considerably improve the necessarily "long course of instruction in the use of the English characters." Appealing to a broadening understanding of Native-language relations, he also reminded the board that his system "would also apply to the Chickasaw language with very little varia- tion." Similarly, after "reckon[ing]" that Seneca had "about 480 syllables," the missionary T. S. Harris and his interpreter James Young devised a syllabary composed of 120 characters, each denoting "what might be called the radical sound" and each of which could be turned at one of four angles to "represent" its "variation." Asher Wright, the Seneca mission's main philologist in the 1830s–1840s, deadpanned that a "considerably reduced" system would be more practical, but Pickering's alphabet seemed little better.[40]

Native missionaries also pursued syllabaries, even if they had already devised alphabetic systems of their own. Eleazer Williams, a native speaker of Mohawk, apparently experimented with a syllabary for missionary work among the Oneidas. Those closely related Iroquoian languages, which Williams tended to blend in practice, were distantly related to Cherokee, but unlike in the latter, their syllables do not necessarily end in vowels. Whereas Sequoyah needed only eighty-five characters, a northern Iroquoian syllabary would be far more cumbrous, as the Seneca missionaries discovered for them- selves. Williams attached close to two hundred syllables to distinct characters before discontinuing what must have seemed a Sisyphean task, since he had needed merely twelve English letters to convey all of the Mohawks' sounds. Peter Jones (Ojibwe), on the other hand, converted to the idea of using a syl- labary. He had used the "simple sounds of the English alphabet" in his first

This untitled page sits unlabeled in the papers of Eleazer Williams, a Mohawk missionary to the Oneidas. It is an attempt to distinguish syllables of the mutually intelligible languages, which he tended to blend in his work, and mark each by an invented character. Such attempts proliferated among whites and Indians in the years after word of Sequoyah's invention spread. Compared to the dozen roman letters that he needed to write Mohawk, the two hundred characters he devised would have seemed far too numerous for effective use. (Courtesy of the Newberry Library, Chicago, IL) translated works, but the remarkable spread of syllabaries among Cherokees and especially Crees, who spoke a language closely related to Ojibwe, convinced him that similar "characters should be invented" for his own language. These would be "easy and simple. All that the Indian has to do is to learn the characters, and . . . he can read and write the language."[41]

The Cree system was the most successful syllabic system in North America besides Sequoyah's. James Evans, superintendent of the Wesleyan Methodist missions in Rupert's Land (Manitoba, Canada), invented the system, but it had varied sources. Some have called attention to the similarity of its characters—angles, curves, circles, lines, hooks, and dots, each pointed up, down, left, or right to denote the vowel sound—to the Devangari script of India and British shorthand systems. The concept of a syllabic system, however, emerged from the interest that Sequoyah had inspired in North America. One community, in particular, embarked upon intense orthographic experimentation. In the 1830s, nonalphabetic systems for recording Ojibwe proliferated at Sault Ste. Marie, a center of the fur trade located at the rapids between lakes Superior and Huron, on the U.S.–Canada border that bisected the Anishnaabe homeland. Despite the importance Schoolcraft attached to Indians' familiarity with English letters, the Indian agent tinkered with a "purely . . . mathematical" set of marks "based, as a principle, on divisions and combinations of a cube, circle, quadrangle, &c." The Baptist missionary Jotham Meeker meanwhile, gave up on a "syllabic system" only after he became convinced that it could "not include all the Chippewa sounds." Evans's work on Ojibwe in this milieu became the basis for Cree syllabics, which first appeared in print in the *Cree Syllabic Hymnbook* (1841).[42]

The "Indian character" spread quickly among the Crees, producing a "rapid and astonishing progress of the Gospel" that merged with a prophetic movement that called for cultural revitalization as game in northern hunting grounds declined. Like Cherokees, Crees taught the system to their countrymen without waiting for missionaries. According to William Mason, the "desire of the Indians for the word of God in their own language and in the syllabic characters . . . is very great." Syllabic religious translation, which was mainly the work of the missionary's Cree wife, Sophia Mason, and the Cree teachers John Sinclair and Henry B. Steinhauer, culminated in 1861–1862, when the British and Foreign Bible Society published a complete Bible (the first in any Native language since Eliot's Massachusett Bible two centuries earlier). By that point, syllabics and communal hymn singing had spread to Crees living far from the missions, and as those Crees learned, white traders with the Hudson's Bay Company could not read the unfamiliar marks. Cree attachment to "their own characters," combined with knowledge of the graphic systems of their ancestors and relations, had already created a sense that syllabics were truly theirs and, perhaps, always had been. Long before any Europeans arrived among them, according to a Montana Cree tradition, the "spirits came to one good man and gave him some songs," and demonstrated "how to write on white birch bark." He recorded all that had occurred since creation, and he "faithfully detailed all of the teachings of *Ki-sei-men'-to*" as a guide for how "to live properly." Either from Cree or Cherokee inspiration or exchange, or through independent invention, Native linguists also created syllabaries for the closely related Odawa and Potawatomi, the more distant Mesquakie (Fox), and the Siouan Winnebago between 1827 and 1884. Recognizing the appeal of characters that did not resemble English letters, white missionaries adapted Evans's syllabics to unrelated Athapaskan and Eskimoan languages as well.[43]

The evident appeal of syllabaries to Native people led to considerable speculation. Since single Native words contained complex sets of ideas, some suggested, perhaps a system that marked multiple discrete sounds as single syllables might be more fitting for Native languages. Sequoyah's syllabary developed naturally from "the Indian mind, accustomed to view and express objects in the gross or combined form," according to Henry Schoolcraft. From a developmentalist standpoint, scholars viewed a system based on syllables as more "natural" because it ostensibly required less analysis than a system that divided syllables into elementary sounds marked with their own letters. Lending credence to this view, in the minds of some philologists, the two modern inventions of scripts by non-Europeans that whites knew of in the mid-nineteenth century—Sequoyah's and Doalu Bukara's nearly simultaneous invention of a script (which the Cherokee syllabary may have inspired) for Vai, a Niger–Congo language spoken in the West African colony of Liberia—were both syllabic. While missionaries such as James Hunter recognized that syllabaries were "much easier to the Indians" and offered them "profit of the soul, without any injury of mind," some philologists wondered if that might be, in itself, a mark of essential difference. For his part, Francis Lieber was convinced, "Had our race fallen on syllabic alphabets . . . our civilization must have been incalculably retarded."[44]

Syllabaries also contributed to a broader shift in how whites understood the physical aspects of Native speech. Even before Sequoyah's invention, missionaries had complained about pronouncing Cherokee. The *Religious Intelligencer* put it simply: Sequoyah's system was "adapted to express, what cannot be expressed by any other known alphabet." Similar commentary

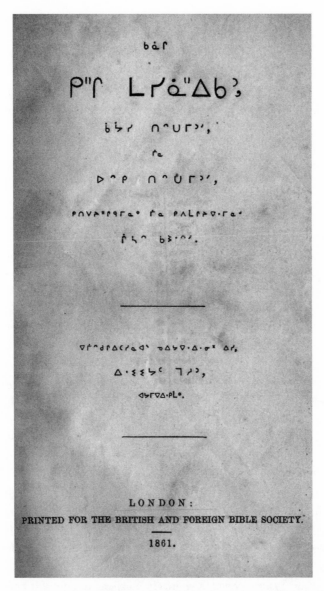

Nearly two centuries after the Massachusett Bible, the British and Foreign Bible Society published the second complete translation of the Old and New Testaments into a Native language, this time using Cree syllabics, an invention of the British Wesleyan missionary James Evans. Large numbers of Crees adopted the "Indian character," as it was sometimes called, and missionaries found the system to be effective in conveying Cree sounds, but its shapes and squiggles were dramatically unlike other orthographies then in use in North America. (Courtesy of the American Philosophical Society, Philadelphia)

surrounded Ojibwe and Cree. James Evans began his linguistic work by studying "the true position of the organs in the various sounds of the Ojibway
language." He attempted to find "analogous" letters for those sounds, but none
could "convey the exact sounds of the voice," which led him to create Cree
syllabics. With that system, his colleague William Mason found it "truly
astonishing" in 1855 to see "with what ease the Indian becomes master of their
sounds, and how well adapted they are both in his circumstances and his language." The "American Indian Phonetic Syllabic Scheme, Mnemonically
Arranged: With More Especial Regard to the Algonquian Dialects, Particularly the Cree," a table that prefaced James Hunter's edition of the Anglican
Book of Common Prayer the following year, linked "whispered" and "spoken"
Cree syllables with movements of the hand and body in an attempt to facilitate learning. Syllabaries seemed to record bodily aspects of language. One
could "transmute" syllabics into English sounds and letters into syllabics, as
Hunter put it, but difficult pronunciations and strange characters produced
mutually reinforcing notions of physical and visible linguistic difference.[45]

The work of Jotham Meeker illustrates especially clearly that the convergence of Native demands for their own written languages, distinct from that
of whites, and the latter's suspicion that English letters could not truly represent Native speech, propelled orthographic experimentation in this era.
Meeker began experimenting with a syllabary at the Sault because he believed
that "each Indian language" possessed "peculiar sounds, which cannot be
maintained by the use of the English alphabet." After his attempt failed,
according to the missionary booster Isaac McCoy, he came to believe that
only a "New System" would "avoid the complexity attending a universal application" of the Cherokee syllabary. Meeker, therefore, devised a method in
which "characters designate, not syllables, but certain positions of the organs
of speech." He used roman letters but discarded their English values, finding
that twenty-three letters or fewer recorded "the exact Indian sounds" in several different languages. Combining roman type with a method that taught
letters as nothing more than unvarying positions of the throat, tongue, and
lips, the New System provided relatively inexpensive publishing while cap-
turing syllabaries' advantage of eliminating spelling as such. Saying the character required "placing the organs of speech, or uttering a sound," so at that
moment "*he is actually reading.*" Following Odawa removal to Indian Territory,
Meeker adapted his plan to the languages of other Algonquians as well.
Within a few years, more than one hundred Shawnees, Delawares, and
Potawatomis, many of them adults, learned to read. Although the Cherokee
example had inspired Methodists to create a Shawnee syllabary, Shawnees "in

public council decided to drop their mode of writing and to adopt" Meeker's system because books were available. Focusing on the physical processes of Native speech, the "New System" provided the illusion of aiding Native assimilation in its use of roman letters, even as it assumed the fundamental difference of Native sounds.[46]

Attention to Native sounds increased as U.S. citizens simultaneously consolidated dispossession in the easternmost portions of the country and pushed settlement southward and westward. After a tour of the Great Lakes in 1830, Calvin Colton, an opponent of Cass and the Jackson administration on removal, asserted that the "dependent, child-like feelings" of Ojibwes had "produced a physical effect." Reliant upon one another in their ostensibly uncultivated social condition and, Colton left unsaid, receiving annuities from the federal government, the "entire character of the Indian voice . . . is altogether peculiar," having hardened into "an affectionate, tender, and dependent cast." Conducting an ethnographic survey for the state of New York fifteen years later, Henry Schoolcraft described the two hundred or so Oneidas who had remained on their traditional lands as a "mild people . . . with a mild enunciation." In contrast, writing in the immediate aftermath of the Third Seminole War (1855–1858), the Baptist missionary H. F. Buckner stressed the "majestic and warlike . . . tone" of Muskogee and reminded his readers that Creeks and their Florida kinsmen, who spoke the same language, "have been more successful in resisting our military forces than any other nation of the same population." Such observations combined eighteenth-century understandings of what constituted "savage" sounds and a desire on the part of U.S. citizens to hear to what extent a Native group posed some danger or could be valorized for their manly, but ultimately doomed, opposition to U.S. colonialism.[47]

Increasing knowledge of eastern Native languages corresponded to increasing assertions of the difference of Native sounds. Whereas travelers in the early nineteenth century noted that "the *Irish, Scotch,* the *Germans* . . . the *Iroquois,* and some other *North-American* tribes" possessed similarly guttural sounds, as the decidedly Anglophilic Timothy Dwight observed, or that, in the opinion of the adopted Mohawk John Norton, "Nations of the Algonquin race use the labials, and speak like English or French," commentators increasingly stressed difference as the century progressed. Heckewelder "could not commit to paper" a "*whistled* sound" in Delaware. Eugene Vetromile heard a "very peculiar strong aspiration" in Abenaki, which "cannot be expressed . . . neither in English, nor in any other language that I know." Even as he insisted that the English alphabet was "adequate" for Native languages, Henry Schoolcraft was forced to admit that he simply ignored "several semi-tones" in Ojibwe "for which no certain character exists." Caleb Atwater, who negotiated a cession of mineral-rich lands from Algonquian and Siouan speakers of the upper Mississippi after gaining prominence as an archaeologist, made the sweeping assertion that "our alphabet does not, and cannot convey the sounds, in any Indian language." Missionaries and federal officials alike pondered the divergence between Native vocal organs and what English letters could represent.[48]

Fixation on the physiology of pronunciation and the resistance of Native sounds to alphabetic assimilation increased with U.S. expansion westward. John Marsh, sub-agent at Prairie du Chien, labored to describe "an unex-pressible, uncomprehensible, inarticulate sound" in Dakota, which one "pro-duced by an aspiration, the end of the tongue at the same time pressed against the roof of the mouth." He denoted it with *tt*, but that gave "no idea of the sound itself—it seems requisite that a new character should be invented." Reporting to Congress on materials gathered by the army surgeon Charles Henry, Schoolcraft described Apache as a language that "abounds equally with guttural, hissing, and indistinctly uttered mixed intonations," which were "difficult to be caught and recorded by the English alphabet." William Hamilton and S. M. Irvin noted that the "position of the organs of speech" in Iowa were "*nearly*, but not quite the same" as in English, with speakers required to keep "the larynx . . . more open" to pronounce Iowa gutturals. These Presbyterian missionaries, who worked among Sauks as well, reflected, "different Indian languages have sounds that none of our characters represent, and which an ear, not familiar with the language, can with difficulty detect." The power of letters to contain Native languages faded across the prairies and up and down the Great Plains.[49]

Attention to the physical difficulty that Native languages posed for Europeans was greatest on the Pacific coast. Speaking of the languages of California generally, the federal surveyor George Gibbs averred that many of their "sounds are not susceptible of representation by any characters of our alphabet." Observations along these lines appeared with the earliest European explorers of the Pacific Northwest in the late eighteenth century, but they increased in frequency and in derision in the nineteenth century. James G. Swan, U.S. Indian agent in the Washington Territory, struggled to describe a Chehalis sound "produced by the tongue pressing against the roof of the mouth." It faintly resembled "*tl* as if there was the letter *k* at the end," but, it was "impossible, in any form of spelling that I know of, to convey the proper guttural clucking sound." Paul Kane, a Canadian printer and artist traveling through Oregon, could not provide a "specimen" of Chinook because he found it impossible "to represent by any combination of the letters of our alphabet the horrible harsh spluttering sounds which proceed from their throats, apparently unguided either by the tongue or lips." That articulation made it "difficult to acquire a mastery of their language." In the logic of colonialism, resisting Anglo-American "mastery" signaled barbarism.[50]

Increasing understanding of the difference of Native sounds was one reason that by midcentury the American Board abandoned Pickering's orthography and eagerly grasped the attempt, by the Prussian Egyptologist Richard Lepsius, to "bring orthography . . . into more exact conformity with the laws of physiology." It too proved imperfect, however, which made the American philologist Samuel Haldeman's efforts toward a "reformed orthography" compatible with "*Laws of the Mechanism of Speech,* and the Physiology and Physiognamy of words" of interest to learned societies and the Smithsonian Institution, a new federal organ of science. Knowledge of the phonemic diversity and difference of Native speech, as experienced viscerally in face-to-face encounters and virtually through the press, spurred whites to listen for signs of difference, even as missionaries and philologists continued to be frustrated by their unsuccessful attempts to assimilate Native sounds to an English alphabet or even to fix that foreignness in a reliable form on the page. Hardening ideas of human diversity in this era were physical and visual, in the realm of speech as well as in ideas of skin color, hair type, and cranial size and shape. Most observers did not choose between understanding Native bodily difference or Native linguistic difference. Rather, they merged them.[51]

Native vocal organs seemed to resist assimilation. Since the eighteenth century, inquirers had devised a plethora of reasons to explain why word lists, vocabularies, and other representations of Native speech seemed to contain discrepancies when compared against one another: the deficiencies of interpreters, the varying nationalities of recorders, the peculiarities of individual pronunciation, or even a whole tribe's inconsistent articulation. By the mid-nineteenth century, following trends in European comparative philology, U.S. philologists and missionaries also acquired greater understanding of regular phonetic differences among dialects and closely related languages, which promised knowledge of shared descent and even, some hoped, of the direction and duration of divergence. By then, however, a more fundamental explanation of apparent discrepancies had also appeared. To some, Native sounds and European sounds were ultimately incommensurate, so any attempt to identify one with the other was bound to fail. James Evans and Peter Jones each pointed out that Ojibwe did not contain the sounds *b* or *p, g* or *k, d* or *t, z* or *s, zh* or *sh, j* or *ch.* Instead, the language possessed sounds that existed somewhere between each pair, commencing with a "guttural or murmuring sound in the throat; exactly that which precedes the English g, b, d, z, and j, and ending with that formation of the organs under which our k, p, t, s, and ch are pronounced." A few decades later, Washington Matthews, an army surgeon who had learned Hidatsa, drew the broader conclusion that "there are labial, lingual, and dental sounds which *we* have not yet learned to distinguish, and which we have no characters to represent." Matthews's work highlights the growing importance of scientifically minded individuals who held various forms of federal commissions to the collection of linguistic information after midcentury. His recognition that the language we speak influences how we hear another language anticipated an insight that Franz Boas reached at the end of the century, which became one of the bases for that anthropologist's broader insistence upon cultural relativity.[52]

In the mid-nineteenth century, however, whites' dawning conviction in the fundamental difference of Native sounds played into white anxieties about assimilation. The physiologist Robley Dunglison, for instance, suggested that "savages" heard things that cultivated people did not. Jones and Evans, for their parts, took different things from their phonemic observations. One of Jones' hymns gave voice to the relative insignificance of articulation for faith, and because "white friends" and "Many of the more educated Indians . . . expressed a desire to possess the hymns in both languages," it, like all the others, appeared in English and Ojibwe on facing pages. "My thoughts lie open to thee, Lord, / Before they're form'd within; / And ere my lips pronounce the word, / Thou know'st the sense I mean" *(Min zhe shuh go ke wah bun don / Mon duh a nain duh mon, / Che bwah suh go kee ge do yon, / Kuh yut keg e kain don)*. While the hymn suggested the universality of thought and prayer, Evans echoed the Old Testament story of the "shibboleth" in stressing the physical tenacity of one's native speech. He insisted that an Ojibwe speaker's softer *j*, longer, "hissing" *s*, and throaty *u*, meant that whenever he "utters the word Jesus, every English ear would in a moment detect him as a foreigner." It must be so, Evans claimed, since an English sound would "require a formation of the organs, differing from that to which he is accustomed." Evans was not alone. Amid their lengthy correspondence, Du Ponceau had wondered how easily Native youth learned English and how correct was the pronunciation that resulted. Heckewelder denied any problems, but missionaries farther west articulated different opinions about the physical difficulties that English posed to Native speakers. Joseph H. Frost, a Methodist in Oregon, concluded, "as their organs of speech are formed, they cannot make our English sounds." The notion that different nations or races produced different sounds, perhaps due to differing climates or sentiments, was as old as ancient Greece;

interpreting the significance of Native tongues' "lack" of certain sounds as evidence of ostensible Native deficiency was as old as colonization. Rooting linguistic difference in the body as a basis for denying assimilation, however, emerged only in the era of removal and "manifest destiny."[53]

Philologists and naturalists interpreted these kinds of observations along a spectrum that ranged from social stage to national habits to biological essentialism. Discussing the "difficulty, and sometimes the impossibility, of rendering the native sounds by the already existing alphabet," Francis Lieber noted that some "may have been so rude, and so little different from the cries of animals (as is sometimes the case with the languages of savages), that they could not be expressed by signs for articulate sounds." Others spoke of national habits. One eager interviewer was curious to know which non-Native languages "the organs" of an Osage speaker "were best adapted to express." National lines, however, could also blur into essentialist demarcations. Refuting ideas of "barbarous" sounds, Du Ponceau stressed that they "exist in nature, since there is at least one nation to which they are familiar." Indeed, he suspected that "Nature has formed" Indians with a "quicker intelligence of words . . . and a quicker ear" than Europeans.[54]

Physiologists offered less ambiguously racialist formulations. The "sounds *xl kl* and *tl*" prevailed in the languages of California, according to the entomologist and traveler John L. LeConte, because of the "physical peculiarity" of Native people. To LeConte's ear, the "harsh, spasmodic sounds of the Africans are not the gutturals of the American Indians, nor are these the same as the uncouth sounds of the Australians." Arguing against the idea that California Indians were "Malay," a common view as territorial expansion and growing commerce brought mid-nineteenth century U.S. citizens knowledge of the indigenous peoples of western North America and the Pacific islands, LeConte told the philologist Samuel Haldeman that the prevailing sounds "prove their affinity with the ancient Aztecs," as did their "projecting lips, & conformation of the upper part of the skull," which was an "exact repetition" of figures on Mexican manuscripts. Louis Agassiz also linked vocal organs and the mental organ, seizing on the combined testimony of grammatical organization and sounds to argue for polygenesis. The "difference which has been observed in the structure of the language of the wild races . . . [and] the power the American Indians have naturally to utter gutturals which the white can hardly imitate, afford additional evidence that these races did not originate from a common stock, but are only closely allied as men."[55] While some scholars and missionaries continued to believe that habit or history or social condition shaped language, the sounds of Native speech combined with other notions of Native linguistic difference to cast Indian languages as racially distinct and essentially different.

The philology of Du Ponceau and Heckewelder gave a renewed push to Native-language education. A crucial first step in this process was developing an orthography that both recorded Native sounds and would be appealing to potential students. Native learners regularly pushed missionaries to accommodate their orthographic preferences, especially the Cherokees, who forced the American Board to adopt Sequoyah's syllabary in place of the uniform orthography of John Pickering. The syllabary itself was a polarizing invention. Its advocates held it up as the invention of writing that philosophers had conjectured was the harbinger of civilization, and they stressed that as a vehicle for spreading religious and political knowledge, it would extend that civilization as well. However, the traditionalists who adopted the syllabary did so because it offered an avenue for education that aided the maintenance of cultural and political sovereignty. American officials and scholars realized that the syllabary opposed the possibility of assimilation. Although some during the removal debates attacked the syllabary as insufficiently "Indian" because of the role of white influence and intermarriage, it concerned others because it inhibited the adoption of English, recognized to be crucial to the development of American nationhood.

The number of syllabaries that proliferated in the wake of Sequoyan literacy made the seeming foreignness of Native languages more visible. As increased knowledge of more and more diverse Native languages intensified the perceived strangeness of Native sounds and the inability of different races to produce others' sounds properly, missionaries and scholars alike inquired more deeply into the bodily bases of language, which converged with a simultaneous push to understand Native grammatical difference in psychological terms.

5

The Unchangeable Character
of the "Indian Mind"

Henry R. Schoolcraft began an extensive study of Ojibwe (or, as it was commonly known, Chippewa) when he became U.S. Indian agent at Sault Ste. Marie in 1822. His superintendent, Lewis Cass, had pushed the task upon him, hoping to obtain material to combat the supposedly elevated ideas of Indian speech and thought that John Heckewelder's and Peter S. Du Ponceau's publications had produced, but Schoolcraft also hoped to cultivate "the best understanding of this powerful and hitherto hostile tribe." He arrived at the Sault at a tumultuous moment, as the fur trade had begun to decline and as pressure on Native land, resources, and ways of life had begun to intensify. White settlement was expanding; the search for lead, copper, and other minerals was becoming more intrusive; and a missionary effort involving U.S. Presbyterians, Baptists, and Catholics as well as British Methodists was growing more assertive. Tensions also remained high along the border, with officials disturbed by the ease with which Anishnaabeg (the collective name for closely related peoples that included Ojibwes) crossed the imaginary line separating British Canada from what U.S. citizens called Michigan Territory. While an "imperfect state of oral translation" had produced "Distrust and misapprehension . . . [and] wars," according to Schoolcraft, linguistic knowledge could produce intelligibility that would lead to Native assimilation into U.S. society.[1]

Learning Ojibwe was difficult for Schoolcraft. Because his interpreter, unable to "tell a verb from a noun, and . . . incapable of translating the simplest sentence literally," provided little help, gaining the friendship of John Johnston, a prominent trader from Ireland, proved crucial. Johnston knew the language's "curious philosophical traits" and his wife, Ozhaguscodaywayquay

(Susan Johnston), and their family provided continuous instruction. During the business season, Schoolcraft would "interrogate all persons visiting the office, white and red," who could provide information, and "test" what he had learned "by reference to the Johnstons." Early on, he believed, it "scarcely seems possible that any two languages should be more *unlike*" than Ojibwe and English. As the family provided a philological "course," Schoolcraft courted their daughter Jane, or Bamewawagezhikaquay (Woman of the Sound the Stars Make Rushing through the Sky). "Her first conceptions had been expressed" in Ojibwe, and she "was an adept in the flow of its stately poly-syllables," according to Schoolcraft, but she also spoke English fluently and composed verse in both tongues. The two married in 1823. Jane Johnston School-craft explained the languages' similarities and differences and aided her husband in the analysis of the component parts of Ojibwe and related Algonquian words. Whiling away long winter months provided time to replace a vocabulary that his dog Ponty (short for Pontiac) had devoured, "revise and extend" notes, and read some philology and language philosophy. He worried that these pursuits unduly distracted him from prayer, but, thinking of St. Paul, Schoolcraft reflected, "all languages are given to men with an exact significance of words and forms," which provided "the highest warrant for their study." He remained wary of allowing the "literary element" of his philology to "palliate our delin-quencies in philanthropic efforts," but he believed that the two would be reciprocally beneficial. As Indian agent, he represented U.S. claims to the con-tested region, but his marriage into the family of Ozhaguscodaywaquay linked Schoolcraft to a long-established system within Native and métis (mixed-race) worlds increasingly under siege from settlers and their governments. It also allowed him to become one of the era's most prominent U.S. ethnologists.[2]

Throughout his scholarly and administrative career, Schoolcraft wavered between imagining a "savage mind" capable of improvement and a fixed "Indian mind," seemingly "doomed to extinguishment by some inscrutable fiat . . . like the primitive inhabitants of Canaan." The contradictory views flowed from his work in the removal era, a period that also included his per-sonal evangelical conversion. By 1834, Schoolcraft decided that Native languages' "vacillation between barbarism and refinement, poverty and redundance" indicated that "the people themselves . . . were formerly in a more advanced and cultivated state." Their languages had "degenerated . . . into barbarism and confusion, as one tribe after another separated from the parent stock" amid emigration to America. Yet, lexical change only underlined, according to Schoolcraft, that the "structure and philosophy of the Indian mind" seemed fixed. Indeed, believing that Indians descended from the Lost Tribes,

Schoolcraft adapted Du Ponceau's grammatical terminology to suggest that Native languages evinced a "Shemitic plan of thought." The very depth of grammatical knowledge that Native participation allowed presented new possibilities for misunderstanding and distortion. Schoolcraft, for instance, occasionally alluded to Jane Johnston Schoolcraft's indispensability in these studies, but he presented himself as the authority who transformed "Indian" opinion into ostensibly scientific material. Some of his conclusions echoed the prejudices of eighteenth-century philosophers, others went further; but each was based on a level of grammatical knowledge that depended on the participation of the Johnstons.[3]

As an Indian agent who had married into a prominent métis family, Schoolcraft was well positioned not only to collect reliable philological material but also to put it to use. Insisting that the Native future depended upon Christianization preparing the way for civilization, he advocated Native-language education of adults, reasoning that revelation could be conveyed "in the most jaw-breaking Wyandot, or flat chopping Sioux." Hoping to shape public opinion about Native peoples and minds, he incorporated studies of Native traditions and graphic practices into an expanded philology that he marketed to a popular audience in a series of periodicals, travel narratives, and other books. He also applied what he learned to U.S. Indian affairs. Besides supplying Cass with material during the removal debates, Schoolcraft's political connections, expertise, and religion landed him a commission from Congress to compile a definitive body of ethnological facts in 1847. This research, and the incalculable aid it received from the Johnstons and other Native consultants around the Sault, was crucial to philology's development in the years of simultaneous removal and continental expansion. Schoolcraft admitted that "business and science, antiquities and politics are curiously jumbled," though he disingenuously insisted that "the stream of inquiry" remained unclouded. Language, as an assumed mirror and lens of thought, was central to questions surrounding Native social condition and the possibility of assimilation. Schoolcraft, like other philologists, worked to convey their researches to scholarly, missionary, popular, and official audiences, in competition with other modes of studying "the Indian."[4]

Philologists, other ethnologists, missionaries, and many others constructed an "Indian mind" from the 1820s to the 1850s, at the same time that they put forward a racialized understanding of Native vocal organs. As in the latter, there was considerable debate over whether this "Indian mind" was fixed or if it in some way corresponded to Native peoples' state of society, conceived either as a primitive precursor to "civilization" or the end result of a process of degeneration. For some, this was a by-product of refuting facile notions that Indian, or any other, languages were "savage." For others, numerous struggles with translation, ranging from practical difficulties to loftier speculation about the incapacity of Native people to conceive of ideas that their speech seemed to lack, fueled the conviction that language both reflected and channeled thought. Understanding Native grammatical organization—and perhaps applying it to oratory, traditions and legends, and graphic systems—promised insight into the descent and difference of "the Indian mind." Language seemed to contain traces of Native peoples' pasts and held implications for their ability to accept the demands of "civilization" in the present and future. For this very reason, a number of scholars sought to present philology to the broader public, stressing its practical importance. Although Du Ponceau, Schoolcraft, and other philologists were unsuccessful at creating a popular audience for philology, they successfully presented its importance to officials within the federal government, which acted upon an essentialist understanding of Native languages as it moved to prohibit their use in federal schools.

Philology and Removal

Even as the work of Du Ponceau and Heckewelder inspired a surge in missionary philology aimed at Native-language education in Christianity, literacy, and Euro-American agriculture and arts, it provoked considerable skepticism and animosity. The startling claims and immediate influence of their work prompted Lewis Cass, the governor and superintendent of Michigan Territory, to suspect that the new philology was little more than fiction inspired by misguided benevolence. To his mind, Heckewelder "thought, and reasoned, like an Indian" and Du Ponceau was "a visionary and an enthusiast." So, the man who had called for a "war of extermination" against "the savages" in the War of 1812, and who eagerly extinguished Native title in Michigan Territory thereafter, began to collect materials. Secretary of War John C. Calhoun approved the plan and authorized paying collectors as part of an attempt to rationalize his department's operations (which also included the creation of a distinct office, later Bureau, of Indian Affairs) as it oversaw the "civilization" program, the growth of private trading that accompanied Congress's abolition of the federal factory system, and more extensive relations with diverse Native peoples. Anticipating, like so many others, Indians' imminent extinction if they did not comply with U.S. demands for "civilization," Calhoun believed that successful policies required the "most satisfactory information respecting the Indians that can be obtained."[5]

In 1821 Cass printed a set of *Inquiries*, which he sent to his Indian agents and to missionaries and fur traders in the region. It was the first such federal ethnological questionnaire, but it was a logical extension of Jeffersonian exploration and collection. The long and detailed *Inquiries* focused on the "constitution of their [Indians'] minds, or their moral habits." Although Cass sought any information that would highlight Native savagery, philology (including long excerpts from Du Ponceau and Heckewelder) took up nearly two-thirds of the whole. After all, there was "so close a connection between words and ideas, that the progress which has been made . . . may, in some degree, be measured by the terms which are used." Here, precision was necessary. Indians could recognize a "coward," but Cass suspected that the "passion of fear, abstracted from its operation upon any person, may be beyond their comprehension." Corneille de Pauw—a target of Thomas Jefferson's and Benjamin S. Barton's ire for his derogative characterization of North American productions and peoples—had expressed similar ideas in the eighteenth century. That the superintendent leaned on him for support suggests the different intellectual priorities of the younger generation. Cass urged his agents to analyze, or decompose, "compound words into their primitives." Excited by the task, Benjamin Stickney, a sub-agent studying Odawa, believed he had discovered the "opperations of the human mind," as they had been "independently devised" by "a portion of the human race, living apart from the rest."[6]

Young men eager for patronage and preferment heeded Cass's call, but accurate information was difficult to obtain. Philologically useful interpreters were *"pretty impossible"* to find, according to Alexander Wolcott, so linguistic information usually had to be obtained from a Native source. Charles C. Trowbridge recorded his experience of the attendant difficulties. His consultant, Le Gros, a Miami orator and prominent anti-removal chief, was hesitant to begin, "even under the stipulation that no information would be required of him which he felt reluctant to give." Once they began, Le Gros was evasive, offering only *N'kikelindasoa* ("I don't know"). That was "the most perplexing course and at the same time the most provoking one, which he could take," for Trowbridge, who "sometimes despair[ed] of obtaining any important facts on the subject of language." Eventually, he discovered that thirty dollars eased the process. Edwin James began linguistic studies in the same milieu. Attempting to learn the notoriously difficult Menominee, his consultant unhelpfully offered only "a Menomenie does not speak in that manner." Would-be philologists in the field faced considerable difficulty in framing the right question, and U.S. officials often found Native people, who recognized the utility of a degree of insulation, tight-lipped in linguistic matters.[7]

Aware of such problems, Cass dismissed his agents' conclusions if they failed to refute what he insisted, with no real knowledge, were Heckewelder's and Du Ponceau's "erroneous representations." Trowbridge, for instance, pointed out the pair's minor mistakes, but to his "astonishment," the agent became firmly "convinced of the wonderful regularity and order" of Delaware. After "infinite questionings and cross-questionings," Alexander Wolcott similarly found Potawatomi verbs "far more varied, more perfect, and beautiful" than in any other language, which more than compensated for the language's other "deficiencies." He had "amazing difficulty" reaching even these "pitiful gleanings," but Wolcott concluded that Potawatomi was "a strange mixture of rudeness and refinement." Frustrated that novice philologists, hastily compiling uncertain information from wary Native consultants, could provide "no systematic arrangement—no analytical process, and, in fact, no correctness of detail," the superintendent complained of the "obtuseness of intellect manifested in both collector and contributor."[8]

Conditions were different, however, at Sault Ste. Marie, where the Johnstons chose to help Schoolcraft overcome the "insuperable difficulties" that philologists usually faced. Schoolcraft's responses regarding Ojibwe, more extensive than any others that Cass received, reveal the importance of Native and métis participation for a "perfect analysis of the language." Supplying rules for tense, mood, number, gender, and voice, with guidelines for euphony and accent, Schoolcraft documented a language of "philosophical principles." More thoroughly than his colleagues, however, Schoolcraft also speculated about Ojibwe difference. Hardening Heckewelder's musings on the animate–inanimate distinction in Algonquian languages, he described the "principle of gender" being "lost in that of vitality." Inseparable pronouns and their "habit of using participles," moreover, made the language both overly concrete and in a perpetual present. Schoolcraft conjectured that these "imperfect forms of syntax" were common among all "rude languages," and he believed that the language was degenerating amid what he saw as a broader decay in Ojibwe communities. The agent's intimacy with Jane Johnston Schoolcraft and her family allowed far deeper philological knowledge than U.S. officials were accustomed to enjoy. They refuted the crude savage-language stereotypes of the eighteenth century, but they also led to new misrepresentations.[9]

Circumstances pushed Cass to publish his findings in early 1826 and to elaborate them in 1828, in response to a barrage of criticism. While Schoolcraft had hoped that Cass would write an authoritative work on Indians for the public, Cass himself had intended to submit a comprehensive report to the War Department. That changed when the *Quarterly Review,* one of Britain's most influential publications, cited the views of Heckewelder and others to denounce western settlers' vices and to accuse the U.S. government of seeking Indians' "extermination." The article's "crude notions" and "peculiar malignancy" irritated Cass. In a series of articles for the *North American Review,* the leading American literary journal and a natural venue for an ambitious westerner of Yankee stock, Cass targeted imperial competitors and domestic philological rivals. Among his most important goals was to give legislators in Congress "a correct estimate . . . of the situation and prospect of our aboriginal neighbors" as they were about to consider an Indian removal bill.[10]

These essays, a cross between literary reviews and policy papers, argued that the work of Heckewelder and Du Ponceau "elevates the Indian character far above its true standard, and . . . depresses that of the frontier settlers as far below it." Romanticization of noble savages—such as James Fennimore Cooper's *Last of the Mohicans* (1826), which drew upon Heckewelder's "History"—could be parried easily enough. By wrapping ostensibly analogous ideas in the authority of a science then dominating Europe, however, Du Ponceau's philology was encouraging Native education on traditional lands, which Cass opposed. Because of the "intimate connexion between the powers and process of the mind, and the means by which its operations are disclosed," refuting the new philology was central to Cass's defense of U.S. pioneers and policy.[11]

Cass could not disprove Du Ponceau and Heckewelder as easily as he might have wished. Despite the authority he claimed from his experience "among some of the wildest and most remote of our Indian tribes," he spoke no Native language, and Indian and métis consultants had convinced his agents that their languages were not "savage" in the ways commonly supposed. Ignoring some aspects of his agents' reports and capitalizing on others, however, Cass argued that Native languages reflected lack of cultivation and perhaps something deeper. Drawing on Schoolcraft, for instance, Cass argued that the distortion of the "natural distinction of gender" in the animate–inanimate classification system was the "feature" that "most distinctly marked" Algonquian languages. Polysynthesis was nothing but the result of "physical and moral" causes—such as Indians being "more prone to action than reflection"—that had given "a particular direction to their thoughts." Uncultivated languages were necessarily "harsh in the utterance, inartificial in their construction, indeterminate in their application, and incapable of expressing a vast variety of ideas, particularly those which relate to invisible objects." Sweeping generalizations aside, he avoided challenging Du Ponceau's grammatical theories directly.[12]

Instead, Cass criticized the new philology in its missionary foundations. Heckewelder's partiality to Delawares led him to believe theirs was the mother language to Ojibwe rather than its "most remote" relation, and, as Trowbridge had explained, Zeisberger had unwittingly mixed together words from different Delaware dialects because the Moravian mission itself brought together Unami and Munsee speakers. Based on Schoolcraft's delineation of the differences between the types of speech used in "public council" and in "ordinary conversation," Cass dismissed the "extravagances" of Heckewelder's depiction of Indian eloquence. Veteran of many land cession treaties, Cass had a low opinion of Native oratory, which he associated with Native dissimulation and the still pernicious influence of the British around the Great Lakes. Cass also contended that any Native consultants who lived near white civilization had lost traditional knowledge, so "any information derived from them must be vague and unsatisfactory." Where Heckewelder had used the most cultivated form of the language as its standard, the Democrat Cass insisted that it was only the language of the mass of Native speakers, and more specifically those who had most opposed the U.S. "civilization" program, that mattered for philology.[13]

Most deeply, Cass believed that the new philology obscured, perhaps deliberately, the fact that the "range of thought of our Indian neighbors is extremely limited." He asserted that Native languages were originally monosyllabic and that adequate communication required the continual accretion of root words. This could create as many compounds "as the most ecstatic philologist could require," but the result was neither poetic nor precise. Moreover, the "looseness" of Heckewelder's translations was "utterly incompatible" with the "severity" and "exactness" necessary for "investigations into the philosophy of language." Rather than convey the spirit of a speaker, philologists must analyze the component parts of words and phrases. Heckewelder's *Eluwantowit* ("God above all"), for instance, should have been rendered *"Aloo wontoowit . . .* 'more God.'" Thus, he hinted that Indians conceived not of an incorporeal absolute ruler but only a being merely greater in quantity or stature. Imposing European categories rather than accepting an alternative means to achieve a coherent and effective whole, declaring each sundered part deficient, and using that judgment to justify further settlement and expansion, Cass used philology to express what had been the governing assumptions of Anglo-American colonialism to that point. The social and spiritual adaptation that Native people had undertaken at Moravian missions, and the desire of a former missionary to aid that process and advertise its successes was worse than irrelevant, according to Cass, because the missionary foundations of the new philology discredited its scientific objectivity. Native languages reflected savagery, Cass insisted, and they could not be cultivated without ceasing to be truly "Indian."[14]

Cass's articles in the *North American Review* produced an immediate effect. They established his reputation as an expert on Indian character and affairs, and they lent support to advocates of removal, even though, at first, Cass himself warned that the policy would be unwieldy and expensive. A month after his first article appeared, Cass gloated that it "takes well" in Washington. Daniel Webster admitted that Cass, an old schoolmate, possessed only a "superficial" knowledge of the subject, but the Massachusetts senator joined him in the "heresy" of rejecting the "new doctrines about the Indian languages." Like Cass, Webster considered them the "rudest forms of speech" and found "as little in the languages of the tribes as in their laws, manners, and customs, worth studying or worth knowing."[15]

Cass's articles also sparked widespread debates about the new philology and its implications for understanding Native psychology and U.S. Indian affairs, with their varied interconnections. These spilled into diverse literary genres in the United States, and they prompted some comment from British scholars as well. Since Cass shifted the arena from the learned to the wider circle of readers of the *North American Review,* others entered the lists in periodicals as well, prompting further exchanges. Privately, Cass called Du Ponceau a "quack," while John Pickering anonymously but publicly accused Cass of "charlatanism" and of embodying the "perverted sentiments" of the frontier. Western allies of Cass, such as army officer Henry Whiting, defended those who had "long stood sentinels upon the outskirts of our population" and rebuked easterners, "born and brought up in all the security of a dense population," for daring to speak on the character of either Indians or pioneers. Schoolcraft elaborated his most essentialist views in "The Unchangeable Character of the Indian Mind" and other essays in a short-lived magazine, in addition to a travel narrative that mixed philology, geology and geography, and anecdote. Edwin James, an assistant army surgeon at the Sault who had given up Menominee and was learning Ojibwe from the former captive John Tanner, wrote to Du Ponceau, charging the "would-be philosopher" Cass and the "toad-eaters" who collected his information with deliberately "misleading public opinion and misinforming the public mind." Assertions of savagery and inevitable extinction only obscured that Indians suffered the "greatest evils from the ungoverned cupidity of these very men." He chose his words more carefully in a review of David Zeisberger's Delaware grammar, edited and published by Du Ponceau amid this debate in 1827, in the *American Quarterly Review.* James also appended some philology to Tanner's captivity narrative and then took it on the lyceum circuit. Farther afield, the former Hudson's Bay Company trader Joseph Howse thought Heckewelder's observations were "unimportant," praised Du Ponceau's work as "very valuable," and bashed Cass for his "complete misrepresentation" of Native languages.[16]

In Washington when Cass's initial review appeared, Albert Gallatin recognized that it had "excited a lively interest and thrown new light on the philosophy of the mind," even as the respective biases of "philanthropists" and their opponents each possessed what he considered undue sway among legislators and the public. Two months earlier, John Quincy Adams had called for the national promotion of learning in his first presidential message to Congress, and Secretary of War James Barbour continued his predecessor's efforts to systematize Indian information. Recognizing an "opportune time" to push federal philology, Gallatin also hoped to convince U.S. officials of the nation's "sacred duty" to educate Indians, whose "faculties are equal to ours." Previously engaged in the results of federal exploration while in the Jefferson administration, and prodded by Alexander von Humboldt to devote his talents to ethnology, Gallatin sought to trace lineal descent and evolutionary development. As he told Du Ponceau, "all that belongs to human knowledge and its progress, to the formation of language & to political institutions is connected together and belongs to *us*."[17]

Most of the continent remained, in Gallatin's words, "as to language terra incognita," especially in the West, but information was also uncertain for peoples south of the Ohio River. The Moravian missionary to the Cherokees, John Gambold, opposed philology because he feared it would discourage the adoption of English and distract the public from the pressing issue of removal. After all, "What can the preservation of their Language Customs & so forth avail if themselves become extinct?" The American Board of Commissioners for Foreign Missions mistakenly expected the grammar of Pickering and David Brown to "aid in systematizing" Choctaw and Chickasaw, languages entirely unrelated to Cherokee. Philologically, Creeks were only dimly known, especially the languages spoken by non-Muskogees in the multiethnic nation. Natchez, "totally distinct" and bordering on "extinction," was especially interesting, according to Gallatin, because it was spoken by people among whom colonial travelers had observed "a highly privileged class, a despotic government, and something like a regular form of religious worship." The language of the last of the Mississippian chiefdoms, in other words, tantalized with potential clues for civilization. Though Cass agreed with Du Ponceau and Heckewelder on little, they concurred that the languages of the large southern nations, acknowledged to be both the most advanced and the most immediate objects of removal, were almost entirely unknown.[18]

Hoping to extend its linguistic knowledge as the country debated removal, in May 1826 the War Department informed its Indian superintendents and agents, agents of John Jacob Astor's American Fur Company, and federally subsidized missionaries, that it was "the intention of the Government to collect and preserve such information as may be obtained concerning the Indian languages." Enclosed with the circular were Gallatin's preliminary classification of Native groups into language families, an explanation of Pickering's uniform orthography, and lists of English words and sentences to be translated, which Gallatin and Du Ponceau had jointly devised. Reflecting the terms of the Du Ponceau–Cass debate, James Barbour instructed respondents not to "confound" parts of speech, to "ascertain" the "general features and peculiarities" that distinguished these languages from one another and from English, and to provide a "literal translation." With the president approving $2,000 for the project (a sum equal to 20 percent of the "civilization fund"), Gallatin expected the "whole to be published at the expense of Govt. on a large scale and as a national work."[19]

This ambitious project, however, came to little. There was no consensus on just what the role of government should be in collecting or publishing philological or ethnological information in the 1820s–1830s. Debates over publicly funded philology paralleled contemporary disputes over internal improvements. Supporters insisted on its utility while pointing out that it was "so unprofitable that Govt. alone can do it." Opponents, on the other hand, suspected that it amounted to nothing but public support for an elite few, or they worried that the government was "making a monopoly of science." Moreover, there was confusion over whether it was truly a national work or simply a private project, and over whether Indian agents or missionaries were the appropriate respondents. Either way, although Du Ponceau was confident that the circular would solicit reliable information, Pickering was skeptical. Thomas L. McKenney, director of the Indian office, who contributed an Ojibwe vocabulary, "as far as it goes," and purchased a Muskogee vocabulary from a missionary, discovered that most of those who should have replied were "wholly incompetent" for the investigations. Cass and some others contributed to the project, but ambivalence, uncertainty, incompetence, and Gallatin's diplomatic assignment to England stalled the project. By the time sufficient materials had been collected, Andrew Jackson occupied the presidency and refused to publish the results.[20]

That is not to say that the philological debates had no effect on Jackson's presidency. Philology was part of a wider recasting of Native savagery as a condition that precluded indigenous rights and, thus, undergirded white settlers' claims to the land. In 1826 Cass had confessed, "our fears are stronger than our hopes" regarding assimilation, and in his final article for the *North American Review,* which appeared in January 1830, he penned an influential statement in support of removal. Though he alluded to philology only in passing in that essay, he addressed Native ways of thought and life. He and Heckewelder agreed that Indians in closest proximity to settlers lived in the worst conditions, but where the latter exhorted whites to better conduct, Cass demanded separation. He had insisted in 1828 that Native languages must reflect the "character" of their speakers. That conclusion was not simply a regurgitation of eighteenth-century views about stages of society, for in 1830 Cass was explicit that he believed that some "inherent difficulty" had left Indians "stationary" in "their moral and their intellectual condition." He ignored Ojibwe, Cherokee, and others' adaptations, or dismissed them as the imitations of a few "half-breeds," though without métis people Cass would have been unable to exercise much power in Michigan Territory. He repeatedly reminded his readers that John Marshall's decision in *Johnson* v. *M'Intosh* (1823) based U.S. sovereignty on past and continuing Indian "savagery." Cass had "attracted a good deal of exterior notoriety" through his *North American Review* articles, and Andrew Jackson named him secretary of war in 1831. While in that office, Cass would turn again to philology to administer removal and its aftermath.[21]

Philology's Audiences

Philologists attempted to reach multiple audiences at home and abroad, sometimes successfully and other times not, developing their linguistic theories as they did so. As a result, the antebellum era witnessed substantial debate about the implications of philology. Among the most natural people to be receptive to philological advances were missionaries, given their responsibility to use Native languages in their evangelization. Popular audiences could be difficult to reach, given the difficulty of the subject matter, though that did not stop certain philologists from attempting the feat. By midcentury, philologists and ethnologists had successfully convinced the federal government that philology should receive federal support beyond mere calls for collecting specimens.

Theorization about Native languages occurred throughout the antebellum era, as problems of translation suffused the expanding missionary effort. Missionaries, like others, were troubled by "missing" terms, like "law" (in Clatsop) and "time" (in Iowa), which were significant in terms of republican government and capitalist discipline on the one hand and in terms of sin and salvation on the other. They also found, as had their predecessors, that attempting to apply specific Christian meanings to preexisting Native terms, such as the word for "sacred" or "hallowed" in Walla Walla *(aut-ni),* carried the substantial risk of confusing heathen superstition and godly piety. Peter Paul Wzokhilain provides us with a rare Native description of how frustrating, yet important, this process could be. "I often find no word to meet the English word" in Abenaki, he related, "and in such case I have to make as it were a new word . . . so descriptive that there will be no difficulty for any Indian reader to understand it." He claimed to devise 200 possible renderings of "Spirit" before he was satisfied. It was difficult, Wzokhilain concluded, "to find the meaning and shape them into Indian words." Hoping to sow the seeds of faith, while at the same time avoiding the potential theological error that resulted from the fact that Nez Perce frequently "obliged" them "to say more than we wish to, & more than the bible itself says," missionaries, in the words of Asa Bowen Smith, had to cultivate a "taste for philological inquiries."[22]

The continued cross-fertilization between missionary and scholarly philology also produced deeper concerns about the grammatical traits of Native languages. Frederic Baraga, just a few years from elevation to bishop in the Catholic church, discerned particular importance in a feature of Ojibwe that requires speakers to mark whether one personally observed what he or she described. This *"Dubitative"* form, Baraga incorrectly believed, was "peculiar to the Indian languages." From this faulty premise, he concluded that it "bears testimony to the fact, that the habit of lying is a strong trait in the Indian character." Precisely because it suggested the "idea . . . of possibly being imposed upon," Baraga warned fellow missionaries not to use it when speaking of revelation. Henry Buckner, a Baptist, pointed to Creek speakers' supposedly unnatural gender categories in language and labor. Noting that women seemed to speak Muskogee differently than men, and noting that this was "common with many other tribes; such as the Natchez, Osages, Quappas, Dekotas, etc.," he concluded that this "common fact must be traced to a common cause—the oppression of the females." Because Native women were supposedly forced to "perform most of the drudgery" and because they were ritually separated from men at certain times, it came to be "regarded as indelicate or unwomanly for a female to speak to men in the language of men." Baraga, Buckner, and many other missionaries deepened ideas of Native grammatical difference in Native-language texts, and they did so while explicitly extending their work to the labors of philologists.[23]

The reciprocal relationship of missionary work and philology can be seen in how Du Ponceau chose to respond to Cass's challenges: by preparing Zeisberger's Delaware grammar for publication (separately and in the *Transactions of the American Philosophical Society*). That the "border-spirit" of Cass and his allies could produce such prejudiced notions did not surprise Du Ponceau, especially since he had "no great opinion" of Cass's learning, and he doubted that his sources were "men of science." Their philology, inextricable from justifying dispossession, sought only to make "Indians . . . appear the most stupid as well as the most barbarous race of men." Du Ponceau was concerned, however, because Cass's views were not all that different from those of leading European savants, who "justly admired" the grammatical intricacy of languages related to their own, such as Greek and Sanskrit, while deriding those of "our Indians." Here Du Ponceau singled out Wilhelm von Humboldt, who, in a memoir presented to the Berlin Academy in 1829, insisted that "agglutination" in the American languages was fundamentally different and on a "lower plane" than the "inflection" of Indo-European languages. Humboldt's language philosophy, Du Ponceau fumed, assigned the American languages "an inferior rank in the scale of languages, considered in the point of view of their capacity to aid the development of ideas."[24]

Du Ponceau hoped that the Delaware grammar would circulate among those responsible for communication in the part of "Indian country" inhabited by speakers of Algonquian languages, but his primary goal was to demonstrate to the learned the perfection of Native grammatical forms and that these flowed from "nature" and "instinct," not from the "*arts of civilization.*" Some languages were "more poetical," and others "better suited to . . . logical reasoning," the philologist explained. "Every mode of speech has its peculiar qualities, susceptible of being developed and improved by cultivation; but like flowers and plants, all languages have a regular organization, and none can be called *barbarous* in the sense which presumption has affixed to that word." Cultivation could "*polish* a language to a certain extent; but can no more alter its organization, than the art of the gardener can change that of an *onion* or a *potato.*" This "ideology" departed significantly from the version that prevailed in France, which insisted upon human capacity for intellectual progress based upon linguistic improvement. Du Ponceau praised the beauty of the American languages' organization and acknowledged its fundamental value, since "language is the instrument of thought and must always be adequate to its object," but he conceded languages' varying intellectual and moral features even as he stressed limits to the possibilities of linguistic change.[25]

While Du Ponceau intended Zeisberger's grammar for missionaries, army officers, and the learned, he presented his broadest philological conclusions to a general audience. In "Language," a long entry in the *Encyclopaedia Americana,* Du Ponceau stressed that "ideas can only occur to the mind in the shapes given to them by the peculiar structure and grammatical forms of that language," and the historical record showed that those were fixed. Chinese, for instance, had retained its form over the four thousand years of its historical record. It was unlikely that the "organic structure" of a language would have thoroughly changed in the two thousand years that were assumed, by traditional scripturally based calculations, to have preceded it. Thus, Du Ponceau concluded, "in all languages there is a strong tendency to preserve their original structure." This made it "impossible to suppose" that different forms were "successively produced." As early as 1808, the German scholar Friedrich von Schlegel had likened philology to comparative anatomy in its attempts to reveal the interior of an organism. Du Ponceau drew upon that science just as deeply, though only implicitly. Like the anatomical "plans of organization" at the center of Georges Cuvier's revolutionary biology in this era, one grammatical "plan of ideas" would not evolve into another. Du Ponceau concluded that the "organization" (another term adopted from biology) of different languages "must be divided into classes or genera, to which must be assigned separate and distinct origins." It was an argument that had some influence upon philologists and even upon some physiologists.[26]

This naturalistic, but scripturally compatible, theory posited the polygenesis of languages within the monogenesis of peoples. Du Ponceau believed that at the "confusion of tongues, the primitive language, its words and forms, were entirely effaced from the memory of man, and men were left to their own resources to form new ones." Each tamed the "rapid perceptions . . . continually flitting before the mental eye" differently, with some describing the "ever-changing shapes" in a single word, and others fixing successive impressions with discrete labels. The world's "various organic or grammatical characters and forms" resulted from "the tempers and capacities of the nations that first formed them, and of the men that took the lead in that formation." Subsequent speakers followed the "impulse first given." Du Ponceau noted similarities between this view and that which Dante had described in *Paradiso,* but it also shared affinity with the assertions of Lord Kames, which had proven so controversial decades earlier, with the important distinction that Du Ponceau insisted that the grammatical character of a language was essentially fixed at the moment of initial organization. In that way, it echoed the work of Wilhelm von Humboldt. Reconciling revelation and empirical evidence of diversity, Du Ponceau dispatched facile theories of Indian origins and linguistic evolution, even as he asserted the tenacity of a distinctly Indian plan of ideas. In challenging the supposed savagism of the American languages, while maintaining the strong link between speech and perception, Du Ponceau stressed the racial distinctness and the fixity of the American languages and the thought they shaped, denying that they could be molded by natural or social environment.[27]

Du Ponceau penned the culmination of his studies on the American languages not for an American audience but rather for the Institut de France,
which offered the illustrious Prix Volney for the best essay on the character of
the Algonquian languages. Despite misgivings "in seeking reputation through
any but the legitimate channel of the American press," he suspected that
Wilhelm von Humboldt would enter the contest and, as he said, he wanted an
American to win the prize. He had failed in a previous attempt, on the question of whether a writing system or its absence shaped a language. At a moment
when European philologists debated whether etymology or grammar should
be the basis for historical linguistic comparison, Du Ponceau argued that
grammatical organization, if anything, shaped the mode of writing adopted,
not vice versa. In 1835, however, he won the prize. Shortly thereafter he sold the
copyright to a French printer, who published the *Mémoire* in Paris. To supplement his scanty knowledge of Ojibwe, Du Ponceau included extracts, which
he translated personally, of one of Schoolcraft's essays, stressing that the author
had a métis wife whose native tongue was Ojibwe. The essay was "one of the
most philosophical works on the Indian languages that I have ever read." He
joked to Gallatin, "*a Chippeway wife . . .* is a great help to an Indianologist."
Du Ponceau's *Mémoire*, along with his highly regarded *Dissertation on the
Nature and Character of the Chinese System of Writing*, each of which appeared in
1838, were his final philological publications, as he grew increasingly blind.
Much of the prize-winning essay reviewed arguments about language that Du
Ponceau had articulated in response to Cass and Humboldt and which Du
Ponceau had published over the previous fifteen years. Although he sought
recognition from the country of his birth, Du Ponceau's choice to publish his
Mémoire in Paris, without an American edition, hints at the degree to which
U.S. philologists felt spurned by the public.[28]

There were limited possibilities in the 1820s-40s for publishing philology in
the United States outside of learned societies, and even there funds could be
tight. Most Americans had no "taste" for Indian philology and, as Pickering
complained, U.S. editors neglected to "instruct" readers in their "duty" to
understand important intellectual currents. Learned societies presented problems, too. After a flurry of publications in the 1820s, Du Ponceau had difficulty raising funds within the APS to publish more philology, including
Eleazer Williams's Mohawk grammar. Having presented it to the APS on the
"express condition" that it be published, and cognizant of his rights as an
author, Williams "regretfully" requested its return when it lay dormant for
more than a decade. After the Jackson administration had refused to publish

the War Department's material, the AAS only agreed to publish Gallatin's "Synopsis" with the understanding that he would introduce it with a long essay that combined history and geography with ethnology. In the 1820s, Du Ponceau had worried that the federal government might monopolize the energies of aspiring philologists, thus closing off a role for learned societies, but by the 1830s, he hoped that it would publish Schoolcraft's work, which he believed to be "indispensably necessary for the instruction of our Agents & Interpreters, & . . . Military Officers." Schoolcraft agreed; the Bureau of Indian Affairs (BIA) did not. When the nation assembled the U.S. Exploring Expedition (1838–1842), which would travel to South America, Australia, the Pacific islands, the northwest coast of North America, and southern Africa, it took determined pressure from Pickering, Du Ponceau, and others to avert "the shipwreck of our *Philology*" on the expedition. With the federal government less eager to publish work than to collect it and learned societies only able to publish material when its members would subscribe sufficient funds, philologists had difficulties seeing their work appear in print.[29]

The broader public encountered philology nonetheless. One question that received consistent attention was the relevance of the work of Du Ponceau and those scholars who built upon it, for the question of Indian origins. After the initial, tremendous success of European philology in successfully establishing the surprising connections among the tongues of far-flung people who looked dissimilar and lived in divergent ways, many scholars and readers had expected philologists to provide evidence for the shared ancestry of the entire human race. That, however, did not occur, and the American languages were one of the field's greatest stumbling blocks. While some scholars continued to insist that they found analogies between the American languages and others, most marginalized this view between the 1820s and 1850s. The "hope" of Congressman Edward Everett, who had studied in Germany, that philology would "unravel" the question of Indian origins proved false. Greater knowledge did not help. In a lecture before Providence's Franklin Society, John Russell Bartlett stressed that "without historic annals, traditions, or sculptured monuments . . . every step we take" in the American languages, "instead of bringing us nearer to the object of which we are in search, only throws new obstacles in our path." Even scholars committed to monogenesis, such as the British ethnologist James Cowles Prichard, confessed that "facts of late discovered have turned out so contrary to previously entertained opinions" that "we are not authorized to draw any positive conclusion as to their origin." Thomas Jefferson was more decisive. Near the end of his life, learning more of

the ways that Cherokees "bundled together" their ideas after reading a portion of Pickering and Brown's grammar, he concluded, "if man came from one
stock, his languages did not."[30]

The relevance of philology for racial difference, and even perhaps for polygenesis, appeared before readers across the country. The *Yankee and Boston
Literary Gazette* informed its readers that those who studied "the style, spirit,
and structure of the language" had found that "if entire difference of language
supposes a difference of origin, the question respecting the origin of the
Americans, is settled at once and for ever." Although it admitted that philology had not proven that Indians "sprung up on the soil from an entirely
distinct stock," Charleston's *Southern Literary Journal and Magazine of the Arts*
averred, "as far as language is conclusive of the point, it justifies the inference,
that the Indians are an original people and not of European, Asiatic, or
African extraction." Explaining "American Ethnology" to readers of New
York City's *American Whig Review,* the archaeologist Ephraim G. Squier
stressed that philology and craniology had converged in the conclusion that
Indians were a separate race, sharing no common descent with another, even
if "few have ventured to make public the deductions to which they inevitably
lead" because it was "generally esteemed . . . a heresy." In a midcentury account
of his experiences in Washington Territory, the former Indian agent James G.
Swan cited Du Ponceau and others in denying northwestern Indian languages
any linguistic links to Asia. The philology of Du Ponceau and many of his
successors seemed to support theories of polygenesis, and those aiming for a
non-scholarly audience proved far less restrained than philologists themselves
in drawing that conclusion.[31]

Some Native historians and philologists reinforced views of essential linguistic differences and, perhaps, polygenesis. Because words such as *koo-koo-
ko-ooh* (owl) and *sah se-je-won* (rapids) expressed the "the very sounds" that
those things made, according to George Copway, Ojibwe was "a natural language." Previous descriptions, such as appeared in the grammar of his coun-
tryman John Summerfield, had forced Ojibwe into ill-fitting English
categories, but Copway stressed that it was quite different. Because it was
"derived . . . from the peculiarities of the country in which it is spoken,"
Ojibwe "must, necessarily, partake of its nature." Peter Jones—whose religious translations provided "a foundation—a rock that cannot be shaken" for
some philologists—similarly stressed that his tongue's "great strength" was
that Ojibwe "words express the nature, use, or resemblance of the things
spoken of," while other languages were "composed of arbitrary . . . sounds."
This view resonated with Judeo-Christian conceptions of the Adamic language

and with some versions of sensationalist philosophy, but these descriptions of inextricable links between the Ojibwe language and Ojibwe lands also expressed Native beliefs that owed nothing to those European traditions. These views also hinted at a deeper significance that Ojibwe tradition ascribed to linguistic difference. Jones personally believed that Indians descended from "Asiatic Tartars," but his nation's sachems told that "every nation speaking a different language is a separate creation." As another Ojibwe scholar, William W. Warren, stressed, Ojibwes had "given to their race" the name *An-ish-in-aub-ag* ("Spontaneous Man") because they believed "they are a spontaneous people," emerged from the ground. As Anishnaabeg and other Native people faced threats of removal in both the United States and British Canada, these Native philologists suggested that their languages were essentially different from European languages, tied to the American land in a way that colonizers' tongues could never be, and they did so in histories that aimed to reach broad readerships.[32]

Moving beyond the socially exclusive circle of learned societies and the pious and distant fields of missions in the 1820s–1840s, philology and ethnology followed the channels carved by an expanding print culture and increasingly varied middle-class cultural life, echoing in lyceum halls, providing common detours in travel accounts, surfacing occasionally in a captivity narrative or epic poem, and filling the pages of literary journals. Yet philology was but part of a broader set of ethnological studies that spiked in the removal era. While language study gained the greatest amount of attention from the 1820s to the mid-1830s, coinciding with a brief but noticeable decline in archaeological interest among the learned, other modes of studying "the Indian" ascended. Samuel G. Morton published the highly regarded and influential *Crania Americana* in 1839. Two years later, George Catlin published the illustrated *Letters and Notes on the Manners, Customs, and Condition of the North American Indians,* based on years of travel among Plains peoples, and drummed up publicity for it by touring U.S. and British cities. In archaeology, the 1840s included John L. Stephens's popular *Incidents of Travel in Central America, Chiapas, and Yucatan* (1841), stirring American interest in Mesoamerica, and Ephraim G. Squier's and Edwin Davis's *Ancient Monuments of the Mississippi Valley* (1848), the inaugural publication of the Smithsonian Institution, offered a methodical description of sites, excavations, artifacts, and skeletons that lent scientific weight and federal authority to the notion that the "Mound Builders" were a race distinct from American Indians. That same decade, Lewis H. Morgan began studies of Iroquois society that broadened into a comparative study of Native kinship. These other modes of ethnology occasionally converged and sometimes competed with philology, and with less learned conjectures on the same subjects.[33]

Surging popular interest in archaeological antiquities and ethnographic descriptions and depictions caught the attention of an increasing number of bookmakers and scholars in the 1830s–1840s. George Bancroft, for instance, described at length the relevance of philology for understanding *The History of the Colonization of the United States.* Recognizing that "this curious subject, has not its *only* admirers within the pales of Antiquarian Societies," Josiah Priest and many others compiled worn tales and new linguistic, mythological, and archaeological discoveries into cheap and widely circulating editions. More rigorous exploration of the "immensity of our country . . . beyond the settlements of men, towards the Pacific," according to the Albany printer in *American Antiquities, and Discoveries in the West,* promised "more definite conclusions" to unanswered ethnological questions. Writers and policymakers anticipated that the physical expansion of the United States would bring with it a more comprehensive understanding of Indians as a race, including their thoughts and sentiments, and that an expanding circle of interested citizens would consume that information. Even when authors avoided the methods of philology, commentary on Native languages appeared. To take one rather dark example, in *The California and Oregon Trail* (1849), Francis Parkman described being taught some Lakota by an Oglala man named The Panther, which generated a series of reflections upon the "impassable gulf" that separated Indians and whites and the "cannibal warfare" that characterized nature "from minnows up to men."[34]

"Indian" subjects—including oratory and "superstitions," monuments and "hieroglyphics," descriptions and illustrations—sparked considerable curiosity in the antebellum era. Heckewelder, Cass, and many others heightened interest in Native traditions. "Indian eloquence," expressing what the *Knickerbocker* described as "hopeless resistance against the march of civilization," filled the pages of newspapers and periodicals, rang out from the stage, and was recited in classrooms. The ubiquity and diversity of Native graphic practices, which included painted buffalo robes that recorded notable events on the Plains, tall poles elaborately adorned with animals that represented genealogy in the Pacific Northwest, and even a system of "Hand-Writing" among Mi'kmaqs in Maine, became more known. Discoveries in Central America, a flurry of excavations in North America, Joseph Smith's alleged translation of the Book of Mormon, and hoaxes involving inscribed tablets and plates led breathless Americans, such as Pliny Miles, to wonder at "the *language* of the builders of the western mounds." Serious ethnologists competed with sensationalistic

This illustration, titled "Collecting a Vocabulary," accompanied "A Visit to the Guajiquero Indians," which appeared in *Harper's New Monthly Magazine* in 1859. The story detailed the humor of Ephraim G. Squier's attempts to collect a vocabulary from these Native people of Honduras, who foiled his attempts to learn the word for "woman" by providing proper names, relationships, and a deadpan response to the exasperated question of how one distinguishes women from men ("They are dressed differently"). The engraving indicates that philology was a communal process that joined whites and Natives, while the story illustrates the dual expansion of U.S. philology in the 1840s–1850s: to Central America and to a popular white audience interested in ethnological topics. (Courtesy of the American Antiquarian Society, Worcester, MA)

accounts in the popular press, and philologists worked to capitalize upon an engaged readership. Several writers, for instance, penned popular accounts of vocabulary collection that played up the funny side of the language barrier in the U.S. Southwest, Mexico, and Central America, while also conveying the difficulties philologists faced, in the words of Ephraim G. Squier, from "Indians incapable of comprehending your interest in the matter, and naturally disposed to think that you have a sinister purpose."[35]

It was difficult for a scholar to appeal simultaneously to learned and popular audiences, as the career of one of the most prolific and least influential philologists of the era makes plain. On account of his dubious character, abrasive competitiveness, and disturbing evolutionism in natural history, elite scholars barred Constantine S. Rafinesque from their learned societies, blocking that potential avenue for publication. So he attempted to speak directly to a popular audience throughout the 1820s–1830s in venues like the *Saturday Evening Post* and his own self-financed *Atlantic Journal, and Friend of Knowledge,* publishing open letters addressed to the likes of Du Ponceau and Jean-François Champollion, the decipherer of Egyptian hieroglyphics. Challenging the new philology, Rafinesque denied the "erroneous" view that the American languages possessed a "common exclusive grammatical structure" and insisted that lexical roots outweighed grammar in importance in language study (especially, he claimed, if studied by using a mathematical formula of his own invention). Challenging elite philologists, and competing with bookmakers like Josiah Priest who plagiarized his work, Rafinesque merged fantastic etymologies with archaeology and speculations on lineages and migrations in philanthropically minded work that aimed to prove that "monuments and arts, as well as languages and human features . . . rise and fall like the nations, mingle or blend." His record was mixed. It included real insights, such as the fact that Maya glyphs were partially syllabic, and brazen fictions. In 1835, Rafinesque claimed to have "obtained" and "translated" what he called the *Wallam-Olum,* a Lenni Lenape "painted record" of the creation and deluge, Delawares' migration from Asia to eastern North America, and European colonization. It was part of an unsuccessful bid to win the Prix Volney in 1835, and he published the "translation" of his invention in the popularly aimed *The American Nations; or, Outlines of a National History; of the Ancient and Modern Nations of North and South America* the following year. Its "symbols" were "inexplicable," he explained, until he discovered that each "applies to a verse or many words; as if the ideas were amalgamated in the compound system." In fact, he took philology and traditions from the work of Du Ponceau and Heckewelder, and pulled "glyphs" from other sources. Although distrusted and ignored at first, Ephraim Squier published it in the *American Whig Review* after the Ojibwe historian George Copway "unhesitatingly pronounced it authentic," both in its "original signs" and in the "fidelity of the translation." This philological hoax, perversely, was Rafinesque's culminating scholarly achievement. The *Wallam-Olum* garnered considerable popular and scholarly attention in the United States, as debates between monogenists and polygenists intensified in the 1840s–1850s.[36]

The significance of some philologists' attempts to reach a popular audience is even clearer in the career of Henry Schoolcraft, precisely because he never suffered from the kind of marginalization that plagued Rafinesque. Although he complained of his scholarly isolation while serving as U.S. Indian agent, he was a member of the Historical Society of Michigan. After the modest popular success of his *Algic Researches, Comprising Inquiries Respecting the Mental Characteristics of the North American Indians* (1839), and after he lost his post in 1841 amid political change and charges of corruption, he moved to New York to make a living as a writer, joining literary and scientific circles there, including the new American Ethnological Society (established in 1842). His initial grammatical studies, as he conceived them, had been a way of "clearing the ground of inquiry," but he had greater ambitions. Schoolcraft sought to democratize philology by expanding its readership, increasing the numbers of those who could understand "the philosophy of the Indian mind"; but he came to recognize what other philologists had long known. As Gallatin advised him, "Your 'Indian Tales and Hieroglyphics' would sell here; but grammatical materials on the languages will not do." To the famous writer Washington Irving, Schoolcraft admitted, "Researches on philology" were seldom read, "unless mixed with other matters for the popular eye," such as "tales and traditions . . . chants & songs . . . hieroglyphic inscriptions & symbol-craft." So, through a series of journals, streams of books, and an abortive "Cyclopedia Indianensis," Schoolcraft sought to integrate these subjects for a popular audience.[37]

Schoolcraft's ambitions were partly literary, but they drifted toward a practical application of ethnology that would inform U.S. colonialism as well. On the one hand, these disparate goals existed in tension. Schoolcraft hoped to lay a foundation for "a purely vernacular literature," doing for the United States what the brothers Grimm had done for Germans. As a text maker, however, Schoolcraft lurched from the ethnological imperative of leaving examples of Native oral literature "as nearly as possible, in their original forms of thought and expression," to the literary goal of creating an "Indo-American series of tales; a cross between the Anglo-Saxon and the Algonquin." The reading public was largely indifferent to Schoolcraft in this regard, though one work that leaned heavily upon him, Henry Wadsworth Longfellow's *The Poem of Hiawatha* (1855), was far more successful. U.S. and European scholars, moreover, criticized Schoolcraft's hybrid texts because they possessed little ethnological value. That was all the more problematic because, with the same publications, Schoolcraft aimed to "disenchant the public mind" regarding Indian affairs. As his supporters insisted, they provided "facts . . . for the information of Congress and the people." There was remarkable (and unlikely) congruence in what Schoolcraft believed would sell in the literary marketplace and what he thought was crucial for Americans to know to pursue an informed Indian policy. To understand "the mental character and capacities of the aborigines," he reported to Congress in 1851, required studying "the principles of their languages—the style of oratory—the oral imaginative lodge lore which they possess—and their mode of communicating ideas by the use of symbolic and representative devices."[38]

Schoolcraft never gained the popular audience he sought through his expansive philology, but he rose in prominence when he received a federal commission. In November 1846, members of the American Ethnological Society petitioned Congress, stressing that more authoritative information was "necessary, to enable government to perform its high and sacred duties of protection and guardianship over the weak and still savage race placed by Providence under its care." The annexation of Texas and the settlement of the Oregon boundary, combined with the ongoing U.S.–Mexican War, drastically changed the scope of U.S. colonialism. The federal government was poised to assert control over a vast number of little-known Native groups, reported to possess an ethnographic and linguistic diversity unknown in the East at a moment when ethnologists debated whether Indians could be civilized, whether they and whites shared a common ancestor, and what mode of study could be relied upon to answer those questions. An act of Congress on March 3, 1847—by which time the army had won victories in Alta California, Nuevo Mexico, and farther south—required the secretary of war "to collect and digest such statistics and materials as may illustrate the history, present condition, and future prospects of the Indian Tribes of the United States." Schoolcraft was the natural choice to direct the project. Besides being an experienced Indian agent and published author, he had just completed an ethnological survey for New York State, arguing that the Iroquois there deserved citizenship. Importantly, he was also an outspoken Christian, which was a politically important consideration, given that Congress had withheld one of the Wilkes Expedition's reports for its polygenism. Following Congressional instructions to include all that was known about "the Indian," he distributed questionnaires of some 350 multipart items to Indian agents, missionaries, military men, and scholars, adding twenty additional "Queries and Suggestions for Travelers South" (i.e., Latin America). William Medill argued that the "Government . . . owes it to itself to originate a body of facts on this subject, from which the race at large may be correctly judged by all classes of its citizens, and its policy towards the Indian tribes under its guardianship, and its treatment of them, appreciated." Ethnology, according to the commissioner of Indian affairs, was necessary for educating the people and their government. Both would be disappointed.[39]

Despite popular ambivalence about philology, philologists occupied a place of considerable cultural prestige. Cass and Schooolcraft each achieved prominence through philology. When Du Ponceau died in 1844, he was president of the APS, the Historical Society of Pennsylvania, and the Athenaeum of Philadelphia, as well as provost of the city's Law Academy. Of the nation's other most renowned philologists, Pickering was president of the American Academy of Arts and Sciences at his death in 1846, and Gallatin of the New-York Historical Society at his death in 1849. Each was instrumental in the creation of new philological-ethnological institutions as well, with Pickering and Gallatin serving as the first presidents, respectively, of the American Oriental Society and the American Ethnological Society. Philologists occupied some of the foremost intellectual positions available in the antebellum United States, and they earned recognition from European savants as well. This cultural status translated into a considerable degree of intellectual influence, which contributed to the way in which debates about separate creations and racial fixity increasingly circulated among the learned and those who sought to popularize their work.[40]

Essentialism, Evolutionism, and Efforts toward Language Eradication

While we usually think of physical ethnologists as the most important theorists of esentialism, Du Ponceau articulated his theories in the twenty years before Samuel George Morton's *Crania Americana* (1839). Diverse writers and speakers responded with questions or even theories of their own, but the cumulative result was open discussion of views of Native languages that were far harsher than Du Ponceau's. They did so amid a sustained assault by polygenists, mainly concerned with supporting slavery by stressing racial fixity and debunking the Bible as a historical text, which discredited degenerationist theories. Meanwhile, advances in geology, archaeology, and biology vastly extended the tenure of human existence and breathed new life into evolutionary notions of human development from primitive savagery.[41]

Schoolcraft was among the most important theorists of a language-based "Indian mind" that was far more pejorative than Du Ponceau's theories. As he told readers of *Oneóta*, one of his ephemeral ethnological magazines, languages "exercise a strong, though silent sway, both upon the question of the mental character, and its true development." Throughout his popular and official writing, Schoolcraft suggested that language, oral literature, and graphic systems functioned within a complex set of reciprocal influences that shaped Indian savagery. He was a disorganized writer, but views scattered across numerous volumes can be pieced together. At treaty councils, he claimed, those with a "native ear" could perceive the etymology of orators' highly wrought compounds, which "transport with their idealty, an audience of glowing foresters." In light of U.S. intentions to impose white ways on Native youth, elders' use of "oral imaginative tales"—stories of permeable boundaries between human and natural worlds and pervasive spiritual power—to convey "instruction, moral, mechanical, and religious, to the young," was especially important. This mythology gave narrative form to firmly embedded linguistic features. Storytellers relied on "metaphor, the doctrine of metamorphosis, and the personification of inanimate objects; for the latter of which, the grammar of the language has a peculiar adaptation." Ojibwe's animate–inanimate classification, according to the philologist, allowed Native speakers to "invest the whole of inanimate creation with life, and thus . . . throw a charm over the most barren waste." An expansive philology, in Schoolcraft's mind, could provide new insights into Native ways of thinking, which he found particularly important as he fixated upon Native resistance to Christianity.[42]

Native "oral lore," moreover, was "connected . . . with a hieroglyphic method of notation," which Schoolcraft explained at length in short-lived magazines, such as *The Literary Voyager, or Muzzeniegun,* and in federally sponsored volumes. Ozhaguscodaywayquay had first brought this to Schoolcraft's attention, and Jane Johnston and her brother George Johnston provided examples and explanations, but Schoolcraft's most important partnership for understanding the interrelationship of Ojibwe oral literature and graphic practices was with Shingwauk, an Ojibwe elder responsible for conducting the rites of the Mide Society. Upon seeing "a thin quadrangular tubular piece of wood, covered with hieroglyphics, cut in the surface, and painted . . . red, black, green, and other colors," Schoolcraft asked for an explanation. When he learned that only the initiated could know such things, Schoolcraft requested admittance to the society and offered his agency office for the ceremony. Shingwauk agreed. When the time came, he laid the "inscribed music-board" in front of Schoolcraft and "commenced his songs . . . figure by figure." Although he grew impatient with the ceremony's "necromantic tricks," Schoolcraft insisted that he "was minute . . . in noting down the original words and translations of each song, with its pictographic signs." Years later, Schoolcraft presented Shingwauk with copies of the inscription on Dighton Rock in Massachusetts. Although many believed it to be Norse, "the Algonquin pictographist" pronounced definitively, "It is Indian." In addition to teaching one how to live properly and access spiritual power, Mide ceremonies were also meant to foster shared identity rooted in place among members. Shingwauk's decision to initiate Schoolcraft, therefore, was an adroit attempt to use the U.S. agent's curiosity to make him an ally in maintaining Ojibwe lands and autonomy amid calls for removal and in increasing understanding of and respect for traditional ways in the face of a multipronged missionary assault on Anishnaabe beliefs and practices. Acting as an ethnological consultant afterward, Shingwauk both maintained those ties and affirmed Native peoples' history on the continent.[43]

Native instruction allowed Schoolcraft to understand the connectedness of the spoken language and graphic practices, but he built upon earlier philology and his own prejudices as well. Mindful of Champollion's decipherment of Egyptian hieroglyphics, Rafinesque had suggested the interconnectedness of graphic practices and speech, and Du Ponceau had voiced the opinion that Aztec pictographs depicted spoken Nahuatl. By 1846, Schoolcraft decided that Algonquians' "system of picture-writing" operated similarly to the "power of amalgamation"—foreign to "Saxon syntax"—that allowed Native languages to combine abbreviated forms of diverse incidents with "ideographic" roots to create "compound terms . . . replete with meaning." A picture of a bird, for example, referred to a bird and, if joined by an arrow, one understood its death. Even a part, such as a talon, could stand for the whole. Whereas verbs dominated spoken Ojibwe, the figures that recorded "*medicine, hunting,* and *war* songs" was "a system of substantives." As he explained to Squier, the *Wallam-Olum*'s "symbols" were "often highly compounded," just like spoken Ojibwe, with a "dot" or "mark" acting as a "picto-grammatical adjunct, giving force or expression to noun-figures." Demonstrating that Native consultants could not, ultimately, control how whites used what they shared with them, Schoolcraft blended Native knowledge with the fabrications of Rafinesque. He also applied them in a way at odds with Shingwauk's intentions. Grammatical processes, tales, and pictographs combined, according to Schoolcraft, to convey a "concreteness" that fostered "idolatry" because it "filled the human mind with gross material objects of veneration." Schoolcraft concluded that it was Indians' "mental bondage to . . . their priests and soothsayers" that allowed prophets from Pontiac to Black Hawk to manipulate Indians' "superstitious observances" to threaten white settlements. The "laws of syntax" and a "peculiar mythology and necromancy" combined in "the Indian mind."[44]

Schoolcraft returned to these issues repeatedly, while addressing the difficulties of extending U.S. colonialism across the continent, in the six volumes of *Information Respecting the History, Condition, and Prospects of the Indian Tribes of the United States* (1851–1857) that were the fruition of his federal project. While reviewers praised the volumes as the finest books an American press had yet produced, they panned the content. The Democratic-aligned *New*

York Herald bemoaned the nearly $200,000 "drawn from the pockets of the
people to pay for the . . . 'whimabams' of some garrulous old man, who should
have been left to mumble his rubbish to the urchins at the fireside, or under
the porch of the corner grocery." The Whig-friendly *North American Review*
feared that the "ill-digested and valueless compilation" would cast "reproach
on American science" abroad and "discredit the whole system of publishing
works at the government expense." A few decades later, the philologist James
Hammond Trumbull expressed common sentiments. The "work contains
much valuable material, though this, unfortunately, cannot be easily separated
from the worthless mass in which it is buried." The volumes' covers depicted
the essence of his ideas. On a midnight blue background, as dark as Schoolcraft's
portrayal of Indians' future, is a gold-inset engraving, done by Seth Eastman,
of a Native warrior taking a scalp ("Death Whoop"). Surrounding that image,
far less visible in contrast with the bright and violent image at the center, are
stamped Ojibwe pictographs, abstracted from any context but Schoolcraft's
own insistence upon the interrelation of Indians' languages, mental life, and
savagery.[45]

The volumes did not fulfill his ambitions. On the one hand, he had intended
the final volume to conclude with three sections. The first would have explained
the respective roles of "Linguistic Principles and Phenomena," "Oral Fiction
and Legends," and "Mnemonic Pictography" in three chapters of "Desiderata
Respecting the Mental Character of the Indian." The second would have delin-
eated Indians' origin and relations. The third would have offered his definitive
views on "Indian Policy and the Indian Future." Each, he alerted the reader,
had been "precluded by the limitation of the work." The lack of a summation
notwithstanding, he addressed these issues throughout. Alluding to European
comparative philology, he asserted that linguistic change occurred over time,
as in pronunciation, but human beings never consciously altered language. It
constituted a system of "mental laws, older than letters, prescribing the practical bearing of one idea upon another." Even amid the "syllabical mutation"
through which languages diverged, their "plan of thought" remained basically
fixed. Lexical change occurred, though grammatical-psychological change did
not, amid degeneration from Judaism and civilization as Indians' ancestors
migrated from Asia to the Americas. The result was an "Americo-Shemitic"
racial type. Throughout these volumes, Schoolcraft had targeted those "who
believe, that our duties to the unenlightened aboriginal nations are overrated"
and those whose "theories of human origin, existence, and development" contradicted the biblical narrative that "binds man to God, and links communities
together by indissoluble moral obligations." Ironically, his descriptions of an

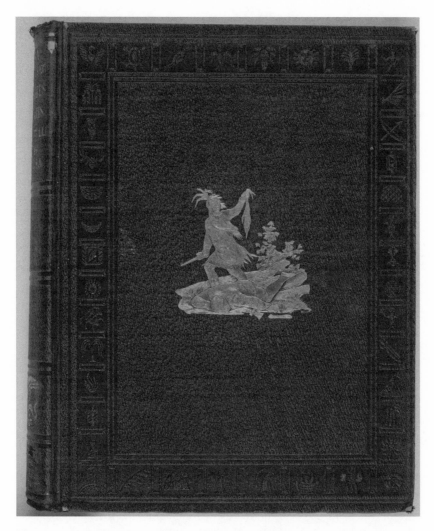

The covers of the six volumes, ordered by Congress, of *Information Respecting the History, Present Condition, and Prospects of the Indians of the United States* (1851–1857) bear the gold stamped engraving "Death Whoop," depicting an Indian who has just taken a scalp, surrounded by Ojibwe pictographs. It aptly conveys the opinion of the volumes' author, Henry R. Schoolcraft, of the relationship between Native savagery and language, which he believed the pictographs expressed. His knowledge depended upon the tutoring he received from Ozhaguscodaywayquay and Shingwauk, but those consultants could not control Schoolcraft's distortion or its publicly funded dissemination. (Courtesy of the American Antiquarian Society, Worcester, MA)

unchanging Indian mind and his recurrent pessimism regarding Indian "civilization," scattered aimlessly across six volumes with little discernable order, led some readers to conclude that he was a polygenist.[46]

As whites became ever more convinced of the grammatical difference of Native and European languages, considerable speculation arose about grammatical difference accounting for the difficulty of interracial language learning. Because of the difficulty of religious translations, missionaries stated these views especially clearly. Although he praised the instruction of his "teacher," the Nez Perce orator Lawyer, Asa Bowen Smith blamed the "peculiarities" of Nez Perce for the fact that "No white man has yet mastered the language & perhaps never will fully do it." After close collaboration with Goliah Herrod, a Creek who had studied at the Choctaw Academy and who superintended his nation's schools, Henry Buckner averred that while white children could learn to speak Muskogee, white adults could not, at least not without "abandon[ing] his own," because their "method of expressing ideas in Creek is so entirely different from that to which our minds have been accustomed, that it is extremely difficult to learn to think or speak according to the idiom of their language." He believed, "in proportion to our success" in learning Muskogee, whites would suffer "loss in the command of English." Such statements were not explicitly determinist or essentialist, but they contributed to broader consideration of the epistemological gulf that supposedly separated Indians and whites, while stressing their inhibiting effects on the "civilizing" process.[47]

Related speculation centered on the widespread assumption that Native people learned other, even lexically unrelated, Native languages more easily than they did English. The missionary Cyrus Byington told the American Board that he "presume[d]" Adin Gibbs, a Delaware teacher, could speak Choctaw "more *naturally* than any of us." Despite the stark phonological contrast of "the rapid *Cóotoonay* of the Rocky Mountains, and the stately *Blackfoot* of the plains, the slow embarrassed *Flat-head* of the mountains, the smooth-toned *Pierced-nose*, the guttural difficult *Sússee* and *Chépewyán*, the sing-song *A'ssinneboigne*, the deliberate *Cree*, and the sonorous majestic *Chíppeway*," Joseph Howse stressed "that the different tribes, or nations of that hemisphere discover a much greater aptitude or facility in acquiring the language of each other than they do in learning any European tongue." The former trader explained, "Their turn of mind leads them to group their ideas and combine their thoughts after their own peculiar manner." Narrating his travels in South America, but building on the theories of his brother, Alexander von Humboldt stated this view as a general principle. Germans easily learned Danish, the Spanish Italian, or Indians another Native language because of "an instinctive and regulating principle, differently modified among nations not of the same race."[48]

The prominent philologist-philosopher Wilhelm von Humboldt developed these ideas most fully. He had spent time poring over Jesuit materials in the Vatican archives, and his brother the explorer had passed along considerable materials. Through the offices of George Bancroft, a young New Englander studying at Göttingen, who had brought U.S. philology to his attention, Humboldt opened a correspondence with John Pickering, which led to a broader conversation with Du Ponceau. They developed their theories in conversation with one another. Although they diverged over their aesthetic evaluations of the American languages and whether those languages utilized inflection, as Indo-European languages did, or a distinct and inferior process (originally "agglutination," but Humboldt later distinguished that process, found in Basque and several Central Eurasian tongues, from the "incorporation" found in the American languages), their views were similar in two important respects. Each presented a view of language simultaneously psychological and lineal, and each believed that language both recorded the historical experiences of a nation and molded the contours of that experience. Despite Pickering's belief that Humboldt had "yielded" to Du Ponceau's criticisms of the philologist's portrayal of the American languages, the central question for Humboldt remained whether their "peculiarities" and "natural beauties" reflected a stage "through which all languages in their origin must at some time have passed" or a "certain train of thought and intellectual individuality altogether peculiar to the American nations." Humboldt believed the answer was both. All languages "began with agglutination," but "essential and real graduated difference" developed among languages. The American languages illustrated his highly developed general theory. A tongue could change, advancing from a "*more youthful* state" to a more mature one, but only within "the limits prescribed to it by the *original design of the language*." He rejected physiologically intrinsic intellectual differences and admitted the possibility of limited development; but linguistic organization would persist over time. The "mental tendency of the nation" had imprinted "a defective variety" of grammatical organization on the American languages, which, in turn, created a "*world-view*" that shaped their speakers' subsequent perceptions and reflection and inhibited (but did not prevent) analytical and artistic thought. Even after a speaker rejected his native worldview "by stepping over at once into the circle of another," he would partially retain his original "conceptual fabric."[49]

These philological ideas, which would prove so important for U.S. colonialism, were also relevant to broader debates over the common origin of the races or their separate creations, which gained prominence in the 1830s–1850s, as they intersected with debates over slavery and abolition in the United States and with debates overseas about the role of "Aryans" and "Semites" in the history of Christianity and Europe and about Britons' relationship with those they colonized in India. Wilhelm von Humboldt's writing could be difficult, and some of his assertions seemingly contradictory, but his views gained prominence in the decades following his death in 1835. While Humboldt's work would be enlisted for evolutionary arguments later in the century, some scholars at midcentury, such as Arthur de Gobineau, used his work in support of polygenism. The "American School of Ethnology" eagerly appropriated another such work. According to the French philologist Alfred Maury, "Languages are organisms that are all conceived upon the same plan . . . the same *skeleton*, which, in their development and their composition, follow fixed laws," but "each family of tongues has its own special evolution, and its own destinies." This "faculty" in the human genus "corresponds, under its different forms, to races of mankind possessing different faculties, as well as for speech as ideas." The "American languages have . . . passed through very different phases of development," according to Maury, but none had "overcome the elementary forms upon which they had been scaffolded." Even philologists who rejected the racial essentialism of Gobineau and Maury, such as August Friedrich Pott and Ernest Renan, articulated essentialist views of peoples' speech and cultures. [50]

Speculation about linguistic essentialism and ostensibly unchanging "Indian" minds converged with the search for a physiological basis of language in the brain. Phrenologists occasionally addressed "Indian" subjects, though not necessarily in essentialist tones. Take two articles that appeared in the *American Phrenological Journal,* one of which capitalized on a defeated prophet's forced tour of eastern cities, the other of which took advantage of the eager self-promotion of a former missionary. Black Hawk's "comparisons and similes" in speech, and his fluency in "several Indian dialects" allegedly stemmed from a "large" language faculty, while George Copway's "Indian style of expression" apparently flowed from a "moderate" language faculty. Other authors addressed the range of faculties, including hearing, memory, speech, that affected one's linguistic abilities. While phrenologists might discuss language in individual terms, others who were physiologically inclined did not. The British physiologist Robert Knox, for instance, insisted that "transcendental anatomy" alone could explain why "the very essence of language is distinct" among the "races of men." At mid-century, the French physical anthropologist Paul Broca discovered a correlation between speech impairments and damage to the frontal lobe. At the same time that missionaries and scholars turned increased attention to Native vocal organs, philology focused on grammar and thought inspired increased attention to a physical language organ in the brain. Reviewing the state of ethnology for the

Smithsonian Institution, Samuel F. Haven argued, "the philosophy of American speech, the phenomena constituting its genius, will not be fully comprehended until the metaphysical, physiological, and possibly phrenological traits of the aborigines are accurately determined." Regardless, the American Antiquarian Society librarian argued, echoing Du Ponceau and Humboldt in sharper tones, a language could only be cultivated in a limited way because "the system of progression has been determined by the laws of intellectual and physical organization peculiar to the race." Anatomists declined to focus their attention on Indians' language organ, while philologists refused to reduce speech to a question of physiology, though later in the century some hoped that attention to "Broca's convolution" in buried remains might shed light on the evolution of human language.[51]

Even among those who rejected essentialism, scholars merged lineal and stadial interpretations of Native languages that adapted, and transformed the meaning of, theories that Du Ponceau, Schoolcraft, and others had put forward since the 1820s. Denying that Indian languages suggested previous "civilization," Albert Gallatin argued that the American languages "bear the impress of primitive languages," which had "assumed their form from natural causes." Although he was uncertain whether *"plans d'idees"* reflected something innate or merely historical accident, he thought languages passed through "different states in . . . successive formation," and he believed that "the character of the language adopted . . . has a strong influence on the progress and knowledge & civilisation of that people." In one of Schoolcraft's reports to Congress, the German émigré Francis Lieber elaborated these kinds of ideas, while adding "holophrastic" to the increasingly crowded terminology that attempted to describe "the Plan of Thought of the American Languages." William W. Turner, a philologist working for the Smithsonian Institution, believed that Native grammatical forms reflected "phases of the human mind," but these were "a true organism, the spontaneous growth, as it were, of the mind of the nation that uses it." Although Du Ponceau believed an Indian plan of ideas was fixed, and Schoolcraft that it resulted from degeneration, many of those who built upon their work reconciled lineal and stadial views of Native languages by embracing evolutionism in a process that was already under way before the Darwinian Revolution.[52]

Evolutionary ideas became increasingly important after midcentury, just as the proliferation of ethnographic information in the United States and throughout European empires threatened to subvert all attempts at ethnological order. Several scholars had articulated developmentalist interpretations of Native cultures in the 1830s–1850s, and other writers, such as the

British sociologist Herbert Spencer, theorized "savage" and "civilized" institutions as stages of a process that proceeded inexorably toward greater perfection. Such theories were joined by, and gained authority from, archaeological advances in the decade before Darwin's *Origin of Species* (1859). A decades-old typology of material used in tools (stone, bronze, iron) came to represent a sequence of cultural development, and excavations of human remains with the bones of extinct animals, demonstrating that human beings had existed thousands of years longer than had been previously accepted, produced a "revolution in human time." With the historical record suddenly representing only a fraction of human existence, cultural change could be imagined over an immeasurably longer interval, which effectively neutralized polygenists' historical arguments that racial differences had always existed and some philologists' claims that language was at least as permanent as physical type. What emerged was a hybrid of biological monogenism and cultural polygenism that rejected degenerationist assumptions. On the one hand, scholars renewed their efforts to connect Indians to the people of Asia in light of increasing knowledge of the world's diverse tongues. On the other hand, the spectrum of cultural evolutionism ranged from a deeply pessimistic focus on race as an inherited collection of physical, intellectual, and moral traits that resisted change with the weight of the tens of thousands of years over which it had developed, to an arrogant and destructive optimism about the possibility and necessity of transforming Native peoples.[53]

Whether adhering to degenerationism or, as became more common after midcentury, evolutionism, few accepted that Indian languages were fixed: in some way, a so-called savage's language must reflect his social condition, though racial makeup perhaps constrained possibilities of change. Contradictory theories about the trajectory of Indians' histories, however, produced perfectly compatible prescriptions for "civilization." Schoolcraft, a degenerationist, believed that "English must be the language of civilization to them." Gallatin, the most important evolutionary-minded ethnologist in the United States in the 1830s–1840s and a native French speaker, believed that Indians must be taught "the English language . . . so thoroughly that they may forget their own." The pervasiveness of this view can also be seen in the fact that one Native intellectual, George Copway, supported it. Although he had praised his language's natural beauty and its ties to Ojibwe lands, Copway urged missionaries to abandon laborious translations that "perpetuated" Indians' traditional "views, ideas, and feelings." In his estimation, survival required linguistic assimilation, and "the sooner he learned the almost universal English and forgot the Indian, the better." Theories about Native psychological difference—whether degenerationist, essentialist, or evolutionist in conception—suggested that assimilation required forcing language change.[54]

The work of one missionary-philologist, Stephen R. Riggs, brings these issues into sharper focus. When he arrived in what is today Minnesota in 1837, charged by the ABCFM to learn Dakota, the language initially "seemed . . . barren and meaningless" to him. After "invaluable" tutoring by Joseph Renville, a métis former trader and interpreter, and his kinsman Wamdiokiya (Eagle Help), a holy man and war chief, Riggs learned more of the language. The former aided him because he was a "friend to the mission," the latter only because he received "good pay," but their extended instruction allowed Riggs to grasp the language's "power and beauty." The realization that "all languages, barbarous as well as civilized, present but different shades of the same mental philosophy," moreover, provided "one of the strongest arguments" for human "unity," a point he made in an address on "The Dakota Language" to the Minnesota Historical Society in 1850. Yet, he conceded, its "method of expressing ideas, so entirely different from that to which our minds have been accustomed, makes it difficult to learn to think in Dakota." Despite that, Riggs called for granting Dakotas "the rights of citizens," just as Brothertown Indians had successfully claimed in neighboring Wisconsin. The society published the address in its *Collections.*[55]

Riggs and his colleagues, with the wider public, diverged on the ultimate significance of Dakota linguistic difference. Riggs did not think it "desirable" that Dakota "continue as a living language," since its speakers could not "preserve their national existence," but he still believed that the language was "capable of vast improvement." Because of the mission's translating work, one could read schoolbooks, scripture, hymns, John Bunyan's *A Pilgrim's Progress,* a newspaper, and the Minnesota constitution, all in Dakota. At the mission station of Hazlewood, open only to Christian Dakotas who rejected traditional practices, Dakota had "ceased to be the language of a barbarous nation, but was that of a community, living in every respect as white or civilized people." Riggs's colleagues (and rivals for scholarly recognition), however, thought differently. Samuel Pond believed that Dakota, "in its present state could not be used as the language of a civilized people." His brother held even more essentialist views. "Indians know better how to *use* their own language than any of us ever did or ever shall," Gideon Pond explained to Riggs. "There is something in the constitution of the Ind. mind & heart that forbids the near approach of a white man."[56]

Linguistic theories of intellectual difference bound up with ancestry, in turn, had concrete consequences in colonialism. In 1861, just a year before the region would erupt in the Dakota War, partially because of divisions among

Dakotas that the mission deepened, a Minnesota judge examined nine Dakota men to determine whether they had adopted the "language, customs and habits of civilization." That was what the new state's constitution required of "full blood" Indians who sought citizenship, though those of "mixed blood" faced no language requirement. *Dred Scott v. Sanford* (1857) had affirmed the constitutionality of Native citizenship, and the Treaty with the Sioux (1858) had explicitly offered it to those who dissolved their tribal ties. The men before the judge had cut their hair, dressed like whites, farmed individually owned plots, lived in houses rather than tipis, refrained from traditional ceremonies, and elected governing officers. Only one of them, however, spoke English. The judge conferred voting rights on that man, Lorenzo Lawrence, but denied citizenship to the other eight men because an "intelligent exercise" of the franchise required a "civilized language." Over the protests of Riggs, who stressed how far Dakota had been cultivated, the judge pronounced, "Sioux was a barbarous language, and the State constitution evidently considered it as such." Although Minnesota established different criteria for those with and without European ancestry, citizenship was available to "full blood" Dakota men, but only upon a condition of language.[57]

Steeped in such views, the Bureau of Indian Affairs began pressing for more deliberate efforts to eliminate Native languages as a means to force language change. Riggs felt pressure to offer instruction in "English and English alone" by the 1850s. Despite teachers' suspicions that "inherited characteristics" made English acquisition "of peculiar difficulty," the Indian Peace Commission—an expression of the fervent Christian nationalism prominent among supporters of the Union in the Civil War, responding to appalling episodes of violence, such as the Dakota War and the massacre of Cheyennes at Sand Creek in 1864—recommended establishing schools where "their barbarous dialects should be blotted out and the English language substituted." After all, the commission reported, "through sameness of language is produced sameness of sentiment and thought." The BIA declared that Native children had to be compelled to learn English in 1881, and it mandated English-only instruction in 1886. Racialized linguistic theories, blending notions of descent and intellectual difference, fueled federal efforts to make Native languages extinct.[58]

Even as the studies of Du Ponceau and other practitioners of the new philology inspired a wave of missionary work in the 1820s, so too did they inspire a sustained counterattack. Lewis Cass, governor and Indian superintendent of

Michigan Territory, led an extensive effort at federal collection of linguistic information to prove that, despite what philologists might claim, Native languages mirrored undeveloped and unchanging savage minds. Cass's views, based as they were on the work of Henry R. Schoolcraft and other Indian agents in the field, were influential in the popular press and in the halls of government. By 1830, Cass drew upon these ideas to justify Indian removal. The era of removal witnessed a remarkable proliferation of varied forms of ethnology, which philologists attempted to capitalize upon. Schoolcraft, for instance, elaborated an expanded philology that combined grammatical studies with information gleaned from Native oral literature and graphic forms in an attempt to reach a broader audience. Those efforts failed, but they did help him become the first federally paid ethnologist. In these studies, and in continuing efforts to transform Native societies, scholars and missionaries fully elaborated notions of a linguistic "plan of ideas" or "plan of thought." Du Ponceau's attempts to deny that the American languages possessed "savage" features, ironically, provided the crucial foundation for an understanding of Indians' languages as racially unique and fixed, or at least nearly so. While Du Ponceau had heaped praise on those tongues, those who built on his ideas stressed their deficiencies. Philologists' speculations about an "Indian mind"— whether it was fixed or the product of degeneration or the initial stage of evolutionary development—fueled a federal effort of terrible cultural violence to eradicate Native languages.

Philology remained important in the aftermath of removal, as federal administrators sought linguistic information that could rationalize policies and as U.S. scholars increasingly looked beyond national borders, especially in the Far West and in Latin America, for linguistic information. These efforts in the decades after 1840 took place amid extraordinary expansion and ethnological disputes over whether different races shared a common ancestor, whether and how they could evolve, and the relative value of philology and physical ethnology for tracing descent and studying "race." After midcentury, as a result of its perceived importance, the federal government itself took on an increasing role in collecting and systematizing linguistic information. Among the results was a fuller elaboration of a racial understanding of language and, eventually, the collapse of that view.

6

Of Blood and Language

In March 1864, the Smithsonian Institution invited William Dwight Whitney to deliver a series of lectures on "The Principles of Linguistic Science." For most of these lectures, the relatively young but already respected Sanskrit scholar explained how philologists studied language and what they had learned in the previous decades, devoting particular attention to English and the Indo-European family. They had begun as monosyllabic languages, he argued, but ongoing "processes" of combining old words into new ones and allowing old ones to pass into disuse had created "our modern speech." While Europeans at the forefront of what was becoming increasingly known as linguistics described language as an "organism," Whitney insisted that language was an "institution," existing only "in the minds and mouths of those who employ it." While speaking habits and the art of writing tended to promote stability, tongues changed nonetheless, due to "subtle and recondite causes" and to the presumably more apparent "individual character of different languages and the qualities of the peoples who speak them."[1]

The first secretary of the federally sponsored Smithsonian, Joseph Henry, had hoped that Whitney would address not only the discoveries and methods of linguistic science but also its relationship to ethnology. Scholars and those who kept abreast of their work expected the world's languages to provide information on the "qualities" and psychologies of diverse peoples, many of whom were subjects of European empires. For most of the previous century and a half, the claim that language indicated descent was a commonplace, and the remarkable findings since the late eighteenth century had intensified the longstanding association of languages and peoples. Philologists had established language families that encompassed large portions of Asia, Africa, and the Pacific, and they had discovered patterns of phonetic shift among the Indo-European languages that seemed so remarkably regular as to result from nothing less than a natural law. In the United States, knowledge of the sounds and grammatical principles of Native languages and relationships among them also grew dramatically. Whitney knew all this, of course, and he gestured toward ethnology early on, noting that linguistic science "determine[s] the fact and degree of relationship among nations" and provides unique "information . . . respecting their moral and intellectual character, and growth of their civilization." After stating these premises, however, he quickly moved on. Only in the final lecture did he return to the subject, addressing "the important question as to the comparative value of linguistic and physical evidence of race." Perhaps he intended to cap his performance with the topic that possessed broadest appeal, but he might have simply wished to postpone what had become a deeply controversial subject since the 1840s.[2]

Divisive social and political issues intertwined with methodological disputes among ethnologists to push the refinement of "race" as a concept. The clashes of nations in Europe, and the opposition of subordinate peoples to the rule of European empires, inspired scholars and polemicists there to explain conflict in terms of inherent or evolutionary difference. In the United States, the creation of federal reservations, a more bellicose expansionism that brought Anglos into increasing contact with non-Anglos, the emergence of more assertive abolitionist and proslavery arguments, the Civil War and Reconstruction, and increasing immigration from Asia and non-Protestant portions of Europe produced interrelated debates around the character of diverse peoples and the terms of racial subordination or interracial coexistence. Those who studied peoples' beliefs and customs advocated their ethnographic approach to answering such questions, and archaeology steadily gained scientific authority. Several physical ethnologists, including members of the American School of Ethnology, insisted that language could reveal nothing of race. Some philologists agreed.[3]

Whitney, however, dissented. As a product of education, he granted, language was "no certain evidence of descent" of peoples. The "imported African" provided a particularly relevant example as the Civil War raged on, since he "forgets, in a generation, his Congo or Mendi, and is able to use only a dialect of his master's speech." The linguist cautioned, however, that this fact "must not be exaggerated." As increasing knowledge of the American languages joined advances in archaeology that had immeasurably deepened the understood duration of human existence after midcentury, and as the Darwinian Revolution gave evolutionary theories new authority, Whitney insisted that there were different modes by which an investigator could discover a people's race. "In laying down grand outlines, in settling ultimate questions, the authority of physiology may be superior," Whitney conceded, "but the filling up of details, and the conversion of barren classification into a history, must be mainly accomplished by linguistic science." The latter, as Whitney stressed, also possessed "greatly superior practical value" since differences in speech were "more easily apprehended, described, and recorded." In subsequent years, Whitney pushed the Smithsonian to devote its energies to discovering, elaborating, and clarifying the genetic relationships among Native American languages and peoples, a project he assisted by working on a new standardized orthography. In *The Life and Growth of Language* (1875), an influential book that elaborated his lectures, he continued to insist on the pragmatic usefulness of linguistic science for understanding race. "To admit that a language can be exchanged," Whitney insisted, "is by no means to deny its value as a record of human history, even of race-history." Although language was an institution that could be adopted, altered, or abandoned, "it still remains true that, upon the whole, language is determined by race, since each human being usually learns to speak from his parents and others of the same blood." Language was intimately linked with race in this view; indeed, it stemmed from it. For that very reason, even as ideas about race and its duration were changing amid the Darwinian Revolution, philologists like Whitney still expected language to provide the key.[4]

The conviction, even in the face of growing criticism by some philologists and physical ethnologists alike, that language corresponded in some way to something essential to peoples themselves, continued well beyond midcentury. Just as speculation regarding Native grammatical organization and vocal organs gained credence from preexisting assumptions about language as a guide to descent, so too did increasing speculation about the ostensible peculiarity of "Indian" vocal and mental organs fuel theorization about language and "blood." At the same time, the United States sought useful taxonomic information in an era of aggressive territorial and commercial expansion and the establishment of federal reservations. Yet a number of factors converged to undermine philology's usefulness for colonialism. Native people resisted consolidation along linguistic lines. The ascent of the biological race science of the American School of Ethnology challenged the notion that language could guide the study of either descent or "race." As the United States annexed Texas, divided Oregon with Great Britain, provoked a war with Mexico to gain California, and increased its commercial, missionary, and political influence in Central America and the Caribbean, philologists became aware of language families that upset assumptions that languages would correspond to cultural inheritance and levels of social progress. Yet philology became more secure in the federal government. The Smithsonian Institution came to play a crucial role in supporting the study of Native languages by publishing missionary philology, compiling materials collected on federal expeditions, and employing philologists directly. A long tradition of federal philology, in collaboration with other forms of scholarly and missionary philology, prepared the ground for the formal institutionalization of linguistic taxonomy and evolutionary anthropology in the Bureau of Ethnology.

Federal Philology: Collection and Reservation Consolidation

As did the learned in other modes of scientific inquiry, philologists increasingly turned to the federal government to support linguistic collection and publication at midcentury, and the government sought increasingly specialized knowledge that only experts could provide. Although support for philology had emerged haltingly in the form of instructions to explorers and Indian agents in previous decades, such patronage grew as the federal government surveyed the West and sought to order it in ways that would be useful for an expanding and increasingly integrated U.S. economy. A combination of federal commissions and appointments that were inextricable from the United States' growing ambitions for additional territory in the hemisphere and increasing Pacific commerce, such as army topographic engineers, surveyors, treaty commissioners, and, more rarely, positions as philologists or ethnologists, supported the study of Native languages. The federal government also created entities to organize the collection, systematization, and publication of information, such as the Smithsonian Institution and, later, the Bureau of Ethnology. Language, as a manifestation of psychology and as a record of ancestry, and as such a facet of race, remained prominent. Those who sought federal patronage for their work continued to insist that philology would prove practically useful.[5]

As important as federal support became in these years, especially in the form of the army exploration and federal surveying of the trans-Mississippi West that began in the 1850s in response to mineral strikes, a rapidly rising tide of migration, and increasing calls for railroads, and as important as scholarly expertise was to federal efforts at ordering the steady flow of new materials, Native participation remained crucial as non-missionaries increasingly undertook field philology. George Gibbs, for instance, who collected dozens of vocabularies while working on treaty commissions and surveys of the U.S.–Canada border and a northern route for the transcontinental railroad, acknowledged that efforts at collection would prove abortive if Native people jealously guarded knowledge of their language as "a State secret." In California, a Yurok man demanded from Stephen Powers, "Me talk you Injun talk, you give me piece of bread and meat." Powers paid because he realized that Native consultants could explain their language with "accuracy, clearness, and philosophic insight," and they could recognize which languages were only "somewhat different from their own." F. V. Hayden, who eventually rose to direct the U.S. Geographical and Geological Survey, confessed "surprise" at "how much of the grammatical structure of a language may be obtained from a wholly uneducated but intelligent native by judicious management." He recommended allowing a consultant to "answer freely, and then by a variety of cross questions, arrive at an approximation to the truth." Among the Algonquian, Siouan, and Caddoan speakers he met on army surveying expeditions of the Missouri and Yellowstone valleys, Hayden found it especially advantageous "to enlist the aid of the chiefs and leading men" because they tended to "take great pride in being regarded as the censors of the purity with which their language is spoken." Applying an understanding of natural selection, he reasoned that amid the "nomadic and precarious life" of the central and northern Plains, "the struggle for existence" ensured that "the position of an Indian in his tribe is an almost certain index to his mental status." Grasping the importance of Native consultants to philology, Hayden appended to his essay, which he published in the American Philosophical Society's *Transactions,* a series of portraits, including likenesses of some of his consultants, along the lines suggested by another philologist, William W. Turner.[6]

The Smithsonian Institution, established by Congress in 1846 and working with a variety of private scholars and organizations, was crucial for those who attempted to order the ballooning quantity of linguistic information that came in from the West. Its dual purpose, according to the bequest that provided for its foundation, was to increase and diffuse knowledge. Those proved to be competing rather than complementary enterprises, as different figures in the Smithsonian, the Interior Department, and Congress struggled to create an institution that focused its energies either on facilitating scientific research or upon exhibiting what was known to the general public. From the beginning, the institution solicited the advice of the American Ethnological Society (AES), and the country's philologists and ethnologists, in turn, sought to influence the new society. At the Smithsonian's first meeting, for example, Henry Schoolcraft urged the Board of Regents to create "a library of philology" since "Nothing is more characteristic of the intellectual existence of man than language," which provided "a more enduring monument of ancient affinities than the physical type." Schoolcraft, who grew increasingly marginalized and bitter in the years before his death in 1864, came to consider the institution's first

This portrait of a Crow man was one of several to appear at the end of F. V. Hayden's "Contributions to the Ethnography and Philology of the Indian Tribes of the Missouri Valley." Taking the idea from another philologist, William W. Turner, Hayden intended to convey some sense of his consultant's intellectual abilities. The publication, appearing in the American Philosophical Society's *Transactions* (1863), but the fruit of Hayden's federal surveying work, indicates the continuing importance of Native consultation to philology and the increasing role of federal patronage to the practice of philology. (Courtesy of the American Philosophical Society, Philadelphia, PA)

secretary, Joseph Henry, "defective in ethnology," but the Smithsonian sponsored and facilitated an expansive, in methodological and geographic scope, form of federal philology that would provide psychological, genealogical, and practical information of Native people within and without the United States.[7]

The institution's philology, like other philology, rested on a wide foundation of contributors, but Henry also relied on those with expertise, the most important of whom were William W. Turner and George Gibbs. Turner consulted for the institution as a member of the AES, contributing to AES-designed and Smithsonian-published blank vocabularies to be used on the Pacific Railroad Surveys. Appointment as librarian of the U.S. Patent Office in 1852 allowed him to work more closely with the Smithsonian's materials, analyzing vocabularies and editing dictionaries and grammars (including one of the West African language Yoruba, the Smithsonian's only title of African philology in those years). While impressing upon Henry the importance of such texts, Turner wanted to add to them "some original production of the native mind—some speech, fable, legend, or song, that may afford samples of aboriginal modes of thought as well as expression." While remaining active in the American Ethnological and the American Oriental societies, he worked with the Smithsonian's materials until his death in 1859. George Gibbs took up the mantle while working on a claims commission related to the partition of Oregon, and he worked with the Smithsonian until his death in 1873. Charged with preparing *Instructions for Research Relative to the Ethnology and Philology of America* (1863), which included a 211-term vocabulary and new orthography (for which he received assistance from William Dwight Whitney), Gibbs informed would-be collectors that the "greatest deficiencies" still concerned the land stretching from Texas to California, though the Smithsonian eyed "British and Russian America and . . . Mexico" as well. For Gibbs, "ascertaining the more obvious relations between the various members of existing families" and discovering more "remote affinities" remained major goals. Both Turner and Gibbs left ambitious, unfinished projects. Gibbs had hoped to use knowledge of linguistic relations to create a map that traced Indians' migrations from what he believed had been the original point of dispersion (after their arrival in North America) in the Great Plains. Turner intended a comprehensive work on Indian languages that would include portraits of Native consultants and illustrate the "mental status of the man, as the representative of his tribe or language," or at least that is how a fellow philologist described the plan. In its first two decades, mainly through Turner and Gibbs, the Smithsonian evaluated and published grammars and dictionaries of Dakota and Chinook Jargon, included shorter linguistic sketches in its *Annual Reports,* partially subsidized the private publication of John G. Shea's

Library of American Linguistics (1860–1863), and organized and analyzed nearly three hundred vocabularies.[8]

The Smithsonian's role in the publication of two missionary grammars and dictionaries illustrates how the institution augmented and channeled, rather than replaced, individuals and voluntary associations in the practice of philology. Stephen Riggs studied Dakota as an American Board missionary, but he also sought to influence the politically influential and the intellectually curious. After Riggs presented the paper "The Dakota Language" to the Minnesota Historical Society, members and territorial legislators "became interested in the matter" and joined with the American Board to fund publication of a Dakota lexicon. To secure national prestige and additional funds, Riggs and his supporters turned to the Smithsonian, for which the philologist William W. Turner, a professor of Oriental languages at Union Theological Seminary, edited the lexicon as a scholarly work. As a tool for evangelization and English instruction, an aid to communication for Indian agents and military officers, and a boon to scholars interested in psychological or genealogical questions relating to Dakota or other Siouan languages, it would serve "practical, philosophical, or philological" functions. Riggs hoped that the final product, the *Grammar and Dictionary of the Dakota Language* (1852), which appeared as the fourth of the Smithsonian's *Contributions to Knowledge,* would serve a philanthropic purpose as well by being "the means of interesting some in behalf of the Dakotas." For similar reasons, the board missionary Cyrus Byington labored for years, through several revisions, to produce a Choctaw grammar. Though it was approved for publication, the Smithsonian never printed it. Instead, further demonstrating the permeable boundaries between public and private philology, an emerging philologist and ethnologist, Daniel G. Brinton, published Byington's grammar in the American Philosophical Society's *Proceedings.* Nonetheless, the Smithsonian under Henry's direction recognized value in philology and ethnology for increasing knowledge of humanity and of Native people, and he hoped that the institution's work in this field would further scientific and social purposes.[9]

As the United States gathered ever more linguistic material and augmented resources for making sense of it, federal officials and scholars hoped and expected that knowledge of linguistic relations would simplify Indian affairs. Among the few concrete proposals that Schoolcraft offered in his multivolume report to Congress, other than teaching Native children English, was to propose a system whereby Native people would be consolidated along linguistic lines. "As a race," Schoolcraft believed, Native people were "bent on a nameless principle of *tribality.*" Believing each "little difference in language" to be a "radical difference," he argued, "Tribes will not run into groups—

groups into great families or ethnographical circles." To bring order to this linguistic and social "anarchy," Schoolcraft advised that the "true object" of philology should be to "group and classify them into families on philosophical principles." That would provide a basis to "restore" their "ancient relations." "In our future policy," Schoolcraft concluded, "they should be removed or colonized in reference to this relationship, and foreign groups not be commingled with the cognate tribes."[10]

This vision was not unique. Several federal officials had proposed similar plans in the previous two decades. In response to several challenges in the 1820s–1830s—deepening tensions regarding "civilization" policy and removal, increasing numbers of white settlers and miners trespassing on Native lands, rapid expansion of the upper Missouri fur trade and the southwestern overland trade along the Santa Fe Trail—a number of public figures began calling for the consolidation of Native groups into more easily managed units. William Clark, superintendent of Indian affairs in St. Louis, was foremost among them. After the Treaty of Prairie du Chien (1825), which demarcated tribal territory among Siouan-speaking Iowas, Winnebagos, and Dakotas, as well as Algonquian-speaking Sauks and Foxes, Menominees, Ojibwes, and Potawatomis, Clark recommended that "as many of the tribes or of the scattering bands as possible, understanding one language, should be collected near each other," under the authority of a single agent. This, he believed, would instill "the idea of submission to the authority of a civil government." Consolidation, in this theory, beyond simply easing the burden of colonialist administration, might create the conditions for social-political advancement.[11]

Such a plan would also support U.S. efforts to restrain intertribal warfare, which might endanger white emigrants and settlements. Whites routinely pointed to linguistic difference as a cause of violence in Native America. "Inveterate and interminable hostility existing, time out of mind, between the people of the different stocks," the U.S. army surgeon and philologist Edwin James predicted, "nothing but mutual destruction could be the consequence of crowding them together into a region already more than filled with warlike and jealous hunters." Faced with hostilities between Algonquian Ojibwes and Siouan Dakotas, Schoolcraft devoted similar attention to such "war of races." Although contrary evidence existed, as in the alliance of Algonquian Sauks and Foxes and Siouan Iowas against Dakotas, commentators drew general conclusions. On the floor of Congress in May 1830, Edward Everett drew his colleagues' attention to the very real violence on the central Plains as eastern groups migrated, voluntarily and involuntarily, across the Mississippi. Early Cherokee emigrants made war on Osages, who responded in kind, and they existed "in a state of hereditary hostility" with Choctaw arrivals. Pointing to their varied languages, the "seventy-five thousand Indians whom you propose to collect in this region," Everett told the House, "are not cognate tribes." Significantly, some Native people pointed to this very same problem. A couple months after Everett's speech, the Cherokee General Council warned U.S. citizens of the consequences of forcing Cherokees alongside those "with languages totally different." Indian removal heightened fears that ancestrally different peoples would not live alongside one another peaceably, which elevated the importance of recognizing linguistic similarity and difference in the minds of policymakers.[12]

As secretary of war in 1832, Lewis Cass acted upon these hopes and fears in his attempt to refashion federal administration in response to the dramatic effects and horrific toll of Indian removal. As superintendent of Indian affairs for Michigan Territory, Cass confronted linguistic diversity in many a treaty council, including at Prairie du Chien in 1825, where he worked alongside Clark. Cass was certain that language offered the key to an ethnologically informed policy, though he was somewhat uncertain as to why. On the one hand, Cass urged President Andrew Jackson that the federal government should create "union[s]" between "kindred tribes, connected by blood and language" to create a more efficient administration. On the other hand, Cass instructed the Stokes Commission, which was responsible for establishing destinations for removed peoples that would inhibit intertribal warfare, to bring together "bands, which are connected by language & habits." Confusion of biological and cultural inheritance notwithstanding—and he never commented upon the divergent formulations—Cass merged Chickasaw and Choctaw administration into a single agency, and he did the same for Ojibwes, Odawas, and Potawatomis. Cass's views provided the most likely direct inspiration for Schoolcraft's proposals, but they were part of broader attention to languages and consolidation.[13]

Native responses to such programs were mixed. Responding to a request from the House committee on Indian affairs, George Copway, a one-time missionary and now a newspaper editor and celebrity speaker, urged the federal government "to locate the Indians in a collective body" between the Mississippi and Missouri rivers, where they would enjoy secure title to land and "amalgamate" with one another. The plan was practically possible, he argued, because it rested on a linguistic basis that would allow Native émigrés to "soon understand each other." Mindful both of his people's extensive linguistic relations and of the use of Ojibwe and the closely related Cree in the fur trade, Copway stressed that the "great family language of all the Algonkin tribes" had once extended over much of northern and eastern North America. He averred that his countrymen supported consolidation on this linguistic basis. "Tradition says we were all one people once, and now to be reunited will be a great social blessing. Wars must then cease."[14]

Chickasaws, in contrast, had maintained a distinct identity for centuries and sought to preserve their national independence thereafter: they rejected consolidation. In the Treaty of Doaksville (1837), the United States had assigned the removed Chickasaws to a district of the Choctaw nation. This portended, for Chickasaws, the possibility of "losing their name and becoming merged" into the larger nation. This did not trouble whites, who considered them distinct only in dialect. Ethan Allen Hitchcock, an army officer familiar with philology, for instance, drew attention to the languages' similar structures and to the fact that significant lexical differences existed only in recently coined words, such as those for European things. Chickasaws, however, told him that "there was a considerable difference between the Choctaw and Chickasaw languages." Sloan Love, a Chickasaw chief and prominent planter who continued to oppose the consolidation even after settling in Indian Territory, conceded to Hitchcock only that his theory "might be so." Chickasaw insistence upon maintaining a distinct nationhood, which Love expressed in his equivocal remarks on his people's linguistic relationship with Choctaws, pushed the United States to acknowledge Chickasaw distinctness in 1855.[15]

Demands for "civilization," cheap administration, and peace, especially as the flood of overland emigrants intensified, meant that ideas of linguistic consolidation remained prominent as the Oregon boundary settlement and the Mexican Cession erased the supposedly permanent frontier line that removal had established. Despite the hopes of some administrators and legislators, however, general consolidation was unworkable, mainly because Native people did not accept it. A Choctaw planter and former teacher at the Choctaw Academy made this case forcefully in a remonstrance to Congress. Among his various objections to a consolidation bill, Peter Pitchlynn stressed that the various tribes had "been separate and independent from time immemorial," they occupied "different platforms in civilization," and "their languages are totally different; most of the tribes do not understand each other."[16]

Precisely because of Native diversity, however, many hoped that language provided a possible guide for limited but feasible consolidation as the United States formulated a reservation system to facilitate settlement of the Pacific coast by separating Indians from whites and concentrating them in smaller areas. Commissioner of Indian Affairs William Medill suggested that the "proper position" of "tractable" Omahas, who sought defense against Pawnees and Lakotas, "would be with the Osages or Kanzas, as they speak nearly if not quite the same language, and are probably of the same primary stock." Medill found "reasons of a similar kind" for merging Otoes, Missouris, and Iowas, who shared "affinities of character and language." Commenting upon this "excellent suggestion" the following year, his successor, Orlando Brown, asserted that such "suitable situations . . . in connexion with other Indians of kindred stock" would "open a wide sweep of country . . . for the expansion and egress of our white population westward."[17]

In the Far West, this same logic opened land for agriculture, timber, mining, ranching, and the roads and rails that linked newcomers to distant markets in the 1850s–1860s. The philologist and treaty commissioner George Gibbs pushed for linguistically specific reservations in the Pacific Northwest in 1854. Although he opposed the Donation Land Act (1850), by which Congress granted settlers title to lands in Oregon that neither the government nor individuals had purchased, Gibbs advocated "one principle of policy . . . the union of small bands under a single head." Walla Wallas and Nez Perces spoke closely related languages and acknowledged their shared descent. Cayuses had adopted Nez Perce as they intermarried extensively following the deadly measles outbreak that had sparked the notorious "Whitman Massacre," in which a group of Cayuses and others attacked and killed American Board missionaries in 1847, which in turn produced white reprisals dubbed the Cayuse War. Gibbs urged that all these peoples be consolidated under a single agency. Illustrating the distance that separated early and mid-nineteenth century U.S. colonialism, he opined that the "maxim of divide and conquer does not apply among these people. They are never so disposed to mischief as when scattered and beyond control."[18]

Officials held similar views farther south. As whites organized militias to hunt down small groups of Indians in northern California, either in response to wild rumors of Native violence or simply to clear the land of its inhabitants, the superintendent Charles Maltby argued that for small groups of Yukis and others "speaking the same language," it was "an act of justice and humanity to them, that they be united." After large numbers of Apaches had fled from appalling conditions at Bosque Redondo in New Mexico, where they had to compete for scarce resources with Navajos, who were linguistic relations but longtime rivals, Indian agent Lorenzo Labadi hoped that Mescalero Apaches and Jicarilla Apaches could be "induce[d]" to merge, since "they are all of the same race, speak the same language, and for many years have lived in peace."[19]

In time, however, federal officials learned that linguistic affinity was not a sure basis for peaceful consolidation. In the Northwest, Modocs left the reservation to their rivals and relations the Klamaths, just as Bannocks rose up against reservation life with Shoshones at Fort Hall in Idaho. These marked the first stages in the series of events that produced the notorious Modoc War

(1872–1873) and the less sensational, though no less meaningful, Bannock War (1878). In the latter, and perhaps in the former as well, a new ceremony known as the Ghost Dance, taught by the Paiute prophet Wodziwob and meant to bring about the destruction of whites and renewal of the Native world, galvanized ethnic identity and resistance. Even as the federal government attempted to push together particular peoples, prevailing policies and attitudes among whites tended to treat all "Indians" similarly, which pushed some Native people toward embracing a common racial identity. Yet, relationships and histories that preceded and persisted through colonization collided with related peoples' differing experiences of life on reservations, where federal efforts to produce economic dependency and eliminate traditional ceremonies, and often arbitrary treatment at the hands of agents and missionaries, made ethnic distinctions starker. The determination to impose and benefit from Indian "civilization" blinded reformers and ethnologists to these facts. John Wesley Powell, a one-time treaty commissioner who had failed to convince Paiutes to merge with Western Shoshones in 1873–1874, superficially reflected that the "linguistic tie has often proved to be an insufficient bond of union" since "feuds and internecine conflicts were common between members of the same linguistic family." The violent failure of consolidation flowed into a broader movement for reform, which emerged from economic interests seeking to open reservation lands to white settlement and resource extraction, public disgust with the incompetence and corruption of Indian agents, and a desire to immerse Indians in "civilization" by breaking apart reservations and tribes alike.[20]

Against this backdrop, Powell would successfully build support for the formal institutionalization of ethnology in the federal government. He only did so, however, after several decades that included intense methodological dispute between philologists and other ethnologists and new understanding of extensive and surprising language families in western North America. The cumulative result of those debates and discoveries severely undermined the authority of philology on questions of descent and race.

Philology versus Other Ethnologies

Contests between philologists and other ethnologists expanded with the country's territory and influence. As the United States surged in population and Americans asserted ever more loudly their superiority as "Anglo-Saxons," they looked beyond national borders to fulfill their economic, military, and scholarly ambitions. Oregon, Mexico, and Central America contained peoples, languages, and physical remains that could shed light on the still pressing questions of the origin, relations, and abilities of Native people. Questions of descent, throughout the antebellum era, were thoroughly intertwined with questions of historical change and the possibility of social development in the future. As they challenged one another and competed for public influence, philologists, physical ethnologists, archaeologists, and ethnographers often engaged broader fields of study, ranging across Europe, Africa, and the Pacific, even as they addressed slavery and colonialism in the United States.

Two methods, one based on language, the other based on the body, competed for authority in tracing human descent in the era of removal, reservations, and "manifest destiny." The linguistic mode proved important not only among administrators but also among missionaries aiming to extend evangelization and the distribution of texts efficiently and who favored studying people according to a trait that distinguished them from animals. Albert Gallatin's work, hailed by scholars abroad and at home, represented the most authoritative statement of linguistic ethnology in the antebellum United States. He combined an unusual awareness of the arbitrary line between language and dialect with the firm conviction that a useful taxonomy must aim toward consolidation. Because he affirmed Du Ponceau's argument that all (or nearly all) the American languages shared a common grammatical organization, Gallatin's taxonomy was primarily lexical. Languages that shared a "sufficient" number of "primitive words . . . must, at some remote epoch, have had a common origin." The assumption, centuries old, was that because languages shared ancestry, so too must the people who spoke them. To corroborate linguistic evidence, and to determine the direction of descent and migrations, he relied on Native traditions. Many were merely "pretended," such as traditions of emergence from underground or descent from an animal, but others, Gallatin believed, were "founded on a true fact." Delawares' tradition of western migration, for example, had been "confirmed by the affinities of their language with the Black-Feet," who lived in what is now Montana. Although he admitted doubt privately, Gallatin hoped that his taxonomic order had reduced Native linguistic diversity to the point where there was "nothing . . . inconsistent with the Mosaic chronology."[21]

Gallatin's shifting interests in the final decade of his life provide an important illustration of the ways in which questions of lineage and social condition intertwined with the country's widening territorial, commercial, and scholarly ambitions. He extended a genealogical and evolutionary approach to Latin America in long articles published in the AES *Transactions*. While others had described a region of linguistic and racial multiplicity, in "Notes on the Semi-Civilized Nations of Mexico, Yucatan, and Central America" (1845),

Gallatin reduced the region to "two principal languages," those related to "Mexican" (Nahuatl) and those related to Maya. These possessed the same "distinctive character" as the other American languages, which indicated their common origin in the remote past. The lexical difference of the Maya and Nahuatl, however, suggested that "perpetual wars and frequent revolutions must have taken place." Regardless, the fact that each practiced arts (cultivation of maize, a distinct mode of calculating time) unknown in the old world before colonization, meant that "American civilization" was indigenous even if its creators' distant ancestors had migrated from Asia. He sent copies of his book to the Secretary of War, hoping the department would subsidize its distribution to Indian agents and missionaries, and to Winfield Scott, requesting that the general procure or have copied $400 worth of vocabularies, grammars, or other manuscripts. Though Gallatin had opposed the U.S.–Mexican War, he admitted that "the occupation of the city of Mexico by the American army may . . . be highly useful to those who occupy themselves with ethnological, antiquarian, and philological researches." Gallatin rejected the notion that ethnology justified "manifest destiny"; yet he relied on U.S. conquest and expanding influence to prove that "savage tribes can, of themselves, and without any foreign assistance, emerge from the rudest and lowest social state, and gradually attain even the highest degree of civilization," and he refuted speculation on "the presumed inferiority of some races." In its emphasis upon progress independent of intervention, either white or divine, Gallatin's view was distinctively evolutionary, despite his belief in the uniqueness of humanity and his hopes to reconcile ethnology with scripture.[22]

Members of "the American School of Ethnology" attacked the arguments, commitments, and methodological assumptions of Gallatin and other philologists. The most influential criticism came from Samuel G. Morton, who published *Crania Americana* in 1839. Previous historians have focused on Morton's arguments regarding fixed, separately created races, but his work was as important for the explicit challenge it posed to philology's authority as a science of racial descent. Following Johann Friedrich von Blumenbach, Morton thought that the shape of the skull alone proved to which of five races a person belonged because, he believed, no environmental factors could change it. After measuring the internal capacity of crania, Morton arranged them in an intellectual and moral hierarchy in which "Caucasians" and "Ethiopians" occupied the highest and lowest places. In a median position, the "American Race" was superior to "Malays" and inferior to "Mongolians." As importantly, it was distinct from both of those Asiatic races. Morton subdivided physically unchanging races into twenty-two families, according to speech, customs, and character. He counted himself a member of the "Anglo-American" branch of the "Germanic Family" of the "Caucasian Race," for example, and he divided the "American Race" into two groups. The "Toltecan" family included Peruvians, Mesoamericans, and North American "Mound Builders," each of whom had achieved "demi-civilization" (a term that signified not only incomplete ascent but also a racially distinct trajectory). Excepting only the "Mongolian" inhabitants of the far north, "all the barbarous nations of the new world" belonged to the "American" family, which possessed a mental "structure . . . different from that of the white man" and an "inaptitude . . . for civilization." In succeeding publications, he argued that these fixed and unequal races shared no common ancestor. Among the three conclusions in *Crania Americana*, Morton insisted that the "feeble analogies of language" possessed no value in tracing descent.[23]

Attempts to assign the Inuit and Aleut peoples of the Arctic to an American or Mongolian race illustrate how philologists and physical ethnologists diverged over the classification of certain peoples. Maintaining the "entire similarity of the structure and grammatical forms of their language [Inuit and Aleut] with those of various Indian tribes," Albert Gallatin argued, "affords an almost conclusive proof of their belonging to the same family of mankind." Physical ethnologists, on the other hand, believed that "the Eskimaux . . . obviously belong to the Polar family of Asia." Morton rejected the idea that they "pass insensibly into the American race, and thus form the connecting link between the two." The two races possessed such "widely different" bodily features that they could not share ancestry, despite what one might glean through the "fathomless depths of philology." While "climate & other physical agents . . . never efface the essential or typical character of the race," Morton stressed that language changed through contact with others. "Asiatics having arrived at various and distant periods, and in small parties, would naturally, if not unavoidably, adopt more or less of the language of the people among whom they settled, until their own dialects finally merged in those of the Chiepewyan and other Indians who bound them on the south."[24]

This debate surfaced in the AES, which Gallatin and John R. Bartlett established in New York City in 1842. Although Gallatin, who hosted and bankrolled the society, was a philologist and a monogenist, the ranks of the AES included those of differing ethnological persuasions. Indeed, by the 1850s, disputes between polygenists and the theologically orthodox fractured the society. Even before then, these divisions produced tension. As a resident of Philadelphia, Morton did not attend meetings, but he did submit a letter, upon request, describing his famous collection of crania in 1846. The letter was most important because it clarified something left unclear in his earlier book. Here he made explicit that each of the "American nations," excluding the Inuit and

Aleut, were "true *autochthones*, the primeval inhabitants of this vast continent." He also explicitly denied—unlike many other American and European ethnologists, who spoke of race and heredity interchangeably—that people of the same "race" necessarily shared a common ancestor, since "several, perhaps even many pairs" produced each race. Gallatin, who believed Indian origins lay in Asia, and suspected that the likeliest emigration route included the Aleutian Islands, requested that Bartlett, the society's corresponding secretary, pass along his objections to the craniologist. Bodies could not reliably indicate descent, Gallatin argued, because they were susceptible to environmental influences. For corroborating evidence, he turned to northern members of the well-understood Finno-Ugric family, citing the "historical fact, supported by an analogy of language, that the Finns and Laplanders are the same race; yet they differ greatly in their physical conformation." Gallatin was accustomed to a degree of deference from correspondents, and Morton had a reputation as a warm and generous scholar, but the latter's reply was sharp. In northernmost Europe, as in northernmost America and elsewhere, "mere proximity, the necessity of the case, has fused their totally diverse tongues into a single language." Speech did not indicate ancestry. Dismissing the previous century of ethnology, Morton declared, "Philology, however important in Ethnography, is not unfrequently a broken reed." It was a view that gained prominence, through his own efforts and those of his followers.[25]

Collectively, the coterie of polemicists and scholars that called themselves the American School of Ethnology elaborated a varied but sustained assault on language as a guide to human descent in the 1840s–1850s, beginning slightly earlier than analogous disputes between physical ethnologists and philologists in Europe. While members of the American School did not adhere to a single position on language study, none accepted that it alone could indicate racial descent. Ephraim G. Squier, who attended to philology while attempting to negotiate an interoceanic canal treaty with Nicaragua and working for a firm attempting to build a railroad across Honduras, turned to language to trace "ancient migrations . . . of vast families of men" and to unlock what he correctly believed to be the phonetic values of Maya glyphs. Squier, whose belief in the possibility of different races' evolution was atypical in this set, also insisted that philology joined archaeology and craniology in proving polygenesis. Others agreed. Alfred Maury's "On the Distribution and Classification of Tongues,—Their Relation to the Geographical Distribution of Races; and on the Inductions Which May Be Drawn from Their Relations" argued that language emerged spontaneously with each separately created race and was "as ancient as that of the races themselves," so "families of tongues" corresponded "to races of mankind possessing different faculties, as well for speech as ideas." Although he warned colleagues to "beware the Philologist!" in matters of classification, the Egyptologist George R. Gliddon translated the French scholar's essay for *Indigenous Races of the Earth* (1857) because it offered a rebuttal to "philological monogenism." Properly circumscribed, Gliddon believed philology could be the "handmaiden, not the mistress, of 'Ethnology.'" Conversely, Josiah Nott determined to exclude even supportive philology. When he edited Arthur de Gobineau's notorious *Moral and Intellectual Diversity of Races* for an American audience (1856), he cut a chapter that declared, "Languages, unequal among themselves, are in perfect correspondence with the relative merit of races." Despite some scholars' claims to have found distinctly "Indian" sounds and a seemingly fixed "Indian mind," the American School rejected the notion that philology could be an autonomous science of race.[26]

Part of these writers' objections stemmed from philologists' perceived uncritical acceptance of the Bible. Schoolcraft's efforts to make philology compatible with the Lost Tribes theory was especially prominent, given its federal stamp, but numerous other works also put forward sweeping claims that supported narratives compatible with scripture by asserting connections between Indians, Inuit and Aleut, and the inhabitants of Asia. Missionaries mindful of orthodoxy, such as Eugene Vetromile, a Jesuit among the Abenakis, claimed that it was "impossible to tell where the Indians became Esquimaux, or where the Esquimaux became Indians." Some scholars agreed, even suggesting a linguistic continuum connecting North America and Asia. Robert Gordon Latham, Britain's preeminent ethnologist after the death of James Cowles Prichard, and a corresponding member of the AES, described the "phenomena of *transition*," in which subarctic Athapaskans "recede from the Sioux and Iroquois type, and approach" that of the Inuit and Aleut. Those peoples, in turn, "pass into the populations of North-eastern Asia." Wilhelm von Humboldt had expressed a similar opinion about the languages of northeastern Asia and the Americas. Rasmus Christian Rask and Friedrich Max Müller put forward an even more ambitious theory, namely that a "Scythian" or "Turanian" family encompassed the American languages and all of the non-Indo-European and non-Semitic Asian languages in "one great chain of speech."[27]

Such theories earned the ire of the American School. In the polemical compendium *Types of Mankind* (1854), Josiah Nott and George R. Gliddon attacked the religious assumptions that underlay much of philology and hoped to bolster support for polygenism by stressing that archaeological discoveries had extended recorded history to the point that the known existence of "nations and languages" was "entirely irreconcilable with the Jewish date for the 'confusion of tongues.'" Gliddon "repudiate[d]" the theory that "Scythia" had "vomited forth . . . men of absolutely different stocks" and ridiculed the "modern evangelical hypothesis of the *unity* of all languages." He would not accept the idea that American Indians were "connect[ed], through one omnific name" with Hungarians, Turks, Mongols, and other peoples of Central Eurasia. In the literally titled *Indigenous Races of the Earth* (1857), he declared, on behalf of those who accepted ostensibly scientific proof that the different races had been separately created, that philology was "the last refuge for alarmed protestant monogenism." The American School's explicit attack on the idea that all human beings shared ancestry through Adam placed them outside the bounds of most U.S. Christians' faith and limited their influence. Religious skepticism was one of the defining features of the American School, and that influenced its opposition to much philology.[28]

In addition to accepting polygenism, the members of the American School extended their skepticism to the moralism of evangelicals and other reformers, whose belief in human unity allegedly tainted their social views. Distancing themselves from missionary and reform organizations, learned societies that worked with them, and allegedly misguided federal efforts, Nott and Gliddon congratulated themselves for publishing *Types of Mankind* without "patronage from Governments, Institutions, or Societies." They wrote to convince policy-makers and the public that whites were "destined eventually to conquer and hold every foot of the globe where climate does not interpose an impenetrable barrier. No philanthropy, no legislation, no missionary labors, can change this law." Readers understood these implications. William B. Hodgson, a Georgia planter and former diplomat in Algiers and Constantinople who studied northern and central African languages and dabbled in American Indian ethnology, provides an illuminating example. Early in his career he corresponded with Du Ponceau, believing "the Author of the Universe has made as great a distinction in the *Speech,* as in the *Skins* of men," and he insisted that "comparative philology is the modern science, which chiefly guides the classification of tribes and nations." Yet he lost faith in philology under the influence of Morton and Gliddon, whose assertions about white civilization and black slavery in Egypt meant that "in the South, we shall not be so much frightened hereafter by the voice of Europe or Northern America." In an account of Creek society for the Georgia Historical Society, Hodgson saw philology as nothing more than a memorial to a vanishing people. Vocabularies and "the books of missionaries printed in their idioms" were the only "fossil, organic remains of [their] intellectual humanity" that would persist. Philology and philanthropy remained linked, in the minds of opponents, as ethnologists confronted deepening divisions over slavery amid continuing processes of colonialism.[29]

Methodologically, members of the American School also rejected the complacent blurring of peoples and their languages that formed the core of philology in the first half of the nineteenth century. As early as 1830, in *Thoughts on the Original Unity of the Human Race,* Charles Caldwell dodged the emphasis on grammatical organization that had prevailed in philology since the work of Du Ponceau and argued that human vocal organs could only form a limited number of "articulate sounds," which expressed "things and their relations, as they appear to the human mind." Since these were supposedly constant, argued the man who was the first to translate Blumenbach for an American audience and among the first to praise *Crania Americana,* "all languages resemble each other . . . because from the nature of the case, it must be so." Besides, linguistic similarities might indicate merely previous interaction. It was "unsound logic" to infer that affinities indicated the common descent of the languages, according to the former Barton student, much less the common descent of their speakers. Mouthing an argument that was at least as old as Antoine Desmoulin's *Histoire naturelle des races humaines* (1826), American School ethnologists repeatedly pointed to the fact that the descendants of Africans spoke European languages to argue that speech and descent were entirely distinct. "Although languages indicate national affiliation," according to Charles Pickering, nephew of the philologist and himself the physical ethnologist of the United States Exploring Expedition (or Wilkes Expedition) whose report Congress had withheld for its polygenesis, "their actual distribution, is to a certain extent independent of physical race."[30]

These arguments converged with a broader intention of the American school to study human beings as scientists studied other animals (as opposed to philologists, who privileged the trait that most clearly distinguished humanity). According to Louis Agassiz, the most prestigious scientist in the antebellum United States, simply because all human beings possessed language did not indicate that all languages or their speakers shared a common descent. After all, "who ever thought that the robin learned his melody from the mocking-bird, or the mocking-bird from any other species of thrush?" They could not share an ancestor because God had created things perfectly adapted to their environments. Against those who supported theories of Indians' Asian origins, Agassiz presented an example of distant but physically similar organisms, who shared no common ancestor in the polygenist scheme, producing similar vocalizations. The fact that "brumming" of distinct species of bears were analogous across the globe, as were the "roaring and miawing" of distinct species of cats, must force scholars "to question the reliability of philological evidence as proving genetic derivation." Agassiz would become one of the world's most important opponents of natural selection, but confronting philology's claims to trace ancestry led him to reject the idea of gradual divergence from a common ancestor in the decade before Charles Darwin first published his evolutionary views.[31]

Arguments for the fixity of racial types, and the sole authority of anatomy and physiology to determine these, depended upon countering philology's premise that substantial divergence could result from the slow accretion of seemingly insignificant changes. Instead, the American School insisted upon intermixture as the driver of change. Explicitly targeting Gallatin's work, Nott admitted "the close *affinity*" of diverse Native languages that shared grammatical traits, but he denied that it "affords any satisfactory proof of the unity of their linguistic derivation." Since the "aboriginal races of America . . . display a certain similarity in their physical and intellectual characters," the Mobile physician continued, "it is probable that their primitive languages would in consequence, more or less, resemble each other." Millennia of "migrations, wars, amalgamations," moreover, would produce collisions and, as a result, they "would necessarily become fused into one heterogeneous mass." This was what Morton had suggested to Gallatin in their private exchange. Elaborating the idea, Gliddon suggested that languages must have radiated out from many primitive centers ("less . . . than a dozen," he estimated), later merging at their respective boundaries, as did races. Alfred Maury went so far as to suggest that when peoples of "alien speech" lived in "perpetual contact" with one another, one would "penetrate" the other in a process of "grammatical dispossession." Understanding linguistic change in terms of encounter, collision, and conquest, echoed eighteenth-century theories that had been rejected by European comparative philologists, but it supported the American School's aims of denying change outside certain confines. Despite their theory that the "amalgamation" of races would naturally produce "extermination," these scholars accepted the likelihood of intermixture within races and used it to explain linguistic features in a way that countered philological arguments about divergence.[32]

Scholars of Native ancestry differed on the question of whether language indicated descent at midcentury. As he tried to stir public sentiment against the exploitative and murderous practices toward Indians during the Gold Rush, John Rollin Ridge, a California newspaper editor and son of the Cherokee leader, wrote articles on ethnological topics that categorized Native groups by "affinities, either proximate or remote, of blood and language." One métis historian, on the other hand, scattered criticisms of ethnologists throughout his *History of the Ojibway People* (written circa 1852). Mindful of his people's differences with Dakotas and others, William W. Warren rejected philologists' claims that "all the tribes of the red race inhabiting America have ever been . . . one and the same people, speaking the same language, and practicing the same beliefs and customs." Tradition recorded the shared descent only of those who spoke Algonquian languages. Besides, the "old men of the Ojibway" knew of at least one instance in which linguistic affinity had nothing to do with shared descent. The "Odugamies" (Foxes), according to tradition, "do not really belong to the Algonquin council fires" since they had only learned their language after "close intercourse" with Sauks. Most importantly, according to Warren, linguistic differentiation from a common ancestor was "secondary" to the "first and principal division, and certainly the most ancient . . . that of blood and kindred, embodied and rigidly enforced" in the "Totemic" system. Although he was silent on the views of Cass, Copway, or others regarding consolidationist efforts, Warren made clear the primacy, in sequence and importance, of this clan system, or *doodemag,* and the relative ranks of these clans within the Ojibwe "civil polity." It was U.S. agents' and superintendents' interference with this system by bestowing illegitimate authority upon "chiefs" willing to sign treaties that had undermined the authority of hereditary chiefs and produced both social disorder among Ojibwes and hostility toward U.S. settlers. Warren suspected that a similar pattern explained the "Creek, Seminole, and Black Hawk wars" of the previous decades. He drew upon personal observations and traditional knowledge to offer a multipronged challenge to the legitimacy of philologists' claims that language was the best means to trace descent, linking it to "beliefs and customs" but separating it from "blood and kindred." He did not, however, accept the theories of the American School. Conveying Ojibwe elders' views that their ancestors had emerged from the land, he ridiculed polygenists' theories of separate creations as no better than those devised by "ignorant sons of the forest." A Christian himself, Warren suggested his people descended from the Lost Tribes, Dakotas from "the roving sons of Tartary," and that multiple migrations from Asia accounted for the "several stocks of the American aborigines." The exact relationship between language, ways of life, and ancestry continued to be hotly debated at midcentury and beyond.[33]

Physical ethnologists and other scholars mounted a formidable challenge to philologists' claims to trace descent. Although polygenists presented this case most forcefully, many of those who opposed theories of separate creations came to accept the legitimacy of the criticism. The monogenist antiquarian Alexander Bradford, who suspected Indians' Malay origins, stressed that since "conquest and other causes" often led either to the adoption or "eradication" of languages, speech did not reliably indicate descent. More and more philologists, especially in Europe, came to accept this view. Shared speech indicated "affiliation or intercourse," as Robert G. Latham put it at midcentury. "One to the exclusion of the other it does *not* exhibit." This trend became even more pronounced after archaeology's vast extension of human duration raised questions about the relative emergence of physical features and languages. According to Friedrich Max Müller, a German-born Sanskritist who was the most renowned Anglophone philologist in the latter half of the nineteenth century, continuous processes of migration, colonization, subjugation, and sexual intermixture had combined to make it "impossible . . . that race and language should continue to run parallel" over the course of human existence. Yet, many U.S. philologists continued to dissent and the federal government intensified its efforts to collect linguistic information. What philologists learned from the 1840s–1870s, however, disrupted language-based understandings of race.[34]

Linguistic Classification and the Problem of Race—or Maybe Races

In western North America, according to the popularizer Charles De Wolf Brownell, the "races vary by such slight shades of distinction, and such analogies exist between their languages, that . . . the line of demarcation can with difficulty be drawn." Many scholars, however, expected that increasing information would naturally produce appropriately simplified understandings. Among the most important contributions of Henry R. Schoolcraft's reports to Congress were reliable vocabularies of languages such as Blackfoot, Arapaho, Cheyenne, Comanche, Navajo, Pima, the pueblos of Tesuque and Zuñi, and eighteen California languages. While admitting that the "enlargement of the boundaries of the United States, by New Mexico, southern Utah, and California, has greatly increased and complicated the classification of the Indian languages," he confidently predicted that that the "number of generic families" would "melt away under the power of analysis."[35]

Those who actually heard the bewildering variety of languages in the West, however, disagreed. While on the Wilkes Expedition (1838–1842), Horatio Hale collected linguistic material in South America, Australia, and the Pacific islands before arriving in the Oregon country to classify and create a linguistic map of the region. He recognized and extended Athapaskan, Salish, Sahaptian, and Shoshonean groupings over considerable areas, but he was convinced that"no other part of the world" could compare to the long slender region between the coast and the Rocky Mountains, from Russian Alaska to Mexican Baja California, for "so many tribes, with distinct languages, crowded together in a space so limited." The region's complexity baffled Hale's attempts to determine whether there was a single "American race" or whether there were several "distinct aboriginal races on this continent." Indians along the Sacramento

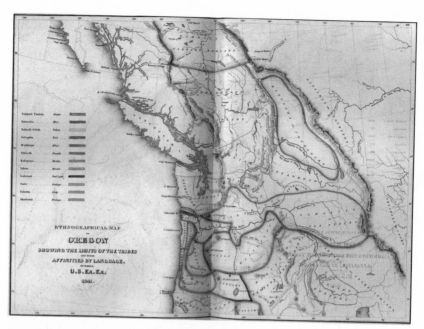

The work of Horatio Hale, the official philologist of the Wilkes Expedition, in *Ethnography and Philology* (1846), illustrates increasing federal sponsorship of philology, especially in the Far West, and the increasing linguistic knowledge of the region, which had been little known when Gallatin had published his language map a decade earlier. This "Ethnographical Map of Oregon, showing the Limits of the Tribes and Their Affinities by Language" attempted to impose visual order on an audibly diverse region. (Courtesy of the Library Company of Philadelphia)

River in the vicinity of Sutter's Fort, for example, "might be referred to two races," similar "in every respect but language." The ethnographer George Catlin mocked most philologists as "off-hand theorists of the scientific world, who do not go near these people." Dissenting from their "very clever" attempts "to *simplify* the subject," he claimed to have heard thirty "distinct and radically different" languages on the Plains. Such diversity was "unaccountable, whether these people are derived from one individual stock . . . or one thousand." Others who attempted to impose taxonomic order on the linguistic terrain reached similar conclusions.[36]

Most philologists understood taxonomic problems in the West to stem from linguistic divergence, a process that occurred in all languages but that was thought to occur especially quickly among "savage" peoples whose languages were not fixed in writing. Illustrating the degree to which many philologists found ways to confirm their preconceptions, some blamed the nomadism of equestrian peoples for fragmentation, others the sedentary life of earth-lodge villagers for allowing languages to grow apart. Most linguists in Europe, and some in the United States, insisted that real languages did not truly intermix. Rather, dialects and languages diverged to an ever greater extent, never converging. The premise of a branching tree of languages and lineages, which had prevailed from the beginning of European philology, received fuller elaboration in a reciprocal relationship with Charles Darwin's description of descent with modification. Despite linguistic contact and exchange, including lexical borrowing and some grammatical simplification, languages could still be traced to a single ancestor (motley English, for example, was Germanic).[37]

Growing ethnographic knowledge disrupted these expectations. Schoolcraft noted apparent "admixture" in Blackfoot, an Algonquian language spoken alongside an Athapaskan language within a multiethnic confederacy. Observing widespread intermarriage among distinct peoples in the Oregon country, John Scouler, a British doctor, found that "intimate relations" had produced "languages . . . mixed together in every imaginable proportion." The U.S. topographical engineer C. R. Collins pointed to the widespread practice of adoption among the peoples of the Great Basin, arguing, "Captives taken and absorbed into the tribe must necessarily have an influence upon the language." Conquest also played its part, at least according to Stephen Powers, a federal surveyor in California. He painted a graphic picture of linguistic cannibalism, in which Hupas had "sapped" the lexicons of Chimarikos, their "tributaries." They left "the dry bones of substantives, but the flesh and blood of verbs were sucked out." Making the task more difficult still for would-be taxonomists, a variety of Native languages had become "hopelessly intermingled and confused" in Spanish missions. From his experience on the Plains, Catlin drew a general rule: it was "far easier and more natural for distinct tribes, or languages, grouped and used together, to *assimilate* than to *dissimilate*." Regardless of the theoretical premises of European linguistics, those with knowledge of Native practices realized that a given duration of time might lead not to ever greater differentiation but rather to classification-defying intermixture.[38]

Horatio Hale provided the most remarkable description of linguistic collision in an account of a pidgin in wide use among diverse Native and European people throughout the Oregon country, then under joint British–U.S. administration (1818–1846). Chinook Jargon—called Chinook (or Chinuk) Wawa by its speakers—presented a "very singular phenomenon." A scanty lexicon, partially derived through onomatopoeia (a gun, for instance, was *pŏ*), had sufficed for coastal trade, but as Chinook, Nootka, Chehalis, Cree, Hawaiian, French, and English people established more extensive and more intimate relationships, their languages provided "the sinews and tendons, the connecting ligaments, as it were, of a speech." Because diverse peoples needed to pronounce its varied elements, speakers modified words to suit "tongues accustomed to different sounds," softening Chinook's "exceedingly rugged" gutturals, dropping French's nasal *n*, and changing English's *f* and *r* to *p* and *l*. Speakers also dramatically simplified Chinook's grammatical features, as is typical in pidgins. Many complained about its limited range of expression, but Hale believed that it could express "every circumstance and qualification of their ideas" with "minuteness" because it retained "the faculty of combining and compounding . . . from its connexion with the Indian tongues." Commentators had long noted how the fur trade produced forms of linguistic intermixture among Native and European participants, but Hale, in far greater detail, described how a process of mutual linguistic accommodation had created a "fusion" of Native and European sounds and words, operating according to a Native grammar.[39]

Most remarkably, increased "intercourse" was transforming this pidgin into a "real language." This was particularly true around the Hudson's Bay Company's Fort Vancouver, where "Canadians and half-breeds married to Chinook women . . . can only converse with their wives in this speech." As a result, "strange as it may seem . . . many young children are growing up to whom this factitious language is really the mother tongue, and who speak it with more readiness and perfection than any other." Hale mused, "Could the state of things which now exists be suffered to remain for a century longer, the result might be the formation of a race and idiom whose affinities would be a puzzle for ethnographers." He had observed such results on Fiji, where bodies, arts, and especially language pointed to an "amalgamation" of distinct peoples. In a generation or more, scholars might have recognized an analogous "hybrid origin" for Chinook Wawa speakers. In 1846, however, he believed that such an event was unlikely. "The tide of population," Hale explained, "which is now turning in that direction, will soon overwhelm all these scattered fragments of peculiar lineage and speech." In presenting evidence of what bellicose expansionists called "the mongrels and hybrids" around the British fort as part of an information gathering campaign inextricable from U.S.–British rivalry in the region, and assuring readers of the inexorable triumph of American settlers, sovereignty, and speech, Hale fueled notions of "manifest destiny."[40]

This report and similar accounts challenged fundamental conceptions of race and language. Some philologists and at least one U.S. Indian agent affirmed Hale's interpretation that this intermixture was producing a new language. Despite the American School's claims that language did not indicate race, many who heard Chinook Wawa described it in terms—"barbarous mixture," "mongrel language," "vile compound"—which suggested that unacceptable intercourse had audible, as well as visual, features. While debates over abolitionism were crucial for understanding the era's obsession with "miscegenation," this issue also resonated with Americans who felt their racial and sexual ideologies challenged by métis and mestizo populations in the Pacific Northwest, the Southwest, and Latin America. By the end of the century, long after whites had dispossessed the region's Natives, Hale realized that his prediction had been wrong. Chinook Wawa was "destined to a long life and wide usefulness." Revisiting the issue also provided an occasion to make explicit why he thought language was the "only certain test for the affinities of races." Challenging the views of the American School and others, Hale asserted that African American and métis history actually provided the best proof of philologists' claim to trace race, since "no people ever yet changed its language until it had become so intimately mingled with another people as to receive from them, along with their language, a large infusion of their blood."[41]

Other taxonomic questions engaged the degree to which linguistic lines shed light on cultural advancement or corresponded to cultural similarities. Consider a question that focused Gallatin's attention in his final ethnological publication, a revised linguistic classification and evolutionary ethnology that addressed the discoveries of federal surveying and exploration, and which appeared a year before his death in 1849. He was particularly interested in an "insulated semi-civilized population" in portions of the Rio Grande and Gila River valleys. He considered these Pueblos "difficult to be explained."[42] They cultivated maize but were distant from Mesoamerican centers and practiced nothing of Mesoamerican astronomy or religion. Pueblos' languages were little known—those vocabularies were "the most desirable" of any on the continent—but Gallatin knew that they were linguistically diverse, and he doubted any affinities to Maya or Nahuatl, which weighed against the notion that they represented a "residue" from a southward migration recorded in the latter's traditions. Villagers averred that they had inherited their customs, beliefs, and languages, but Gallatin stressed that a people might not know whether "remote ancestors" or more recent "intercourse" was responsible for what their "immediate progenitors" had bequeathed. Regardless of the details, the Pueblos provided proof of "the progress which a people may make, when almost altogether insulated, and unaided by more enlightened nations." In Gallatin's opinion, they also disrupted notions that conflated language, lineal descent, and cultural transmission.[43]

Not only were culturally similar peoples linguistically distinct, but linguistic investigation revealed surprising relations. Comparing Apache and Navajo linguistic materials at the Smithsonian Institution, including some that Horatio Hale and John Bartlett had collected, respectively, on the Wilkes Expedition and the Mexican Boundary Commission, the philologist William W. Turner opened "a new chapter in American ethnology" when he discovered that those languages were related not, as had been reported, to Comanche or Pawnee, but rather to Athapaskan languages in Canada, Oregon, and California, which posed important questions about origins, migrations, and social development over time. A German philologist, Johann Buschmann, suggested that Tlingit, spoken by a coastal people near the Alaska–Canada border, was part of this group as well. For scholars and missionaries predisposed to believe in Indians' Asian origins, this amounted to evidence of north-to-south migration, and anthropologists today urge us to recognize its compatibility with Native traditions of emergence, since peoples who lived in recognizably "Navajo" or "Apache" ways only came into being in the Southwest. Knowledge of Siouan peoples had already suggested the varying modes of subsistence that linguistically related peoples might pursue, but the Nadene family (as it is now known) fueled speculation about how "different branches" of a "widespread family," in Turner's words, could become isolated from one another and come to possess distinct "character and habits." The discovery highlighted ongoing debates about Indian origins, evolution, and the divergence of biological ancestry and cultural inheritance.[44]

Between and beyond the Oregon and Santa Fe trails, a vast range that included the California gold fields and the Mormon Zion, peoples who spoke related languages and who recognized ties among themselves, yet who varied in ethnological "rank," posed an even greater problem to taxonomists. Comanches, at one extreme, were equestrian hunters who tended large herds of horses and exercised dominant power on the southern Plains in the first half of the nineteenth century. They were, in the atypically precise formulation of one early nineteenth-century Indian agent, "rather Barbarians than Savages." At the other extreme, Western Shoshones and Paiutes, often derided as "Diggers," were labeled "miserable" because, as increased trading and settlement in the arid Great Basin stretched precarious resources to their limit in the 1840s–1850s, they relied upon roots and larvae for subsistence and were reputed to exchange children for food in an Indian slave trade. Beginning in the 1860s, others drew attention to the affinities between these Numic languages and those spoken in the Hopi pueblos and in the former Aztec Empire. Linguistic affinity, combined with a tradition of migration from the north, made it "probable that they are kindred races," according to the British anthropologist E. B. Tylor; but that muddled evolutionary theories. While Comanches "die out whenever white men come within reach of them," Nahuatl speakers had proven themselves "capable, not only of mixing with European races and co-existing with them, but even of raising themselves to . . . semi-civilization." Although linguists accept it today, philologists debated the existence of the Uto-Aztecan family through the end of the nineteenth century, and scholars continue to examine whether it sheds light on the relationship between linguistic dispersion and cultural diffusion (regarding, for example, the spread of maize cultivation). Those who recognized these linguistic relationships in the late nineteenth century implied that dramatic differences in ways of life, even among apparently related Native peoples, amounted to racial multiplicity.[45]

Even as federal publication of philology intensified, scholars continued to publish their work on the United States and Latin America individually and through learned societies, and besides a broader survey of the terrain, philologists also acquired deeper linguistic knowledge. As European linguistics insisted upon discovering laws of sound shift within families as the only means to prove genetic relationships conclusively, philologists such as James Hammond Trumbull and Albert Gatschet, each whom did work for the Smithsonian while also participating in newer organizations like the American Philological Association (established in 1869), called for applying increasing understanding of the regularity of variation within Indian language families to the discovery of such "laws and limits of phonetic change." Grammatical diversity among Native language families also became clearer. Charles Frederic Hartt, for instance, who accompanied Louis Agassiz on an expedition to Brazil, argued that the Tupí-Guanarí stock lacked polysynthesis. This did little to change prevailing theories about an "Indian mind" and nothing to alter the explicit aim of the federal government and so-called philanthropists of eradicating Native languages. That was true even of those philologists who were outspoken in criticizing the philology of Du Ponceau and his generation for its imprecision and its erroneous theory that features of Algonquian languages would also characterize other Native languages. Trumbull, for instance, spoke of multiple "Indian races" but clung to the notion that they possessed some "common likeness . . . in their *plan of thought*." Daniel G. Brinton, philology incorporated archaeology and traditions and whose *The American Race* (1891) attempted a comprehensive linguistic classification of Latin America, recognized several "native races of this continent," which possessed the same "logical sub-structure." Philological knowledge grew as the United States exercised increasing power over the continent and as American ethnologists imagined Latin America as an empty canvas that their studies could fill. Just as belief that language evolved did nothing to change the conviction that Native assimilation rested upon the elimination of the American languages, neither did confusion over whether there was a single "Indian" plan of ideas or perhaps several distinct plans, a single American race or several indigenous races on the continent.[46]

In 1879, reporting to the Smithsonian on the materials that the Army Corps of Engineers had collected on geographic surveys west of the hundredth meridian, Albert Gatschet noted, the "former unsatisfactory state of western linguistic topography has of late been remedied effectually by an abundance of new and reliable data." Just what that information revealed was not entirely certain, however, especially with regard to the relationship between language and race. Some figures, such as the monogenist Gallatin, suggested that languages could indicate racial identity even among those with differing bodies. Others, including polygenists like Maury, considered language families and races one and the same because they emerged simultaneously. Knowledge of western Native languages, and the perceived divergence of ways of life among linguistically related peoples, pushed yet other scholars to recognize multiple races even within language families. Other still, like Hale and Whitney, accepted the effective identity of language and race because each followed blood. Because language—with its sounds perhaps indicating racially distinct vocal organs and its grammar ostensibly indicating racially distinct ways of thinking—seemingly bridged the body and behavior, many scholars continued to conceive of language genealogically, a tendency reinforced by an understanding that intermarriage produced language shift. Such views made explicit the difference that many philologists recognized between language and other institutions. However, the conflation of physical and cultural inheritance, at least as far as it concerned language, came to be increasingly distrusted in the second half of the nineteenth century, in no small part because of federal efforts to attain linguistic mastery.[47]

Evolution, Genealogy, and the Bureau of Ethnology

Some scholars clung to the notion that language was genealogically reliable because, in some way, it coursed through the body itself. The most important evolutionary synthesis in the United States was Lewis H. Morgan's *Ancient Society, or Researches in the Lines of Human Progress from Savagery through Barbarism to Civilization* (1877). It asserted that "human intelligence, unconscious of design, evolved articulate language." But that subject, "a department of knowledge by itself, does not fall within the scope of the present investigation." A genealogical understanding of language, however, was central to Morgan's most original theories, which centered on kinship. In "Systems of Consanguinity and Affinity of the Human Family" (1871), a comparison of kinship systems among different American Indian language families and of them to other peoples worldwide, published under the aegis of the Smithsonian Institution, Morgan stressed that difference in speech produced incessant violence and that Indians coalesced into nations and confederations according to similarity in language. Philologists had successfully traced these linguistic relationships, and he even offered his own conjectures on the order in which different stocks branched off from their common ancestor in the vicinity of the Columbia River. Morgan began his researches in direct conversation with Schoolcraft and Gallatin; yet he noted that philologists had been unable to trace global ancestry through attention either to grammatical organization or patterns of phonetic shift. He focused, instead, on terms for kinship, which revealed lineage as well as social condition. Native consultation was crucial for this research, especially "matrons of the tribe," who were "skilled in relationships, beyond men." When Morgan found the same system in the Turanian family (excluding Finns and Turks) and what he termed the Ganowánian family (American Indians, but not Inuits and Aleuts), he concluded that each "drew their common system . . . from the same parent nation or stock." While different modes of classifying kindred indicated "progressive changes with the growth of man's experiences," Morgan insisted that these systems were stable because "their use and preservation are intrusted to every person who speaks the common language, and their channel of transmission is the blood."[48]

Morgan's discovery of an apparent connection with the Turanian grouping of Central Eurasia gave new life to attempts to use philology to discover linguistic relationships between Native people and populations in other parts of the globe, despite the possibility of linguistic polygenesis within an evolutionary framework. Scholars such as James Hammond Trumbull stressed that the grammatical organization of the American languages was not "peculiarly American." The surveyor W. H. Dall and many more, in federal and private publications, pointed to the roughly similar "agglutinative" character of American languages and the Finno-Ugric, Turkic, or Mongolic languages (sometimes grouped as "Ural-Altaic"). Occasionally, a scholar pointed to more specific linguistic features. In a publication for the Smithsonian, for example, the army officer F. L. O. Roehrig drew connections between Dakota and the Ural-Altaic languages. Specifically, he noted that each used "reduplication" of words for emphasis, particularly regarding color and other external qualities. Efforts to include Native languages in a "Turanian" or "Ural-Altaic" family flourished in the 1850s–1870s. Intriguingly, speculation about links with the European isolate Basque resurfaced amid calls for the exclusion of Asian immigrants in the 1870s–1890s. Increasing study of the lesser-known tongues of Asia and the Americas, within a broader context in which the Darwinian Revolution affirmed the shared descent of the human species, continued to inspire attempts to fit Native people into a broader human history that rejected many Natives' own traditions of immemorial and inextricable links to North America.[49]

Increasing philological knowledge also contributed to further refinement of just what linguistic relationships demonstrated in the 1860s–1870s, amid a backdrop of growing cries for reform. Although early in his career as a surveyor, treaty commissioner, and philologist in the Pacific Northwest, George Gibbs thought that a "whole people speaking a common language" should be considered a "nation," he revised his views in 1870. "There are no *nations* in our sense of the word among these Indians," Gibbs reported one year before Congress discontinued the treaty process and asserted the power simply to dictate laws that would apply to Indians, because "those speaking even the same dialect . . . are often broken up into separate bands under different chiefs." Beginning work in southern Oregon in the late 1870s on the U.S. Geographical and Geological Survey of the Rocky Mountain Region, Albert Gatschet observed relations between Klamaths and Warm Springs (or Tenino) Indians in southern Oregon, who speak distinct languages within what linguists today identify as the Plateau Penutian family. Gatschet, a Swiss immigrant who had studied philology in Germany, interpreted their "friendly intercourse" in light of centuries of assumptions about linguistic and social relationships, concluding that "racial and linguistic affinity" explained their closeness, "just as inveterate enmity is often founded upon disparity of race and language." Yet the impulse to demarcate races produced complications, especially when taxonomists tried to reconcile linguistic similarity with cultural difference, as Gatschet revealed in a discussion of the Uto-Aztecan family. Lexical, grammatical, and phonological traits confirmed "a common parentage" of the "Numa race" and the "Nahuatl race," according to Gatschet, despite their separation by territory "inhabited by the Yuma, Tinné-Apache, and Pueblo races." All but the Pueblos were linguistically defined, and racial diversity existed not only from one language family to another but even within those families. More importantly, with Indians unrecognized as sovereign political entities, some philologists associated linguistic affinity with race rather than nationhood. Yet, as Gatschet complained elsewhere, much of the public was ignorant of philologists' findings and philology suffered from insufficient public encouragement.[50]

In an atmosphere of evolutionism, determination to impose a more efficient colonialism, and lingering views of language as genealogical and tied in some way to race, John Wesley Powell pushed for Congress to increase its support for ethnology. While in charge of the U.S. Geographical and Geological Survey of the Rocky Mountain Region, he had already used its resources to publish a series of *Contributions to North American Ethnology*, including the work of Powers and Gatschet on California peoples, posthumous work on Oregon and Washington by Gibbs, and W. H. Dall's work on Alaska Natives that had stemmed from the privately funded Western Union Telegraph Survey.

To gather more information, he also published an *Introduction to the Study of Indian Languages* (1877), with "Schedules" of words and sentences to be collected, and the rather daunting assurance that it would "assist" any would-be philologist "in overcoming the difficulties which he is sure to encounter." As evidence that "a thorough investigation of North American ethnology would be of great value to our Indian Office," Powell addressed his dual aims of civilization and pacification in the idioms of evolution and lineage. Rather than view savagery as "inchoate civilization," Powell stressed that it was a social state that possessed its own variety of institutions, all of which needed to be overcome before "civilization" would take hold. That, in turn, required understanding those institutions, and "little of value can be accomplished in making investigations in other branches of the field without a thorough knowledge of the languages."[51]

Powell drew particular attention to the genealogical advantages of linguistic study as he urged Congress to create an ethnological bureau. He pointed to the Nez Perce War (1877), the misleading name given to an attempt by fewer than a thousand Nez Perces to escape reservation life and U.S. efforts toward national integration by riding more than a thousand miles toward Canada. During this conflict, the army and the Bureau of Indian Affairs had expressed "much fear" that Shoshones and Paiutes would rise up as well, and "the papers were filled with rumors that such a coalition had been made." As Powell, who had a "tolerable speaking acquaintance" with Shoshone dating to his time as a federal surveyor, had "confidently predicted," however, "no such alliance" between speakers of unrelated Sahaptian and Numic languages came to pass. In fact, he reminded the Secretary of the Interior, "Shoshones and Pai Utes were enlisted to fight against the Nez Perces." Despite numerous instances of alliances among unrelated peoples in the centuries since initial colonization, and although as he wrote Klamaths and Modocs (speakers of Plateau Penutian languages related to Sahaptian tongues) were learning the Ghost Dance from a Paiute prophet and his followers, Powell insisted that translinguistic political alliance was impossible because "no coalition between tribes of different stocks has ever been successful." For such reasons, Powell argued, "further knowledge of the extent of the several stocks as they can be classed by linguistic affinities, would be of great value in the administration of our Indian affairs." He made a convincing case for the importance of such knowledge, for an institution to compile it, and for his own qualifications as director. Established in 1879, the Bureau of Ethnology pursued the interrelationship of human languages, beliefs, arts, and institutions within evolutionary and taxonomic frameworks.[52]

Congress may have supported the bureau in expectation of its practical use-fulness, but Powell provided no policy recommendations on the basis of lin-guistic taxonomy, despite the bureau's substantial linguistic work in its opening decades. Indeed, on the question of taxonomy, it is hard to see how he might have. Powell's foremost goal was to address the "complex, mixed, and inconsistent" system that had accreted over the previous decades, as inquirers sought a "classification of these languages and a corresponding classification of races." Powell rejected the American School's arguments for polygenism and comparative philologists' claims that determining laws of sound change was the only means to establish language families, but he accepted the view that physical race was distinct from language. The discoveries of U.S. philologists over the preceding decades had foiled assumptions about the relationship between languages and ways of life, a disjuncture that was even more glaring when viewed through evolutionary assumptions. As Powell stated in the bureau's *First Annual Report* (1883), "the classification of languages is not, to the full extent, a classification of peoples." Eight years later, he published his linguistic classification and the accompanying "Map of the Linguistic Stocks of the American Indians Chiefly within the Present Limits of the United States" (1891).[53]

It did not go as far as some wanted. That same year, Daniel G. Brinton, an ethnologist active in the American Philosophical Society and excluded from the manuscript materials that Powell and the bureau were working on, published *The American Race* (1891), an attempt to offer a full linguistic classification and ethnographic description of North and South America. Two years later, in a paper delivered before the World's Fair Congress of Anthropology, Brinton stressed how much there remained to be done in classifying the languages of Mexico and South America. At the same meeting, a young philologist and anthropologist, Franz Boas, offered suggestions for further refining the classification of the languages of the Northwest coast, suggesting that languages that showed no resemblance in words might still share grammatical features amounting to evidence of shared descent. On this basis, he suggested joining Haida to Tlingit and the Athapaskan family, among other consolidations.[54]

Powell, on the other hand, focused on the peoples under U.S. colonialism, and he rejected morphology as a basis of genealogy because it violated his evolutionary views, which held that languages developed through processes of linguistic fusion and grammatical specialization. Human beings shared a common evolutionary ancestor, in Powell's view, but "languages have sprung from innumerable sources after the dispersion of mankind," with "simple tribal speech" being "little superior to that of some of the lower animals." Over time, "linguistic materials" passed "out of the exclusive possession of cognate peoples"

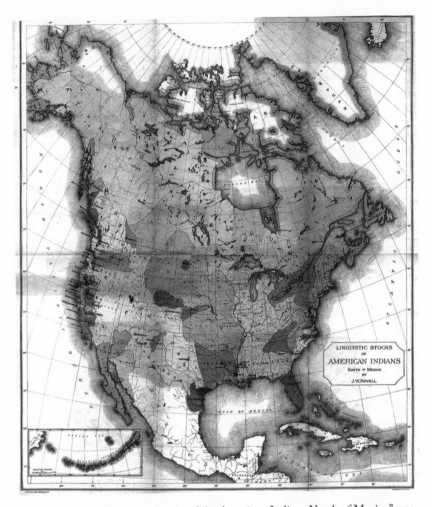

LINGUISTIC STOCKS
OF
AMERICAN INDIANS
NORTH OF MEXICO
BY
J.W. POWELL.

This "Map of the Linguistic Stocks of the American Indians North of Mexico" was the first comprehensive, continental updating of Gallatin's earlier effort, which benefited from the vast accretion of linguistic information of the Far West in the intervening years. The degree to which it benefited from federal exploration and surveying, and its publication in the *Seventh Annual Report of the Bureau of Ethnology* (1891), indicates the central role that federal government had come to play in the collection and creation of linguistic information. J. W. Powell's careful distinction that his map illustrated "linguistic stocks" and not "Indian tribes" reflects his conviction that languages and peoples's ancestry were not necessarily one and the same. (Courtesy of Walsh Library, Seton Hall University, South Orange, NJ) through trade and conquest. Against linguists' insistence that languages naturally diverged from a common source, Powell argued that "differentiation of languages within a single stock is mainly due to the absorption of materials from other stocks." Although ethnographers had documented that peoples who had long been neighbors and allies, such as Hidatsas and Mandans, or Pimas and Maricopas, had deliberately maintained their own mother tongues and discrete identities, Powell stressed the importance of colonization in producing linguistic collision. Wracked by disease and seeking allies and new means of prosperity, "new associations of tribe with tribe and of the Indians with Europeans" formed, producing "quite elaborate jargon languages." His assertion that "the grand process of linguistic development among the tribes of North America has been toward unification rather than toward multiplication" was a facet of his belief that European and U.S. colonization had furthered, and would continue to further, progressive evolution. Whereas some philologists, from Du Ponceau to Boas, argued that grammatical similarities could indicate descent, Powell insisted that grammar represented nothing more than an evolutionary "phase." Just as the Industrial Revolution relied on laborers performing ever more subdivided tasks, as the grammatical "plan of a language" evolved, isolated words with precise functions would replace elaborate declensions and inflections. Since English had ostensibly advanced furthest of all languages in this process, and since "baneful superstitions" were "woven" into Native languages, Powell believed that Indians must be taught English.[55]

Powell's map, measuring an imposing sixteen feet by twelve feet, sat at the center of one wall of the National Museum's ethnological exhibit at the World's Columbian Exposition in 1893. "So far as possible," Otis T. Mason "arranged" life-sized models, wearing traditional dress and using traditional tools in natural environments, according to more than a dozen of the largest of the fifty-eight language families that Powell had identified. The proper organization of the exhibit was the subject of some controversy. Evolutionary arrangements of artifacts had met increasing criticism in the previous decade on the grounds that by ignoring the differing functions and cultural significance of objects that happened to look alike, in favor of some ostensible ladder of technological progress, such displays obscured more than they revealed. Rejecting the possibility of displaying artifacts by tribe, but skeptical of the ultimate utility of linguistic classification, Mason, the director of the National Museum, introduced the new category of "culture areas" that included groups of peoples who made use of the natural environment in similar ways but differed in their mental lives. On the one hand, peoples in the "pueblo region" belonged to four different stocks, differing "essentially in language and totemic system and mythology," and although peoples of numerous stocks used arrows of similar shapes and materials to hunt bison on the Great Plains, "the feathering, the streaking, the symbolism on the arrow, were distinct for each tribe and tongue." Mason, like many before him, believed that languages, "being the product of a people who are blood kindred, form the best guide to the study of race." On the other hand, some language families, such as the Athapaskan and Uto-Aztecan, crossed culture areas. According to the Smithsonian Institution administrator G. Brown Goode, Powell's classification and map were "the crowning result of ethnological labors on our continent for fifty years," and he praised the exhibit for bringing "into sharp comparison, the concepts of race, speech, and activities."[56]

That only a small number of missionaries, officials, and scholars viewed Albert Gallatin's ethnographic map earlier in the century, while Powell's volume circulated more widely at public expense and was displayed for millions at the world's fair, illustrates a simultaneous professionalization and popularization of ethnology. Powell's map diverged from earlier taxonomic projects. In contrast to the "Indian tribes" that Gallatin's map had claimed to depict, Powell's map claimed only to represent "linguistic stocks." Rather than depict Native migrations, long a goal of U.S. ethnologists, the map provided "conclusive proof" that before colonization Indians had been "sedentary." Viewers could see that most of the continent was covered with broad swaths of single colors, representing related languages, rather than speckled with countless languages unrelated to their neighbors, as would surely have been the case if the wandering hordes of popular imagination had existed in reality. At the same time, while Powell's map, like Gallatin's had before, made colonialism visible to U.S. citizens, its place in a broader ethnological exhibit displayed the incoherence of what the United States knew about its ostensible wards. Indians had been dispossessed of their "fixed and definitely bounded habitats" and confined to reservations, which by 1893 were being broken up in the name of assimilation, and the federal government was pursuing the elimination of Native languages altogether in favor of forcing Indians to speak English. Language did not indicate biological ancestry, a linguistic taxonomy was "wholly arbitrary" for classifying arts, and, at least to Powell's mind, ethnologists had never established just what a "race" was. He doubted that taxonomic efforts would ever advance beyond "multifarious groupings for multifarious purposes." Powell's classification and map, despite his claims in 1878, offered little aid to the administrators of colonialism. The exhibit brought multiple taxonomies into comparison and left language hanging on the wall, above a visitor's direct line of sight, off to the side.[57]

When Franz Boas prepared the bureau's new *Handbook of American Indian Languages* (1914), he intended his work as part of an anthropology that offered cultural relativity in place of evolutionary-racial hierarchy and cultural diffusion and convergence in place of inheritance. He opposed the evolutionism of Powell as much as the racial essentialism of other scholars, but he affirmed the need to separate language, culture, and race.[58] That view dominated the twentieth century.

Scholars and federal administrators considered it important to trace the descent of Native peoples not only to hypothesized relations in the Old World but also to their relations in the Americas. This was not merely a matter of abstract scholarly mastery symbolizing continental dominion, but rather philologists and officials believed that classification would ease the administration of colonialism, especially in the early years of federal reservations. Administrators' hopes in this regard came to little, mainly because of Native opposition to programs that ignored meaningful identities and the brute coercion of dispossession. The idea upon which such hopes had been based, the centuries-old assumption, still prominent in the nineteenth century, that linguistic affinities provided a reliable indication of shared ancestry also met considerable opposition. Some ethnologists provided a multipronged rebuttal as part of intertwined campaigns in support of slavery and conquest and in opposition to religious orthodoxy, philanthropy, and notions of evolutionary development. Archaeology and Darwinian biology combined to vastly extend known human existence far beyond the span represented in the linguistic record. Philologists themselves puzzled over newly discovered relationships between languages widely separated by geography, spoken by peoples widely divergent according to Euro-American evolutionary notions. This knowledge emerged from the expansion of the United States through invasion and economic influence. Exploration, military reconnaissance and occupation, and various surveys collected linguistic information of diverse peoples. Federal support, especially through the Smithsonian Institution, allowed for the analysis and publication of philology.

Administrators and Congress still hoped that philology could provide information useful for pacification and assimilation, and Powell played on these hopes in pushing for the creation of the Bureau of Ethnology. Yet, while some of his contemporaries, including Whitney, Hale, Morgan, and Mason, continued to conceive of language and blood as in some way linked, the evolutionary taxonomist Powell argued that they were not. In this view, he and other U.S. scholars belatedly joined their European counterparts. They did so in conversation with them and as a result of the tremendous increase in linguistic knowledge that various arms of U.S. colonialism had produced.

Epilogue

In 1893 the Anthropological Society of Washington published the paper "Polysynthesis in the Languages of the American Indians" in its journal *The American Anthropologist*, which targeted the theory that had dominated study of Native languages for most of the nineteenth century. In it, J. N. B. Hewitt, a scholar at the Bureau of Ethnology, dismissed Peter S. Du Ponceau's "cursory" work and "imperfect" materials, but he also went on to challenge Daniel G. Brinton and several other philologists who had adapted Du Ponceau's theory to evolutionary assumptions about "savage tribes" and "languages . . . at the bottom of the scale." He blasted, in respectable tones, the "lamentable confusion" and "fanciful assumptions" that had governed much of philology, especially in its psychological speculations. Challenging the conflation of Native languages and an "Indian mind," he charged that philologists, as a group, were guilty of "confounding . . . mode of expression with mental analysis." The science of languages had advanced beyond such "romance." Hewitt, who was Tuscarora, was a native English speaker but learned Tuscarora from schoolmates. He drew upon his own deep but acquired knowledge of Iroquoian languages and he consulted James Owen Dorsey, a former missionary and a fellow laborer in the bureau, on Siouan languages. But he was also familiar with Indo-European work as well, citing William Dwight Whitney's description of Slavic languages to counter the view (held by the director of the bureau, among others) that languages uniformly evolved toward more simplified grammatical forms. Hewitt held broad evolutionary views, but he stressed that contemporary Native languages were "distant from the beginnings of human speech." [1]

Hewitt never addressed the federal policies then attempting to destroy the linguistic inheritance of Native people, and he avoided the word "race" in this essay. Yet, it is difficult to read the essay without appreciating those issues. Hewitt recognized the social importance of ethnology. Indeed, over the next twenty years, he came to advocate that it be taught in federal Indian schools. He stressed that there was "no proof" that Native people were intellectually or physically "inferior," and he noted that they faced "often hostile" circumstances. Against those who overemphasized the influence of environment, however, Hewitt stressed the greater importance of "inherited traits or tendencies, abilities or capacities." He urged the Society of American Indians, a pan-Indian reform organization, to study "the peculiar cultural attainments of the various tribes and stocks of American Indians throughout the entire western hemisphere" to learn how best to promote its goal of Native advancement. If conveyed to Native students, the same study would convey ancestral cultures and instill "race pride." He spent his career compiling Iroquois texts, explaining the concepts they illustrated, and working on a Tuscarora grammar and dictionary. He also applied philology to other Native peoples, suggesting that the isolate Cayuse was related to Nootka and other Wakashan languages, for instance, and using language to refute the theory of a bureau archaeologist that Mayas were Polynesian in origin. Despite this taxonomic work, and despite his own dual convictions that language illustrated mental life and that different Native "stocks" possessed varying inherited traits, he cautioned against using grammar to trace racial ancestry. Aware of the pernicious uses to which such notions had been put, Hewitt was unequivocal in his essay on polysynthesis that Indians possessed no "peculiar construction of language . . . or 'plan of ideas.'"[2]

Hewitt confronted the studies of human descent and difference that had prevailed for the first century and more of the United States. That approach had begun with discrete assumptions about the way in which language indicated ancestry and that language reflected thought. Those convictions informed early European colonization, which, in turn, broadened and deepened, and eventually transformed, such theories. The sounds a people formed, the words they spoke, and the manner in which they arranged them inspired extensive projects to trace genealogies among Native groups and between them and the old world (or not). The aural and written evidence that colonizers, and more distant scholars benefiting from empire, found in language also impelled attempts to define how Native people thought, almost always in a way that highlighted ostensible differences between Native and Euro-American psychologies. At times, philosophers cast a "savage mind" that was but one stage in a universal scheme of human development; other times scholars imagined a racially particular and static "Indian mind." By the mid-nineteenth century, fixation upon Native sounds, Native thoughts, and Native blood produced an understanding of language as a crucial component in an expansive, extra-biological understanding of race. In the minds of some, it was race itself. Only the determined criticisms of physical ethnologists to establish race as a strictly biological category and, as importantly, the discoveries of philologists of the extent to which linguistic relation was unconnected to cultural inheritance overturned this view.

The contexts in which these theories arose were varied. In everyday inter-actions in and near Indian country, people strained to hear audible evidence of social boundaries. Native people, at one degree of remove or another and for a variety of motives, provided Euro-Americans with linguistic information. Native wives taught their husbands to form and distinguish Native sounds, Native consultants offered words to be scratched into lists in exchange for gifts, bilingual Native tutors explained grammatical processes to Euro-American students, and Native elders and orators sometimes shared traditions of earlier ages and past migrations and relations. Traders, settlers, or officials sometimes conveyed their linguistic impressions and information to scholars, but mis-sionaries provided most of the linguistic knowledge that philosophers used to construct theories about human descent and difference. By the mid-nineteenth century, federal explorers, military officers, and surveyors took on increasing importance in contributing to what was more and more recognized as a science of language. Frequently, these parties deliberately created close and mutually beneficial ties with philologists and, later, linguists, who asserted expertise on the significance of linguistic material that men, and occasionally women, in the field communicated. Philologists debated theories with one another, with ethnologists who preferred other methodologies (such as archaeological exca-vation, craniological measurement, or close study of customs and beliefs), and frequently with the broader public. Linguistic studies were esoteric in method, but scholars deliberately communicated their theories to a broader audience through addresses before learned societies, which were often published in those societies' transactions or, on rarer occasions, in their own right and exchanged for the similar volumes of other societies and scholars. Such studies were reviewed in periodicals, frequently producing debate among those who were not philologists, properly speaking, but who either felt their own exper-tise on the subject or who recognized the significance of philological theories for the administration of colonialism in the United States, which provided the basis for expanding settlement and economic development.

Understandings of Native languages helped to create a Euro-American philosophy and science of language, and much of the story that this book has traced has analogues in other parts of the world that experienced colonization. Throughout Africa, Asia, Australia, and elsewhere in the Americas, European empires sought linguistic means to exercise power, whether through immediate administrative control or more indirect cultural transformation, and they justified rule according to evolutionary or essentialist theories of linguistic-mental difference, and through stories of ancient population movements and resulting patterns of relatedness.

The study of Native languages in the United States partakes of this common history, but it cannot be understood apart from the sometimes constant, sometimes shifting priorities of U.S. colonialism. Theorizing a "savage mind" justified the hypothetically temporary rule of a "civilized" empire. Seeking evidence of linguistic diversity not only undergirded notions of savagery but also provided a more practical means to demarcate one Native group from another and establish what groups had authority to cede land. Fuller, and more favorable, understandings of Native grammatical organization justified an education program that, it was thought, would increase the assimilation of Native people and, in the minds of many, make the colonizing project simpler. The vastly increased Native-language transcription and translation project that resulted created entirely new understandings of the seemingly fixed difference of Native vocal organs and minds, which supported calls for removal. These were embodied understandings of language that reinforced developing notions of biological race; yet they supported an understanding of race that transcended physical characteristics. Even as physical ethnologists and others began to question the identity of languages and peoples, however, the War and Interior departments, and occasionally Congress, intensified efforts to collect linguistic information about Indians and use it as evidence of descent. Some officials hoped to use to create administratively convenient reservations and to anticipate, or dismiss the possibility of, threatening alliances. As the federal government sought to benefit from knowledge of linguistic relations in Native America, it implemented an assimilationist program—founded upon ideas that were simultaneously psychological and genealogical, evolutionary and racial—to eradicate Native languages.

Most of us recognize the distinction between language and biological race, but unexamined notions of the relationship between language and ancestry, language and psychology, and language and identity continue. Some scholars still point to language as supplementary evidence on human origins and migrations, especially when they corroborate other findings, such as the claim of a group of geneticists to have traced the Native population of the Americas to three distinct waves of migration from Asia. Supporters noted that this theory matched Joseph Greenberg's controversial tripartite classification of the languages of the Americas into relatively small Eskimo-Aleut and Nadene families and an immense and richly varied Amerind phylum that contains each of the hundreds of other Native languages in the hemisphere. Given many Native traditions of emergence, and the moral force that they provide to continuing adjudication of tribal claims, many Indians remain justifiably skeptical toward the ideological neutrality of these recent representations of Indian languages, which so clearly echo older theories.[3]

At the same time, the early twenty-first century marks a moment of renewed interest in the evolution and differentiation of language and the question of whether language shapes perception or cognition, with familiar answers to old questions gaining new authority from computer modeling, magnetic imaging, and other forms of evidence that possess scientific authority in the minds of researchers and the general public. As was the case in the eighteenth and nineteenth centuries, studies of indigenous languages have proven crucial to attempts to form comprehensive theories. Perhaps the clearest example of this trend can be found in work on Pirahã, a language spoken among people in the Amazon and unrelated to any other living language. Linguists have claimed that it lacks terms for colors and almost all numbers, and it might possess fewer phonemes than any other known language. In addition, Daniel Everett, an academically trained linguist and former missionary, has claimed that recursion—the capacity to embed units of meaning within units of meaning—is impossible in the language. If all this is true, as articles ranging from academic journals to respected general periodicals have stressed, Pirahã would disprove the theory that all human beings share a universal grammar (at least in that theory's most prominent current iteration). Besides meeting technical opposition from linguists, Everett's claim that the language lacks an essentially human trait has produced accusations of racism. Other scholars, however, have seized on his findings to reassert notions that all languages must have passed through similar stages in the distant past. From the sixteenth century through the present, Native languages have provided an effective platform for people with diverse motives to speak about human difference.[4]

Scientific trends regarding notions of language and race must be understood within the broader cultural history of colonialism. The past three decades have seen a simultaneous surge in calls to establish English as the official language of the United States and a new federal commitment to Native-language revitalization. Attention to the latter issue in the United

States has converged with broader attention to languages that colonial lega-
cies, nationalism, and globalization have endangered the world over, as
scholars estimate that about 90 percent of the world's 6,000 current languages
will no longer be spoken by 2100. Of the 400 languages estimated to have
been spoken in North America north of Mexico circa 1492, only about 5 percent of those Native languages are projected to survive six centuries of
European colonization. Congressional legislation in 1990 and 1992 reversed
longstanding federal efforts to accelerate this process by affirming Native
people's right to speak their ancestral languages in all public venues, including
federally funded schools, though financial support has been slight, and other
educational reforms have excluded Native elders who are often the only qualified teachers of Native languages.[5]

The relationships between these efforts and the history described in this
book are complex. On the one hand, the moral force of language revitalization
efforts in large part rests upon the conviction that what linguists describe as
language shift amounts to cultural loss, devastating to individuals severed
from their cultural inheritance, and harmful to humanity at large because the
disappearance of a language closes off a set of human possibilities. Languages,
in this view, represent frameworks that organize experience in culturally particular ways. Diversity is not superficial, as some supporters of universal
grammar might argue. Rather, in the words of W. Richard West (Southern
Cheyenne), founding director of the National Museum of the American
Indian, "In many ways, language determines thought." In some articulations
of this view, the linguistic-mental legacy is a product of education only; in
others, it is intertwined with ancestry. One might interpret such a view as an
adaptation of colonialist ideas of linguistic relativity and determinism that
have some of their deepest roots in the work of the philologists, missionaries,
and federal officials that this book has examined. Yet neither they nor more
recent linguists and anthropologists are necessarily the source for these ideas
among those working in Native communities to preserve and strengthen their
linguistic inheritances. Native people, like Euro-Americans, have long felt an
intimate connection between language, place, way of living, and one's sense of
self and community. Native efforts to sustain and revitalize their languages,
ironically, often appropriate old missionary texts that were produced for the
purpose of cultural transformation. Understandings of Native languages and
use of those languages have shaped and been shaped by histories of colonialism and race, but they remain open to redefinition, for ill and good.[6]

Abbreviations

Institutions

AAS	American Antiquarian Society, Worcester, MA
APS	American Philosophical Society, Philadelphia, PA
DPL	Burton Historical Collection, Detroit Public Library
Clements Library	William L. Clements Library, University of Michigan, Ann Arbor
HSP	Historical Society of Pennsylvania, Philadelphia
MHS	Massachusetts Historical Society, Boston
NYHS	New-York Historical Society, New York

Manuscript Collections

AAS Archives	AAS Archives, Correspondence and Documents, AAS
AAS Indians	Indians of North America, Miscellaneous Papers, 1620–1895, AAS
ABCFM Papers	Papers of the American Board of Commissioners for Foreign Missions, Houghton Library, Harvard University, Cambridge, MA
Atwater Letters	Caleb Atwater Letters and Drawings, AAS
Bartlett Papers	John Russell Bartlett Papers, John Carter Brown Library, Brown University, Providence, RI
Barton Papers	Benjamin Smith Barton Papers, 1778–1813, HSP
Cass Papers	Lewis Cass Papers, Clements Library

Delafield-Barton Collection	Violetta Delafield-Benjamin Smith Barton Collection, APS
Douglass Papers	David Bates Douglass Papers, Clements Library
Dreer Collection	Ferdinand J. Dreer Autograph Collection, HSP
Du Ponceau Collection	Peter Stephen Du Ponceau Collection, 1781–1844, APS
Du Ponceau Letters	Peter S. Du Ponceau Letters, Wisconsin State Historical Society, Madison
Du Ponceau Notebooks	Peter S. Du Ponceau, Notebooks on Philology, 9 vols., APS
Du Ponceau Papers	Peter Stephen Du Ponceau Papers, 1663–1844, HSP
Du Simitière Collection	Pierre Eugène Du Simitière Collection, LCP
Gallatin Papers	Albert Gallatin Papers, NYHS (microfilm)
Gratz Collection	Simon Gratz Collection, HSP
Heckewelder Communications	John Gottlieb Ernestus Heckewelder, "Communications to the Historical and Literary Committee of the American Philosophical Society, 1816–1821," APS
HLC Letter Books	Letter Books of the Historical and Literary Committee, 3 vols., APS
HLC Vocabularies	HLC Vocabularies and Miscellaneous Papers Pertaining to Indian Languages, APS
LeConte Papers	John L. LeConte Papers, APS
Letters to Scientists	Letters to Scientists, APS
Meeker Papers	Jotham Meeker Papers, Kansas State Historical Society, Topeka (microfilm)
Moravian Archives	Moravian Archives, Bethlehem, PA
Morton Papers (APS)	Samuel George Morton Papers, 1819–1850, Series I. Correspondence, APS
Morton Papers (LCP)	Samuel George Morton Papers, 1832–1862, Series I. Correspondence, LCP
OIALS	Records of the Office of Indian Affairs, Letters Sent, National Archives, Washington, DC (microfilm)
Pickering Papers	Timothy Pickering Papers, microfilm edition, 69 reels, MHS
Poinsett Papers	Joel Roberts Poinsett Papers, HSP

Schoolcraft Papers (DPL)	Henry R. Schoolcraft Papers, DPL
Schoolcraft Papers (LC)	Henry Rowe Schoolcraft Papers, Library of Congress, Washington, DC (microfilm)
Schoolcraft-Johnston Correspondence	Henry R. Schoolcraft–George Johnston Correspondence, DPL
Society Collection	HSP Autograph Collection, 1673–1981, HSP
Trowbridge Papers	Charles Christopher Trowbridge Papers, DPL
Trowbridge Materials	Charles C. Trowbridge's Miscellaneous Indian Research Materials, Trowbridge Papers
Turner Papers	William Wadden Turner Papers, 1838-1859, National Anthropological Archives, Smithsonian Institution, Washington, DC
WDLR	Letters Received by the Office of the Secretary of War Relating to Indian Affairs, 1800–1823, National Archives, Washington, DC (microfilm)
WDLS	Letters Sent by the Office of the Secretary of War Relating to Indian Affairs, 1800–1823, National Archives, Washington, DC (microfilm)
Williams Papers	Eleazer Williams Papers, Newberry Library, Chicago IL

Published Primary Sources

AAAS Memoirs	*Memoirs of the American Academy of Arts and Sciences*
AAAS Proc.	*Proceedings of the American Academy of Arts and Sciences*
AAS Proc.	*Proceedings of the American Antiquarian Society, 1812–1849* (Worcester, MA: American Antiquarian Society, 1912)
AAS Trans.	*Archaeologia Americana: Transactions and Collections of the American Antiquarian Society*
AES Trans.	*Transactions of the American Ethnological Society*
APA Trans.	*Transactions of the American Philological Association*
APS Proc.	*Proceedings of the American Philosophical Society*
APS Trans.	*Transactions of the American Philosophical Society*
ARBE	*Annual Report of the Bureau of Ethnology to the Secretary of the Smithsonian Institution*
ARSI	*Annual Report of the Board of Regents of the Smithsonian Institution, Showing the Operations, Expenditures, and Condition of the Institution for the Year*

Am. State Papers	*American State Papers, Class II. Indian Affairs,* 2 vols. (Washington, DC, 1834)
Barton, *New Views*	Benjamin Smith Barton, *New Views of the Origin of the Tribes and Nations of America,* 2nd ed. (Philadelphia, 1798)
Carver, *Travels*	Jonathan Carver, *Travels through the Interior Parts of North America, in the Years 1766, 1767, and 1768,* 2nd ed. (London, 1779)
Catlin, *Letters and Notes*	Geo. Catlin, *Letters and Notes on the Manners, Customs, and Condition of the North American Indians . . . Written during Eight Years' Travel amongst the Wildest Tribes of Indians in North America. In 1832, 33, 34, 35, 36, 37, 38, and 39,* 2 vols. (London, 1841)
Charlevoix, *Journal*	Pierre François Xavier de Charlevoix, *Journal of a Voyage to North-America. Undertaken by Order of the French King,* 2 vols. (London, 1761)
CNAE	U.S. Geographical and Geological Survey of the Rocky Mountain Region, *Contributions to North American Ethnology*
Du Ponceau, "Correspondence"	Peter S. Du Ponceau, "A Correspondence between the Rev. John Heckewelder, of Bethlehem, and Peter S. Du Ponceau, Esq., . . . Respecting the Languages of the American Indians," *HLC Trans.* 1 (1819)
Du Ponceau, *Dissertation*	Peter S. Du Ponceau, *A Dissertation on the Nature and Character of the Chinese System of Writing, in a letter to John Vaughan, Esq.* (Philadelphia, 1838)
Du Ponceau, "Report"	Peter S. Du Ponceau, "Report of the Corresponding Secretary to the Committee, of His Progress in the Investigation Committed to Him of the General Character and Forms of the Languages of the American Indians,—Read 12th Jan, 1819," *HLC Trans.* 1 (1819)
Early Western Travels	Reuben Gold Thwaites, ed. *Early Western Travels, 1748–1846,* 32 vols. (Cleveland: Arthur H. Clark, 1904–07)

Encyclopaedia Americana	*Encyclopaedia Americana: A Popular Dictionary of Arts, Sciences, Literature, History, Politics and Biography; Brought Down to the Present Time; Including a Copious Collection of Original Articles in American Biography; on the Basis of the Seventh Edition of the German* Conversations-Lexicon, ed. Francis Lieber, 13 vols. (Philadelphia, 1829–35)
Gallatin, "Synopsis"	Albert Gallatin, "A Synopsis of the Indian Tribes within the United States east of the Rocky Mountains, and in the British and Russian Possessions in North America," *AAS Trans.* 2 (1836)
Gallatin *Writings*	*The Writings of Albert Gallatin,* ed. Henry Adams, 3 vols. (Philadelphia, 1879)
GW Papers	*Papers of George Washington, Confederation Series,* ed. W. W. Abbott, 6 vols. (Charlottesville: University Press of Virginia, 1992–97)
Heckewelder, "History"	"An Account of the History, Manners and Customs of the Indian Nations Who Once Inhabited Pennsylvania and the Neighbouring States," in *HLC Trans.* 1 (1819)
Historical and Statistical Information	Henry R. Schoolcraft, *Information Concerning the History, Condition, and Prospects of the Indian Tribes of the United States: Collected and Prepared under the Direction of the Bureau of Indian Affairs, Department of the Interior, per Act of Congress of March 3d, 1847,* 6 vols. (Philadelphia, 1851–57)
HLC Trans.	*Transactions of the Historical and Literary Committee of the American Philosophical Society*
Howse, *Grammar*	Joseph Howse, *A Grammar of the Cree Language; with Which Is Combined an Analysis of the Chippeway Dialect* (London, 1844)
HSP Memoirs	*Memoirs of the Historical Society of Pennsylvania*
Humboldt, *Personal Narrative*	Alexander de Humboldt, *Personal Narrative of Travels to the Equinoctial Regions of the New Continent, during the Years 1799–1804,* 7 vols. (London, 1815–29)
Humboldt, *Political Essay*	Alexander de Humboldt, *Political Essay on the Kingdom of New Spain* (1811; New York: AMS Press, 1966)

James, *Account* Edwin James, *Account of an Expedition from Pittsburgh to the Rocky Mountains, Performed in the Years 1819, 1820 . . . under the Command of Maj. S. H. Long* (1823), in *Early Western Travels*, vols. 14–17

Jesuit Relations Reuben Gold Thwaites, ed., *The Jesuit Relations and Allied Documents: Travels and Explorations of the Jesuit Missionaries in New France*, 73 vols. (Cleveland: Burrows Brothers, 1896–1901)

Lafitau, *Customs* Joseph Francois Lafitau, *Customs of the American Indians Compared to the Customs of Primitive Times*, ed. William N. Fenton and Elizabeth L. Moore, 2 vols. (1724; Toronto: Champlain Society, 1977)

Le Page du Pratz, *History* Antoine Simon Le Page du Pratz, *The History of Louisiana, or of the Western Parts of Virginia and Carolina: Containing a Description of the Countries That Lye on Both Sides of the River Mississippi: With an Account of the Settlements*, 2 vols. (London, 1763)

MHS Coll. *Collections of the Massachusetts Historical Society*

NYHS Coll. *Collections of the New-York Historical Society*, ser. 1 (New York: AMS Press, 1974)

Prix Volney Joan Leopold, ed., *The Prix Volney*, vol. 2. *Early Nineteenth-Century Contributions to General and Amerindian Linguistics: Du Ponceau and Rafinesque* (Dordrecht: Kluwer Academic Publishers, 1999)

RIHS Coll. *Collections of the Rhode-Island Historical Society*

Smithsonian Contrib. *Smithsonian Contributions to Knowledge*

Schoolcraft, *Personal Memoirs* Henry R. Schoolcraft, *Personal Memoirs of a Residence of Thirty Years with the Indian Tribes on the American Frontiers, with Brief Notices of Passing Events, Facts, and Opinions, A.D. 1812 to A.D. 1842* (Philadelphia, 1851)

TJ, *Notes* Thomas Jefferson, *Notes on the State of Virginia*, ed. William Peden (Chapel Hill, NC, 1954)

TJ Papers Julian P. Boyd, ed., *The Papers of Thomas Jefferson* (Princeton, NJ: Princeton University Press, 1950–)

TJ Papers RS J. Jefferson Looney, ed., *The Papers of Thomas Jefferson: Retirement Series* (Princeton: Princeton University Press, 2004–)

TJ Writings	Andrew A. Lipscomb, ed. *The Writings of Thomas Jefferson,* 20 vols. (Washington: Thomas Jefferson Memorial Association, 1903–1905)
Williams, *Key*	Roger Williams, *A Key into the Language of America or, an Help to the Language of the Natives in That Part of America, Called New-England; Together, with Briefe Observations of the Customes, Manners and Worships, &c. of the Aforesaid Natives* (1643), in *RIHS Coll.* 1 (1827)
Zeisberger, "Grammar"	"A Grammar of the Language of the Lenni Lenape or Delaware Indians. Translated from the German ms. of the Late Rev. David Zeisberger," trans. Peter S. Du Ponceau, *APS Trans.* n.s. 3 (1830)
Zeisberger, "History"	Archer Butler Hulbert and William Nathaniel Schwarze, ed., *David Zeisberger's History of the Northern American Indians* (Ohio State Archaeological and Historical Society, 1910)

Published Secondary Sources

AHR	*American Historical Review*
EAS	*Early American Studies*
Handbook	Ives Goddard, ed., *Languages,* vol. 17, *Handbook of the North American Indians,* gen. ed. William C. Sturtevant (Smithsonian Institution, 1996)
JCS	*Journal of Cherokee Studies*
JER	*Journal of the Early Republic*
JHI	*Journal of the History of Ideas*
NEQ	*New England Quarterly*
PMHB	*Pennsylvania Magazine of History and Biography*
WMQ	*William and Mary Quarterly,* series 3

Notes

Introduction

1. Henry D. Thoreau, *The Maine Woods* (Boston, 1864), 139–40; Henry David Thoreau, *The Writings of Henry David Thoreau: Journal X, August 8, 1857–June 29, 1858*, ed. Bradford Torrey (Boston: Houghton Mifflin, 1906), 295. Thoreau perused John Pickering, ed., "A Dictionary of the Abenaki Language, in North America; by Father Sebastian Rasles," *AAAS Memoirs*, n.s. 1 (1833). On the journey, see Lisa Brooks, *The Common Pot: The Recovery of Native Space in the Northeast* (Minneapolis: University of Minnesota Press, 2008), 247–48. Joshua D. Bellin, "In the Company of Savagists: Thoreau's Indian Books and Antebellum Ethnology," *The Concord Saunterer*, n.s., 16 (2008): 1-32, stresses that Thoreau was in the mainstream of his era's ideas about Native people. On hearing as a historically constructed experience, see Sophia Rosenfeld, "On Being Heard: A Case for Paying Attention to the Historical Ear," *AHR* 116.2 (Apr. 2011): 316–34, esp. 319–26.

2. On the similarity–difference tension, see Nancy Shoemaker, *A Strange Likeness: Becoming Red and White in Eighteenth-Century North America* (New York: Oxford University Press, 2004), 3, 8; Joseph Errington, *Linguistics in a Colonial World: A Story of Language, Meaning and Power* (Malden, MA: Blackwell, 2008), viii, 3; Ann Fabian, *The Skull Collectors: Race, Science, and America's Unburied Dead* (Chicago: University of Chicago Press, 2010), 3.

3. "Constitution of the American Ethnological Society," *AES Trans.* 1 (1845), iii; TJ, *Notes*, 101; Howse, *Grammar*, v; William W. Warren, *History of the Ojibway People* (1887; St. Paul: Minnesota Historical Society Press, 1984), 61–62, 212.

4. Barton, *New Views*, xxiii–xxiv; H. F. Buckner, *A Grammar of the Maskoke or Creek Language, to Which Are Prefixed Lessons in Spelling, Reading, and Defining . . . Assisted by His Interpreter G. Herrod* (Marion, AL, 1860), 5.

5. Henry R. Schoolcraft, "Article V. Mythology, Superstitions and Languages of the North American Indians," *Literary and Theological Review* 2.5 (Mar. 1835): 96–121, at 117; Thomas L. McKenney to James Barbour, Nov. 15, 1825, OIALS, 2:235.

6. Peter S. Du Ponceau to John Pickering, Nov. 2, 1820, Du Ponceau Papers, Box 3; Charles Mackenzie, "The Missouri Indians: A Narrative of the Four Trading Expeditions to the Missouri, 1804–1805–1806, for the North-West Company" in *Les Bourgeois de la Compagnie du Nord-Ouest: Récits de voyages, lettres et rapports inédits relatifs au Nord-Ouest Canadien,* ed. L. R. Masson, vol. 1 (1889; New York: Antiquarian Press, 1960), 336–37. See also Bernard Cohn, *Colonialism and Its Forms of Knowledge: The British in India* (Princeton, NJ: Princeton University Press, 1996), chap. 2; Eric Cheyfitz, *Poetics of Imperialism: Translation and Colonization from* The Tempest *to* Tarzan, rev. ed. (Philadelphia: University of Pennsylvania Press, 1997); Maya Jasanoff, *Edge of Empire: Lives, Culture, and Conquest in the East, 1750–1850* (New York: Knopf, 2005), 313.

7. On language and colonialism, see Stephen J. Greenblatt, "Learning to Curse: Aspects of Linguistic Colonialism in the Sixteenth Century," in *Learning to Curse: Essays in Early Modern Culture* (London: Routledge, 1990); Cohn, *Colonialism and Its Forms of Knowledge,* chap. 2; Errington, *Linguistics in a Colonial World.* On language and sovereignty, see Tom Holm, J. Diane Pearson, and Ben Chavis, "Peoplehood: A Model for the Extension of Sovereignty in American Indian Studies," *Wicazo Sa Review* 18.1 (Spring 2003): 7–24, esp. 11–13; Thomas Belt and Margaret Bender, "Speaking Difference to Power: The Importance of Linguistic Sovereignty," in *Foundations of First Peoples' Sovereignty: History, Education and Culture,* ed. Ulrike Weithaus (New York: Peter Lang, 2007); Scott Richard Lyons, "There's No Translation for It: The Rhetorical Sovereignty of Indigenous Languages," in *Cross-Language Relations in Composition,* eds. Bruce Horner, Min-Zhan Lu, and Paul Kei Matsuda (Carbondale: Southern Illinois University Press, 2010). On translation, see David J. Silverman, "Indians, Missionaries, and Religious Translation: Creating Wampanoag Christianity on Seventeenth-Century Martha's Vineyard," *WMQ* 52.2 (Apr. 2005): 141–74. On European dependence upon indigenous knowledge in philology and anthropology, see Thomas R. Trautmann, *Languages and Nations: The Dravidian Proof in Colonial Madras* (Berkeley: University of California Press, 2006); Peter Pels and Oscar Salemink, "Introduction: Locating the Colonial Subjects of Anthropology," in *Colonial Subjects: Essays on the Practical History of Anthropology,* eds. Pels and Salemink (Ann Arbor: University of Michigan, 2000). On Native participation in political-ethnological debates, see Scott Michaelsen, *The Limits of Multiculturalism: Interrogating the Origins of American Anthropology* (Minneapolis: University of Minnesota Press, 1999); Maureen Konkle, *Writing Indian Nations: Native Intellectuals and the Politics of Historiography, 1827–1863* (Chapel Hill: University of North Carolina Press, 2002); Paige Raibmon, *Authentic Indians: Episodes of Encounter from the Late-Nineteenth-Century Northwest Coast* (Durham, NC, 2005).

8. Peter S. Du Ponceau to Thomas Jefferson, Dec. 11, 1817 HLC Letter Books, 1:61–63; Pierre-Louis Moreau de Maupertuis, "Réflexions philosophiques sur l'origine des langues et la signification des mots," in *Maupertuis, Turgot et Maine de Biran sur*

l'origine du langage, ed. Ronald Grimsley (Geneva: Librarie Droz, 1971), 31; Zeisberger, "Grammar," 97. See also Du Ponceau, "Correspondence," 371–72.

9. Du Ponceau, "Report," xxxiv–xxxv.

10. James H. Merrell, *Into the American Woods: Negotiators on the Pennsylvania Frontier* (New York: Norton, 1999); Shoemaker, *A Strange Likeness,* stress increasing understanding and hardening lines in the eighteenth century. On translation as an idealized way to counteract that trend, cf. Patrick M. Erben, *A Harmony of the Spirits: Translation and the Language of Community in Early Pennsylvania* (Chapel Hill: University of North Carolina Press, 2012), 301–23, esp. 317. On intercultural communication more broadly, see Edward G. Gray and Norman Fiering, eds., *The Language Encounter in the Americas, 1492–1800: A Collection of Essays* (New York: Berghahn Books, 2000); Richard Cullen Rath, *How Early America Sounded* (Ithaca, NY: Cornell University Press, 2003), chap. 5. On literacy and lines of difference, see Walter D. Mignolo, *The Darker Side of the Renaissance: Literacy, Territoriality, and Colonization* (Ann Arbor: University of Michigan Press, 1995); Jill Lepore, *The Name of War: King Philip's War and the Origins of American National Identity* (New York: Vintage, 1999), chap. 1–2; Phillip H. Round, *Removable Type: Histories of the Book in Indian Country, 1663–1880* (Chapel Hill: University of North Carolina Press, 2010).

11. Edward G. Gray, *New World Babel: Languages and Nations in Early America* (Princeton, NJ: Princeton University Press, 1999), 7, 160–67, is a stimulating history of ideas about Native languages to about 1820, which, due to its endpoint, finds that few Americans saw any direct link between language and race. See also Julie Tetel Andresen, *Linguistics in America, 1769–1924* (London: Routledge, 1990); Laura J. Murray, "Vocabularies of Native American Languages: A Literary and Historical Approach to an Elusive Genre," *American Quarterly* 53.4 (December 2001): 590–623; Sarah Rivett, *The Science of the Soul in Colonial New England* (Chapel Hill: University of North Carolina Press, 2011), 125–72; Erben, *Harmony of the Spirits,* 1–61, 301–23. On language and race, see Maurice Olender, *The Languages of Paradise: Race, Religion, and Philology in the Nineteenth Century* (1989; Cambridge, MA: Harvard University Press, 2008); Trautmann, *Languages and Nations,* 220–25; Tuska Benes, *In Babel's Shadow: Language, Philology, and the Nation in Nineteenth-Century Germany* (Detroit: Wayne State University Press, 2008), 189–239.

12. On science and empire, "Nature and Empire: Science and the Colonial Enterprise," *Osiris,* 2nd ser., 15 (2000); "Focus: Colonial Science," *Isis* 96.1 (Mar. 2005): 52–87; James Delbourgo and Nicholas Dew, eds., *Science and Empire in the Atlantic World* (New York: Routledge, 2008). For older work on attitudes and expansionism, see Roy Harvey Pearce, *Savagism and Civilization: A Study of the Indian and the American Mind* (1953; Baltimore: Johns Hopkins University Press, 1971); Bernard W. Sheehan, *Seeds of Extinction: Jeffersonian Philanthropy and the American Indian* (Chapel Hill: University of North Carolina Press, 1973), 15–88; Robert F. Berkhofer, *White Man's Indian: Images of the American Indian from Columbus to the Present* (New York: Vintage, 1979); Reginald Horsman, *Race and Manifest Destiny: The Origins of American Racial Anglo-Saxonism* (Cambridge, MA: Harvard University Press, 1981).

13. For Native shaping of the terms of interaction, see Kathleen Du Val, *The Native Ground: Indians and Colonists in the Heart of the Continent* (Philadelphia: University of Pennsylvania Press, 2006); Pekka Hämäläinen, *The Comanche Empire* (New Haven, CT: Yale University Press, 2008); Michael Witgen, *An Infinity of Nations: How the Native New World Shaped Early America* (Philadelphia: University of Pennsylvania Press, 2012). On Native people as producers of knowledge, see Nancy Shoemaker, "How Indians Got to Be Red," *AHR* 102.3 (June 1997): 625–44; Susan Scott Parrish, *American Curiosity: Cultures of Natural History in the Colonial British Atlantic World* (Chapel Hill: University of North Carolina Press, 2002), 215–58; Marcy Norton, "Tasting Empire: Chocolate and the Internalization of Mesoamerican Aesthetics," *AHR* 111.3 (2006): 660–91. On Native participation in political-cultural debates, see note 7, above.

14. On historical perceptions of race, see Mark M. Smith, *How Race Is Made: Slavery, Segregation, and the Senses* (Chapel Hill: University of North Carolina Press, 2006); Matthew Frye Jacobson, *Whiteness of a Different Color: European Immigrants and the Alchemy of Race* (Cambridge, MA: Harvard University Press, 2001). On the social construction of race, see Shoemaker, *A Strange Likeness;* John Wood Sweet, *Bodies Politic: Negotiating Race in the American North, 1730–1830* (2003; Philadelphia: University of Pennsylvania Press, 2006). Michael Banton's *Racial Theories,* 2nd ed. (New York: Cambridge University Press, 1998), usefully distinguishes aspects of race (as "lineage," "type," "designation," etc.) that are usually conflated. On extra-physical understandings of race, see Rebecca Anne Goetz, *The Baptism of Early Virginia: How Christianity Created Race* (Baltimore: Johns Hopkins University Press, 2012); Roxann Wheeler, *The Complexion of Race: Categories of Difference in Eighteenth-Century British Culture* (Philadelphia: University of Pennsylvania Press, 2000); Dror Wahrman, *The Making of the Modern Self: Identity and Culture in Eighteenth-Century Britain* (New Haven, CT: Yale University Press, 2004), 116–22; George W. Stocking, Jr., *Victorian Anthropology* (New York: Free Press, 1987), 63–64, 106, 235; Matthew Frye Jacobson, *Barbarian Virtues: The United States Encounters Foreign People at Home and Abroad, 1876–1917* (New York: Hill and Wang, 2000), 101–72.

15. D. M. Dooling, ed., *The Sons of the Wind: The Sacred Stories of the Lakota* (1985; Norman: University of Oklahoma Press, 2000), 121–22 (quote). For the Onondaga, Navajo, Crow, and Choctaw traditions, see, respectively, John Norton, *The Journal of Major John Norton, 1816,* eds. Carl F. Klinck and James J. Talman (Toronto: Champlain Society, 1970), 98; Washington Matthews, *Navaho Legends* (Boston, 1897), 143; Robert H. Lowie, *The Crow Indians* (1935; Lincoln: University of Nebraska Press, 2004), 128; Catlin, *Letters,* 2:128.

16. Gray, *New World Babel,* has examined many of the themes discussed in this and the following paragraph, though its emphases and interpretations differ from my own. See also Anthony Pagden, *Fall of Natural Man: The American Indian and the Origins of Comparative Ethnology,* rev. ed. (Cambridge: Cambridge University Press, 1986), 15–23, 127–31, 179–91, 201–8; Umberto Eco, *The Search for the Perfect Language* (Malden, MA: Blackwell, 1995), 86–91; Mignolo, *Darker Side of the Renaissance;* David B. Paxman,

Voyage into Language: Space and the Linguistic Encounter, 1500–1800 (Burlington, VT: Ashgate, 2003). On travelers' use of these ideas, see Anthony Pagden, *European Encounters with the New World* (New Haven, CT: Yale University Press, 1993), 126–40.

17. On the range of European language thought in this era, see Peter Burke, *Languages and Communities* in Early Modern Europe (New York: Cambridge University Press, 2004); Hannah Dawson, *Locke, Language and Early-Modern Philosophy* (New York: Cambridge University Press, 2007), 91–182; Matthew Lauzon, *Signs of Light: British and French Theories of Communication, 1648–1789* (Ithaca, NY: Cornell University Press, 2010). On hopes of repairing the damage of Babel, see Erben, *Harmony of the Spirits,* 1–15, 104–26, 301–23; Rhodri Lewis, *Language, Mind and Nature: Artificial Languages in England from Bacon to Locke* (Cambridge: Cambridge University Press, 2007). On Native-language learning and the new science, see Rivett, *Science of the Soul,* 125–72. On eighteenth- and nineteenth-century philosophy, see also Hans Aarsleff, *From Locke to Saussure: Essays on the Study of Language and Intellectual History* (Minneapolis: University of Minnesota Press, 1982); Ulrich Ricken, *Linguistics, Anthropology and Philosophy in the French Enlightenment: Language Theory and Ideology,* trans. Robert E. Norton (London: Routledge, 1994); Thomas R. Trautmann, *Aryans and British India* (1997; New Delhi: Yoda Press, 2003), 28–98; Benes, *In Babel's Shadow,* chap. 1–2; Avi Lifschitz, *Language and Enlightenment: The Berlin Debates of the Eighteenth Century* (New York: Oxford University Press, 2012).

18. Peter Fidler, "Journal of a Journey with the Chepewyans or Northern Indians, to the Slave Lake, & to the East & West of the Slave River, in 1791 & 2," in *Journals of Samuel Hearne and Philip Turnor,* J. B. Tyrrell, ed. (Toronto: Champlain Society, 1934), 543. On environmentalism and race, see Joyce E. Chaplin, *Subject Matter: Technology, the Body, and Science on the Anglo-American Frontier* (Cambridge, MA: Harvard University Press, 2001) 116–80, 323; Richard H. Popkin, "The Philosophical Basis of Eighteenth-Century Racism," in *Racism in the Eighteenth Century,* ed. Harold E. Pagliaro (Cleveland, OH: Press of Case Western Reserve University, 1973); Ronald L. Meek, *Social Science and the Ignoble Savage* (Cambridge: Cambridge University Press, 1976); Wahrman, *Making of the Modern Self,* 83–126. For a concise view of early racial taxonomies, see Ivan Hannaford, *Race: The History of an Idea in the West* (Baltimore: John Hopkins University Press, 1996), 187–233, esp. 202–13.

19. For "hereditary heathenism," see Goetz, *Baptism of Early Virginia,* 10. On race and lineage, see Nicholas Hudson, "From 'Nation' to 'Race': The Origin of Racial Classification in Eighteenth-Century Thought," *Eighteenth-Century Studies* 29.3 (1996): 247–64; Colin Kidd, *The Forging of Races: Race and Scripture in the Protestant Atlantic World, 1600–2000* (New York, 2006), 21–22, 26–27; Thomas C. Holt, María Elena Martínez, and Guillaume Aubert, "Forum: Purity of Blood and the Social Order," *WMQ* 61.3 (July 2004): 435–520. On eighteenth-century hereditarian but extra-bodily understandings of "race," see; Wahrman, *Making of the Modern Self,* 116–22; William Max Nelson, "Making Men: Enlightenment Ideas of Racial Engineering," *AHR* 115.5 (Dec. 2010): 1364–94, esp. 1365. On nineteenth-century ideas of race, see Stocking, *Victorian Anthropology;* Trautmann, *Aryans and British India,*

131–216. See also Bruce Dain, *A Hideous Monster of the Mind: American Race Theory in the Early Republic* (Cambridge, MA: Harvard University Press, 2002); Horsman, *Race and Manifest Destiny;* Robert E. Bieder, *Science Encounters the Indian, 1820–1880: The Early Years of American Ethnology* (Norman: University of Oklahoma Press, 1986).

20. Errington, *Linguistics in a Colonial World,* provides an excellent overview. See also Mignolo, *Darker Side of the Renaissance;* Cohn, *Colonialism and Its Forms of Knowledge,* chap. 2; Johannes Fabian, *Language and Colonial Power: The Appropriation of Swahili in the Former Belgian Congo, 1880–1938* (Cambridge: Cambridge University Press, 1986); Vicente L. Rafael, *Contracting Colonialism: Translation and Christian Conversion in Tagalog Society under Early Spanish Rule* (Durham, NC: Duke University Press, 1993); Sara Pugach, *Africa in Translation: A History of Colonial Linguistics in Germany and Beyond, 1814–1945* (Ann Arbor: University of Michigan Press, 2012).

21. On colonization and linguistic studies, see note 16, above. On Atlantic patterns of knowledge, see Parrish, *American Curiosity;* James Delbourgo, "The Newtonian Slave Body: Racial Enlightenment in the Atlantic World," *Atlantic Studies* 9.2 (June 2012): 185–207; Kariann Akemi Yokota, *Unbecoming British: How the United States Became a Postcolonial Nation* (New York: Oxford University Press, 2011), 153–225.

22. On whites' ambivalent identification with Indians and "savagery," see Philip J. Deloria, *Playing Indian* (New Haven, CT: Yale University Press, 1998). On Indians and an American *volk,* see Helen Carr, *Inventing the American Primitive: Politics, Gender, and the Representation of Native American Literary Traditions, 1789–1936* (New York: New York University Press, 1996), 108–9; Gray, *New World Babel,* 165. On philology, ethnology, and nationalism, see Benes, *Babel's Shadow,* 113–57; Benedict Anderson, *Imagined Communities: Reflections on the Origin and Spread of Nationalism,* rev. ed. (London: Verso, 1991), 144–46; Martin Thom, *Republics, Nations and Tribes* (London: Verso, 1995). On the U.S. institutionalization of linguistics and anthropology, see Andresen, *Linguistics in America;* Regna Darnell, "Toward Consensus on the Scope of Anthropology: Daniel Garrison Brinton and the View from Philadelphia," *Philadelphia and the Development of Americanist Archaeology,* eds. Don Fowler and David R. Wilcox (Tuscaloosa: University of Alabama Press, 2003); Curtis M. Hinsley, *The Smithsonian and the American Indian: Making a Moral Anthropology in Victorian America* (1981; Washington: Smithsonian Institution Press, 1994).

23. On languages and identities in the early republic, see Birte Pfleger, "'Miserable Germans' and Fries's Rebellion: Language, Ethnicity, and Citizenship in the Early Republic," *EAS* 2.2 (Fall 2004): 343–61; Friederike Baer, *The Trial of Frederick Eberle: Language, Patriotism, and Citizenship in Philadelphia's German Community, 1790 to 1830* (New York: New York University Press, 2008). On nationalism and linguistic projects, see David Simpson, *The Politics of American English, 1776–1850* (New York: Oxford University Press, 1986); Kenneth Cmiel, *Democratic Eloquence: The Fight over Popular Speech in Nineteenth-Century America* (Berkeley: University of California Press, 1991); Jill Lepore, *A is for American: Letters and Other Characters in the Newly United States* (New York: Knopf, 2002). Timothy Blum Cassedy, "The Character of Communication, 1790–1810" (Ph.D. diss., New York University, 2012) traces Anglo-American debates.

On semiotic concerns, see Christopher Looby, *Voicing America: Language, Literary Form, and the Origins of the United States* (Chicago: University of Chicago Press, 1996); Philip Gura, *The Wisdom of Words: Language, Theology, and Literature in the New England Renaissance* (Middletown, CT: Wesleyan University Press, 1981); John Howe, *Language and Political Meaning in Revolutionary America* (Amherst: University of Massachusetts Press, 2004). On print culture, see Round, *Removable Type;* Oz Frankel, *States of Inquiry: Social Investigations and Print Culture in Nineteenth-Century Britain and the United States* (Baltimore: Johns Hopkins University Press, 2006). On voluntary associations, see Albrecht Koschnik, *"Let a Common Interest Bind Us Together": Associations, Partisanship, and Culture in Philadelphia* (Charlottesville: University of Virginia Press, 2007), 205–27; Johann N. Neem, *Creating a Nation of Joiners: Democracy and Civil Society in Early National Massachusetts* (Cambridge, MA: Harvard University Press, 2008), 82–90. On evangelical impulses in the Second Great Awakening, see Richard Lee Rogers, "'A Bright and New Constellation': Millennial Narratives and the Origins of American Foreign Missions," in *North American Foreign Missions, 1810–1914,* ed. Wilbert R. Shenk (Grand Rapids, MI: William B. Eerdmans, 2004). On struggles over learned authority, see Andrew J. Lewis, *Democracy of Facts: Natural History in the Early Republic* (Philadelphia: University of Pennsylvania Press, 2011).

24. Charles Caldwell, *Thoughts on the Original Unity of the Human Race* (New York, 1830), 138; E. G. S., "American Ethnology," *American Review, A Whig Journal Devoted to Politics and Literature* 3.4 (Apr. 1849): 385–98, at 385–86. On the American Revolution heightening racial theorization, see George M. Frederickson, *The Black Image in the White Mind: The Debate on Afro-American Character and Destiny, 1817–1914* (1971; Middletown, CT: Wesleyan University Press, 1987), 2–3; Dain, *Hideous Monster of the Mind,* vii–ix; Sweet, *Bodies Politic,* 3–5, 271–311. Patrick Griffin, *American Leviathan: Empire, Nation, and Revolutionary Frontier* (New York: Hill and Wang, 2007); Peter Silver, *Our Savage Neighbors: How Indian War Transformed Early America* (New York: Norton, 2008), stress popular racialization in the revolutionary era. On understandings of Native difference, see Sheehan, *Seeds of Extinction,* 15–116; Chaplin, *Subject Matter;* Bieder, *Science Encounters the Indian.* On broader ethnological debates, see Horsman, *Race and Manifest Destiny;* Jacobson, *Barbarian Virtues,* 101–72. On ethnology as education, see Hinsley, *Smithsonian and the American Indian,* 34–57, 83–117, 145–83; Steven Conn, *Museums and American Intellectual Life, 1876–1926* (Chicago: University of Chicago Press, 1998), 75–114; Frankel, *States of Inquiry,* 1–23, 235–301. On narratives of progress, see Carol Sheriff, *The Artificial River: The Erie Canal and the Paradox of Progress, 1817–1862* (New York: Hill and Wang, 1996); Alan Trachtenberg, *The Incorporation of America: Culture and Society in the Gilded Age* (New York: Hill and Wang, 1982).

25. Eric Hinderaker, *Elusive Empires: Constructing Colonialism in the Ohio Valley, 1673–1800* (New York: Cambridge University Press, 1997), xi–xiv, 185–86, 226–67, at 267, characterizes the U.S. "empire of liberty" as "voluntarily constituted, racially defined, indefinitely expansive, and democratically governed." The terms "liberal democratic colonialism" in Jodi A. Byrd, *The Transit of Empire: Indigenous Critiques of*

Colonialism (Minneapolis: University of Minnesota Press, 2011), 228; and "settler empire" in Aziz Rana, *The Two Faces of American Freedom* (Cambridge, MA: Harvard University Press, 2010), 3, 8–14, convey similar points. On democratic institutions in this context, see Berkhofer, *White Man's Indian*, 143–66; Brendan C. Lindsay, *Murder State: California's Native American Genocide, 1846–1873* (Lincoln: University of Nebraska Press, 2012). See also Jeffrey Ostler, *The Plains Sioux and U.S. Colonialism from Lewis and Clark to Wounded Knee* (New York: Cambridge University Press, 2004); Gray H. Whaley, *Oregon and the Collapse of* Illahee: *U.S. Empire and the Transformation of an Indigenous World, 1792–1859* (Chapel Hill: University of North Carolina Press, 2010); Lisa Ford, *Settler Sovereignty: Jurisdiction and Indigenous People in America and Australia, 1788–1836* (Cambridge, MA: Harvard University Press, 2010).

26. On the central importance of acknowledging the violence of U.S. colonization, see Ned Blackhawk, *Violence over the Land: Indians and Empires in the Early American West* (Cambridge, MA: Harvard University Press, 2006). The most comprehensive overview of U.S. policy aims is Francis Paul Prucha, *The Great Father: The United States Government and the American Indians* (Lincoln: University of Nebraska Press, 1984). See also Stephen J. Rockwell, *Indian Affairs and the Administrative State in the Nineteenth Century* (New York: Cambridge University Press, 2010).

27. The best overview of seventeenth- and eighteenth-century colonization from a Native perspective is Daniel K. Richter, *Facing East from Indian Country: A Native History of Early America* (Cambridge, MA: Harvard University Press, 2001). For an overview of the West in the early nineteenth century, which focuses especially on intermarriage, see Anne F. Hyde, *Empires, Nations, and Families: A History of the North American West, 1800–1860* (2011; New York: HarperCollins, 2012). On Native incorporation of Euro-Americans, see Du Val, *Native Ground;* Witgen, *Infinity of Nations.* On missions and ethnogenesis, see Gary Clayton Anderson, *The Indian Southwest, 1580–1830: Ethnogenesis and Reinvention* (Norman: University of Oklahoma Press, 1999), 67–92; Julius H. Rubin, *Tears of Repentance: Christian Indian Identity and Community in Colonial Southern New England* (Lincoln: University of Nebraska Press, 2013). On competing Native visions of "race," see David J. Silverman, *Red Brethren: The Brothertown and Stockbridge Indians and the Problem of Race in Early America* (Ithaca, NY: Cornell University Press, 2010); Gregory Evans Dowd, *A Spirited Resistance: The North American Indian Struggle for Unity, 1745–1815* (Baltimore: John Hopkins University Press, 1992). On prophecy and tribal identity, see Gregory E. Smoak, *Ghost Dances and Identity: Prophetic Religion and American Indian Ethnogenesis in the Nineteenth Century* (Berkeley: University of California Press, 2006).

28. Samuel L. Knapp, *Lectures on American Literature, with Remarks on Some Passages of American History* (New York, 1829), 25. On the linguistic effects of colonization, see Colin G. Calloway, *New Worlds for All: Indians, Europeans and the Remaking of Early America* (Baltimore: Johns Hopkins University Press, 1997), 172–77; John K. Thornton, *A Cultural History of the Atlantic World, 1250–1820* (Cambridge: Cambridge University Press, 2012), 315–41. On Michif in particular, see Peter Bakker, *A Language*

of Our Own: The Genesis of Michif, the Mixed Language of the Canadian Métis (New York: Oxford University Press, 1997).

29. Francis La Flesche, *The Middle Five: Indian Boys at School* (1900; Boston, 1909), xiv–xv. See also Ruth Spack, *America's Second Tongue: American Indian Education and the Ownership of English, 1860–1900* (Lincoln: University of Nebraska Press, 2002).

30. *Historical and Statistical Information,* 4:666.

31. Horatio Hale to Brantz Meyer, Oct. 1843, in Meyer, *Mexico as It Was and as It Is* (New York, 1844), 382.

1. Language Encounters and the "Mind of Man, while in the Savage State"

1. Chrestien Le Clercq, *New Relation of Gaspesia: With the Customs and Religion of the Gaspesian Indians,* trans. and ed. William F. Ganong (Toronto: Champlain Society, 1910), 311; Cadwallader Colden, *The History of the Five Indian Nations of Canada, Which Are Dependent on the Province of New-York, and Are a Barrier between the English and the French in That Part of the World,* 2nd ed. (London, 1750), 15; James G. Swan, *The Northwest Coast; or, Three Years' Residence in Washington Territory* (New York, 1857), 308–9.

2. Thomas Harriot, *A Briefe and True Report of the New Found Land of Virginia* (London, 1588), [22]; George Percy, "Observations by Master George Percy, 1607," in *Narratives of Early Virginia, 1606–1625,* ed. Lyon Gardiner Tyler (New York: Scribner's, 1907), 12; Charlevoix, *Journal,* 1:299; Edward Umfreville, *The Present State of Hudson's Bay: Containing a Full Description of That Settlement, and the Adjacent Country; and Likewise of the Fur Trade* (London, 1790), 199. On colonists' experience of Native voices, see Richard Cullen Rath, *How Early America Sounded* (Ithaca, NY: Cornell University Press, 2003), chap. 5; Glenda Goodman, "'But They Differ from Us in Sound:' Indian Psalmody and the Soundscape of Colonialism," *WMQ* 69.4 (Oct. 2012): 793–822. The linguistic observations in China and Africa are quoted in Liam Mathew Brockey, *Journey to the East: The Jesuit Mission to China, 1579–1724* (Cambridge, MA: Harvard University Press, 2007), 245–71, at 245; David B. Paxman, *Voyage into Language: Space and the Linguistic Encounter, 1500–1800* (Burlington, VT: Ashgate, 2003), 42. For another important comparison, see Patricia Palmer, *Language and Conquest in Early Modern Ireland: English Renaissance Literature and Elizabethan Imperial Expansion* (Cambridge: Cambridge University Press, 2001). See also Even Hovdhaugen, "The Great Travelers and the Study of 'Exotic' Languages,'" in *History of the Language Sciences . . . An International Handbook on the Evolution of the Study of Language from the Beginnings to the Present,* vol. 1, ed. Sylvain Auroux et al. (Berlin: Walter de Gruyter, 2000). On Europe in this era, see Peter Burke, *Languages and Communities in Early Modern Europe* (Cambridge: Cambridge University Press, 2004).

3. [Louis Armond de Lom d'Arce,] Baron Lahontan, *New Voyages to North-America, containing an Account of the Several Nations of That Vast Continent,* 2 vols.

(London, 1703), 2:287; Williams, *Key,* 18; Louis Hennepin, *A New Discovery of a Vast Country in America,* ed. Reuben Gold Thwaites, 2 vols. (1698; Chicago: McClurg, 1903), 1:215; "From the 'New World,' by Johan De Laet, 1625, 1630, 1633, 1640," in *Narratives of New Netherland, 1609–1664,* ed. J. Franklin Jameson (New York: Charles Scribner's Sons, 1909), 57; William Stith, *History of the First Discovery and Settlement of Virginia: Being an Essay toward a General History of This Colony* (Williamsburg, VA, 1747), 13. On observations of North American linguistic diversity, see Edward G. Gray, *New World Babel: Languages and Nations in Early America* (Princeton, NJ: Princeton University Press, 1999), 8–27. See also the excellent collection Edward G. Gray and Norman Fiering, eds., *The Language Encounter in the Americas, 1492–1800: A Collection of Essays* (New York: Berghahn Books, 2000). On Lahontan, see H. Christoph Wolfart, "Lahontan's Bestseller," *Historiographia Linguistica* 16.1/2 (1989): 1–24.

   4. William Wood, *New England's Prospect,* ed. Alden T. Vaughan (Amherst: University of Massachusetts Press, 1977), 110; "The Humble Address of the Governour and Councill of Your Majesty's Prouince of New Yorke and Dependenceys [Aug. 6, 1691]," in *The Documentary History of the State of New-York,* ed. E. B. O'Callaghan, 4 vols. (Albany, 1849–1851), 1:409; Titus King, *Narrative of Titus King of Northampton, Mass.: A Prisoner of the Indians in Canada, 1755–1758* (Hartford: Connecticut Historical Society, 1938), 17; William M. Beauchamp, ed., *Moravian Journals Relating to Central New York, 1745–1766* (Syracuse, NY: Dehler Press, 1916), 187. On language and transgression, see Anthony Pagden, *European Encounters with the New World* (New Haven, CT: Yale University Press, 1993), 40–41. On language and identity more broadly, see Burke, *Languages and Communities;* Teresa L. McCarty and Ofelia Zepeda, "Native Americans," in *Handbook of Language and Ethnic Identity,* 2 vols., eds. Joshua A. Fishman and Ofelia García (New York: Oxford University Press, 2010), 2:323–39.

   5. Williams, *Key,* 17. On "contact zones," see Mary Louise Pratt, *Imperial Eyes: Travel Writing and Transculturation,* rev. ed. (London: Routledge, 2008), 7–8; Joseph Errington, *Linguistics in a Colonial World: A Story of Language, Meaning, and Power* (Malden, MA: Blackwell, 2008), 2–3, 20 n.1. On improved communication heightening perceived difference, see Jane T. Merritt, "Metaphor, Meaning, and Misunderstanding: Language and Power on the Pennsylvania Frontier," in *Contact Points: American Frontiers from the Mohawk Valley to the Mississippi, 1750–1830,* eds. Andrew R. L. Cayton and Fredrika J. Teute (Chapel Hill: University of North Carolina Press, 1998), 86–87; James H. Merrell, *Into the American Woods: Negotiators on the Pennsylvania Frontier* (New York: Norton, 1999), 38–40; Robert Michael Morrissey, "'I Speak It Well': Language, Cultural Understanding, and the End of a Missionary Middle Ground in Illinois Country, 1673–1712," *EAS* 9.3 (Fall 2011):617–48. On commonalities across empires, see Anthony Pagden, *Lords of All the World: Ideologies of Empire in Spain, Britain and France, c.1500–c.1800* (New Haven, CT: Yale University Press, 1995); Richard Grove, *Green Imperialism: Colonial Expansion, Tropical Edens, and the Origins of Environmentalism* (New York: Cambridge University Press, 1995); Jorge Cañizares-Esguerra, *Puritan Conquistadors: Iberianizing the Atlantic, 1550–1700*

(Stanford, CA: Stanford University Press, 2006), 9; "AHR Forum: Entangled Empires in the Atlantic World," *AHR* 112.3 (June 2007): 710–99. Cf. Eric Hinderaker, *Elusive Empires: Constructing Colonialism in the Ohio Valley, 1673–1800* (Cambridge: Cambridge University Press, 1997); J. H. Elliott, *Empires of the Atlantic World: Britain and Spain in America, 1492–1830* (New Haven, CT: Yale University Press, 2006).

6. For early labeling of the Native languages of North America as "the language of America," "American languages" and "the American language," see Williams, *Key; Jesuit Relations,* 10:120; Cotton Mather, *The Triumphs of the Reformed Religion in America: The Life of the Renowned John Eliot* (Boston, 1691), 90.

7. Williams, *Key,* 135; Thomas Campanius Holm, "A Short Description of the Province of New Sweden, now called, by the English, Pennsylvania, in America," trans. Peter S. Du Ponceau, *HSP Memoirs* 3 (1834), 152–53; John W. Jordan, ed., "James Kenny's 'Journal to ye Westward,' 1758–1759," *PMHB* 37.1 (Jan. 1913): 395–449, at 420; idem, "Journal of James Kenny, 1761–1767," ibid. 37.2 (Apr. 1913): 152–201, at 169. Laura J. Murray, "Vocabularies of Native American Languages: A Literary and Historical Approach to an Elusive Genre," *American Quarterly* 53.4 (Dec. 2001): 590–623, esp. 596–99, discusses this dynamic. On varieties of early communication, see James Axtell, "Babel of Tongues: Communicating with the Indians in Eastern North America," in Gray and Fiering, eds., *Language Encounter,* 18–29; Allan R. Taylor, "Nonspeech Communications Systems," in *Handbook.* On trade, see Richard White, *The Middle Ground: Indians, Empires, and Republics in the Great Lakes Region, 1650–1815* (New York: Cambridge University Press, 1991), 75, 94–104; Daniel K. Richter, *Facing East from Indian Country: A Native History of Early America* (Cambridge, MA: Harvard University Press, 2001), 42–53, 174–79; Joseph M. Hall, Jr., *Zamumo's Gifts: Indian-European Exchange in the Colonial Southeast* (Philadelphia: University of Pennsylvania Press, 2009).

8. James Rosier, "A True Relation of the Voyage of Captaine George Waymouth, 1605," in *Early English and French Voyages chiefly from Hakluyt, 1534–1608,* ed. Henry S. Burrage (New York: Scribner's, 1906), 371; Hennepin, *A New Discovery,* 136; George Dixon, *A Voyage Round the World; but More Particularly to the North-west Coast of America: Performed in 1785, 1786, 1787, and 1788, in the King George and Queen Charlotte* (London, 1789), 172, 227–28.

9. John Lawson, *A New Voyage to Carolina,* ed. Hugh Talmadge Lefler (Chapel Hill: University of North Carolina Press, 1967), 35–36. See also "Copy of a Family Register in the handwriting of Conrad Weiser . . . ," trans. Hiester H. Muhlenberg, in *Collections of the Historical Society of Pennsylvania* 1 (1853), 2–3; John Long, *Voyages and Travels of an Indian Interpreter and Trader Describing the Manners and Customs of the North American Indians; with an Account of the Posts Situated on the River Saint Lawrence, Lake Ontario, &c. April 10 1768–Spring, 1782,* in *Early Western Travels,* 36–37, 61. On intermarriage and language learning, see Laura J. Murray, "Fur Traders in Conversation," *Ethnohistory* 50.2 (Spring 2003): 285–314. See also White, *Middle Ground,* 56–75, 214–15; Susan Sleeper-Smith, *Indian Women and French Men: Rethinking Cultural Encounter in the Western Great Lakes* (Amherst: University of Massachusetts Press, 2001).

10. John White, *The Planters Plea, or the Grounds of Plantations Examined, and Vsual Objections Answered* . . . (London, 1630), 52–53; James Isham, *James Isham's Notes and Observations on Hudson's Bay, 1743 and Notes and Observations on a Book Entitled* A Voyage to Hudson's Bay in the Dobbs Galley, *1749*, eds. E. E. Rich and A. M. Johnson (Toronto: Champlain Society, 1949), 178. See also Karen O. Kupperman, *Indians and English: Facing Off in Early America* (Ithaca, NY: Cornell University Press, 2000), 41–43; Murray, "Fur Traders in Conversation," 285–86.

11. Le Jeune in *Jesuit Relations*, 5:113, 115; Lafitau, *Customs*, 2:261–62. On pidgins and jargons, see Axtell, "Babel of Tongues," 30–40; Ives Goddard, "The Use of Pidgins and Jargons on the East Coast of North America," in Gray and Fiering, eds., *Language Encounter in the Americas*, 61, 72; Emanuel J. Drescher, *Mobilian Jargon: Linguistic and Sociohistorical Aspects of a Native American Pidgin* (New York: Oxford University Press, 1997), 257–64.

12. Marc Lescarbot, *The History of New France* (Toronto: Champlain Society, 1914), 125; "Letter of Reverend Jonas Michaëlius, 1628," in Jameson, ed., *Narratives of New Netherland*, 128; [Charles de Rochefort], *The History of the Caribby-Islands, viz, Barbados, St Christophers, St Vincents, Martinico, Dominico, Barbouthos, Monserrat, Mevis, Antego, &c . . . with a Caribbian Vocabulary*, trans. John Davies (London, 1666), 259, 261. On creating new languages, see Johannes Megapolensis, "A Short Account of the Mohawk Indians (1644)," Jameson, ed., *Narratives of New Netherland*, 172–73; Peter Mårtensson Lindheström, *Geographia Americae, with an Account of the Delaware Indians, Based on Surveys and Notes Made in 1654–1656*, ed. and trans. Amandus Johnson (Philadelphia: Swedish Colonial Society, 1925), 203–4. On "sociolinguistic buffer," see Drescher, *Mobilian Jargon*, 348.

13. Le Page du Pratz, *History*, 1:144; Carver, *Travels*, 414–16, at 416; Alexander Walker, *An Account of a Voyage to the North West Coast of America in 1785 and 1786*, eds. Robin Fisher and J. M. Bumsted (Seattle: University of Washington Press, 1982), 88–89. Paul W. Mapp, *The Elusive West and the Contest for Empire, 1713–1763* (Chapel Hill: University of North Carolina Press, 2011), 201–32, examines linguistic diversity and geographic ignorance as intertwined problems for Europeans.

14. Goddard, "Use of Pidgins and Jargons," 66, makes the compelling argument that those forms of speech were partially responsible for Euro-American stereotypes of Indian languages with few words and little morphology or syntax. Cf. George Colpitts, "'Animated Like Us by Commercial Interests': Commercial Ethnology and Fur Trade Descriptions in New France, 1660–1760," *Canadian Historical Review* 83.3 (Sept. 2002): 305–37, esp. 306, for traders contradicting eighteenth-century philosophical assumptions.

15. For an excellent overview of Native attraction to Christianity, see Richter, *Facing East*, 79–90. On Native linguistic mediation of Puritanism and Catholicism, see, respectively, David J. Silverman, "Indians, Missionaries, and Religious Translation: Creating Wampanoag Christianity on Seventeenth-Century Martha's Vineyard," *WMQ* 52.2 (Apr. 2005): 141–74; Tracy Neal Leavelle, *The Catholic Calumet: Colonial Conversions in French and Indian North America* (Philadelphia: University of Pennsylvania Press, 2012), 97–125. Linford D. Fisher, *The Indian Great Awakening:*

Religion and the Shaping of Native Cultures in Early America (New York: Oxford University Press, 2012), 8, urges "religious engagement" and "affiliation" over the Euro-centric and misleadingly totalizing "conversion." On the missionary context for European ideas about Native languages, see Anthony Pagden, *Fall of Natural Man: The American Indian and the Origins of Comparative Ethnology*, rev. ed. (Cambridge: Cambridge University Press, 1986), 179–81, 197–205; Walter D. Mignolo, *The Darker Side of the Renaissance: Literacy, Territoriality, and Colonization* (Ann Arbor: University of Michigan Press, 1995); Sarah Rivett, *The Science of the Soul in Colonial New England* (Chapel Hill: University of North Carolina Press, 2011), 125–72; Matthew Lauzon, *Signs of Light: British and French Theories of Communication, 1648–1789* (Ithaca, NY: Cornell University Press, 2010), 67–101.

16. Le Jeune in *Jesuit Relations*, 14:125; John Gambold, "A Short Account Concerning the Labours of the Brethren among the Heathen in General," [n.d.], Box 3500, folder 17, Moravian Archives. On Protestant–Catholic missionary-translation similarities, see Silverman, "Indians, Missionaries, and Religious Translation," 173–74. Cf. James Axtell, *The Invasion Within: The Contest of Cultures in Colonial North America* (New York: Oxford University Press, 1985), 71–267; Gray, *New World Babel*, 28–84.

17. Michael P. Clark, ed., *The Eliot Tracts: With Letters from John Eliot to Thomas Thorowgood and Richard Baxter* (Westport, CT: Praeger, 2003), 391, 85, 271. For a discussion of Native religious questions, see Kristina Bross, *Dry Bones and Indian Sermons* (Ithaca, NY: Cornell University Press, 2004), 84–111. On Native Puritan communities, see Jean M. O'Brien, *Dispossession by Degrees: Indian Land and Identity in Natick, Massachusetts, 1650–1790* (New York: Cambridge University Press, 1997); David J. Silverman, *Faith and Boundaries: Colonists, Christianity, and Community among the Wampanoag Indians of Martha's Vineyard, 1600–1871* (New York: Cambridge University Press, 2005).

18. Biard in *Jesuit Relations*, 2:219, 11, 221; Le Jeune in ibid., 7:57, 63, 61; Aulneau in ibid., 68:299. On Jesuit centralization and networks, see J. Gabriel Martínez-Serna, "Procurators and the Making of the Jesuits' Atlantic Network," in *Soundings in Atlantic History: Latent Structures and Intellectual Currents, 1500–1830* (Cambridge, MA: Harvard University Press, 2009). The best accounts of how missionaries learned Native languages focus on Jesuits. See Margaret J. Leahy, "'Comment peut un muet prescher l'évangile?': Jesuit Missionaries and the Native Languages of New France," *French Historical Studies* 19.1 (Spring 1995): 105–32; Rüdiger Schreyer, "Take Your Pen and Write: Learning Huron: A Documented Historical Sketch," in . . . *and the Word Was God: Missionary Linguistics and Missionary Grammar*, ed. Even Hovdhaugen (Münster: Nodus Publikationen, 1996); Aliocha Maladavsky, "The Problematic Acquisition of Indigenous Languages: Practices and Contentions in Missionary Specialization in the Jesuit Province of Peru (1568–1640)," in *The Jesuits II: Cultures, Sciences, and the Arts, 1540–1773*, eds. John W. O'Malley, et al. (Toronto: University of Toronto Press, 2006); Morrissey, "I Speak It Well."

19. Gabriel Sagard, *The Long Journey to the Country of the Hurons*, ed. George M. Wrong, trans. H. H. Langton (Toronto: Champlain Society, 1939), 73; Josiah Cotton, "Vocabulary of the Massachusetts (or Natick) Indian Language," ed. John Pickering,

in *MHS Coll.*, 3rd ser., 2 (1830), 242; Bressani in *Jesuit Relations*, 39:105; Le Mercier in ibid., 14:11; Le Jeune in ibid., 7:27. On gesture in language learning, see Céline Carayon, "Beyond Words: Nonverbal Communication, Performance, and Acculturation in the Early French-Indian Atlantic" (Ph.D. diss., College of William and Mary, 2010), 179–232.

20. Brebeuf in *Jesuit Relations*, 10:117; Lalemant in ibid., 46:71; Bressani in ibid., 39:103, 119; Rasle in ibid., 67:143, 145, 133. Ibid., 5:115, 46:69, express the view that Iroquoian and Siouan languages are grammatically similar to Algonquian languages. See also Mariann Mithun, "Overview of General Characteristics," in *Handbook*, 138–42; Victor Egon Hanzeli, *Missionary Linguistics in New France: A Study of Seventeenth- and Eighteenth-Century Descriptions of American Indian Languages* (The Hague: Mouton, 1969), 65–66. On grammatical texts and debates over universal grammar, see Hannah Dawson, *Locke, Language and Early-Modern Philosophy* (New York: Cambridge University Press, 2007), 41–63, esp. 53–63.

21. Gabriel Sagard, *"Dictionnaire de la langue Huron"* in *Histoire du Canada et voyages que les freres mineurs recollects y ont faicts pour la conuersion des infidelles*, 4 vols. (1636; Paris, 1866), 4:10; Le Jeune in *Jesuit Relations*, 7:29.

22. Biard in *Jesuit Relations*, 2:219; Brebeuf in ibid., 10:105, 91; Pierre Joseph Marie Chaumonot, *La Vie du R.P. Pierre Joseph Marie Chaumonot, de la compagnie de Jesus, missionnaire dans la Nouvelle France, ecrite par lui-même par Ordre de son Supérieur, l'an 1688* (New York, 1858), 53; Lafitau, *Customs*, 2:253; John Eliot, *The Indian Grammar Begun: or, an Essay to Bring the Indian Language into Rules, for the Help of Such as Desire to Learn the Same, for the Furtherance of the Gospel among Them* (1666), ed. John Pickering, *MHS Coll.*, 2nd ser., 9 (1822), 312. See also Schreyer, "Take Your Pen and Write," 103–5.

23. Le Jeune in *Jesuit Relations*, 7:63; Brebeuf in ibid., 15:65; Rasles in ibid., 67:146. On the dictionary and raid, see "Biographical Memoir of Father Rasles," *MHS Coll.*, 2nd ser., 8 (1819): 253–54. On the production of Native-language texts in this period, see Phillip H. Round, *Removable Type: Histories of the Book in Indian Country* (Chapel Hill: University of North Carolina Press, 2010), 23–39.

24. Brebeuf in *Jesuit Relations*, 10:259; David Brainerd, *Mirabilia Dei inter Indicos, or the Rise and Progress of a Remarkable Work of Grace amongst a Number of the Indians in the Provinces of New-Jersey and Pennsylvania* (Philadelphia, [1745]), 228; Corinna Dally-Starna and William A. Starna, eds. and trans., *Gideon's People: Being a Chronicle of an American Indian Community in Colonial Connecticut and the Moravian Missionaries Who Served There*, 2 vols. (Lincoln: University of Nebraska Press, 2009), 1:533. For Catholic and Protestant examples of lists of "missing" words, see Sagard, *Long Journey*, 74; Brainerd, *Mirabilia Dei inter Indicos*, 228. Pagden, *European Encounters with the New World*, 127, discusses the significance of "anti-lexica." On religious translation, see Silverman, "Indians, Missionaries, and Religious Translation"; Leavelle, *Catholic Calumet*, 97–125; John Steckley, "The Warrior and the Lineage: Jesuit Use of Iroquoian Images to Communicate Christianity," *Ethnohistory* 39.4 (Autumn, 1992): 478–509. For comparative perspectives, see Alan Durston, *Pastoral Quechua: The History of*

Christian Translation in Colonial Peru, 1550–1650 (Notre Dame, IN: University of Notre Dame Press, 2007); William F. Hanks, *Converting Words: Maya in the Age of the Cross* (Berkeley: University of California Press, 2010). On Native Moravian communities, see Jane T. Merritt, *At the Crossroads: Indians and Empires on a Mid-Atlantic Frontier, 1700–1763* (Chapel Hill: University of North Carolina Press, 2007), 89–166; Rachel Wheeler, *To Live upon Hope: Mohicans and Missionaries in the Eighteenth-Century Northeast* (Ithaca, NY: Cornell University Press, 2008), 67–173.

25. Le Jeune in *Jesuit Relations*, 7:21; Biard in ibid., 2:11, 13, 221; Brainerd, *Mirabilia Dei inter Indicos*, 228–29. Biard accepted the "tentative racial . . . hierarchy," which stressed that Native health inhibited intellectual development, described in Joyce Chaplin, *Subject Matter: Technology, the Body, and Science on the Anglo-American Frontier, 1500–1676* (Cambridge, MA: Harvard University Press, 2001), 8–9, 22. Carole Blackburn, *Harvest of Souls: The Jesuit Missions and Colonialism in North America, 1632–1650* (Montreal: McGill-Queens University Press, 2000), 133–34, stresses that Jesuits constructed savagery as a "rigid" category that would remain "permanent" without their own intervention. Cf. Gray, *New World Babel*, 5, which suggests that seventeenth-century writers saw Native languages as "comparable to other vernacular tongues." Rivett, *Science of the Soul*, 125–72, observes interests in and the racializing function of universal language in seventeenth-century New England. On Moravian missionary engagement in universal language and pansophic projects, see Patrick M. Erben, *Harmony of the Spirits: Translation and the Language of Community in Early Pennsylvania* (Chapel Hill: University of North Carolina Press, 2012), 1–61, 301–23.

26. Eliot, *Indian Grammar Begun*, 252, 272; Cotton Mather, *Magnalia Christi Americana, or, the Ecclesiastical History of New-England, from Its First Planting, in the Year 1620, unto the Year of Our Lord 1698*, 2 vols. (1702; Hartford, 1853), book 3, 3rd part, 1:561; "Letter-Book of Samuel Sewall," *MHS Coll.* 6th ser., 1 (1886), 400–403, at 401. See also Zeisberger, "Grammar," 97. Chaplin, *Subject Matter*, 293, stresses that Eliot interpreted Indians as possessing "peculiar" representation of the world. Rivett, *Science of the Soul*, 144, 169, describes the racial logic of Eliot and Mather.

27. Lafitau, *Customs*, 261, 264, 267; Jonathan Edwards, Jr., *Observations on the Language of the Muhhekaneew Indians* (New Haven, CT, 1788), 3. On Lafitau, see Pagden, *Fall of Natural Man*, 204–9. Cf. Schreyer, "Take Your Pen and Write," 110, which suggests that it was the "vagueness and lack of detail" of missionaries' linguistic descriptions that "stimulated 18th century theoretical history of language." Kenneth Pieter Minkema, "The Edwardses: A Ministerial Family in Eighteenth-Century New England" (Ph.D. diss., University of Connecticut, 1988), 406, notes this use of Mohican in Edwards's diary.

28. Le Page du Pratz, *History*, 2:127

29. Zeisberger, "History," 96; Lawson, *New Voyage to Carolina*, 239;. On the history of treaty councils, see William N. Fenton, "Structure, Continuity, and Change in the Process of Iroquois Treaty Making," in *The History and Culture of Iroquois Diplomacy: An Interdisciplinary Guide to the Treaties of the Six Nations and Their League*, eds. Francis Jennings, et al. (Syracuse, NY: Syracuse University Press, 1985). The best accounts of

treaty councils are Richter, *Facing East,* 129–49; Merrell, *Into the American Woods,* 253–301. On diplomacy more broadly, see Patricia Galloway, "Talking with Indians: Interpreters and Diplomacy in French Louisiana," in *Race and Family in the Colonial South,* eds. Winthrop D. Jordan and Sheila L. Skemp (Jackson: University Press of Mississippi, 1987); Merritt, "Metaphor, Meaning, and Misunderstanding"; Kathleen Du Val, *The Native Ground: Indians and Colonists in the Heart of the Continent* (Philadelphia: University of Pennsylvania Press, 2006), 88–90.

30. "Indian Explanation of a Treaty at Casco Bay, 1727," in *Dawnland Encounters: Indians and Europeans in Northern New England,* ed. Colin G. Calloway (Hanover, NH: University Press of New England, 1991), 117; "An Indian Conference," Sept. 8–10, 1762, in *The Papers of Sir William Johnson,* vol. 10, eds. Milton W. Hamilton and Albert B. Corey (Albany: University of the State of New York, 1951), 505. On falsification, see David L. Ghere, "Mistranslations and Misinformation on the Maine Frontier, 1725–1755," *American Indian Culture and Research Journal* 8.4 (1984): 3–26. On the use of writing and wampum in treaties, see also Michael K. Foster, "Another Look at the Function of Wampum in Iroquois-White Councils," in Jennings et al., eds., *History and Culture of Iroquois Diplomacy;* Merrell, *Into the American Woods,* 187–97; Nancy Shoemaker, *A Strange Likeness: Becoming Red and White in Eighteenth-Century North America* (New York: Oxford University Press, 2004), 61–81. On nativism in this era, see Gregory Evans Dowd, *A Spirited Resistance: The North American Indian Struggle for Unity, 1745–1815* (Baltimore: John Hopkins University Press, 1992); Alfred A. Cave, *Prophets of the Great Spirit: Native American Revitalization Movements in Eastern North America* (Lincoln: University of Nebraska Press, 2006).

31. Edward Porter Alexander, ed., *The Journal of John Fontaine: An Irish Huguenot Son in Spain and Virginia, 1710–1719* (Williamsburg, VA: Colonial Williamsburg Foundation, 1972), 93; Edward P. Hamilton, ed. and trans., *Adventure in the Wilderness: The American Journals of Louis Antoine de Bougainville, 1756–1760* (Norman: University of Oklahoma Press, 1964), 243; Carl Van Doren and Julian P. Boyd, eds., *Indian Treaties Printed by Benjamin Franklin* (Philadelphia: Historical Society of Pennsylvania, 1938), 4, 33. Lawson, *New Voyage to Carolina,* 233, also stresses Native expectations to speak only their own language.

32. Lafitau, *Customs,* 263; Brebeuf in *Jesuit Relations,* 10:259; Zeisberger, "History," 95.

33. Brebeuf in *Jesuit Relations,* 10:257; James Adair, *The History of the American Indians,* ed. Kathryn E. Holland Braund (1775; Tuscaloosa: University of Alabama Press, 2005), 114; Zeisberger, "History," 142, 97; Colden, *History of the Five Indian Nations,* 14–15; [Pierre Maillard], *An Account of the Customs and Manners of the Micmakis and Maricheets Savage Nations, Now Dependent on the Government of Cape-Breton* (London, 1758), 35. Pagden, *Fall of Natural Man,* 180, notes that some Spanish observers believed that formal speech registers indicated Indians' social fragmentation.

34. Brebeuf in *Jesuit Relations,* 10:257; Alexander Henry, *Travels and Adventures in Canada and the Indian Territories, between the Years 1760 and 1776, in Two Parts* (New York, 1809), 75. On the use of metaphor in treaty councils, see "Glossary of Figures of

Speech in Iroquois Political Rhetoric," in Jennings et al., eds., *History and Culture of Iroquois Diplomacy;* Merritt, "Metaphor, Meaning, and Misunderstanding." For accounts of this interest, see Edward G. Gray, "The Making of Logan, the Mingo Orator," in *Language Encounter in the Americas*, eds. Gray and Fiering, esp. 258; Sandra M. Gustafson, *Eloquence Is Power: Oratory and Performance in Early America* (Chapel Hill: University of North Carolina Press, 2000), 111–39, esp. 111, each of which stress Native–European diplomacy as the context for eighteenth-century ideas of Indian eloquence. Cf. Laura J. Murray, "Joining Signs with Words: Missionaries, Metaphors, and the Massachusett Language," *NEQ* 74.1 (Mar. 2001): 62–93, at 63; Lauzon, *Signs of Light*, 67–101, which examine missionary origins of ideas of eloquence and metaphor. For critical readings, see David Murray, *Forked Tongues: Speech, Writing and Representation in North American Indian Texts* (Bloomington: Indiana University Press, 1991), 41, 44; Philip J. Deloria, *Playing Indian* (New Haven, CT: Yale University Press, 1998), 32–34.

35. Van Doren and Boyd, eds., *Indian Treaties*, 252, 45, 142; William Johnson to Earl of Hillsborough, Aug. 20, 1769, in O'Callaghan, ed., *Documentary History of the State of New York*, 2: 946. See also Van Doren and Boyd, ed., *Indian Treaties*, 162–63, 187–88, 197, 224, 255. James H. Merrell, "'I Desire All That I Have Said ... May Be Taken down Aright': Revisiting Teedyuscung's 1756 Treaty Council Speeches," *WMQ* 63.4 (Oct. 2006): 777–826, suggests triangulating Franklin's collection with different manuscript sources. On this era of negotiation, see Merrell, *Into the American Woods*, 276–301; Alan Taylor, *The Divided Ground: Indians, Settlers, and the Northern Borderland of the American Revolution* (New York: Knopf, 2006), 3–104; Leonard J. Sadosky, *Revolutionary Negotiations: Indians, Empires, and Diplomats in the Founding of America* (Charlottesville: University of Virginia Press, 2009), 31–58.

36. Zeisberger, "History," 96, 143; Milton W. Hamilton, ed., "Guy Johnson's Opinions on the American Indian," *PMHB* 77.3 (July 1953): 311–27, at 325. On Zeisberger's ambiguous role in the War for Independence, see Dowd, *Spirited Resistance*, 84–85; Hinderaker, *Elusive Empires*, 180.

37. Sir William Johnson, "Extracts of Some Letters, from Sir William Johnson Bart. to Arthur Lee, M.D.F.R.S. on the Customs, Manners, and Language of the Northern Indians of America," *Philosophical Transactions of the Royal Society of London* 63 (1773–1774): 142–48, at 147; Adair, *History of the American Indians*, 114; Colden, *History of the Five Indian Nations*, 14–15. See also Lauzon, *Signs of Light*, 130.

38. William Robertson, *The History of America* (1792; London: Routledge, 1996), 2:93. On the slow emergence of a temporal concept of "savagery," see Margaret T. Hodgen, *Early Anthropology in the Sixteenth and Seventeenth Centuries* (1964; Philadelphia: University of Pennsylvania Press, 1971), 330-31, 433-71. On the broader importance of travel literature from the Americas, see also Ronald L. Meek, *Social Science and the Ignoble Savage* (Cambridge: Cambridge University Press, 1976), 37–67, esp. 67; Pagden, *Fall of Natural Man*, 119–209, esp. 179–81, 191, 198–201, 209; David Paxman, "Adam in a Strange Country: Locke's Language Theory and Travel Literature," *Modern Philology* 92.4 (May 1995): 460–81. Pagden, *European Encounters*

with the New World, 83–86, stresses the dual insistence on the necessity of empirical observation and the philosophical value of distance. On Atlantic networks in this era, see Susan Scott Parrish, *American Curiosity: Cultures of Natural History in the Colonial British Atlantic World* (Chapel Hill: University of North Carolina Press, 2002); James Delbourgo and Nicholas Dew, eds., *Science and Empire in the Atlantic World* (New York: Routledge, 2008); Caroline Winterer, "Where Is America in the Republic of Letters?," *Modern Intellectual History* 9.3 (Nov. 2012): 597–623. For an excellent collection of essays on the multifarious iterations of a common set of eighteenth-century studies of human beings and society, see Larry Wolff and Marco Cipolloni, eds., *The Anthropology of the Enlightenment* (Palo Alto, CA: Stanford University Press, 2007). Sankar Muthu, *Enlightenment against Empire* (Princeton, NJ: Princeton University Press, 2003), 273, acknowledges that "the egalitarian assumption of a shared humanity . . . lay at the heart of a number of manifestly inegalitarian imperialist arguments."

39. John Locke, *An Essay Concerning Human Understanding,* 7th ed., 2 vols. (London, 1715–1716), 2: 119, 266, 33. For Locke's reliance on travel accounts, see Paxman, "Adam in a Strange Country." On language as convention in the seventeenth century, see Rhodri Lewis, *Language, Mind and Nature: Artificial Languages in England from Bacon to Locke* (Cambridge: Cambridge University Press, 2007), 6–22, 222–29. On Locke, see Dawson, *Locke, Language, and Early-Modern Philosophy.*

40. Etienne Bonnot de Condillac, *Essay on the Origin of Human Knowledge,* trans. and ed. Hans Aarsleff (Cambridge: Cambridge University Press, 2001), 113, 151, 79, 197, 178, 180; idem, *The Logic of Condillac,* ed. Daniel N. Robinson (Washington, DC: University Publications of America, 1977), 62. See also Aarsleff, "Introduction," in Condillac, *Essay,* xxxi–xxxiv; Hans Aarsleff, "The Tradition of Condillac: The Problem of the Origin of Language and the Debate in the Berlin Academy before Herder," in *From Locke to Saussure: Essays on the Study of Language and Intellectual History* (Minneapolis: University of Minnesota Press, 1982); Avi Lifschitz, "The Arbitrariness of the Linguistic Sign: Variations on an Enlightenment Theme," *JHI* 73.4 (Oct. 2012): 537–57, esp. 548–50. On language, hearing, and modernity, see Sophia Rosenfeld, "On Being Heard: A Case for Paying Attention to the Historical Ear," *AHR* 116.2 (Apr. 2011): 316–34, esp. 321; Richard Bauman and Charles L. Briggs, *Voices of Modernity: Language Ideologies and the Politics of Inequality* (New York: Cambridge University Press, 2003), 72–121.

41. On the debate over the "mutual emergence of language, the mind, and society," see Avi Lifschitz, *Language and Enlightenment: The Berlin Debates of the Eighteenth Century* (New York: Oxford University Press, 2012), chap. 1. See also Ulrich Ricken, *Linguistics, Anthropology and Philosophy in the French Enlightenment: Language Theory and Ideology,* trans. Robert E. Norton (London: Routledge, 1994); Nicholas Phillipson, "Language, Sociability, and History: Some Reflections on the Foundations of Adam Smith's Science of Man," in *Economy, Polity, and Society: British Intellectual History, 1750–1950,* eds. Stefan Collini, Richard Whatmore, and Brian Young (New York: Cambridge University Press, 2000). On conjectural history more broadly, see Meek, *Social Science and the Ignoble Savage,* 5–36; Pagden, *Fall of Natural Man,* 146–209,

esp. 197–99; Joseph S. Lucas, "The Course of Empire and the Long Road to Civilization: North American Indians and Scottish Enlightenment Historians," *Explorations in Early American Culture* 4 (2000): 166–190; J. G. A. Pocock, *Barbarians, Savages, and Empires,* vol. 4 of *Barbarism and Religion* (Cambridge: Cambridge University Press, 2005), 157–226, 269–93.

42. Jean-Jacques Rousseau, "Discourse on the Origin and Foundations of Inequality among Men" (1755), in *The First and Second Discourses,* ed. Roger D. Masters (New York: St Martin's Press, 1964), 123–24; Adam Smith, "Considerations Concerning the First Formation of Languages, &c. &c." in *Lectures on Rhetoric and Belles Lettres,* ed. by J. C. Bryce (Indianapolis: Liberty Fund, 1985), 204–5; Charles Marie de La Condamine, *Relation abrégée d'un voyage fait dans l'interieur de l'Amerique méridionale* (Paris, 1745), 54; Robertson, *History of America* 2:93–94. On intermixture and linguistic improvement, see Smith, "Considerations," 220–22. On savage languages generally, see Gray, *New World Babel,* 85–111; Pagden, *European Encounters with the New World,* 126–40; Rudiger Schreyer, "'Savage' Languages in Eighteenth-Century Theoretical History of Language," in *Language Encounter in the Americas;* David B. Paxman, "Language and Difference: The Problem of Abstraction in Eighteenth-Century Language Study," *JHI* 54 (1993): 19–36. On La Condamine, see Neil Safier, *Measuring the New World: Enlightenment, Science and South America* (Chicago: University of Chicago Press, 2009).

43. Hugh Blair, *Lectures on Rhetoric and Belles-Lettres,* 2nd. ed. (1785; Carbondale: Southern Illinois University Press, 2003), 58, 60–62. See also Jean-Jacques Rousseau, *Essay on the Origin of Languages Which Treats of Melody and Musical Imitation,* in *Two Essays on the Origin of Language,* eds. John H. Moran and Alexander Gode (Chicago: University of Chicago Press, 1966), 12–19. On Blair and Ossian, see Meek, *Social Science and the Ignoble Savage,* 177–85. Michael West, "Thoreau and the Language Theories of the French Enlightenment," *English Literary History* 51.4 (Winter 1984): 747–70, at 758, provides Blair's publishing figures.

44. Rousseau, *Discourse,* 123; James Beattie, *The Theory of Language, in Two Parts: Part I. Of the Origin and General Nature of Language; Part II. Of Universal Grammar* (London, 1788), 56; James Burnet, Lord Monboddo, *Of the Origin and Progress of Language,* 2nd ed., 6 vols. (1774; New York: Garland, 1970), 1: 508, 539, 538, 502–03, 480, 483. Ibid., 558, 568–69, asserts that Delaware was "the most perfect" of any barbarous language but that it was overly complicated.

45. Court de Gébelin, *Histoire naturelle de la parole, ou précis de l'origine du langage & de la grammaire universelle; extrait du* Monde Primitif (Paris, 1776); Charles de Brosses, *Traité de la formation méchanique des langues et des principes physiques de l'étymologie* (1765), 1:xiii–xiv; [Charles Marie de La Condamine], *An Account of a Savage Girl, Caught Wild in the Woods of Champagne* (Edinburgh, 1768), ix–x, xviii. La Condamine, *Relation abrégée,* 66, addresses Brazil. On de Brosses's debt to Lafitau, see Pagden, *Fall of Natural Man,* 204. See also Aarsleff, *Study of Language in England,* 33–36; Lifschitz, "Arbitrariness of the Linguistic Sign," 554.

46. [George-Louis Leclerc, comte de Buffon], *Histoire naturelle par Buffon,* vol. 3 (Paris, 1799), 187–88; La Condamine, *Account of a Savage Girl,* xviii; Charles Linné

[Linnaeus], *A General System of Nature, through the Three Grand Kingdoms of Animals, Vegetables and Minerals: Systematically Divided into Their Several Classes, Orders, Genera, Species and Varieties, with Their Habitations, Manners, Economy, Structure and Peculiarities,* trans. William Turton (Swansea, UK, 1800), 1:9; Monboddo, *Origin and Progress of Language,* 1:270; Charles White, *An Account of the Regular Gradation in Man, and in Different Animals and Vegetables; and from the Former to the Latter* (London, 1799), 67–69, at 68; Adair, *History,* 119. The anatomical study is Peter Camper, "Account of the Organs of Speech of the Orang Outang," *Philosophical Transactions of the Royal Society of London* 69 (1779): 139–59. See also Phillip R. Sloan, "The Idea of Racial Degeneracy in Buffon's *Histoire Naturelle,*" in *Racism in the Eighteenth Century,* ed. Harold E. Pagliaro (Cleveland, OH: Press of Case Western Reserve University, 1973); Ivan Hannaford, *Race: The History of an Idea in the West* (Baltimore: John Hopkins University Press, 1996), 195-205; Robert Wokler, "The Ape Debates in Enlightenment Anthropology," *Studies on Voltaire and the Eighteenth Century* 192 (1980): 1164–75, esp. 1174; Lifschitz, *Language and Enlightenment,* 165-70. For a description of the debate over the American environment, see Gilbert Chinard, "Eighteenth Century Theories on America as a Human Habitat," *APS Proc.* 91 (1947): 27–57; Jorge Cañizares-Esguerra, *How to Write the History of the New World: Histories, Epistemologies, and Identities in the Eighteenth-Century Atlantic World* (Stanford, CA: Stanford University Press, 2001).

47. Rousseau, *Essay,* 5; Robertson, *History of America,* 30, 52, 48. See also Nicholas Hudson, "From 'Nation' to 'Race': The Origin of Racial Classification in Eighteenth-Century Thought," *Eighteenth-Century Studies* 29.3 (1996): 247–64, esp. 250, 252; Richard H. Popkin, "The Philosophical Basis of Eighteenth-Century Racism," in Pagliaro, ed., *Racism in the Eighteenth Century,* 249, 256 n. 9

48. Johann Gottfried von Herder, "Treatise on the Origin of Language (1772)," in *Philosophical Writings,* trans. and ed. Michael J. Forster (New York: Cambridge University Press, 2002), 117–18; James Dunbar, *Essays on the History of Mankind in Rude and Cultivated Ages* (London, 1780), 61, 109, 411. Paxman, *Voyage into Language,* 217–46, examines ideas of grammatical difference and national cultures. Dror Wahrman, *The Making of the Modern Self: Identity and Culture in Eighteenth-Century Britain* (New Haven, CT: Yale University Press, 2004), 88–126, esp. 121–22, argues that Dunbar provides the "best example" of the era's confusion about environmentalist versus hereditarian explanations of race. See also Tuska Benes, *In Babel's Shadow: Language, Philology, and the Nation in Nineteenth-Century Germany* (Detroit: Wayne State University Press, 2008), 40-46; William Max Nelson, "Making Men: Enlightenment Ideas of Racial Engineering," *AHR* 115.5 (Dec. 2010): 1364–94.

2. Descent and Relations

1. John Norton, *The Journal of Major John Norton, 1816,* eds. Carl F. Klinck and James J. Talman (Toronto: Champlain Society, 1970), 51, 114–16, 144, at 114, 144. On Cherokee adaptation in these years, see William G. McLoughlin, *Cherokee Renascence*

in the New Republic (Princeton, NJ: Princeton University Press, 1986), 33–91. On captivity and the fluidity of identity among southeastern peoples in the seventeenth and eighteenth centuries, see Christina Snyder, *Slavery in Indian Country: The Changing Face of Captivity in Early America* (Cambridge, MA: Harvard University Press, 2010), 101–26.

2. Norton, *Journal,* 82, 46, 86, 41. For other descriptions of Cherokee, see William Bartram, "Observations on the Creek and Cherokee Indians" (1789), in *Travels and Other Writings,* ed. Thomas P. Slaughter (New York: Library of America, 1996), 529–30; Carver, *Travels,* 414; Zeisberger, "History," 142. See also Duane H. King, "Who Really Discovered the Cherokee-Iroquois Linguistic Relationship," *JCS* 2 (Fall 1977): 401–4; Snyder, *Slavery in Indian Country,* 113, 161, 247.

3. Norton, *Journal,* 117, 139, 85. On Norton's translation of Scott, see ibid., xx.

4. Williams, *Key,* 20; Experience Mayhew, *Observations on the Indian Language* (1722; Boston, 1894), 6–8, 10–11, at 6. For other asserted resemblances, see Thomas Morton, *The New English Canaan,* ed. Charles Francis Adams, Jr. (Boston 1883), 123–27; Le Page du Pratz, *History,* 1:117; Charles Beatty, *The Journal of a Two Months Tour; with a View of Promoting Religion among the Frontier Inhabitants of Pensylvania, and of Introducing Christianity among the Indians to the Westward of the Alegh-geny Mountains* (London, 1768), 25–26; Carver, *Travels,* 213–14. See also Giuliano Bonfante, "Ideas on the Kinship of European Languages from 1200 to 1800," *Journal of World History* 1 (1954): 679–99; Lee Huddleston, *Origins of the American Indians: European Concepts, 1492-1729* (Austin: University of Texas Press, 1967), 9, 33–40, 60, 128–34; Umberto Eco, *The Search for the Perfect Language* (Malden, MA: Blackwell, 1995), 74–85.

5. Morton, *New English Canaan,* 127. On Morton and Merrymount, see Neal Salisbury, *Manitou and Providence: Indians, Europeans, and the Making of New England* (1982; New York: Oxford University Press, 1984), 152–65. On Reland, see Samuel F. Haven, "Archaeology of the United States. Or Sketches, Historical and Bibliographical, of the Progress of Information and Opinion Respecting Vestiges of Antiquity in the United States," *Smithsonian Contrib.* 8 (1856), 56; Rudiger Schreyer, "'Savage' Languages in Eighteenth-Century Theoretical History of Language," in *Language Encounter in the Americas, 1492-1800: A Collection of Essays,* eds. Edward G. Gray and Norman Fiering (New York: Berghahn Books, 2000), 313. See also Eco, *Search for a Perfect Language,* 86-89.

6. G. W. Leibniz, *New Essays on Human Understanding,* eds. and trans. Peter Remnant and Jonathan Bennett (New York: Cambridge University Press, 1981), 333, 285; Charlevoix, *Journal,* 1:279, 52, 49–50. See also [Anne Robert Jacques Turgot], "Etymologie," in *Encyclopédie, ou Dictionnaire raisonné des sciences, et des métiers, par une societé de gens de letters,* eds. [Denis] Diderot and [Jean le Rond] d'Alembert, vol. 6 (1756); Charles de Brosses, *Traité de la formation méchanique des langues et des principes physiques de l'étymologie* (Paris, 1765), iii. On arbitrariness and "genius," see, respectively, Avi Lifschitz, "The Arbitrariness of the Linguistic Sign: Variations on an Enlightenment Theme," *JHI* 73.4 (Oct. 2012): 537–57, esp. 546; Christiane Schlaps, "The 'Genius of Language': Transformations of a Concept in the History of

Linguistics," *Historiographia Linguistica* 31.2/3 (2004): 367-88. On Charlevoix, see also Edward G. Gray, *New World Babel: Languages and Nations in Early America* (Princeton, NJ: Princeton University Press, 1999), 124-26.

7. Leibniz, *New Essays*, 249; Barton, *New Views*, "Preliminary Discourse," lxxv; ibid., "Preface," xix. See also "Affinity," in *Oxford English Dictionary*, at http://proxy .library.upenn.edu:2277/view/Entry/3417?redirectedFrom=affinity#, accessed 3/5/2011; Michel Foucault, *The Order of the Things: An Archaeology of the Human Sciences* (New York: Vintage, 1994), 56-57, 107-10; Paul B. Salmon, "The Beginnings of Morphology: Linguistic Botanizing in the Eighteenth Century," *Historiographia Linguistica* 1.3 (1974): 313-39; Mi Gyung Kim, *Affinity, That Elusive Dream: A Genealogy of the Chemical Revolution* (Cambridge, MA: Massachusetts Institute of Technology Press, 2003), 1-16, 134-38.

8. Leibniz, *New Essays*, 285, 336-37; Philip John von Strahlenberg, *An Histori-Geographical Description of the North and Eastern Parts of Europe and Asia; but More Particularly of Russia, Siberia, and Great Tartary; Both in Their Ancient and Modern State: Together with an Entire New Polyglot-Table of the Dialects of 32 Tartarian Nations* (London, 1736), v, 80, [table]. On the "Tartar" migration thesis, see Huddleston, *Origins of the American Indians*, 48-54, 114-17, 126; Anthony Pagden, *Fall of Natural Man: The American Indian and the Origins of Comparative Ethnology*, rev. ed. (Cambridge: Cambridge University Press, 1986), 193-97. On a "Scythian" language, see Bonfante, "Ideas on the Kinship of European Languages," 691; Eco, *Search for a Perfect Language*, 100-01. On vocabularies' philosophical logic and cultural functions, see, respectively, Thomas R. Trautmann, *Languages and Nations: The Dravidian Proof in Colonial Madras* (Berkeley: University of California Press, 2006), 10-12, 22-41, esp. 27, 31-32; Laura J. Murray, "Vocabularies of Native American Languages: A Literary and Historical Approach to an Elusive Genre," *American Quarterly* 53.4 (Dec. 2001): 590-623. See also Hans Aarselff, "Leibniz on Locke on Language," and "The Study and Use of Etymology in Leibniz," in *From Locke to Saussure: Essays on the Study of Language and Intellectual History* (Minneapolis: University of Minnesota Press, 1982); Henry M. Hoenigswald, "Descent, Perfection and the Comparative Method since Leibniz," in Tullio de Mauro and Lia Formigari, eds., *Leibniz, Humboldt, and the Origins of Comparativism* (Amsterdam: John Benjamins, 1990); David B. Paxman, *Voyage into Language: Space and the Linguistic Encounter, 1500–1800* (Burlington, VT: Ashgate, 2003), 119. On the Enlightenment attack on the auditory, see Sophia Rosenfeld, "On Being Heard: A Case for Paying Attention to the Historical Ear," *AHR* 116.2 (Apr. 2011): 316-34, esp. 321-22.

9. Bernard Romans, *A Concise History of East and West Florida*, ed. Kathryn E. Holland Braund (1775; Tuscaloosa: University of Alabama Press, 1999), 110-11, 119-20; James Adair, *The History of the American Indians*, ed. Kathryn E. Holland Braund (Tuscaloosa: University of Alabama Press, 2005), 72-73, 93-121, at 72-73. See also Eco, *Search for a Perfect Language*, 89-91; David N. Livingstone, *Adam's Ancestors: Race, Religion, and the Politics of Human Origins* (Baltimore: Johns Hopkins University Press, 2008), 30-31, 40-41, 49-51, 72-73.

10. Henry Home, Lord Kames, *Sketches of the History of Man*, 2 vols. (Edinburgh, 1774), 1:24, 38–44; 2:70–74. See also Livingstone, *Adam's Ancestors*, 57–60; Colin Kidd, *The Forging of Races: Race and Scripture in the Protestant Atlantic World, 1600–2000* (Cambridge: Cambridge University Press, 2006), 61–73, 86–87, 95–100.

11. [Antoine] Court de Gébelin, *Monde primitif, analysé et comparé avec le monde moderne, consideré dans divers objets concernant l'histoire, le blason, les monnoies, les jeux, les voyages de phéneiciens autour le monde, les langues Américaines, &c; ou dissertations mêlées*, vol. 8 (Paris, 1781), 57–59, at 59. For its American aspects, see Antoine Court de Gébelin to Benjamin Franklin, May 6, 1781; Franklin to Court de Gébelin, May 7, 1781; Franklin to Court de Gébelin, [after May 7, 1781], *The Papers of Benjamin Franklin*, ed. Barbara S. Oberg (New Haven, CT: Yale University Press, 1999), 35:28–32, 34–36, 41; "Eliot's Indian Bible" ["Notes for a Letter to Mr. Court de Gebelin"] in Du Simitière Collection. See also Frank E. Manuel and Fritzie P. Manuel, *James Bowdoin and the Patriot Philosophers* (Philadelphia: American Philosophical Society, 2004), 195–99; Frank E. Manuel, *The Eighteenth Century Confronts the Gods* (1959; New York: Atheneum, 1969), 250–58, 272–75; Eco, *Search for the Perfect Language,* 93–95. On collection more broadly, see Daniela Blackmar and Peter C. Mancall, ed., *Collecting across Cultures: Material Exchanges in the Early Modern Atlantic* (Philadelphia: University of Pennsylvania Press, 2011).

12. Marquis de Lafayette to George Washington, Feb. 10, [1786], *GW Papers,* 3:555; Pallas and Catherine the Great quoted in John Pickering, *An Essay on a Uniform Orthography for the Indian Languages of North America* (Cambridge, MA, 1820), 4. See also "On an Academy of Arts and Sciences (Letter to Peter the Great, 1716)" in *Leibniz: Selections*, trans. and ed. Philip P. Wiener (New York: Charles Scribner's Sons, 1951), 596–99; James Zug, ed., *The Last Voyage of Captain Cook: The Collected Writings of John Ledyard* (Washington, DC: National Geographic Society, 2005), 243. For descriptions of Catherine II's project, see Gray, *New World Babel,* 112–15; Harriet E. Manelis Klein and Herbert S. Klein, "The 'Russian Collection' of Amerindian Languages in the Spanish Archives," *International Journal of American Linguistics,* 44.2 (Apr. 1978): 137–44. For the broader context, see Han F. Vermeulen, "Origins and Institutionalization of Ethnography and Ethnology in Europe and the USA, 1771–1845," *Fieldwork and Footnotes: Studies in the History of European Anthropology,* eds. Han F. Vermeulen and Arturo Alvarez Roldán (London: Routledge, 1995), 39–45. On Ledyard, see Edward G. Gray, *The Making of John Ledyard: Empire and Ambition in the Life of an Early American Traveler* (New Haven, CT: Yale University Press, 2007).

13. TJ, *Notes,* 101–2; Thomas Jefferson to David Campbell, Mar. 14, 1800, in *TJ Papers,* 31:433; Benjamin Smith Barton, *Observations on Some Parts of Natural History; to which is prefaced An Account of Several Remarkable Vestiges of an Ancient Date, which have been Discovered in Different Parts of North America,* Part I (London, 1787), 19; Washington to Jonathan Edwards, Aug. 28, 1788, in *GW Papers,* 6:480. Benjamin Smith Barton, "Western Boundary Survey," 12–26, in "Journals" (1786–1805), Delafield-Barton Collection, describes his encounter with the Grave Creek mound. On the rejection of colonial patterns of knowledge, see Susan Scott Parrish, *American*

Curiosity: Cultures of Natural History in the Colonial British Atlantic World (Chapel Hill:
University of North Carolina Press, 2002). On antiquarian archaeology in this era, see
Robert Silverberg, *The Mound Builders of Ancient America: The Archaeology of a Myth*
(Greenwich, CT: New York Graphic Society, 1968), 1–58; Annette Kolodny, "Fictions
of American Prehistory: Indians, Archaeology, and National Origin Myths," *American
Literature* 75.4 (Dec. 2003): 693–721; Andrew J. Lewis, *A Democracy of Facts: Natural
History in the Early Republic* (Philadelphia: University of Pennsylvania Press, 2011),
72–105.

14. L. H. Sigourney, "Indian Names," *Select Poems,* 3rd ed. (Philadelphia, 1838),
239–40; Noah Webster, *The American Spelling Book; Containing, the Rudiments of the
English Language, for the Use of Schools in the United States* (Philadelphia, 1804), v;
Moses Greenleaf, "Eastern Indians," in *First Annual Report of the American Society for
Promoting the Civilization and General Improvement of the Indian Tribes in the United
States* (New Haven, CT, 1824), 48. See also John Heckewelder, "Names Which the
Lenni Lenape or Delaware Indians, Who Once Inhabited This Country, Have Given
to Rivers, Streams, Places, &c.," *APS Trans.,* n.s. 4 (1834): 351–96. On claiming "native"
status through narratives of replacement, see Jean M. O'Brien, *Firsting and Lasting:
Writing Indians out of Existence in New England* (Minneapolis: University of Minnesota
Press, 2010), xiii–xiv, 55–104. On the "Christian Origins of the Vanishing Indian"
trope, see Laura M. Stevens, *The Poor Indians: British Missionaries, Native Americans,
and Colonial Sensibility* (Philadelphia: University of Pennsylvania Press, 2004),
160–94.

15. "Circular Letter," *APS Trans.* o.s. 4 (1799), xxxviii; Jefferson to Peter Wilson,
Jan. 20, 1816, in *TJ Writings,* 14:404. On taxonomy and popular confidence in observing
natural phenomena, see Lewis, *Democracy of Facts,* 1–6, 13–45, 52–54. For contrast, see
John Gascoigne, *Science in the Service of Empire: Joseph Banks, the British State and the
Uses of Science in the Age of Revolution* (New York: Cambridge University Press, 1998),
30–33.

16. Benjamin Hawkins to Jefferson, June 14, 1786, in *TJ Papers,* 9:640–41; Hawkins
to James McHenry (Secretary of War), Feb. 23, 1798, in *The Collected Works of Benjamin
Hawkins, 1796–1810,* ed. Thomas Foster (Tuscaloosa: University of Alabama Press,
2003), 293; Jefferson to Peter Wilson, Jan. 20, 1816, *TJ Writings,* 14:402; Jefferson to
William Dunbar, June 24, 1799, in *TJ Papers,* 31:137–38. See also Jefferson to Thomas
Hutchins, Dec. 29, 1783, "Jefferson's Vocabulary of the Unquachog Indians," William
Linn to Jefferson, May 25, 1797, in *TJ Papers* 6:427, 20:467–70, 29:400; Hawkins to
John Parish, Henry Drinker, and Thomas Wistar, Apr. 19, 1797, in *Collected Works,* 128;
"Instructions from the Directors of the New-York Missionary Society, to the
Missionaries among the Indians," *New-York Missionary Magazine, and Repository of
Religious Intelligence* 1.1 (Jan. 1, 1800), 18.

17. TJ, *Notes,* 102; Jefferson to John Sibley, May 27, 1805, *TJ Writings,* 11:81; Jefferson
to Ezra Stiles, Sept. 1, 1786, in *TJ Papers,* 10:316. See also Jefferson to Charles Thomson,
Sept. 20, 1786, Jefferson to Edward Rutledge, July 18, 1788, Sept. 18, 1789, in ibid.,
12:159, 13:377–78; 15:451. Gray, *New World Babel,* 127, notes the contradiction of Buffon.

On Stiles's scholarly interests, see Christopher Grasso, *A Speaking Aristocracy: Transforming Public Discourse in Eighteenth-Century Connecticut* (Chapel Hill: University of North Carolina Press, 1999), 230–78.

18. Henry Marie Brackenridge, "On the Population and Tumuli of the Aborigines of North America. In a Letter from H. H. [sic] Brackenridge, Esq. to Thomas Jefferson," *APS Trans.*, n.s., 1 (1818): 151–59, at 159; Samuel Latham Mitchell, "Communications," *AAS Trans.* 1 (1820): 331–32; Humboldt, *Political Essay*, 137–38; C. F. Volney, *A View of the Soil and Climate of the United States of America; with Supplementary Remarks upon Florida; on the French Colonies on the Mississippi and Ohio, and in Canada; and on the Aboriginal Tribes of America*, trans. C. B. Brown (Philadelphia, 1804), 363. Anthony Pagden, *European Encounters with the New World* (New Haven, CT: Yale University Press, 1993), 121–25, notes the tradition in French literature of using Native figures to critique Christian assumptions.

19 Barton, *Observations*, v, 45–46; Barton to Joseph Banks, May 26, 1793, Barton Papers; Barton, *New Views*, "Preliminary Discourse," xxiv; Henry Dearborn to Barton, Mar. 26, 1802, attached to Henry Dearborn to Col. R. J. Meigs, Mar. 26, 1802, in "Correspondence 1778–1815," Page 50, Barton Papers; *New Views*, "Preface," viii. See also Barton to Charles Gotthold Reichel, Sept. 2, 1793, Joseph Priestley to Barton, June 9, 1796, Nov. 17, 1800, Pages 18, 27, 46, Correspondence, Barton Papers; "Rafinesque, C. S.—Osage Vocabulary," Delafield-Barton Collection, ser. II. American Indian Materials. *New Views*, "Preliminary Discourse," lxiii, lxvii, lxviii, lxxxi; ibid., "Appendix," 5, 13, 20, 22, 26, indicates that Barton personally collected Catawba, Cherokee, Choctaw, Creek, Potawatomi, Unami Delaware, Wyandot, Mohawk, Oneida, Cayuga, Seneca, and Tuscarora words. On U.S. natural historians' positions relative to fellow citizens and to British scholars, see, respectively, Lewis, *Democracy of Facts*; Kariann Akemi Yokota, *Unbecoming British: How the United States Became a Postcolonial Nation* (New York: Oxford University Press, 2011), 153–225. Ibid., 180, notes that Barton claimed Bartram's work as his own.

20 Abbé D. Francesco Saviero Clavigero, *The History of Mexico, collected from Spanish and Mexican Historians, from Manuscripts, and Ancient Paintings of the Indians*, trans. Charles Cullen. 2 vols. (London, 1787), 2:208–10; Barton, *New Views*, "Preliminary Discourse," vi, iii. See also ibid., xx–xxiii; Barton to John Heckewelder, Dec. 4, 1798, Letters to Scientists. On Clavigero, see Jorge Cañizares-Esguerra, *How to Write the History of the New World: Histories, Epistemologies, and Identities in the Eighteenth-Century Atlantic World* (Stanford, CA: Stanford University Press, 2001), 60–62, 235–49.

21. Barton, *New Views*, "Preliminary Discourse," lxxxviii; ibid., "Appendix," 29, 24–25; *Observations*, v; MSS. Notes, Page 126: 229–30, Barton Papers. See also Barton, *New Views*, "Preliminary Discourse," lxxv–lxxvii, lxxxi–lxxxii, xcvii; Joseph Ewan and Nesta Dunn Ewan, *Benjamin Smith Barton: Naturalist and Physician in Jeffersonian America*, eds. Victoria C. Hollowell, Eileen P. Duggan, Marshall R. Crosby (St. Louis: Missouri Botanical Garden Press, 2007), 261. Barton would have found opinions regarding multiple origins in Charlevoix, *Journal*, 6, 52, 59, 299.

22. Benjamin S. Barton, *A Discourse on some of the principal desiderata in natural history, and on the best means for promoting the study of the science, in the U-S, read before the Linnean Society, on the tenth of June, 1807* (Philadelphia, 1807), 79; Barton, *New Views,* "Appendix," 18–19; ibid., "Preface," xi–xii. See also ibid., "Preliminary Discourse, lxv–lxvii; ibid., "Appendix," 17–18, 20–23, 25. On Barton's views of scientific authority, see Lewis, *Democracy of Facts,* 38–40.

23. Barton, *New Views,* "Preliminary Discourse," lxxv, xc–xcvii; Benjamin Smith Barton, "Hints on the Etymology of certain English Words, and on their affinity to words in the languages of different European, Asiatic, and American (Indian) nations, in a letter from Dr. Barton to Dr. Thomas Beddoes," *APS Trans.* o.s. 6 (1809), 148–51, 154, at 154. See also Clavigero, *History of Mexico,* 208–9. On scriptural chronology, see Trautmann, *Languages and Nations,* 16–17.

24. On intermixture and American English, see Noah Webster, *Dissertations on the English Language; with Notes Historical and Critical* (1789; Gainesville, FL: Scholars' Facsimiles & Reprints, 1951), 22–23; John Pickering, "Memoir on the Present State of the English Language in the United States of America, with a Vocabulary; containing various words and phrases which have been supposed to be peculiar to this country," *AAAS Memoirs* 3.2 (Jan. 1, 1815): 439–535, esp. 441, 498, 499, 506, 516, 524, 526. Trautmann, *Languages and Nations,* 10–21, 37–38, treats Mosaic ethnology and the divergence model's supplanting of the intermixture model.

25. See TJ, *Notes,* 92–97, 101–7, at 92, 102; Jefferson to Alexander von Humboldt, Dec. 6, 1813, in *TJ Writings,* 14:23–24; Barton, *New Views,* "Preliminary Discourse," xxxiii–xxxvi, lx–lxi, 35. Nicholas Hudson, "From 'Nation' to 'Race': The Origin of Racial Classification in Eighteenth-Century Thought," *Eighteenth-Century Studies* 29.3 (1996): 247–64; Kidd, *Forging of Races,* 21–22, 26–27, stress the concept of "lineage" tying these together.

26. *Jesuit Relations,* 42:221, recorded Algonquian and Iroquoian groupings in the mid-seventeenth century, and Louis Armand de Lom d'Arce, Baron de Lahontan, *New Voyages to North-America, Containing an Account of the Several Nations of That Vast Continent,* 2 vols. (London, 1703), 1:16, 201, spread the view. Lafitau, *Customs,* 2:262–64; Charlevoix, *Journal,* 1:279, 299, explained a third distinct group, corresponding to Siouan languages. Carver, *Travels,* 414, 417; William Bartram, *Travels through North and South Carolina, Georgia, East and West Florida, the Cherokee Country, the Extensive Territories of the Muscogulges or Creek Confederacy, and the Country of the Chactaws* (London, 1791), 386–87, 463–64, 517, speculated, with errors, on a fourth, southern group. On phonetic differences and their flattening, see Williams, *Key,* 96; Mayhew, *Observations on the Indian Language,* 6.

27. John Lawson, *A New Voyage to Carolina,* ed. Hugh Talmadge Lefler (Chapel Hill: University of North Carolina Press, 1967), 239. *Jesuit Relations,* 3:91; Inca Garcilasso de la Vega, *First Part of the Royal Commentaries of the Incas* (London, 1688), 10, also discuss language and alliance. See also Andrew Keith Sturtevant, "Jealous Neighbors: Rivalry and Alliance among the Native Communities of Detroit, 1701–1766" (Ph.D. diss., College of William & Mary, 2011), 45–59; J. Leitch Wright, Jr.,

Creeks and Seminoles: The Destruction and Regeneration of the Muscolge People (Lincoln: University of Nebraska Press, 1986), 7–19, 110–16; Gregory Evans Dowd, *War under Heaven: Pontiac, the Indian Nations, and the British Empire* (Baltimore: Johns Hopkins University Press, 2004).

28. On dashing the wampum string, see Richard Butler, "General Butler's Journal, Continued" *Olden Time* 2.11 (Nov. 1847): 481–525, at 524. On the Ohio Valley, see Richard White, *The Middle Ground: Indians, Empires, and Republics in the Great Lakes Region, 1650–1815* (New York: Cambridge University Press, 1991), 366–412; Eric Hinderaker, *Elusive Empires: Constructing Colonialism in the Ohio Valley, 1673–1800* (New York: Cambridge University Press, 1997), 186–225; Gregory Evans Dowd, *A Spirited Resistance: The North American Indian Struggle for Unity, 1745–1815* (Baltimore: John Hopkins University Press, 1992), 90–115. In the context of revolutionary diplomacy, see Leonard J. Sadosky, *Revolutionary Negotiations: Indians, Empires, and Diplomats in the Founding of America* (Charlottesville: University of Virginia Press, 2009), 127–40.

29. Jonathan Edwards, Jr., *Observations on the Language of the Muhhekaneew Indians* (New Haven, CT, 1788), [4], 8, 12; Richard Butler to Washington, Nov. 30, 1787, in *GW Papers*, 5:461–64. See also Washington to Jonathan Edwards, Aug. 28, 1788, in ibid., 6:479–80.

30. Washington to Lafayette, Jan. 10, 1788, Lafayette to Washington, Feb. 10, 1786, in *GW Papers*, 6:29–30, 3:555. Cf. Gray, *New World Babel*, 113, for a philosophy-focused interpretation. On Native–white conflict in the 1790s, see White, *Middle Ground*, 413–21, 440–45; Hinderaker, *Elusive Empires*, 226–36; Dowd, *Spirited Resistance*, 90–103.

31. "The Speech of Captain Hendrick Aupaumut," [June 20, 1791], Pickering Papers, 60:71A. See also Samuel Kirkland to Henry Knox, Apr. 22, ibid., 61:201; [Hendrick Aupaumut], "A Narrative of an Embassy to the Western Indians, from the Original Manuscript of Hendrick Aupaumut, with Prefatory Remarks by Dr. B. H. Coates," *HSP Memoirs* 2 (1827), 126–29. On Aupaumut, see Alan Taylor, "Captain Hendrick Aupaumut: The Dilemmas of an Intercultural Broker," *Ethnohistory* 43.3 (Summer 1996): 431–57; Rachel Wheeler, "Hendrick Aupaumut: Christian-Mahican Prophet," *JER* 25.2 (Summer 2005): 187–220; Lisa Brooks, *The Common Pot: The Recovery of Native Space in the Northeast* (Minneapolis: University of Minnesota Press, 2008), 106–21, 127–49.

32. Timothy Pickering to Arthur St. Clair, July 8, 1791; "Questions Relative to the Proposed Indian Treaty—and Hendrick's Answers. Feby. 24, 1793"; Pickering to Benjamin H. Coates, Apr. 15, 1826, Pickering Papers, 60:88A, 59:55, 16:116A–17; Aupaumut, "Narrative of an Embassy," 113; "Memorandum, for the Information of the Commissioners, River LaTranchée, from June 17. to June 23. 1793," Pickering Papers, 59:185; Aupaumut, "Captain Hendrick's Narrative of his Journey in July, Aug., Sept, and Oct. [1791]," ibid., 59:8. See also Pickering to Knox, July 1, 1791, ibid., 60:77. On Mohican–Ojibwe unintelligibility, see Eugene F. Bliss, trans. and ed., "Diary of David Zeisberger; A Moravian Missionary among the Indians of Ohio," in *Historical and Philosophical Society of Ohio Transactions*, n.s., 2–3 (1885), 2:287; Peter Jones, *Life and*

Journals of Kah-Ke-Wa-Quo-Na-By (Toronto, 1860), 122. On identities at New Stockbridge and Brothertown, see David J. Silverman, *Red Brethren: The Brothertown and Stockbridge Indians and the Problem of Race in Early America* (Ithaca, NY: Cornell University Press, 2010). On the uncertainty of translation and its openness to misunderstanding and manipulation, see James Merrell, *Into the American Woods: Negotiators on the Pennsylvania Frontier* (New York: Norton, 1999), 221.

33. David Cusick, "Sketches of Ancient History of the Six Nations" (1828), in *The Iroquois Trail, or Foot-Prints of the Six Nations in Customs, Traditions, and History*, ed. W. M. Beauchamp (Fayetteville, NY, 1892), 11–13, at 12; Onondaga man in MSS. Notes, Barton Papers, Page 127, p. 234; Occom quoted in David M'Clure, *Diary of David M'Clure* (New York, 1899), 99; Hendrick Aupaumut et al., "Mahican-Stockbridge Tribe to Samson Occom," Aug. 27, 1787, in Joanna Brooks, ed., *Collected Writings of Samson Occom, Mohegan: Literature and Leadership in Eighteenth-Century Native America* (New York: Oxford University Press, 2006), 153–54, 403; Heckewelder, "History," 78–79, 42.

34. Norton, *Journal*, 91, 84–85, 98; John Heckewelder, "A Short Account of the Mengwe—Maqua—(or Mingoes as These Are Called by the White People), According to the Sayings & Reports of the Lenni Lennape, Mahicanni (Mohegans) & Other Tribes Connected with These," [1–2], and "Answers to Queries Respecting Indian Tribes &c. Addressed to Me by the Revd. Samuel Miller of N. York," in Heckewelder Communications; Capt. Pipe in Charles C. Trowbridge, "Traditions of the Lenēē Lenāūpee or Delawares," [1], in "Account of the Traditions, Manners, & Customs of the Lenee Lenauppee Indians . . . ca. 1825," University of Michigan [microfilm at APS]. On Delawares in the War for Independence, see Dowd, *Spirited Resistance*, 65–89; White, *Middle Ground*, 380–400.

35. Aupaumut, "Narrative of an Embassy," 76; E. A. Cruikshank, ed., *The Correspondence of Lieut. Governor John Graves Simcoe, with Allied Documents Relating to His Administration of the Government of Upper Canada*, 5 vols. (Toronto: Ontario Historical Society, 1923), 1:381, 5:34, 1:225, 2:7. For ties with Wyandots, see Aupaumut, "Narrative of an Embassy," 77. For an account of Mohican–Delaware relationship that ignores language entirely, see "It Is a Tradition Handed down from Our Ancestors . . . ," WDLR, folder 1821, 2. On Aupaumut's and Brant's rival visions for the Ohio Valley, see Taylor, "Captain Hendrick Aupaumut," 445; Brooks, *Common Pot*, 121–62. On Native skin color and identity, see Nancy Shoemaker, "How Indians Got to be Red," *AHR* 102.3 (June 1997): 625–44. On Mohican–Delaware rivalry with the Iroquois, see Heckewelder, "History," 9–24; Norton, *Journal*, 83–84. See also Daniel K. Richter, *The Ordeal of the Longhouse: The Peoples of the Iroquois League in the Era of European Colonization* (Chapel Hill: University of North Carolina Press, 1992), 50–58, 97–104, 133–37; Gunlög Fur, *A Nation of Women: Gender and Colonial Encounters among the Delaware Indians* (Philadelphia: University of Pennsylvania Press, 2009), 160–98.

36. Heckewelder, "History," 324–25. For his work in 1792–1793, see Paul A. W. Wallace, ed., *The Travels of John Heckewelder in Frontier America* (Pittsburgh: University of Pittsburgh Press, 1958), 258–333; Dowd, *Spirited Resistance*, 84–85.

37. TJ, *Notes*, 282 n.12. I date this undated fragment from his personal copy of *Notes* to the early nineteenth century because as late as 1805, Jefferson considered the question of American origins "undecided" and because his only other reference to Indian linguistic "barrenness" came in his retirement. See Jefferson to John Sibley, May 27, 1805, Jefferson to Peter Wilson, Jan. 20, 1816, in *TJ Writings*, 11:79, 14:403. Logan's Lament in *Notes*, 62–63, was evidence of Native–European intellectual equality, not a specimen of savage eloquence. Cf. Gray, *New World Babel*, 130–32.

38. Jefferson to Ezra Stiles, Sept. 1, 1786, in *TJ Papers*, 10:316; Jefferson to John Adams, June 11, 1812, Aug. 15, 1820, in Lester J. Cappon, ed., *The Adams–Jefferson Letters: The Complete Correspondence between Thomas Jefferson and Abigail and John Adams* (Chapel Hill: University of North Carolina Press, 1959), 306, 323. The first letter echoes Humboldt, *Political Essay*, 137–38. See also TJ, *Notes*, 103–6; William Linn to Jefferson, Feb. 8, 1798, in *TJ Papers*, 30:86–87; Jefferson to John Manners, Feb. 22, 1814, in *TJ Writings*, 14:101; Jefferson to John Pickering, Feb. 20, 1825, in "Jefferson's Letters to Pickering," ed. Thomas A. Kirby, in *Philologica: The Malone Anniversary Studies*, eds. Thomas A. Kirby and Henry Bosley Woolf (Baltimore: Johns Hopkins University Press, 1949), 262–63. Against public support for linguistic collection, see Charles Brockden Brown's remark in Volney, *View*, 425. While Christopher Looby, "The Constitution of Nature: Taxonomy as Politics in Jefferson, Peale, and Bartram," *Early American Literature* 22.3 (1987): 252–73, at 257, describes Jeffersonian attempts to represent an "immutable" nature; and Peter Thompson, "'Judicious Neology: The Imperative of Paternalism in Thomas Jefferson's Linguistic Studies," *EAS* 1.2 (2003): 187–224, esp. 221, describes his interest in linguistic "filiation" as abstract, I argue that linguistic taxonomy represented a practical effort to find useful information in a changing social entity. See also Foucault, *Order of Things*, 71–76, 125–62; Joseph Errington, *Linguistics in a Colonial World: A Story of Language, Power, and Meaning* (Malden, MA: Blackwell, 2008), 83–88, 107–20.

39. Jefferson to Meriwether Lewis, June 20, 1803, Jefferson to José Correa de Serra, Apr. 26, 1816, in Donald Jackson, ed., *Letters of the Lewis and Clark Expedition with Related Documents, 1783–1854* (Urbana: University of Illinois Press, 1962), 62, 612; Jefferson to Peter S. Du Ponceau, Dec. 30, 1817, in *TJ Writings*, 15:158. See also Jefferson to Barton, Feb. 27, 1803, in Jackson, ed., *Letters*, 18–19; Jefferson to Thomas Freeman, Apr. 14, 1804, in *Thomas Jefferson and Early Western Explorers*, ed. Gerard W. Gawalt, Library of Congress, American Memory, at http://memory.loc.gov, accessed 7/24/2013; John C. Calhoun to S. H. Long, Mar. 8, 1819, in W. Edwin Hemphill, ed., *The Papers of John C. Calhoun* (Columbia: University of South Carolina Press, 1967), 3:639–40. For European linguistic neglect, see Heckewelder, "History," 114. Cf. Carver, *Travels*; Alexander Mackenzie, *Voyages from Montreal on the River St. Laurence, through the Continent of North America, to the Frozen and Pacific Oceans; in the Years 1789 and 1793. With a Preliminary Account of the Rise, Progress, and Present State of the Fur Trade of That Country* (1801; Ann Arbor: University Microfilms, 1966). The total number of vocabularies is in John Conrad to Meriwether Lewis [c. Apr. 1, 1807], in Jackson, ed., *Letters*, 396. The captains describe some of these recordings in Gary E. Moulton, ed., *The*

Journals of the Lewis and Clark Expedition (Lincoln: University of Nebraska Press, 1987), 3:27, 319; 5:189, 292–94, 345, 347. On the expedition, see James P. Ronda, *Lewis and Clark among the Indians* (Lincoln: University of Nebraska Press, 1984); Jenry Morsman, "Securing America: Jefferson's Fluid Plans for the Western Perimeter," and Alan Taylor, "Jefferson's Pacific: The Science of Distant Empire, 1768–1811," in *Across the Continent: Jefferson, Lewis and Clark, and the Making of America*, eds. Douglas Seefeldt, Jeffrey L. Hantman, and Peter S. Onuf (Charlottesville: University Press of Virginia, 2005). On the Trade and Intercourse Acts, see Francis Paul Prucha, *The Great Father: The United States Government and the American Indian* (Lincoln: University of Nebraska Press, 1984), 89–92.

40. Moulton, ed., *Journals*, 3:402, 2:438, 3:27; [Nicholas Biddle], *The Lewis and Clark Expedition* [retitled facsimile of *History of the Expedition under the Command of Captains Lewis and Clark, to the Sources of the Missouri, across the Rocky Mountains down the River Columbia to the Pacific Ocean; Performed during the Years 1804–6*, ed. Paul Allen (1814)], eds. Archibald Hanna and William H. Goetzmann (Philadelphia, 1961), 614.

41. John Johnston, "Account of the Present State of the Indian Tribes Inhabiting Ohio," *AAS Trans.* 1 (1820), 274–75; Henry Rowe Schoolcraft, *Narrative Journal of Travels through the Northwestern Regions of the United States, Extending from Detroit through the Great Chain of American Lakes, to the Sources of the Mississippi River in the Year 1820*, ed. Mentor L. Williams (East Lansing: Michigan State College Press, 1953), 202–3; James, *Account*, 17:152–53. Philip C. Bellfly, *Three Fires Unity: The Anishnaabeg of the Lake Huron Borderlands* (Lincoln: University of Nebraska Press, 2011), describes this alliance. Michael Witgen, *An Infinity of Nations: How the Native New World Shaped Early North America* (Philadelphia: University of Pennsylvania Press, 2012), 85–96, stresses the fluidity of identity among Anishinaabeg. Richard E. Jensen, "Introduction," in *The Pawnee Mission Letters, 1834–1851* (Lincoln: University of Nebraska Press, 2010), xxxi, notes that Loup Pawnee lived and hunted apart and spoke a dialect divergent from other Pawnee bands.

42. TJ, *Notes*, 92, 202, at 92; Secretary of War [Henry Dearborn] to Benjamin Hawkins, Nov. 11, 1804, WDLS, B:26; John Sibley, "Historical Sketches of the Several Indian Tribes in Louisiana, South of the Arkansas River, and Between the Mississippi and River Grande," in *American State Papers*, 2:721; Edwin James, "Some Account of the Menomonies with a Specimen of an Attempt to form a Dictionary of their Language, by Edwin James, an Assistant Surgeon of the U.S. Army" [1827], 1–2, APS.

43. Biddle, *Lewis and Clark Expedition*, 128, 515; Cruikshank, ed., *Correspondence of Lieut. Governor John Graves Simcoe*, 1:226; "Captain Hendrick's Narrative of His Journey to Niagara & Grand River, in February 1792," Pickering Papers, 59:19. On Jeffersonian expansion, see Drew R. McCoy, *The Elusive Republic: Political Economy in Jeffersonian America* (Chapel Hill: University of North Carolina Press, 1980); Adam Rothman, *Slave Country: American Expansion and the Origin of the Deep South* (Cambridge, MA: Harvard University Press, 2005).

44. On nativism, see Dowd, *Spirited Resistance*, 123–47; Alfred A. Cave, *Prophets of the Great Spirit: Native American Revitalization Movements in Eastern North America* (Lincoln: University of Nebraska Press, 2006), 45–139. For Jeffersonian policies, see Anthony F. C. Wallace, *Jefferson and the Indians: The Tragic Fate of the First Americans* (Cambridge, MA: Harvard University Press, 1999), 229, 239, 275, esp. 239; Robert M. Owens, "Jeffersonian Benevolence on the Ground: The Indian Land Cession Treaties of William Henry Harrison," *JER* 22.3 (Autumn 2002): 405–35. Cf. Reginald Horsman, *Expansion and Indian Policy 1783–1812* (1967; Norman: University of Oklahoma Press, 1992), 113, 170; Sheehan, *Seeds of Extinction*, 3–12, 243–50, which present Jeffersonian policy as a continuation of Federalist policy, though the latter emphasizes philanthropic ideas over the popular land hunger that the former stresses. Peter S. Onuf, *Jefferson's Empire: The Language of American Nationhood* (Charlottesville: University Press of Virginia, 2000), 39–46, examines Jefferson's Indian policy in light of his political ideals.

45. Moses Dawson, *A Historical Narrative of the Civil and Military Services of Major General William H. Harrison, and a Vindication of His Character and Conduct, as a Statesman, a Citizen, and a Soldier, with a Detail of His Negotiations and Wars with the Indians, until the Final Overthrow of the Celebrated Chief Tecumseh, and His Brother the Prophet* (Cincinnati, 1824), 109; George Stiggins, "A Historical Narration of the Genealogy Traditions and Downfall of the Ispocaga or Creek Tribe of Indians, Written by One of the Tribe" [c. 1831–44], in Theron A. Nunez, Jr., "Creek Nativism and the Creek War of 1813–1814: Part 2 (Stiggins Narrative, continued)," *Ethnohistory* 5.2 (Spring 1958): 131–75, at 151, 168. The Shawnee Prophet's tradition is in Vernon Kinietz and Erminie W. Voegelin, eds., *Shawnese Traditions: C. C. Trowbridge's Account*, Occasional Contributions from the Museum of Anthropology of the University of Michigan, 7 (1939), 6–9. For traditions of Shawnee relations, see Charles C. Trowbridge to Lewis Cass, Jan. 22, 1825, in "Account of the Traditions, Manners and Customs of the Twaatwaa or Miami Indians," Trowbridge Materials, 161–64; Ethan Allen Hitchcock, *A Traveler in Indian Territory: The Journal of Ethan Allen Hitchcock, Late Major-General in the United States Army*, ed. Grant Forman (1930; Norman: University of Oklahoma Press, 1996), 145–46; Heckewelder, "History," 69. On the Red Sticks, see Wright, *Creeks and Seminoles*, 162, 226; Joel W. Martin, *Sacred Revolt: The Muskogees' Struggle for a New World* (Boston: Beacon Press, 1991), 160.

46. Kinietz and Voegelin, eds., *Shawnese Traditions*, 61–62. See also Noel W. Schutz, Jr., "The Study of Shawnee Myth in an Ethnographic and Ethnohistorical Perspective (Ph.D. diss., Indiana University, 1975), 114–15, 300–302, 465–78; Stephen Warren, *The Shawnees and Their Neighbors, 1795–1870* (Urbana: University of Illinois Press, 2005), 14–17. On Black Hoof's program, see ibid., 43–67. Anthony F. C. Wallace, *The Death and Rebirth of the Seneca* (1969; New York: Vintage, 1972), 40, 42, stresses the prominence of "ethnic confederacies" in eastern Native America. For ethnogenesis along linguistic lines, see Patricia Galloway, *Choctaw Genesis, 1500–1700* (Lincoln, NE, 1995), 320–23; Daniel K. Richter, *Before the Revolution: America's Ancient Pasts* (Cambridge, MA: Harvard University Press, 2011), 148–49. Cf. David Dixon, "We

Speak as One People: Native Unity and the Pontiac Indian Uprising," in *The Boundaries between Us: Natives and Newcomers along the Frontiers of the Old Northwest Territory, 1750–1850*, ed. Daniel P. Barr (Kent, OH, 2006), 47, 57, on ethnogenesis transcending linguistic bounds. Michael D. McNally, *Ojibwe Singers: Hymns, Grief, and a Native Culture in Motion* (2000; St. Paul: Minnesota Historical Society Press, 2009), 28, discusses songs as linguistic expressions that transcend lexical content.

47. Tecumseh quoted in *Messages and Letters of William Henry Harrison*, ed. Logan Esarey, vol. 1 (Indianapolis: Indiana Historical Commission, 1922), 469, 465; Harrison quoted in Benjamin Drake, *Life of Tecumseh, and of His Brother, the Prophet; with a Historical Sketch of the Shawanoe Indians* (Cincinnati, 1841), 127–28. See also Dawson, *Historical Narrative*, 156–58. On the Treaty of Fort Wayne (1809), in which U.S.-supported Delaware, Miami, and Potawatomi chiefs sold three million acres in Indiana and Illinois, see John Sugden, *Tecumseh: A Life* (New York: Henry Holt, 1997), 182–90; Robert M. Owens, *Mr. Jefferson's Hammer: William Henry Harrison and the Origins of American Indian Policy* (Norman: University of Oklahoma Press, 2007), xxiv, 200–209. On the possibility of Tecumseh using sign language at Vincennes, see Robert L. Gunn, "John Dunn Hunter, Pan-Indianism, and the Politics of Indian Languages," paper delivered at Native American and Indigenous Studies Association Conference, Uncasville, CT, June 6, 2012.

48. Caleb Swan to Henry Knox, May 2, 1791, in Delafield-Barton Collection, ser. III., vol. 32, 21; Gallatin, "Synopsis," 94. On Miamis, see Vernon Kinietz, ed., *Meearmeear Traditions by C. C. Trowbridge*, Occasional Contributions from the Museum of Anthropology of the University of Michigan 7 (1938), 12–13; Dowd, *Spirited Resistance*, 131–32; Owens, "Jeffersonian Benevolence on the Ground," 416. On U.S. practice of creating "nations" that could cede land, see Warren, *Shawnees and Their Neighbors*, 8; Witgen, *Infinity of Nations*, 346–47.

49. Jefferson to Edward Rutledge, Sept. 18, 1789, in *TJ Papers*, 15:451; S. H. Long to the Secretary of War, June 15, 1818, WDLR, 2:1818.2; "Department of War, May 15, 1826," [1–2], Gallatin Papers, reel 36. See also Owens, "Jeffersonian Benevolence," 407; Kathleen Du Val, *The Native Ground: Indians and Colonists in the Heart of the Continent* (Philadelphia: University of Pennsylvania Press, 2006), 188–89.

50. Gallatin, "Synopsis," 2–4, 9, 16, 91–92, 96, 122–26, at 96, 2–3, 126, 9, 16. Cf. Adrien Balbi, *L'Atlas ethnographique du globe, ou Classification des peuples anciens et modernes d'apres leur langues* (Paris, 1826), xxv; Malte Brun, *Universal Geography; or a Description of All the Parts of the World, on New Plan, According to the Great Natural Divisions of the Globe*, 6 vols. (Boston, 1824), 5:19–20; C. S. Rafinesque, "CLIO No. I. Ancient History of North America," *Cincinnati Literary Gazette* 1.8 (Feb. 21, 1824): 59–60; idem, "American History. Tabular View of the American Generic Languages, and Original Nations," *Atlantic Journal, and Friend of Knowledge* 1.1 (Spring 1832): 6–8. On Osage hostilities and Lakota–Cheyenne alliance and intermarriage, see, respectively Du Val, *Native Ground*, 185–87; Elliott West, *The Way to the West: Essays on the Central Plains* (Albuquerque: University of New Mexico Press, 1995), 13–50. For evaluations of Gallatin's classification, see Mary Haas, "The Problem of Classifying

American Indian Languages: From Duponceau to Powell," in *Language, Culture and History: Essays by Mary Haas*, ed. Anwar S. Dil (Stanford, CA: Stanford University Press, 1978), 136–39; Roy Goodman and Pierre Swiggers, "Albert Gallatin's Table of North American Native Languages (1826)," *Orbis* 36 (1991–1993): 240–48, esp. 244–46.

51. James, *Account*, 16:122, 263–64, at 122. On the vocabularies, see also Samuel J. Harrison to Gibson and Jefferson, July 16, 1809, Jefferson to Barton, Sept. 21, 1809, in *TJ Papers RS*, 1:348n., 555–56; Jefferson to Du Ponceau, Nov. 7, 1817, in Jackson, ed., *Letters*, 631–33; Gallatin to William Clark, Mar. 31, 1826, Gallatin Papers, reel 36. Gallatin, "Synopsis," 134–35, notes reliance on British traders.

3. Much More Fertile Than Commonly Supposed

1. "Brother John Heckewelder's Account of their Journey by Water from Languntoutenünk to Welhik Thuppeek in April 1773," in *The Travels of John Heckewelder in Frontier America*, ed. Paul A. W. Wallace (Pittsburgh: University of Pittsburgh Press, 1958), 106–7. On language learning, see ibid. 102–3; Heckewelder, "History," 315–20. For judicial inquiries, see "An Account of What Happened in the Indian Affairs at Shekomeko & Pachgatgoch viz. The Arrest, Imprisonment & Examination of Br. Pyrlaeus, Martin Mack & Joseph Shaw at Millford in New-England Mense Jun. A. 1743," 01.33.111.4b; Gottlob Buettner to Peter Böhler, Aug. 13, 1744, Records of the Indian Missions, 01.33.112.3, item 5, p. 11, Moravian Archives. On Moravian work as repairing Babel, see Patrick M. Erben, *Harmony of the Spirits: Translation and the Language of Community in Early Pennsylvania* (Chapel Hill: University of North Carolina Press, 2012), 1–15, 301–23. On Moravian mission communities, see Jane T. Merritt, *At the Crossroads: Indians and Empires on a Mid-Atlantic Frontier, 1700–1763* (Chapel Hill: University of North Carolina Press, 2007), 89–166; Rachel Wheeler, *To Live upon Hope: Mohicans and Missionaries in the Eighteenth-Century Northeast* (Ithaca, NY: Cornell University Press, 2008), 67–173; Herman Wellenreuther and Carola Wessel, "Introduction," *The Moravian Mission Diaries of David Zeisberger*, trans. Julie Tomberlin Weber, eds. Herman Wellenreuther and Carola Wessel (University Park: Pennsylvania State University Press, 2205), 59, 67–68. Linford D. Fisher, "'I Believe They Are Papists!': Natives, Moravians, and the Politics of Conversion in Eighteenth-Century Connecticut," *NEQ* 81.3 (Sept. 2008): 410–37, examines opposition. See also Aaron Spencer Fogleman, *Jesus Is Female: Moravians and the Challenge of Radical Religion in Early America* (Philadelphia: University of Pennsylvania Press, 2007), 156–64, 219; Katherine Carté Engel, *Religion and Profit: Moravians in Early America* (Philadelphia: University of Pennsylvania Press, 2009), 161–225; Gregory Evans Dowd, *A Spirited Resistance: The North American Indian Struggle for Unity, 1745–1815* (Baltimore: John Hopkins University Press, 1992), 84–85. Samuel F. Jarvis, "A Discourse on the Religion of the Indian Tribes of North America," *NYHS Coll.* 3 (1821), 183, suspected, "As long as they were formidable, curiosity was overpowered by terror." James H. Merrell, *Into the American Woods: Negotiators on the Pennsylvania Frontier* (New York: Norton, 1999), 314, suggests the same. On the connection between curiosity and social

reform in the era's literature, see Barbara M. Benedict, *Curiosity: A Cultural History of Early Modern Inquiry* (Chicago: University of Chicago Press, 2002), 228–44.

2. John Heckewelder to Peter S. Du Ponceau, Feb. 3, 1819, Sept. 21, 1818, in Heckewelder Letters; Heckewelder, "History," 326, 110, 319, 362; Heckewelder to Benjamin S. Barton, March 4, 1805, Delafield-Barton Collection, ser. I. See also Heckewelder to Du Ponceau, Nov. 17, 1819, July 15, 1820, Sept. 13, 1821, in Heckewelder Letters.

3. On Zeisberger's participation in the projects of Catherine the Great and Court de Gébelin, see "Diary of the Small Indian Company in a Night Lodge on the Cayahaga," 14, in Box 153, No. 8; David Zeisberger to the Brethren of the Helpers' Conference, Feb. 25, 1787, ibid., No. 14, Moravian Archives; Zeisberger to Josiah Harmar, Jan. 13, 1788, Misc. MSS. Collection, APS; Richard Butler to Washington, Nov. 30, 1787, *GW Papers*, 5:461–64. See also Erben, *Harmony of the Spirits*, 301–2, 322.

4. *Second Report of the American Bible Society, Presented May 14 1818* (New York, 1818), 15; Jefferson to William Ludlow, Sept. 6, 1824, in *TJ Writings*, 16:74–75; Barton, *New Views*, [Dedication], iv–v. See also Maurizio Valsania, "'Our Original Barbarism': Man vs. Nature in Thomas Jefferson's Moral Experience," *JHI* 65.4 (Oct. 2004): 627–45.

5. On eighteenth-century understandings of "civilization" and environmentalism, see Phillip R. Sloan, "The Idea of Racial Degeneracy in Buffon's *Histoire Naturelle*," in *Racism in the Eighteenth Century*, ed. Harold E. Pagliaro (Cleveland, OH: Press of Case Western Reserve University, 1973); Bernard W. Sheehan, *Seeds of Extinction: Jeffersonian Philanthropy and the American Indian* (Chapel Hill: University of North Carolina Press, 1973), 15–44; George W. Stocking, Jr., *Victorian Anthropology* (New York: Free Press, 1987), 12–25; Bruce Dain, *A Hideous Monster of the Mind: American Race Theory in the Early Republic* (Cambridge, MA: Harvard University Press, 2002), 1–26, 59–65. On Native agriculture, see Daniel H. Unser, Jr., "Iroquois Livelihood and Jeffersonian Agrarianism: Reaching Behind the Models and Metaphors," in *Native Americans in the Early Republic*, eds. Frederick E. Hoxie, Ronald Hoffman, and Peter J. Albert (Charlottesville: University Press of Virginia, 1999). On white fears of cultural degeneration, see Drew R. McCoy, *The Elusive Republic: Political Economy in Jeffersonian America* (Chapel Hill: University of North Carolina Press, 1980), 13–47, 84, 115, 122, 198, 219; Harold Hellenbrand, "Not 'to Destroy but to Fulfill': Jefferson, Indians, and Republican Dispensation," *Eighteenth-Century Studies*, 18.4 (Autumn 1985): 523–49, esp. 535–38; Nathan O. Hatch, *The Democratization of American Christianity* (New Haven, CT: Yale University Press, 1989), 62–64.

6. Jacob Behmen, *Mysterium Magnum, or An Exposition of the First Book of Moses Called Genesis: Concerning the Manifestation or Revelation of the Divine Word through the Three Principles of the Divine Essence, and of the Original of the World and the Creation; wherein the Kingdom of Nature and the Kingdom of Grace Are Explained*, vol. 3 (1623; London 1772), 197–203, at 198; Samuel Stanhope Smith, "Strictures on Lord Kames's Discourse on the Original Diversity of Mankind," in *Essay on the Causes of the Variety of Complexion and Figure in the Human Species* (Philadelphia, 1787), 24, 29–30.

[Cornelius de Pauw], *Recherches philosophiques sur les Américains, ou Mémoires intéressants pour server à l'histoire de l'espece humaine,* 2 vols. (London, 1770), 1:138, described a similar natural process. On Böhme's linguistic influence, see Erben, *Harmony of the Spirits,* 19–23, 49–54, 196–213, 301–24. Dain, *Hideous Monster of the Mind,* 40–49, 65–72, describes Smith's non-linguistic ideas.

7. [William Thornton], "Cadmus, or a Treatise on the Elements of Written Language, Illustrating, by a Philosophical Division of Speech, the Power of Each Character, Thereby Mutually Fixing the Orthography and Ortheopy. With an Essay on the Mode of Teaching the Deaf, or Surd and Consequently Dumb, to Speak," *APS Trans.,* o.s. 3 (1793), 297–98; Benjamin Lincoln, "Observations on the Indians of North-America; Containing an Answer to Some Remarks of Doctor Ramsay," *MHS Coll.* 5 (1798), 11; [Thomas Pierronet], "Specimen of the Mountaineer, or Sheshatapooshshoish, Skoffie, and Micmac Languages," ibid. 6 (1799), 16–17; Jefferson to Doctor John Sibley, May 27, 1805, *TJ Writings,* 11:79; Jefferson to Charles Thomson, Sept. 20, 1786, *TJ Papers,* 12:159. See also John C. Greene, *American Science in the Age of Jefferson* (Ames: Iowa State University Press, 1984), 5; Joyce E. Chaplin, "Nature and Nation: Natural History in Context," in *Stuffing Birds, Pressing Plants, Shaping Knowledge: Natural History in North America, 1730–1860,* ed. Sue Ann Prince, *APS Trans.* 93.4 (2003).

8. Benjamin Smith Barton, *Observations on Some Parts of Natural History; to which is prefaced An Account of Several Remarkable Vestiges of an Ancient Date, which have been Discovered in Different Parts of North America, Part I* (London, 1787), 11; Barton to Charles Gotthold Reichel, Sept. 2, 1793, Barton Papers; Barton to Heckewelder, Jan. 15, 1794, Dreer Collection, Box 293, Folder 19; Benjamin Smith Barton, "Observations and Conjectures Concerning Certain Articles Which Were Taken out of an Ancient Tumulus, or Grave, at Cincinnati, in the County of Hamilton, and Territory of the United-States, North-West of the River Ohio, in a Letter from Benjamin Smith Barton, to Joseph Priestley," in *APS Trans.,* o.s. 4 (1799), 197; Barton to Heckewelder, Apr. 17, 1800, Letters of Scientists. Native traditions and linguistic topics are frequent in letters from Barton to Heckewelder in Letters of Scientists, and in the letters from Heckewelder to Barton in Delafield-Barton Collection, ser. I. See also "Zeisberger, D.—Onondaga Dictionary," ibid., ser. II.

9. Barton, "Observations and Conjectures," 189–91, at 190; [Hendrick Aupaumut], "Extract from an Indian History," *MHS Coll.* 9 (1804), 100; Heckewelder, "History," 12, 10. Barton cited the accounts of Daniel Gookin and James Adair, but he also received similar traditions in "A Letter from Major Jonathan Heart, to Benjamin Smith Barton . . . Containing Observations on the Ancient Works of Art, the Native Inhabitants, &c. of the Western Country," *APS Trans.,* o.s. 3 (1793): 214–22, at 216–18, 220–21; William Bartram, "Observations on the Creek and Cherokee Indians" (1789), in *Travels and Other Writings,* ed. Thomas P. Slaughter (New York: Library of America, 1996), 527–31. See also Barton, *New Views,* "Preliminary Discourse," xii, xv, xic–xciii; ibid., "Appendix," 29, in which Barton cites Captain Hendrick, and John Drayton to Barton, Sept. 9, 1803, Barton Papers, Page 61. On colonization, disease, and its effects, see Daniel K. Richter, *Facing East from Indian Country: A Native History of Early*

America (Cambridge, MA: Harvard University Press, 2001), 41–68; Joyce Chaplin, *Subject Matter: Technology, the Body, and Science on the Anglo-American Frontier, 1500–1676* (Cambridge, MA: Harvard University Press, 2001), 157-98, 270-76. On Drayton and Nettles, see James H. Merrell, *The Indians' New World: Catawbas and their Neighbors from European Contact to through the Era of Removal* (Chapel Hill: University of North Carolina Press, 1989), 226–29, 239–43. For traditions that Indians' ancestors did not build the mounds, see "Barton, New Views, misc. notes # 3, Folder 6" in Delafield-Barton Collection, Series II; William Bartram, "Travels through North and South Carolina, Georgia, East and West Florida, the Cherokee Country, the Extensive Territories of the Muscogulges or Creek Confederacy, and the Country of the Chactaws" (1791), in Slaughter, ed., *Travels and Other Writings*, 318, 414.

10. Samson Occom, *A Sermon at the Execution of Moses Paul, an Indian; Who Had Been Guilty of Murder, Preached at New Haven in America* (New-London, 1772), 8; Schoolcraft, *Personal Memoirs*, 125. See also Michel de Montaigne, *Essays of Montaigne*, trans. Charles Cotton, ed. William Carew Hazlitt, 3 vols. (London, 1877), 1:255.

11. Barton, "Observations and Conjectures," 192–96. For examples of commentary on hieroglyphics, see William Johnson, "Extracts of Some Letters, from Sir William Johnson Bart. to Arthur Lee, M.D.F.R.S. on the Customs, Manners, and Language of the Northern Indians of America," *Philosophical Transactions* 63 (1773–1774): 142–48, esp. 143; Pehr Kalm, *Travels into North America; Containing Its Natural History, and a Circumstantial Account of Its Plantations and Agriculture in General, with the Civil, Ecclesiastical and Commercial State of the Country, the Manners of the Inhabitants, and Several Curious and Important Remarks on Various Subjects* (Warrington, UK, 1770), 3:125-27; Bartram, "Observations on the Creek and Cherokee Indians," 532–33. For Barton's earlier opinion about European mound builders, see Barton, *Observations*, 50–51, 60, 65–67. See also Allan R. Taylor, "Nonspeech Communication Systems," in *Handbook*; Lisa Brooks, *The Common Pot: The Recovery of Native Space in the Northeast* (Minneapolis: University of Minnesota Press, 2008), 8-13; Phillip H. Round, *Removable Type: Histories of the Book in Indian Country, 1663–1880* (Chapel Hill: University of North Carolina Press, 2010), 11-13.

12. Barton, "Observations and Conjectures," 191–92. Sources cited extensively in *New Views* contain references to linguistic fertility and retentiveness. See Charlevoix, *Journal*, 1:52, 299–300, 302; Abbé D. Francesco Saviero Clavigero, *The History of Mexico, collected from Spanish and Mexican Historians, from Manuscripts, and Ancient Paintings of the Indians*, trans. Charles Cullen. 2 vols. (London, 1787), 1:106, 391, 394, 2:197. On sociolinguistic variation, see Johnson, "Extracts of Some Letters," 148; William Robertson, *The History of America*, 6th ed., 3 vols. (1792; London: Routledge, 1996), 3:167; Le Page du Pratz, *History*, 1:170–71; Carver, *Travels*, 260–61.

13. Humboldt, *Political Essay*, 175; Johann Severin Vater, "An Enquiry into the Origin of the Population of America from the Old Continent" (1810), trans. Peter S. Du Ponceau, 85–86, 88–89, at APS; Cyrus Kingsbury to the Secretary of War (John C. Calhoun), May 15, 1818, in WDLR 2:1818.2.

14. Barton to Alexander McGillivray, July 29, 1792, Delafield-Barton Collection, ser. I; Barton, *New Views*, [Dedication], v–vi; ibid., 10–11. See Edgar Fahs Smith, "Benjamin Smith Barton," *Historical Papers and Addresses of the Lancaster County Historical Society* 28 (1924): 59–66, esp. 59; Peter Silver, *Our Savage Neighbors: How Indian War Transformed Early America* (New York: Norton, 2008), 195. On the deterioration of Delaware-settler relations in Pennsylvania and resulting Delaware migration, see Merritt, *At the Crossroads;* Amy C. Schutt, *Peoples of the River Valleys: The Odyssey of the Delaware Indians* (Philadelphia: University of Pennsylvania Press, 2007). On McGillivray, see Claudio Saunt, *A New Order of Things: Property, Power, and the Transformation of the Creek Indians, 1733–1816* (New York: Cambridge University Press, 1999), 67–89.

15. Jefferson to Barton, Apr. 3, 1814, *TJ Papers RS*, 7:281; Jefferson to Peter Wilson, Jan. 20, 1816, *TJ Writings*, 14:403. See also Jefferson to James Jay, Apr. 7, 1809, ibid., 12:270–71; Anthony F. C. Wallace, *Jefferson and the Indians: The Tragic Fate of the First Americans* (Cambridge, MA: Harvard University Press, 1999), 287–88.

16. Barton to Jefferson, Apr. 12, 1814, Jefferson Papers, Library of Congress, at http://memory.loc.gov, accessed 7/29/2013; Jefferson to Alexander von Humboldt, Dec. 6, 1813, in Lipscomb, ed., *Writings of TJ*, 14:23. For Seminole, Delaware, and Osage traditions of writing being given to whites, see Thomas L. McKenney, *Memoirs, Official and Personal; with Sketches of Travels among the Northern and Southern Indians; Embracing a War Excursion, and Descriptions of Scenes along the Western Borders* (New York, 1846), 15–17; Thomas Brainerd, *The Life of John Brainerd, the Brother of David Brainerd, and His Successor as Missionary to the Indians of New Jersey* (Philadelphia, 1865), 234–35; James, *Account*, 15:110. See also Wallace, *Jefferson and the Indians*, 229, 275; Donald Jackson, *Thomas Jefferson and the Stony Mountains: Exploring the West from Monticello* (1981; Norman: University of Oklahoma Press, 1993), 203–20; William G. McLoughlin, *Cherokee Renascence in the New Republic* (Princeton, NJ: Princeton University Press, 1992), 33–145; Theda Perdue, *Cherokee Women: Gender and Culture Change, 1700–1835* (Lincoln: University of Nebraska Press, 1999), 115–95.

17. TJ, *Notes*, 282 n. 12; Benjamin Smith Barton, "Hints on the Etymology of Certain English Words, and on their Affinity to Words in the Languages of Different European, Asiatic, and American (Indian) Nations, in a Letter from Dr. Barton to Dr. Thomas Beddoes," *APS Trans.* o.s. 6 (1809), 145, 157; Barton to Alexander Tilloch, Mar. 1813, in "Barton, Benjamin Smith, 1766–1815: 1783 May 27–1815 Feb. 1," Delafield-Barton Collection, ser. I. Joseph Ewan and Nesta Dunn Ewan, *Benjamin Smith Barton: Naturalist and Physician in Jeffersonian America* (St. Louis: Missouri Botanical Garden Press, 2007), 252, identifies the letter's recipient.

18. "Address by Rev. William Jenks" (1813), in *AAS Proc.*, 35; James Cowles Prichard, *Researches into the Physical History of Man*, ed. George W. Stocking, Jr. (1813; Chicago: University of Chicago Press, 1973), 154, 549. On Prichard and degeneration, see Stocking, *Victorian Anthropology*, 47–53; Hannah Franziska Augstein, "Linguistics and Politics in the Early Nineteenth Century: James Cowles Prichard's Moral Philology," *History of European Ideas* 23.1 (1997):1–18.

19. C. F. Volney, *A View of the Soil and Climate of the United States of America; with Supplementary Remarks upon Florida; on the French Colonies on the Mississippi and Ohio, and in Canada; and on the Aboriginal Tribes of America*, trans. C. B. Brown (Philadelphia, 1804), 424; Vater to Jefferson, Nov. 4, 1809, in *TJ Papers RS* 1:651–52; Vater, "Enquiry," 56; Alexander de Humboldt, *Researches Concerning the Institutions and Monuments of the Ancient Inhabitants of America, with Descriptions & Views of Some of the Most Striking Scenes in the Cordilleras!*, trans. Helen Maria Williams (London, 1814), 19–23, at 22–23. See also Jorge Cañizares-Esguerra, *How to Write the History of the New World: Histories, Epistemologies, and Identities in the Eighteenth-Century Atlantic World* (Stanford, CA: Stanford University Press, 2001), 13, 55–59, 124–29.

20. Nicholas Collin, "Philological View of Some Very Ancient Words in Several Languages," *APS Trans.* 4 (1799), 508–09, 482, 478, 483; Heckewelder to Du Ponceau, Nov. 25, 1818, Heckewelder Letters.

21. [William Jones], "Discourse the Ninth. On the Origin and Families of Nations. Delivered 23 February, 1792," in *Asiatic Researches; or, Transactions of the Society, Instituted in Bengal, for Inquiring into the History and Antiquities, the Arts, Sciences, and Literature, of Asia*, 20 vols. (London, 1799–1839), 3:488–89; James H. McCulloh, *Researches on America; Being an Attempt to Settle Some Points Relative to the Aborigines of America*, 2nd. ed. (Baltimore, 1817), v–xi, at vii, xi.

22. John Ledyard, "The Siberian Journal and Letters, 1787–1788," in *The Last Voyage of Captain Cook: The Collected Writings of John Ledyard*, ed. James Zug (Washington, DC: National Geographic, 2005), 188–89; William Dunbar, "On the Language of Signs among Certain North American Indians," *APS Trans.*, o.s. 6 (1809), 3.

23. Clement C. Moore, *Observations upon Certain Passages in Mr. Jefferson's Notes on Virginia, Which Appear to Have a Tendency to Subvert Religion, and Establish a False Philosophy* (New York, 1804), 16–19, 31; Elijah Parish, *A Discourse, Delivered at Byfield, on the Annual Thanksgiving, in the Commonwealth of Massachusetts, November 29, 1804* (Salem, MA, 1805), 3, 17–18. On "evangelical anti-Jacobinism" in ethnology, see Stocking, *Victorian Anthropology*, 42–44. On debates about etymology and materialism, see Hans Aarsleff, *The Study of Language in England, 1780–1850* (Minneapolis: University of Minnesota Press, 1966), chap. 2–3; Olivia Smith, *The Politics of Language, 1791–1819* (Oxford: Clarendon Press, 1984), 122–33; David Simpson, *The Politics of American English, 1776–1850* (New York: Oxford University Press, 1986), 81–90. On reaction against philosophical radicalism and its political uses, see Christopher Grasso, *A Speaking Aristocracy: Transforming Public Discourse in Eighteenth-Century Connecticut* (Chapel Hill: University of North Carolina Press, 1999), 327–85. Ironically, Jefferson's linguistic speculations did not appear in the French edition of *Notes*. See Gordon S. Barker, "Unraveling the Strange History of Jefferson's *Observations sur la Virginie*," *Virginia Magazine of History and Biography* 112 (2004): 135–77, esp. 143, 146.

24. Jonathan Edwards, Jr., *Observations on the Language of the Muhhekaneew Indians* (New Haven, CT, 1788), 8, 12; Elias Boudinot, *A Star in the West: A Humble Attempt to Discover the Long Lost Ten Tribes of Israel, Preparatory to Their Return to Their Beloved*

City of Jerusalem (Trenton, NJ, 1816), 106, 104, 74; William Apess, "A Son of the Forest," in *On Our Own Ground: The Complete Writings of William Apess, a Pequot,* ed. Barry O'Connell (Amherst: University of Massachusetts Press,1992), 74–77, at 74. See also Timothy Dwight, "Observations on Language," *Memoirs of the Connecticut Academy of Arts and Sciences* 1.4 (1816): 124, 365–386, esp. 382; "Daniel S. Butrick on Jews and Indians. Part I. [1840?]," ABCFM Papers, 18.3.3, vol. 3, item 5.

25. [William Jones], "The Third Anniversary Discourse, Delivered 2d February, 1786"; "Discourse the Ninth," *Asiatic Researches,* 1:424, 3:482. On Jones's philology, ethnology, and its influence, see Aarsleff, *Study of Language in England,* chap. 4–5; Thomas R. Trautmann, *Aryans and British India* (1997; New Delhi: Yoda Press, 2003), chap. 2–3. On scriptural accounts, see also Benjamin Braude, "The Sons of Noah and the Construction of Ethnic and Geographical Identities in the Medieval and Early Modern Period," *WMQ* 54.1 (1997): 103–42. Robert A. Ferguson, "The Emulation of Sir William Jones in the Early Republic," *NEQ* 52 (1979): 2–26, mentions philology only in passing.

26. Vater, "Enquiry," 123, 118–19. See also Jefferson to Barton, Oct. 6, 1810; Barton to Jefferson, Oct. 16, 1810, Thomas Jefferson Papers, Library of Congress, at http://memory .loc.gov/, accessed 7/29/2013; Prichard, *Researches,* 154; Humboldt, *Political Essay,* 1:102, 105. On Blumenbach, see Ivan Hannaford, *Race: The History of an Idea in the West* (Baltimore: John Hopkins University Press, 1996), 205–13; Dain, *Hideous Monster of the Mind,* 59–65. On the indistinctness, and interchangeability, of "nation" and "race" in these years, see Thomas R. Trautmann, *Languages and Nations: The Dravidian Proof in Colonial Madras* (Berkeley: University of California Press, 2006), 221.

27. [Charles Caldwell], "Criticism—for the Port Folio," *Port-Folio* 7.6 (June 1812): 507–26, at 522–23, 526, 513; J. Ignatius Molina, *Geographical, Natural and Moral History of Chili,* 2 vols. (Philadelphia, 1808), 2:2; Humboldt, *Researches,* 19; Humboldt, *Personal Narrative,* 3:244–247, at 245. See also Thaddeus Mason Harris, "A Dissertation on the First Peopling of America, as Indicated by the Traditions and Some Peculiar Customs of the Natives, 1822," in *AAS Proc.,* 200. On Molina, see Cañizares-Esguerra, *How to Write the History of the New World,* 253–54. Laura Dassow Walls, *The Passage to Cosmos: Alexander von Humboldt and the Shaping of America* (Chicago: University of Chicago Press, 2009), 5–7, 63, 74–76, 181–85, stresses Humboldt's environmentalist view of human difference. On the broader Euro-American attack on environmentalism before the 1830s, see William Stanton, *The Leopard's Spots: Scientific Attitudes toward Race in America, 1815–59* (Chicago: University of Chicago Press, 1960), 15–30; Reginald Horsman, *Race and Manifest Destiny: The Origins of American Racial Anglo-Saxonism* (Cambridge, MA: Harvard University Press, 1981), 98–118. Dain, *Hideous Monster of the Mind,* demonstrates ongoing debates over environmentalism and fixity. See also Robert E. Bieder, *Science Encounters the Indian, 1820–1880: The Early Years of American Ethnology* (Norman: University of Oklahoma Press, 1986).

28. [Peter S. Du Ponceau], "Philology," in *Encyclopaedia Americana,* 82, 84. See also [Peter S. Du Ponceau], "Translator's Preface," in Zeisberger, "Grammar," 65–74; [John Pickering], "Art. VII," *American Quarterly Review* 4.7 (Sept. 1, 1828): 191–214.

29. Du Ponceau to Jefferson, Dec. 11, Feb. 17, 1817, HLC Letter Books, 1:61–63, 57–59; Peter S. Du Ponceau, "The Autobiography of Peter Stephen Du Ponceau," ed. James L. Whitehead, *PMHB* 64.2 (Apr. 1940): 243–69, at 261; Heckewelder to Du Ponceau, Oct. 5, 1816, Oct. 25, 1821, in Heckewelder Letters; Du Ponceau, "Correspondence," 361. See also ibid., 427–28; Du Ponceau, "Report," xxxiii; Du Ponceau to Theodore Schulz, June 29, 1819, HLC Letter Books, 2:25; Heckewelder to Du Ponceau, Mar. 21, 1819, Heckewelder Letters. R. H. Robins, *A Short History of Linguistics*, 4th ed. (London: Longman, 1997), 194, concludes that *Mithridates* teeters between "older . . . speculation and collection and the later . . . organization of genetically related families."

30. Du Ponceau, "Report," xviii; Du Ponceau to Heckewelder, Aug. 5, 1816, HLC Letter Books, 1:43–45. See also Du Ponceau to Adelung, Dec. 16, 1817, ibid., 2:1–2. Du Ponceau admitted extensive editing of the correspondence, but Heckewelder was active in the process, too. See Du Ponceau to Albert Gallatin, Apr. 18, 1826, Gallatin Papers, reel 36; Heckewelder to Du Ponceau, June 4, July 30, 1818, Heckewelder Letters. I have used both the published and unpublished versions of this correspondence, depending on whether I am treating their private exchanges or the public face that Du Ponceau wanted to provide. Cf. Edward G. Gray, *New World Babel: Languages and Nations in Early America* (Princeton, NJ: Princeton University Press, 1999), 7, 139–58, at 7, which argues that for Du Ponceau "language was distinct from mind."

31. Du Ponceau, "Report," xxii–xxiii.

32. Du Ponceau, "Report," xxviii; "Correspondence," 422; Heckewelder, "History," 116–17.

33. Du Ponceau, "Correspondence," 372; Heckewelder, "History," 247–48; Du Ponceau, "Correspondence," 428, 435; Peter S. Du Ponceau, "Notes and Observations on Eliot's Indian Grammar. Addressed to John Pickering, Esq." *MHS Coll.*, 2nd ser. 9 (1822), xix. See also Du Ponceau, "Report," xxxiii–xxxiv, xxxix–xli; "Correspondence," 367–68, 435–38; Du Ponceau to Heckewelder, Sept. 22, 1818, Du Ponceau Letters.

34. Du Ponceau, "Correspondence," 415, 386, 393; idem, "Report," xxxi, xxvi. See also Pierre Swiggers, "Americanist Linguistics and the Origin of Linguistic Typology: Peter Stephen Du Ponceau's 'Comparative Science of Language,'" *APS Proc.* 142 (1998): 18–46.

35. Du Ponceau, "Correspondence," 423, 417, 384, 418, 401–2; Frederick von Schlegel, "On the Indian Language, Literature, and Philosophy" (1808), in *Aesthetic and Miscellaneous Works*, trans. E. J. Millington (London, 1860), 429–53, at 449; Du Ponceau, "Autobiography," ed. Whitehead, *PMHB* 63.2 (Apr. 1939): 189–227, at 222. He never mentioned Schlegel by name, but the classification in Du Ponceau, "Correspondence," 399–402, seems designed to refute him. For Monboddo, see ibid., 384–86, 415. On resentment at the elevation of peoples of Asia and northern Africa, see Du Ponceau, "Correspondence," 399, 402; Heckewelder, "History," 241–42. Robert Henry Robins, "Du Ponceau and General and Amerindian Linguistics," in *Prix*

Volney, 5, notes that "polysynthesis" conflated the formation of compound words with incorporation.

36. Peter S. Du Ponceau, "Report of the Historical and Literary Committee to the American Philosophical Society—Read 9th January 1818," *HLC Trans.,* xiv; Peter S. Du Ponceau, "English Phonology; or an Essay towards an Analysis and Description of the Component Sounds of the English Language," *APS Trans.,* n.s. 1 (1818), 230; Du Ponceau, "Correspondence," 421, 399. Even proponents of universal grammar, like [James Harris], *Hermes: or, a Philosophical Inquiry Concerning Language and Universal Grammar* (London, 1751), 25–26, 407–8, could believe that particular parts of speech were unnecessary in some languages, and that "Nations, like single Men, have their *peculiar* Ideas." On medieval and early modern universal grammar, see Robins, *Short History of Linguistics,* 100–101, 142–43; Ulrich Ricken, *Linguistics, Anthropology, and Philosophy in the French Enlightenment,* trans. Robert E. Norton (London: Routledge, 1994), 1–60.

37. Zeisberger, "Grammar," 97; [Pierre-Louis Moreau de] Maupertuis, "Réflexions philosophiques sur l'origine des langues et la signification des mots," in *Maupertuis, Turgot et Maine de Biran sur l'origine du langage,* ed. Ronald Grimsley (Geneva: Librarie Droz, 1971), 31, 40, 32. See also John Amos Comenius, *The Great Didactic of John Amos Comenius,* trans. and ed. M. W. Keatinge (New York: Russell and Russell, 1967), 206. For Comenius's influence on the Moravian missionary project, see Erben, *Harmony of the Spirits,* 303–18. On Maupertuis, see Avi Lifschitz, *Language and Enlightenment: The Berlin Debates of the Eighteenth Century* (New York: Oxford University Press, 2012), 65–78; David Beeson, *Maupertuis: An Intellectual Biography* (Oxford: Voltaire Foundation, 1992), 154–62.

38. Du Ponceau Notebooks, 1:85; Du Ponceau, "Correspondence," 371–72; Du Ponceau, "Translator's Preface," 75; Du Ponceau to Gallatin, May 4, 1826, Gallatin Papers, reel 36. See also Du Ponceau, "Essai de solution du problème philologique proposé en l'année 1823 par la Commission de l'Institut Royal de France" (1826), in *Prix Volney,* 40. Du Ponceau to Vater, Oct. 20, 1822, HLC Letter Books, 3:15–17; Du Ponceau, "Notes and Observations," vii, demonstrates awareness of comparative work on phonetic shift. On signs in "ideology" see Brian William Head, *Ideology and Social Science: Destutt de Tracy and French Liberalism* (Dordrecht: Martinus Nijhoff, 1985); Ricken, *Linguistics, Anthropology, and Philosophy,* 206–20; Sophia Rosenfeld, *A Revolution in Language: The Problem of Signs in Late Eighteenth-Century France* (Stanford, CA: Stanford University Press, 2001), 181–246. For its more material dimension, see Elizabeth A. Williams, *The Physical and the Moral: Anthropology, Physiology, and Philosophical Medicine in France, 1750–1850* (Cambridge: Cambridge University Press, 1994).

39. Du Ponceau to Eliza C. Tunstall, Jan. 11, 1819, Du Ponceau to John Crowell (U.S. agent to Creeks), Oct. 27, 1821, Du Ponceau to Vater, Oct. 20, 1822, HLC Letter Books, 2:23, 3:4–5, 15–17; Du Ponceau to John Vaughan, May 21, 1832, APS Archives, Record Group III. On this network, see also HLC Letter Books and HLC Vocabularies, APS.

40. Eleazer Williams, "Grammar of the Mohawk Dialect of the Iroquois Language, of the Five Ancient Confederated Nations. Containing Rules and Exercises, Intended to Exemplify the Indian Syntax, According to the Best Authorities, Preceded by Succinct Rules Relative to the Pronunciation," 170–71, Missouri Historical Society, Columbia [microfilm, APS]; Du Ponceau, "Notes and Observations," xix–xx, at xx. See also Du Ponceau to Vater, Oct. 20, 1822, HLC Letter Books, 3:15–17; Du Ponceau, "Report," xxxiv–xxxv, xxi; Jarvis, "Discourse," 234, 246–48. Robert F. Berkhofer, Jr., *The White Man's Indian: Images of the American Indian from Columbus to the Present* (1978; New York: Vintage, 1979), xv, argues that "the essence of the White image of the Indian has been . . . a separate and single other."

41. Du Ponceau, "Report," xli–xliii, xxxix; Du Ponceau, "Correspondence," 432, 402; Du Ponceau, "Letter . . . to the President of the Society," in William Shaler, "On the Language, Manners, and Customs of the Berbers, or Brebers of Africa," *APS Trans.*, n.s. 2 (1825), 442, 438–39, 442, 443; Du Ponceau to Vater, Oct. 20, 1822, HLC Letter Books, 3:15–17. Extracted specimens of the languages of central and northern Asia are in Du Ponceau Notebooks, 1:48, 2:23–28, of the Pacific islands in ibid., 1:96–98, 3:32, 67–69, 8:43, and of Berber in HLC Vocabularies, No. 51. On Otomi, see Du Ponceau to Gallatin, Mar. 12, Apr. 2, 1835, Gallatin Papers, reel 41; Du Ponceau, *Dissertation*, 38, 45; Pickering to Du Ponceau, May 8, 1839, Du Ponceau Papers, box 3. Emmanuele Naxera's essay appeared in Latin, in "De Linguâ Othomitorum Dissertatio," *APS Trans.*, n.s. 5 (1837): 249–96.

42. Du Ponceau, "Correspondence," 431–32; "Report," xxvii–xxviii, xxii. See also Humboldt, *Personal Narrative*, 3: 245–46, at 246. Du Ponceau to Gallatin, May 8, 1826, Gallatin Papers, reel 36, states that he read Humboldt's narrative "2 or 3 years" after his own publication in 1819, observing "Had I written a little later, I should have been considered a plagiarist." Andrew J. Lewis, *A Democracy of Facts: Natural History in the Early Republic* (Philadelphia: University of Pennsylvania Press, 2011), 107–28, describes a "theology of nature" as a means of "discipline." Cf. ibid., 110, which suggests that such expressions were rare in *APS Trans.*

43. Du Ponceau to Joseph Von Hammer, Apr. 25, 1822, HLC Letter Books, 3:10–12.

44. Du Ponceau to Vater, Sept. 9, 1821, HLC Letter Books, 2:54–55; Peter S. Du Ponceau, *A Discourse on the Necessity and Means of Making Our National Literature Independent of That of Great Britain* (Philadelphia, 1834), 17, 24; Du Ponceau to Von Hammer, Apr. 25, 1822, HLC Letter Books, 3:10–12. For representative efforts to European scholars, see also Du Ponceau to Vater, Feb. 2, 1820, "List of Books Sent to Vater," Feb. 16, 1821, Du Ponceau to Wilhelm von Humboldt, July 28, 1821, Du Ponceau to Klaproth, 1823, HLC Letter Books, 2:27–28, 41, 48–49, 3:28–29. For more on Philadelphia's and New York's exchanges with Göttingen, Leipzig, Halle, and Vienna, see the letters from Frederick Christian Schaffer to Du Ponceau, in Du Ponceau Papers, box 1, folders 2–4. On British influence after independence, see Kariann Akemi Yokota, *Unbecoming British: How the United States Became a Postcolonial Nation* (New York: Oxford University Press, 2011), 153–225; Caroline Winterer, "Where Is

America in the Republic of Letters?," *Modern Intellectual History* 9.3 (Nov. 2012): 597–623, esp. 603–7. Cf. Carl Diehl, *Americans and German Scholarship, 1770–1870* (New Haven, CT: Yale University Press, 1978), which stresses Boston and Cambridge.

45. Du Ponceau to Isaiah Thomas, Mar. 1, 1816, AAS Archives, Correspondence and Documents, box 1, folder 30; Du Ponceau to Gallatin, Mar. 12, 1835, Gallatin Papers, reel 41. See also the letters from Du Ponceau to Rejoice Newton, in AAS Archives, box 3, folder 14; HLC Letter Books; and letters from Du Ponceau to Pickering in Du Ponceau Papers, box 3. On natural history contests over authority, see Lewis, *Democracy of Facts*. On learned societies, see Alexandra Oleson and Sanborn C. Brown, eds., *The Pursuit of Knowledge in the Early American Republic: American Scientific and Learned Societies from Colonial Times to the Civil War* (Baltimore: Johns Hopkins University Press, 1976); Albrecht Koschnik, *"Let a Common Interest Bind Us Together": Associations, Partisanship, and Culture in Philadelphia* (Charlottesville: University of Virginia Press, 2007), 205–27; Johann Neem, *Creating a Nation of Joiners: Democracy and Civil Society in Early National Massachusetts* (Cambridge, MA: Harvard University Press, 2008), 82–90.

46. "Art. V.," *Quarterly Review* 31 (1825): 76–111, at 80–81; "For the Port-Folio" [Review 2], *Port-Folio* 8.3 (Sept. 1819): 248–59, at 259; J R T, "The Indian Languages and Pennsylvania History," *The Friend; a Religious and Literary Journal,* 4.34 (June 4, 1831), 267–68, at 267. On *Port-Folio* satire attempting to preserve British ties, see Catherine O'Donnell Kaplan, *Men of Letters in the Early Republic: Cultivating Forums of Citizenship* (Chapel Hill: University of North Carolina Press, 2008), 9, 140–83, 223–25.

47. Thomas Nuttall, *A Journal of Travels into the Arkansa Territory during the Year 1819, with Occasional Observations on the Manners of the Aborigines* (Philadelphia, 1821), vii–viii, at viii; Jarvis, "Discourse," 220, 267; John D. Clifford, *John D. Clifford's Indian Antiquities; Related Mater by C. S. Rafinesque,* ed. Charles Boewe (Knoxville: University of Tennessee Press, 2000), 9–10. See also Jarvis to Du Ponceau, Jan. 11, Jan. 18, 1820, in Du Ponceau Papers, box 1, folder 3.

48. Caleb Atwater, "Description of the Antiquities Discovered in the State of Ohio and Other Western States," *AAS Trans.* 1 (1820), 188–90, 209–13, 238–41, 244–50, 251–67, at 133; Samuel Latham Mitchell, "Communications," ibid., 340. Ibid., 328–29, suggested that the Mound Builders were Malay. Mitchell, in *Medical Repository of Original Correspondence and Intelligence* 3 (Aug.–Oct. 1811), 160–71, had noted the compatibility of Malay and Hindu theses. John Johnston (U.S. Indian Agent at Piqua), "Account of the Present State of the Indian Tribes Inhabiting Ohio," *AAS Trans.* 1 (1820), 271, 287–99, which provided specimens of Shawnee and Wyandot, was the exception to the volume's neglect of language. For examples of linguistic interest within the early AAS, see Jenks, "Address"; Harris, "Dissertation"; Levi Bartlett to Rejoice Newton, June 2, 1819; Barton to Secretary, July 18, 1814; Charles Caldwell to Isaiah Thomas, Dec. 16, 1816, Sept. 22, 1817; William Jenks to Thomas, Dec. 13, 1816; Mitchell to Newton, Aug. 15, 1819; Roger Alden to Thomas, Mar. 15, 1821; Matthew

Carey to Newton, Jan. 1, 1823; Thaddeus M. Harris to Botta, Aug. 24 (May 1), 1822; Constantine S. Rafinesque to Thomas, July 5, 1824, AAS Archives, box 1, folders 17, 18, 24, box 2, folders 10, 15, box 3, folders 4, 10, 26, box 4, folder 4. See also Lewis, *Democracy of Facts*, 72–105; Robert Silverberg, *The Mound Builders of Ancient America* : The Archaeology of a Myth (Greenwich, CT: New York Graphic Society, 1968), 59–75; Greene, *American Science in the Age of Jefferson*, 350–53, 368–69; Bieder, *Science Encounters the Indian*, 110–11, 125, 131.

49. "Preface," *RIHS Coll.* 1 (1827), 4. See also Sheehan, *Seeds of Extinction*, 119–29; Francis Paul Prucha, *The Great Father: The United States Government and the American Indian* (Lincoln: University of Nebraska Press, 1984), 135–58. For similar connections in the British Empire, see Howse, *Grammar*, [iii]; Stocking, *Victorian Anthropology*, 240–45.

50. Heckewelder to Du Ponceau, Jan. 11, 1817, Heckewelder Letters; John Pickering, "Art. XI," *North American Review* 9.24 (June 1819), 186. See also Heckewelder, "History," 5, 8, 327–29, 345; idem, *Narrative of the Mission of the United Brethren among the Delaware and Mohegan Indians, from Its Commencement, in the Year 1740, to the Close of the Year 1808* (1820; New York: Arno Press and the New York Times, 1971), x–xi. De Witt Clinton, "A Discourse before the New-York Historical Society, at Their Anniversary Meeting, 6th December 1811," *NYHS Coll.* 2 (1814), demonstrates continuing idealization of the Iroquois. Keat Murray, "John Heckewelder's 'Pieces of Secrecy': Dissimulation and Class in the Writings of a Moravian Missionary," *JER* 32.1 (Spring 2012): 91–126, criticizes Heckewelder's elitism but ignores the unsettling connection between democracy and violence in the mid- to late eighteenth-century "backcountry."

51. Du Ponceau to Albert Gallatin, May 19, 1826, Gallatin Papers, reel 36; Daniel S. Butrick, "Conjugation of a Verb in the Cherokee Language," Oct. 29, 1818; "Remarks on the Verbs of the Cherokee Language," n.d., HLC Vocabularies, 41–42; Du Ponceau to Daniel S. Butrick, Sept. 7, 1818, HLC Letter Books, 2:16–18. See also Peter S. Du Ponceau, *A Discourse on the Early History of Pennsylvania; Being an Annual Oration Delivered before the APS* (Philadelphia, 1821), esp. 10, 12, 25–26; Du Ponceau and J. Francis Fisher, "A Memoir on the History of the Celebrated Treaty Made by William Penn with the Indians, under the Elm Tree at Shackamaxon, in the Year 1682" in *HSP Memoirs* 3.2 (1836), esp. 153, 185; Du Ponceau, "Translator's Preface," 78, 95; Du Ponceau Notebooks, 2:inside flap, 3:51; Pickering, *Life of Pickering*, 287. On U.S. consumption of Native oratory, see Carolyn Eastman, "The Indian Censures the White Man: 'Indian Eloquence' and American Reading Audiences in the Early Republic," *WMQ* 65.3 (July 2008): 535–64.

52. Du Ponceau, "Correspondence," 388; Zeisberger, "Grammar," 141. In John O'Meara, *Delaware-English/English-Delaware Dictionary* (Toronto, 1996), xxi, 307, 509, 519, 534, 549, the verb "live" is rendered *pŭmáawsuw;* the verb "move" is rendered *kwchúkwiiw;* and coming closest is seemingly *taláawsuw,* which means "live there," or *ndalŭmóoxwe,* meaning "I walk away." To "own someone" is *nihláaleew* and "own something" is *nihláatam;* to "kill someone" is *nihleew* and "kill something" is *nihtoow.*

53. Walter Bromley to Thomas Wistar, Apr. 26, 1819, HLC Vocabularies; John Adams to Du Ponceau, June 23, July 5, 1819, Du Ponceau Collection; F. C. Schaffer to Du Ponceau, Apr. 2, 1819, Du Ponceau Papers, box 1, folder 2.

54. Du Ponceau to John Pickering, June 24, 1832, in Du Ponceau Papers, 3:83–84; Pickering, "Art. XI," 181–82; "Art. IX," ibid. 14.3 (Jan. 1822), 129; "Art. VII," ibid. 11.28 (July 1820), 113; John Pickering, *On the Adoption of a Uniform Orthography for the Indian Languages of North America, as Published in the Memoirs of the American Academy of Arts and Sciences* (Cambridge, MA, 1820), 9. See also idem, "Indian Languages of America," *Encyclopaedia Americana*, 6:581–600. For his earlier work, see John Pickering, *A Vocabulary, or Collection of Words and Phrases Which Have Been Supposed to Be Peculiar to the United States of America. To Which Is Prefixed an Essay on the Present State of the English Language in the United States* (Boston, 1816); John Pickering, "On the Pronunciation of the Greek Language," *AAAS Memoirs* 4 (1818).

55. John Pickering, "Introductory Observations to John Eliot, *Indian Grammar Begun*," *MHS Coll.*, 2nd ser., 9 (1822), 234, 224; "Doctor Edwards' Observations on the Mohegan Language" in ibid., 10 (1823), 81; [Edwin James], "Article V," *American Quarterly Review* 3.6 (June 1828), 418. See the discussions of "to be" and "*Ultra-Mississippian* Languages" in "Doctor Edwards' Observations," 112–17, 149. Pickering's other editions were "Josiah Cotton's Vocabulary of the Massachusetts (or Natick) Indian Language," *MHS Coll.*, 3rd ser., 2 (1830); "A Dictionary of the Abnaki Language, in North America; by Father Sebastian Rasles," *AAAS Memoirs*, n.s. 1 (1833). See also Heckewelder, "History," 111; Pickering, *Life*, 282, 312. Julie Tetel Andresen, *Linguistics in America, 1769–1924* (London: Routledge, 1990), 101, 104–5, 120–21, overdraws Du Ponceau's and Pickering's respective "French" and "German" orientations and overstates Pickering's influence independent from Du Ponceau. On "physically affectionate and yet nonerotic" male relationships in this era, see Richard Godbeer, *The Overflowing of Friendship: Love between Men and the Creation of the American Republic* (Baltimore: Johns Hopkins University Press, 2009), 6, 155–92, at 6.

56. J. H. McCulloh, *Researches, Philosophical and Antiquarian, Concerning the Aboriginal History of America* (Baltimore, 1829), 42, 56–57; Caleb Atwater to Isaiah Thomas, Oct. 23, 1820, Caleb Atwater Letters and Drawings, AAS; Caleb Atwater, *Remarks Made on a Tour to Prairie du Chien; Thence to Washington City, in 1829* (Columbus, OH, 1831), 78, 146. On Jeffersonian and Jacksonian opposition to the spread of voluntary organizations and attempts to link civil society and the federal government, see Neem, *Creating a Nation of Joiners*.

4. Four Clicks, Two Gutturals, and a Nasal

1. David Brown, "Extract of a Letter to a Lady in Wilmington," *Circular* 3.22 (Oct. 1, 1824): 87; "Extract of a Letter from Mr. Evan Jones to a Friend in This City," *Latter-Day Luminary* 3.10 (Oct. 1822): 310–13, at 311; John Heckewelder to Peter S. Du Ponceau, Mar. 4, 1820, Heckewelder Letters; D. S. Butrick and D. Brown, *Tsvlvki Sqclvclv. A Cherokee Spelling Book, for the Mission Establishment at Brainerd* (Knoxville,

1819), 60; Brown to *Family Visitor* (Richmond), Apr. 27, 1825, in *Religious Intelligencer* 10.6 (July 9, 1825): 87–88, at 88; Brown to *Family Visitor* (Richmond), Sept. 2, 1825, enclosed in Thomas L. McKenney to James Barbour, Dec. 13, 1825, in *Am. State Papers,* 2:651. See also Joyce B. Phillips and Paul Gary Phillips, eds., *Brainerd Journal: A Mission to the Cherokees, 1817–1823* (Lincoln: University of Nebraska Press, 1998), 141, 145, 151; Brown to John Pickering, Sept. 4, 1823, in Mary Orne Pickering, *The Life of John Pickering* (Boston, 1887), 332–33. On the Browns' role in evangelization, see Mary Alves Higginbotham, "The Creek Path Mission," *JCS* 1 (1976): 72–86.

2. Brown to *Family Visitor,* Sept. 2, 1825, 651–52; Brown to Jeremiah Evarts, July 11, 1826, Butrick to Evarts, May 28, 1825, ABCFM Papers, 18.3.1, vols. 4–5, items 290, 13; John Pickering, *On the Adoption of a Uniform Orthography for the Indian Languages of North America, as Published in the Memoirs of the American Academy of Arts and Sciences* (Cambridge, MA, 1820), 15. Pickering uses "corrupting," citing Brown, and Brown may use it himself in the letter to Evarts (illegible). On Brown's translations, see Butrick to Evarts, June 25, 1825, Dec. 8, 1826, Samuel A. Worcester to Evarts, Jan. 8, 1827, ABCFM Papers 18.3.1, vols. 4–5, items 14, 26, 294; Evarts to Brown, Jan. 6, 1824, ibid., 1.01, vol. 4, 96–98; "Cherokees. Progress of Religion," *Missionary Herald* 23.7 (July 1827): 212–13, at 213. For his preaching, see William Chamberlain to Evarts, Mar. 12, 1825, Worcester to Evarts, Sept. 21, 1826, ABCFM Papers 18.3.1, vols. 4–5, items 40, 233. See also William G. McLoughlin, *Cherokee Renascence in the New Republic* (Princeton, NJ: Princeton University Press, 1986), 226, 397.

3. "Address of Dewi Brown, a Cherokee Indian" (1823), *Proceedings of the Massachusetts Historical Society, 1871–1873* (Boston, 1873), 30, 32–33, 36. On the dating of this address, see Pickering, *Life,* 331–32. On language and sovereignty, see Thomas Belt and Margaret Bender, "Speaking Difference to Power: The Importance of Linguistic Sovereignty," in *Foundations of First Peoples' Sovereignty: History, Education and Culture,* ed. Ulrike Weithaus (New York: Peter Lang, 2007); Scott Richard Lyons, "There's No Translation for It: The Rhetorical Sovereignty of Indigenous Languages," in *Cross-Language Relations in Composition,* eds. Bruce Horner, Min-Zhan Lu, and Paul Kei Matsuda (Carbondale: Southern Illinois University Press, 2010). On Brown's career, see Joel W. Martin, "Crisscrossing Projects of Sovereignty and Conversion: Cherokee Christians and New England Missionaries during the 1820s," in *Native Americans, Christianity, and the Reshaping of the American Religious Landscape,* eds. Martin and Mark A. Nicholas (Chapel Hill: University of North Carolina Press, 2010); Hilary E. Wyss, *English Letters and Indian Literacies: Reading, Writing, and New England Missionary Schools* (Philadelphia: University of Pennsylvania, 2012), 150–210. On ABCFM and "civilization" funds, see Ronald N. Satz, *American Indian Policy in the Jacksonian Era* (Lincoln: University of Nebraska Press, 1975), 13.

4. Daniel Gookin, *Historical Collections of the Indians in New England* (1674; Boston, 1792), 82. See also Carol Sheriff, *The Artificial River: The Erie Canal and the Paradox of Progress* (New York: Hill and Wang, 1997), 9–26; John A. Andrew III, *From Revivals to Removal: Jeremiah Evarts, the Cherokee Nation, and the Soul of America* (1992; Athens: University of Georgia Press, 2007), 74–106; Richard Lee Rogers, "'A Bright and New

Constellation': Millennial Narratives and the Origins of American Foreign Missions," in *North American Foreign Missions, 1810–1914*, ed. Wilbert R. Shenk (Grand Rapids, MI: William B. Eerdman's, 2004).

5. *Ne Yakawea Yondereanayendaghkwa Oghseragwegouh, Neoni Yakawea ne Orighwadogeaghty Yondatnekosseraghs Neoni Tekarighwagehhadont* [The Book of Common Prayer . . . Translated into the Mohawk Language] (London, 1787), i; Alfred Wright to Evarts, May 13, 1830, ABCFM Papers 18.3.4, vol. 3, item 108. On the seventeenth-century episode, contrast Jill Lepore, *The Name of War: King Phillip's War and the Origins of American Identity* (New York: Knopf, 1998), 42–44; Edward G. Gray, *New World Babel: Languages and Nations in Early America* (Princeton, NJ: Princeton University Press, 1999), 79–80.

6. Noah Webster, *Dissertations on the English Language; with Notes Historical and Critical* (1789; Gainesville, FL: Scholars' Facsimiles & Reprints, 1951), 21; Thomas Jefferson to William Henry Harrison, Feb. 27, 1803, Jefferson to John Cartwright, June 5, 1824, Jefferson to James Monroe, Nov. 24, 1801, Jefferson to John Waldo, Aug. 16, 1813, *TJ Writings*, 10:373, 16:42, 10:296, 13:345. On language loss, see TJ, *Notes*, 96; "Jefferson's Vocabulary of the Unquachog Indians," *TJ Papers*, 20:467–70; John Sibley, "Historical Sketches of the Several Indian Tribes in Louisiana" (1805), in *Am. State Papers*, 2:721–25, esp. 725. On linguistic colonization, compare Jefferson, "Essay on the Anglo-Saxon Language," in *TJ Writings*, 18:365, with [Timothy] Dwight, "Observations on Language," *Memoirs of the Connecticut Academy of Arts and Sciences* 1.4 (1816), 381. On removal and linguistic homogeneity, see also Sylvestris [St. George Tucker], *Reflections on the Cession of Louisiana to the United States* (Washington City, 1803), 24–25. On a national language, see Jill Lepore, *A is for American: Letters and Other Characters in the Newly United States* (2002; New York: Vintage, 2003), 15–41. On Saxon study, see H. Trevor Colbourn, *The Lamp of Experience: Whig History and the Intellectual Origins of the American Revolution* (Chapel Hill: University of North Carolina Press, 1965), 158–84, 196–98. Peter S. Onuf, *Jefferson's Empire: The Language of American Nationhood* (Charlottesville: University Press of Virginia, 2000), 15–16, 49–52, 75–79, 158–61, 181–82, examines his view of a racially homogenous nation and empire.

7. John Heckewelder to Peter S. Du Ponceau, Sept. 3 1818, in Heckewelder Letters; Secretary of War (Henry Dearborn) to Return J. Meigs, July 1, 1803, vol. A, WDLS; Samuel Worcester to William Jenks, Nov. 15, 1815, ABCFM Papers, 1.01, vol. 1, 48–51; Lyman Beecher, *The Bible a Code of Laws; a Sermon, Delivered in Park Street Church, Boston, Sept. 3, 1817, at the Ordination of Mr. Sereno Edwards Dwight, as Pastor of That Church; and of Messrs. Elisha P. Swift, Allen Graves, John Nichols, Levi Parsons, & Daniel Buttrick, as Missionaries to the Heathen* (Andover, MA, 1818), 63–64; ABCFM, *Ninth Annual Report of the ABCFM* (Boston, 1818), 23. See also Worcester to Evarts, July 1, 1815, ABCFM Papers, 1.01, vol. 1, 22–24; Jedidiah Morse, *A Report to the Secretary of War of the United States on Indian Affairs* (1822; New York: Augustus M. Kelley, 1970), 77–78; *Seventh Annual Report of the ABCFM* (Boston, 1816), 12–13. On Blackburn's mission, see William G. McLaughlin, *Cherokees and Missionaries, 1789–1839* (New Haven, CT: Yale University Press, 1984), 46–47, 56–67, 72–75; Anthony F. C. Wallace,

Jefferson and the Indians: The Tragic Fate of the First Americans (Cambridge: Cambridge University Press, 1999), 287–88. Edwin S. Gaustad, *Sworn on the Alter of God: A Religious Biography of Thomas Jefferson* (Grand Rapids, MI: William B. Eerdmans, 1996), 99–102, discusses Jefferson's views of missionary work within the context of separation of church and state. On the ABCFM and the transatlantic evangelical missionary-translation movement, see Donald Philip Corr, "'The Field Is the World': Proclaiming, Translating, and Serving by the American Board of Commissioners for Foreign Missions, 1810–40" (Ph.D. diss., Fuller Theological Seminary, 1993), 205–12.

8. "Extract from the Indian Journal, being the Sixth Speech That Was Delivered to the Delaware Nation Residing at Waupekum Mekut, or White River, on the 15th Day of April, 1803," in "Letter to the Rev. Mr. Hopkins, of Salem," *Massachusetts Missionary* 1 (Apr. 1804), 9–10. See also Henry Dearborn to John Sergeant, Feb. 10, 1804, WDLS, A:438; [Hendrick Aupaumut], "Extract from an Indian History," *MHS Coll.* 9 (1804); idem, "History of the Muhheakunnuk Indians," in *First Annual Report of the American Society for Promoting the Civilization and General Improvement of the Indian Tribes in the United States* (New Haven, CT, 1824), 41–43. Rowena McClinton, "Introduction," *The Moravian Springplace Mission to the Cherokees*, ed. McClinton, 2 vols. (Lincoln: University of Nebraska Press, 2007), 1:21, 31–33, stresses Cherokee insistence on English education. On Aupaumut's nineteenth-century work, see Rachel Wheeler, "Hendrick Aupaumut: Christian-Mahican Prophet," *JER* 25.2 (Summer 2005): 187–220.

9. Morse, *Report*, 356–57; Speech of Richard Wilde, May 19, 1830, *Register of Debates in Congress, Comprising the Leading Debates and Incidents of the First Session of the Twenty-first Congress* (Washington, 1830), 6:1079–1103, at 1103. On the ABS, see *The First Annual Report of the Board of Managers of the American Bible Society, presented May 8, 1817* (New York, 1817), 18; *Second Annual Report of the American Bible Society, Presented May 14, 1818* (New York, 1818), 15–19. On Wilde, see also Michael Paul Rogin, *Fathers and Children: Andrew Jackson and the Subjugation of the American Indian* (1975; New York: Vintage, 1976), 210–11.

10. *MSS. Notes*, Page 117–18, Barton Papers; Morse, *Report*, 113–14. See also James Axtell, *The Invasion Within: The Contest of Cultures in Colonial North America* (New York: Oxford University Press, 1985), 214; David J. Silverman, *Red Brethren: The Brothertown and Stockbridge Indians and the Problem of Race in Early America* (Ithaca, NY: Cornell University Press, 2010), 7, 151, 192.

11. Butrick to Worcester, Jan. 1, 1819, ABCFM Papers, 18.3.1, vol. 3, item 114; "Art. V," *American Quarterly Review* (Sept. 1830): 108–34, at 131; "Intelligence. United States. Great Osage Mission," *Christian Herald and Seaman's Magazine* (New York, NY) 9.13 (Nov. 16, 1822): 398–401, at 398. See also Butrick to Evarts, Sept. 27, 1825, ABCFM Papers, 18.3.1, vols. 4–5, item 18; Finney and Washburn to Evarts, Jan. 10, 1822, ibid., vol. 1, item 32. Cf. Phillip H. Round, *Removable Type: Histories of the Book in Indian Country, 1663–1880* (Chapel Hill: University of North Carolina Press, 2010), 73–96, at 91, which notes a "surprising" nineteenth-century shift to Native-language education.

12. Tamakoche [Stephen R. Riggs], "Learning English," clipping from *Minnesota Weekly Times* (Mar. 5, 1859) in ABCFM Papers, 18.3.7, vol. 3, item 47; [Peter King], *Dah-ko-tah (Sioux) First Book, or Introduction to the Spelling Book. Designed for the Use of the Mission Schools of the Methodist Episcopal Church* (Pittsburgh, 1839), iii; "The Cherokees," *Religious Intelligencer* (New Haven, CT), 10.6 (July 9, 1825): 87–88.

13. Williams, *Key,* 25; Heckewelder, "History," 318; Henry Perkins, "Journal" (1843–1844), in *People of the Dalles: The Indians of Wascopam Mission: A Historical Ethnography Based on the Papers of the Methodist Missionaries,* ed. Robert Boyd (Lincoln: University of Nebraska Press, 1996), 287.

14. Rufus Anderson, "Instructions of the Prudential Committee to the Rev. Abel L. Barber, destined to the North Western Indians . . . Sept. 25, 1833," ABCFM Papers 8.1, vol 1, 63; Evarts to Butrick, June 20, 1826, ibid., 1.01, vol. 6, 140–41. See also Evarts to Wright, May 19, 1829, ibid., 8:290; Butrick to Evarts, Apr. 19, 1826, ibid., 18.3.1, vols. 4–5, item 20; Stephen R. Riggs to David Greene, Feb. 24, 1841, ibid., 18.3.7, vol. 2, item 65; Joshua Potter to Selah B. Treat, Mar. 21, 1854, ibid., 18.6.3, vol. 3, item 57; [Sarah Tuttle], *Conversations on the Choctaw Mission,* 2nd ed. (Boston, 1834), 132, 142–43, 147. On print culture and reform, see Nathan O. Hatch, *The Democratization of American Christianity* (New Haven, CT: Yale University Press, 1989), 93–97, 204–5; Johann Neem, *Creating a Nation of Joiners: Democracy and Civil Society in Early National Massachusetts* (Cambridge, MA: Harvard University Press, 2008), 82–90; John L. Brooke, "Cultures of Nationalism, Movements of Reform, and the Composite-Federal Polity: From Revolutionary Settlement to Antebellum Crisis," *JER* 29.1 (Spring 2009): 1–33.

15. [William Thornton], "Cadmus, or a Treatise on the Elements of Written Language," *APS Trans.* 3 (1793), 262–63. On the orthographic collaboration, see Pickering, *Life,* 291–92. On previous universal writing systems, see Karen Ordahl Kupperman, *Indians and English: Facing Off in Early America* (Ithaca, NY: Cornell University Press, 2000), 80–83; Lepore, *A is for American,* 42–60; Alan Kemp, "Transcription, Transliteration, and the Idea of a Universal Alphabet," in *Prix Volney,* 477–99.

16. Pickering, *Uniform Orthography,* 11, 33, 13; Noah Webster, *A Grammatical Institute of the English Language, comprising, an Easy, Concise, and Systematic Method of Education, Designed for the Use of English Schools in America. In Three Parts. Part I. Containing, a New and Accurate Standard of Pronunciation* (Hartford, CT, 1783), 5; Horatio Hale, *Ethnography and Philology,* vol. 6., "United States Exploring Expedition during the Years 1838, 1839, 1840, 1841, 1842. Under the Command of Charles Wilkes, U.S.N." (Philadelphia, 1846), x. For suggestions of Greek, Armenian, and Hebrew alphabets, see Peter S. Du Ponceau, "English Phonology; or an Essay towards an Analysis and Description of the Component Sounds of the English Language," *APS Trans.* n.s. 1 (1818), 264; Asher Wright to David Greene, June 4, 1834, ABCFM Papers 18.6.3, vol. 1, item 46; Eugene Vetromile, *Indian Good Book, Made by Eugene Vetromile, S.J., Indian Patriarch, for the Benefit of the Penobscot, Passamaquody, St. John's, Micmac, and Other Tribes of the Abnaki Indians,* 2nd ed. (New York, 1857), 13. On German values,

see Peter S. Du Ponceau, "Notes and Observations on Eliot's Indian Grammar. Addressed to John Pickering, Esq." *MHS Coll.*, 2nd ser. 9 (1822), xi.

17. Pickering, *Uniform Orthography*, 37, 33, 29; John Pickering, *A Grammar of the Cherokee Language* (1825), 12. On the extensive use of the orthography, see Evarts to Thompson S. Harris, Dec. 25, 1829, ABCFM Papers, 1.01, vol. 8, 487–88; David Greene, "Extracts from the Instructions of the Prudential Committee to the Rev. Sherman Hall & Rev. William T. Boutwell, missionaries to the Ojibeways of the North West Territory of the United States, 10 June 1831," ibid., 8.1, vol. 1, item 6; William H. Prescott, *Memoir of the Hon. John Pickering, LL.D.* (Cambridge, MA, 1848), 16.

18. Butrick to Evarts, Aug. 31, 1821, ABCFM Papers, 18.3.1, vol. 3, item 128; Asher Wright to David Greene, Aug. 29, 1834, ibid., 18.6.3, vol. 1, item 47; Stephen R. Riggs, *Mary and I: Forty Years with the Sioux* (Chicago, 1880), 36; Stephen R. Riggs, Journal, Oct. 17, 1840, ABCFM Papers, 18.3.7, vol. 2, item 64; Cyrus Byington to Jeremiah Evarts, May 16, 1825, ibid., 18.3.4, vol. 3, item 68. See also "Extract of a Letter from the Rev. Cyrus Byington," July 1, 1826, in ibid., item 76. On native-language texts as "phonetic prompts," see Michael D. McNally, *Ojibwe Singers: Hymns, Grief, and Native Culture in Motion* (2000; St. Paul: Minnesota Historical Society Press, 2009), 48.

19. Pickering, *Uniform Orthography*, 2; Henry R. Schoolcraft, "Chapter XIV. Hymns, Original and Translated, in the Indian Languages," in "Considerations, on the Art of Picture Writing, & the System of Mnemonic Symbols of the North American Indians" (ca. 1844), [6], in Schoolcraft Papers (LC), reel 59, box 76; Peter Jones, trans., *A Collection of Chippeway and English Hymns, for the Use of the Native Indians* (New York, 1847), v; Eugene Vetromile, *Ahiamihewintuhangan; The Prayer Song* (New York, 1858), vi; Isaac McCoy, *History of the Baptist Indian Missions: Embracing Remarks on the Former and Present Condition of the Aboriginal Tribes; Their Settlement within the Indian Territory, and Their Future Prospects* (Washington and New York, 1840), 476. On the problem of competing alphabets, see also Cyrus Kingsbury to David Greene, Sept. 4, 1834; Cyrus Byington to Greene, Sept. 4, 1834, in ABCFM Papers, 18.3.4. vol. 4, items, 63, 169. Round, *Removable Type*, 91–92, discusses Native influence on literacy and orthography.

20. Asher Wright to David Greene, Aug. 29, 1834, June 30, 1836, June 4, 1834, ABCFM Papers, 18.6.3, vol. 1, items, 47, 62, 46. See also [Jabez Hyde], *Analysis of the Seneca Language, Na na none do wau gau / Ne u wen noo da* (Buffalo, 1827), 2; Jabez Backus Hyde, "A Teacher among the Senecas," *Publications of the Buffalo Historical Society* 6 (1903): 239–74, at 273–74; Evarts to the Chiefs and People of the Seneca Nation residing near Buffalo, N.Y., Dec. 25, 1829, Evarts to Thompson S. Harris, Dec. 25, 1829, ABCFM Papers, 1.01, vol. 8, 485, 487–88; Asher Bliss and Asher Wright to David Greene, Sept. 26, 1839, ibid., 18.5.8, vol. 1, item 42.

21. Pickering to Wilhelm von Humboldt, Nov. 27, 1827, in Pickering, *Life*, 353; "Cherokees, Progress of Religion," *Missionary Herald* 23.7 (July 1827): 212–13; Samuel A. Worcester, "Cherokee Alphabet," *Cherokee Phoenix* 1.1 (Feb. 21, 1828), [3]. See also Pickering, *Life*, 336–38; "Note," Apr. 27, 1850, inside Houghton Library's copy of Pickering, *Grammar*. On Worcester and the Cherokee press, see Althea Bass, *Cherokee*

Messenger (Norman: University of Oklahoma Press, 1936), 31–50, 69–89. For the social-political context, see McLoughlin, *Cherokee Renascence,* 277–427 Round, Removeable Type, 123–49.

22. George Lowrey and John Howard Payne, "Notable Persons in Cherokee History: Sequoyah or George Gist," *JCS,* 2 (1977): 385–93, at 388.

23. Lowrey and Payne, "Notable Persons in Cherokee History," 388–89; Chamberlain to Evarts, Oct. 1826, in ABCFM Papers, 18.3.1, vols. 4–5, item 39. Other details can be found in Samuel L. Knapp, *Lectures on American Literature, with Remarks on some Passages of American History* (New York, 1829), 25–29, esp. 27; "Cherokees, Syllabic Alphabet Invented by a Native," *Missionary Herald* 22.2 (Feb. 1826): 47–49, at 48; Elias Boudinot, "Invention of a New Alphabet" (1832), in *Cherokee Editor: The Writings of Elias Boudinot,* ed. Theda Perdue (Knoxville: University of Tennessee Press, 1983), 58. See also Willard Walker and James Sarbaugh, "The Early History of the Cherokee Syllabary," *Ethnohistory* 40 (1993): 70–94; Grant Foreman, *Sequoyah* (Norman: University of Oklahoma Press, 1938).

24. "Art. VI—Description of the Cherokee Alphabet," *American Annals of Education* 2 (Apr. 1832):181–84, at 184. For Cherokee traditions of whites' stealing literacy, see McClinton, ed., *Moravian Springplace Mission,* 2:87; Boudinot, "Invention of a New Alphabet," 52; "Speech of John Ridge, a Cherokee Chief," *The Liberator* 2.11 (Mar. 17, 1832): 44. Ethan Allen Hitchcock, *A Traveler in Indian Territory: The Journal of Ethan Allen Hitchcock, Late Major-General in the U.S. Army,* ed. Grant Forman (1930; Norman: University of Oklahoma Press, 1996), 124–27, describes a similar Creek tradition. In contrast, see the Seminole, Delaware, and Osage traditions in chap. 3 n. 16. See also McLoughlin, *Cherokee Renascence,* 176, 350–65; Nancy Shoemaker, *A Strange Likeness: Becoming Red and White in Eighteenth-Century North America* (New York: Oxford University Press, 2004), 80; Ellen Cushman, " 'We're Taking the Genius of Sequoyah into This Century': The Cherokee Syllabary, Peoplehood, and Perseverence," *Wicazo Sa Review* 26.1 (Spring 2011): 67–83. On diffusion, see Peter T. Daniels, "The Invention of Writing," in *The World's Writing Systems,* eds. Peter T. Daniels and William Bright (New York: Oxford University Press, 1996), 579.

25. [Antoine Yves] Goguet, *The Origin of the Laws, Arts, and Sciences, and Their Progress among the Most Ancient Nations,* 3 vols. (1758; Edinburgh, 1761), 1:190; Edward Gibbon, *The History of the Decline and Fall of the Roman Empire,* vol. 1 (London, 1776), 222; Samuel Taylor Coleridge, *Logic,* ed. J. R. de J. Jackson, in *The Collected Works of Samuel Taylor Coleridge,* no. 13 (Princeton NJ: Princeton University Press, 1981), xxxix, 15, at 15; [Francis Lieber], "Writing," in *Encyclopaedia Americana,* 12: 273. See also Nicholas Hudson, *Writing and European Thought, 1600–1830* (Cambridge: Cambridge University Press, 1994), 55–160, esp. 141–60; Walter D. Mignolo, *The Darker Side of the Renaissance: Literacy, Territoriality, and Colonization* (Ann Arbor: University of Michigan Press, 1995), 29–122. On Goguet's eighteenth-century prominence, see Francis L. Broderick, "Pulpit, Physics, and Politics: The Curriculum of the College of New Jersey, 1746–1794," *WMQ* 6 (1949): 42–68, at 65–66 n.68; J. G. A. Pocock, *Barbarians, Savages, and Empires,* vol. 4. *Barbarism and Religion* (Cambridge: Cambridge University Press, 2005), 37–64.

26. James Beattie, *The Theory of Language. In Two Parts. Part I. Of the Origin and General Nature of Language. Part II. Of Universal Grammar* (London, 1788), 109. For observations of Native graphic practices, see chap. 3 n. 11, and Heckewelder, "History," 117–18, 288; Lewis Cass, "Extract of a Letter from Gov. Cass to the Secretary of War," *The Philanthropist* 6.1 (May 5, 1821): 3–8, at 6; Catlin, *Letters and Notes*, 2:246–47; Frederic W. Hoxay, ed., *Voyages of the "Columbia" to the Northwest Coast, 1787–1790 and 1790–1793* (Boston: Massachusetts Historical Society), 234; Eugene Vetromile, *The Abnakis and Their History; or, Historical Notices on the Aborigines of Acadia* (New York, 1866), 40.

27. Goguet, *Origin of Laws, Arts, and Sciences*, 1:177–78; Peter S. Chazotte, *An Introductory Lecture on the Metaphysics & Philosophy of Languages; Being the first Number of a Philosophical and Practical Grammar of the English and French Languages* (Philadelphia, 1819), 39. See also Hugh Blair, *Lectures on Rhetoric and Belles Lettres*, eds. Linda Ferreira-Buckley and S. Michael Halloran (1783; Carbondale: Southern Illinois University Press, 2005), 72; James Burnet, Lord Monboddo, *Of the Origin and Progress of Language*, 2nd ed., 6 vols. (1774; New York: Garland, 1970), 2:258; "History of the Progress of Language," *Christian Review*, 4.15 (Sept. 1, 1839): 333–55, esp. 338. Daniels, "Origin of Writing," 585, suggests a syllabic stage.

28. Peter S. Du Ponceau to Albert Gallatin, May 17, 1826, Gallatin Papers, reel 36; P. -Ét. Du Ponceau, "Mémoire sur le système grammatical des langues de quelques nations indiennes de l'Amérique du Nord" (1838), 48, in *Prix Volney;* Du Ponceau to Pickering, Mar. 14, 1835, Du Ponceau Papers, box 3; Gallatin to Theodore Frelinghuysen, Feb. 14, 1835, Gallatin Papers, reel 41. See also Du Ponceau, *Dissertation*, xii–xiv, xxxi–xxxii.

29. [Lewis Cass], "Article III," *North American Review* 30.66 (Jan. 1830): 62–121, at 71; Charles Caldwell, *Thoughts on the Original Unity of the Human Race* (New York, 1830), 143, 136, 138. See also "Literary and Intellectual Statistics," *New-England Magazine* (Dec. 1831): 465–80, esp. 466–67; George R. Gliddon, "Paleographic Excursus on the Art of Writing," in J. C. Nott and Geo. R. Gliddon, *Types of Mankind: or, Ethnological Researches* (Philadelphia, 1854), 630. Cf. "A Cherokee," *Independent Chronicle and Boston Patriot* 61.4584 (Apr. 2, 1825), 1; "Aboriginal Literature," *Christian Register* 4.14 (Apr. 9, 1825), 55. On white ancestry and leadership in cultural adaptation, see McLoughlin, *Cherokee Renascence;* Claudio Saunt, *A New Order of Things: Property, Power, and the Transformation of the Creek Indians, 1733–1816* (Cambridge: Cambridge University Press, 1999). Cf. Theda Perdue, *"Mixed Blood" Indians: Racial Construction in the Early South* (Athens: University of Georgia Press, 2003). On Ridge, Boudinot, and riots, see Thurman Wilkins, *Cherokee Tragedy: The Story of the Ridge Family and the Decimation of a People* (New York: Macmillan, 1970), 119–53.

30. Knapp, *Lectures*, 25–26, 28.

31. Evarts to Rufus Anderson, Mar. 11, 1828, in E. C. Tracy, *Life of Jeremiah Evarts, Late Corresponding Secretary of the ABCFM* (Boston, 1845), 305–7, at 306.

32. Knapp, *Lectures*, 26. See also Lowrey and Payne, "Notable Persons in Cherokee History," 390; Cushman, "We're Taking the Genius of Sequoyah into This Century," 72–74.

33. Elias Boudinot, "An Address to the Whites" (1826), in Perdue, ed., *Cherokee Editor*, 73–74, 78; John Ridge to David Brown, Dec. 13, 1822, in "Indian Youth," *Abolition Intelligencer and Missionary Magazine* 1.11 (Mar. 1823): 175–76, at 175; "Speech of John Ridge," 44. On "civilization" and political institutions, see Ridge to Brown, June 13, 1823, ABCFM Papers, 18.3.1, vol. 11, item 55. See also Barry O'Connell, "Literacy and Colonization: The Case of the Cherokees," in *An Extensive Republic: Print, Culture, and Society in the New Nation, 1790–1840*, eds. Robert A. Gross and Mary Kelley, vol. 2. *A History of the Book in America* (Chapel Hill: University of North Carolina Press, 2010), 503–4; Maureen Konkle, *Writing Indian Nations: Native Intellectuals and the Politics of Historiography* (Chapel Hill: University of North Carolina Press, 2004), 78–96.

34. Catharine Beecher, "Circular. Addressed to Benevolent Ladies of the U. States," *Christian Advocate and Journal and Zion's Herald* (New York) 4.17 (Dec. 25, 1829): 65–66, at 65; Evarts, note, Aug. 31, 1825, ABCFM Papers, 1.01, vol. 4, 371. See also Alisse Portnoy, *Their Right to Speak: Women's Activism in the Indian and Slave Debates* (Cambridge, MA: Harvard University Press, 2005), 16–86; Anderson, *From Revivals to Removal*, 133–228.

35. Henry R. Schoolcraft to Charles C. Trowbridge, Dec. 4, 1825, in Trowbridge Papers; Schoolcraft, *Personal Memoirs*, 549–50; Wilhelm von Humboldt to Elias Boudinot, Nov. 15, 1828, ABCFM Papers, 18.3.1, vols. 4–5, item 365; Humboldt to Pickering, July 12, Nov. 15, 1828, in Kurt Müller-Vollmer, ed., "Wilhelm von Humboldt und der Anfang der amerikanischen Sprachwissenschaft: Die Briefe an John Pickering," *Universalismus und Wissenschaft im Werk und Wirken der Brüder Humboldt* (Frankfurt am Main: Vitorio Klostermann, 1974), 303, 307; Pickering to Humboldt, Nov. 27, 1827, in Pickering, *Life*, 353. A better appraisal, in [John Pickering], "Indian Languages of America," *Encyclopaedia Americana*, 6:581–600, he sent to the man then preparing the prosecution's case in *Worcester v. Georgia*. See William Wirt to Pickering, Aug. 5, 1831, in Pickering, *Life*, 385–86.

36. "Cherokees. Syllabic Alphabet, Invented by a Native," *Missionary Herald* 22.2 (Feb. 1826): 47–49, at 49; Thomas L. McKenney to William Chamberlain, July 25, 1825, OIALS, 2:103; McKenney to Barbour, Dec. 13, 1825, *Am. State Papers*, 651; McKenney to Pickering, Apr. 18, 1826, McKenney to Thomas Henderson, Jan. 30, 1829, OIALS, 3:39–40, 5:285–86. See also Thomas L. McKenney and James Hall, *The Indian Tribes of North America; with Biographical Sketches and Anecdotes of the Principal Chiefs*, 3 vols., ed. Frederick Webb Hodge (1836–1844; Edinburgh: John Grant, 1933), 1:132–34.

37. "Communication of the Cherokee Deputation to the Honble. Secy. of War, Feb. 5, 1818, WDLR, 2:576; William C. Sturtevant, ed., "John Ridge on Cherokee Civilization," *JCS* 6 (1981): 79–91, at 86. On the *Cherokee Phoenix*, see Elias Boudinot, "Prospectus," *Cherokee Phoenix* 1.2 (Feb. 28, 1828), 3. See also Round, *Removable Type*, 132–40; McLoughlin, *Cherokee Renascence*, 225–26, 352, 397.

38. ABCFM, *Seventeenth Annual Report of the ABCFM* (Boston, 1826), 49; S. S. Haldeman, *Analytic Orthography: An Investigation of the Sounds of the Voice and their Alphabetic Notation; including the Mechanism of Speech* (Philadelphia, 1860), 12; "Extract

of a Letter from Mr. Evan Jones," 310; Riggs, "Learning English"; Cyrus Byington to David Greene, Sept. 4, 1834, in ABCFM Papers, 18.3.4, vol. 5, item 169.

39. Nicholson H. Parker, "The American Red Man" (c. 1847–1848), in Arthur C. Parker, *The Life of General Ely S. Parker: Last Grand Sachem of the Iroquois and General Grant's Military Secretary* (Buffalo, NY: Buffalo Historical Society, 1919), 266, 268–69; James Mooney, "Myths of the Cherokee," *Nineteenth ARBE,* Part 1 (Washington, DC, 1900), 147. See also "Se-quo-yah, or George Guess," *Friends' Weekly Intelligencer* 1.46 (Feb. 8, 1845): 366.

40. Loring S. Williams to Evarts, Dec. 28, 1825, "A Plan for Writing the Choctaw Language with Characters denoting Syllabic Sounds," ABCFM Papers 18.3.4, vol. 3, item 57, vol. 4, item 283; Asher Wright to David Greene, June 4, 1834, ibid.,18.6.3, vol. 1, item 46.

41. Jones, *Collection of Chippeway Hymns,* vi; Peter Jones (Kahkewaquonaby), *History of the Ojebway Indians; with Especial Reference to their Conversion to Christianity* (London, 1861), 190. Williams's manuscript syllabic orthography is in Williams Papers, 2:28. See also Eleazer Williams, *Prayers for Families and for Particular Persons: Selected from the Book of Common Prayer; Translated into the Language of the Six Nations of Indians* (Albany, 1816); James Constantine Pilling, *Bibliography of the Iroquoian Languages* (Washington, DC, 1888), 168.

42. "Extract of a Letter from Henry R. Schoolcraft," *American Annals of Education* (Aug. 1835), 356–57; Jotham Meeker to Lucius Bolles, Jan. 1833, Meeker Papers, MS 617. See also Douglas C. McMurtrie and Albert H. Allen, *Jotham Meeker: Pioneer Printer of Kansas; with a bibliography of the known issues of the Baptist Mission Press at Shawanoe, Stockbridge, and Ottawa, 1834–1854* (Chicago: Eyencourt Press, 1930), 45; Bruce Peel, *Rossville Mission Press: The Invention of the Cree Syllabic Characters, and the First Printing in Rupert's Land* (Montreal: Osiris, 1974), 7; John D. Nichols, "The Cree Syllabary," in *World's Writing Systems,* eds. Daniels and Bright, 599. On Evans's missionary work, see Neil Semple, *The Lord's Dominion: The History of Canadian Methodism* (McGill-Queen's Press, 1996), 153, 168–77.

43. William Mason to the Secretary of the Church Missionary Society, Aug. 13, 1852, Sept. 20, 1855, in Peel, *Rossville Mission Press,* 27, 32; Verne Dusenberry, *The Montana Cree: A Study in Religious Persistence* (1962; Norman: University of Oklahoma Press, 1998), 267. See also Jennifer S. H. Brown, "The Wasitay Religion: Prophecy, Oral Literacy, and Belief on Hudson Bay," in *Reassessing Revitalization Movements: Perspectives from North America and the Pacific Islands,* ed. Michael E. Harkin (Lincoln: University of Nebraska Press, 2007), esp. 105, 112; Peel, *Rossville Mission Press,* 38–40; Willard Walker, "Native American Writing Systems," in *Language in the U.S.A.,* eds. Charles E. Ferguson and Shirley Brice Heath (New York: Cambridge University Press, 1981), 157–62.

44. *Historical and Statistical Information,* 6:673; [James Hunter], *Portions of the Book of Common Prayer, According to the Use of the United Church of England and Ireland in the Language of the Cree Indians, of the Diocese of Rupert's Land (Transmuted into the Phonetic Syllabic Symbols)* (London, 1856), iii; Francis Lieber, "A Paper on the Vocal Sounds of Laura Bridgman, Compared with the Elements of a Phonetic Language" (1850), in

Reminiscences, Addresses, and Essays (Philadelphia, 1881), 458. See also Konrad Tuchscherer and P. E. H. Hair, "Cherokee and West Africa: Examining the Origins of the Vai Script," *History in Africa* 29 (2002): 427–486.

45. "The Cherokees," *Religious Intelligencer* 10.6 (July 9, 1825): 87–88, at 87; James Evans, *The Speller and Interpreter, in Indian and English, for the Use of the Mission Schools, and Such as May Desire to Obtain a Knowledge of the Ojibway Tongue* (New York, 1837), 8, 3; William Mason to the Secretary of the Church Missionary Society, Sept. 20, 1855, in Peel, *Rossville Mission Press*, 32; Hunter, *Book of Common Prayer*, [vi–vii], title page. See also McClinton, ed., *Moravian Springplace Mission*, 1:161. Thank you to William Hunting Howell for pushing me to consider pronunciation as a physical process, intersecting with concerns about the body.

46. McCoy, *History of the Baptist Missions*, 472–78, at 472, 478; Meeker to Bolles, Jan. 1833, June 18, 1834, Meeker Papers. See also "New System of Writing," *Christian Watchman* 18.33 (Aug. 18, 1837): 132; "The 'New System' of Writing Indian Languages," *Baptist Missionary Magazine* 18.6 (June 1838): 48; "Explanation of the Putawatomie Characters" (1834), in James Constantine Pilling, *Bibliography of the Algonquian Languages* (Washington, DC, 1891), 354.

47. C. Colton, *Tour of the American Lakes, and among the Indians of the North-West Territory, in 1830: Disclosing the Character and Prospects of the Indian Race*, 2 vols. (London, 1830), 1:84; Henry R. Schoolcraft, *Notes on the Iroquois; or Contributions to American History, Antiquities, and General Ethnology* (1846; Albany, 1847), 88; H. F. Buckner, *A Grammar of the Maskɔke or Creek Language, to Which Are Prefixed Lessons in Spelling, Reading, and Defining . . . Assisted by his Interpreter G. Herrod* (Marion, AL, 1860), 6, 10. On Colton, see Daniel Walker Howe, *The Political Culture of the American Whigs* (Chicago: University of Chicago Press, 1979), 41.

48. Dwight, "Observations on Language," 131[371]–32[372]; John Norton, *The Journal of Major John Norton, 1816*, eds. Carl F. Klinck and James J. Talman (Toronto: Champlain Society, 1970), 86; Du Ponceau, "Correspondence," 396; Eugene Vetromile, *Of Vetromile's Noble Bible, Such as happened Great-Truths* (New York, 1860), ix–x; *Historical and Statistical Information*, 2:361; Caleb Atwater, *Remarks Made on a Tour to Prairie du Chien, thence to Washington City, in 1829* (Columbus, 1831), 80.

49. John Marsh, "Rudiments of the Grammar of the Sioux Language," in Atwater, *Remarks*, 149; *Historical and Statistical Information*, 5:202, 578, at 202; Wm. Hamilton and S. M. Irvin, *An Ioway Grammar, illustrating the Principles of the Language used by the Ioway, Otoe, and Missouri Indians* (Ioway Sac and Mission Press, 1848), 9, iii.

50. George Gibbs, "Observations on Some of the Indian Dialects of California," *Historical and Statistical Information*, 3:420; James G. Swan, *The Northwest Coast; or, Three Years' Residence in Washington Territory* (New York, 1857), 315–16; Paul Kane, *The Columbia Wanderer: Sketches, Paintings, and Comment, 1846–1847*, ed. Thomas Vaughan (Portland: Oregon Historical Society, 1971), 25. For early linguistic observations of the Pacific Northwest, see James Cook, *A Voyage to the Pacific Ocean: Undertaken by the Command of his Majesty, for Making Discoveries in the Northern Hemisphere, to Determine the Position and Extent of the West Side of North America its Distance from Asia; and the Practicability of a Northern Passage to Europe*, vol. 2 (London, 1784), 334–36.

51. R. Lepsius, *Standard Alphabet for Reducing Unwritten Languages and Foreign Graphic Systems to a Uniform Orthography in European Letters* (London, 1855), vi–xi, 17–22, 70–72, at 22; Haldeman, *Analytic Orthography*, 10, vi. See also Haldeman, "On Some Points of Linguistic Ethnology; with Illustrations, Chiefly Drawn from the Aboriginal Languages of North America," in *AAAS Proc.* 2 (1852), 65–78. On Lepisus's system, see Joseph Errington, *Linguistics in a Colonial World: A Story of Language, Power, and Meaning* (Malden, MA: Blackwell, 2008), 104–5. On hardening racial ideas, see George W. Stocking, Jr., *Victorian Anthropology* (New York: Free Press, 1987), 62–69; Reginald Horsman, *Race and Manifest Destiny: The Origins of American Racial Anglo-Saxonism* (Cambridge, MA: Harvard University Press, 1981), 116–297; Bruce Dain, *A Hideous Monster of the Mind: American Race Theory in the Early Republic* (Cambridge, MA: Harvard University Press, 2002), 197–226.

52. Evans, *Speller and Interpreter*, 6; Jones, *Collection of Chippeway Hymns*, vi; Washington Matthews, *Ethnography and Philology of the Hidatsa Indians*, United States Geological and Geographical Survey Miscellaneous Publications No. 7 (Washington, 1877), 75–84, at 81. See also Franz Boas, "On Alternating Sounds" (1889), in *A Franz Boas Reader: The Shaping of American Anthropology, 1883–1911*, ed. George W. Stocking, Jr. (Chicago: University of Chicago Press, 1982). National differences among recorders and imprecise pronunciation of interpreters are in, respectively, Cadwallader Colden, *The History of the Five Indian Nations Depending on the Province of New-York in America* (New York, 1727), xiii; Henry R. Schoolcraft to Lewis Cass, Oct. 26, 1822, Schoolcraft Papers (LC), reel 2, box 3, 558. On continuing speculation on inconsistent pronunciation among Indians, see Vetromile, *Noble Bible*, ix; Frederic Baraga, *A Dictionary of the Otchipwe Language, Explained in English. This Language Is Spoken by the Chippewa Indians, as also by the Ottawas, Potawatamis and Algonquins, with Little Difference. For the Use of Missionaries, and Other Persons Living among the Indians* (Cincinnati, 1853), v; Nathaniel Wyeth, "Indian Tribes of the South Pass of the Rocky Mountains; the Salt Lake Basin; the Valley of the Great Säaptin, or Lewis' River, and the Pacific Coast or Oregon," in *Historical and Statistical Information*, 1:215. On phonetic differences among Algonquians, see Du Ponceau, "Notes and Observations," vii; Henry R. Schoolcraft, "Discourse Delivered before the Historical Society of Michigan," in *Historical and Scientific Sketches of Michigan: Comprising a Series of Discourses Delivered before the Historical Society of Michigan, and other Interesting Papers Relative to the Territory* (Detroit, 1834), 95; Howse, *Grammar*, 316–17. On phonetic differences among Muskogean, Iroquoian, and Siouan speakers, see, respectively, Byington to Worcester, Apr. 1, 1821, ABCFM Papers 18.3.4, vol. 2, item 151; Lewis H. Morgan, *League of the Ho-de'-no-sau-nee, Iroquois*, ed. William N. Fenton (1851; New York: Carol Communications, 1962), 395–96; S. R. Riggs, "The Dakota Language," *Collections of the Minnesota Historical Society* 1 (1851; St. Paul, 1872), 94–95. On seeking the "relative age" of related tongues, see S. S. Haldeman to Rev. Harvey Byington, Apr. 22, 1854, box 1, Turner Papers. On European comparative philology and phonetic shift, see Tuska Benes, *In Babel's Shadow: Language, Philology, and the*

Nation in Nineteenth-Century Germany (Detroit: Wayne State University Press, 2008), 116–27, 146–52, 236–39.

53. Robley Dunglison, *Human Physiology,* 7th ed., 2 vols. (Philadelphia, 1856), 1:204; Jones, trans., *Collection of Chippeway Hymns,* vi, 98–99; Evans, *Speller and Interpreter,* 7; D. Lee and J. H. Frost, *Ten Years in Oregon* (New York, 1844), 311. See also Du Ponceau to Heckewelder, July 31, 1816, HLC Letter Books, 1:39–40; Swan, *Northwest Coast,* 317. On pessimism and race in the Methodist mission, see Gray H. Whaley, *Oregon and the Collapse of Illahee: U.S. Empire and the Transformation of the Indigenous World* (Chapel Hill: University of North Carolina Press, 2010), 160. John E. Joseph, *Limiting the Arbitrary: Linguistic Naturalism and Its Opposites in Plato's* Cratylus *and Modern Theories of Language* (Philadelphia: John Benjamins, 2000), 95–99, esp. 96, discusses environmentalist views of pronunciation. On "lack" of sounds, see Mignolo, *Darker Side of the Renaissance,* 45–48.

54. Lieber, "Writing," 276; "Indian Genius," *The Country Courier* (New York), 1 (Sept. 12, 1816): 446–48, at 446; Du Ponceau, "English Phonology," 228, 230.

55. John L. LeConte, "Distinctive Characters of the Indians of California," *Copway's American Indian* 1.8 (Aug. 30, 1851), 1; John L. LeConte to S. S. Haldeman, Jan. 4, 1854, Le Conte Papers; L. A., "Art. VIII—The Diversity of Origin of the Human Races," *Christian Examiner and Religious Miscellany* 49.1 (July 1850): 110–45, at 141. Benes, *In Babel's Shadow,* 204, 208–10, discusses philologist August Friedrich Pott and physiologists Adolf Bastian and Carl Vogt seeking the bodily foundations of language.

5. The Unchangeable Character of the "Indian Mind"

1. Schoolcraft, *Personal Memoirs,* 97, 101, 106, 109, at 97; Henry R. Schoolcraft, *Algic Researches, Comprising Inquiries Respecting the Mental Characteristics of the North American Indians,* 2 vols. (New York, 1839), 1:11, 36. See also Karl S. Hele, ed., *Lines Drawn upon the Water: First Nations and the Great Lakes Borders and Borderlands,* ed. Karl S. Hele (Waterloo, ON: Wilfrid Laurier University Press, 2008); Michael Witgen, *An Infinity of Nations: How the Native New World Shaped Early America* (Philadelphia: University of Pennsylvania Press, 2012); Lucy Eldersveld Murphy, *A Gathering of Rivers: Indians, Métis, and Mining in the Western Great Lakes, 1737–1832* (Lincoln: University of Nebraska Press, 2007).

2. Henry R. Schoolcraft, "Difficulties of Studying the Indian Tongues of the United States," in *Summary Narrative of an Exploratory Expedition to the Sources of the Mississippi River, in 1820: Resumed and Completed by the Discovery of Its Origin in Itasca Lake, in 1832. By the Authority of the United States* (Philadelphia, 1855), 441–42; Schoolcraft, *Personal Memoirs,* 100, 107, 136, 257, 189; "Dawn of Literary Composition by Educated Natives of the Aboriginal Tribes," [11], in Schoolcraft Papers (LC), reel 52, box 62. Schoolcraft had in mind I Corinthians 14:10. For Jane Johnston's philological role, see Schoolcraft, *Personal Memoirs,* 208, 257, 646. See also Anne F. Hyde, *Empires, Nations, and Families: A New History of the North American West, 1800–1860* (2011; New York: Ecco, 2012), 9–11, 35; Robert Dale Parker, "Introduction," in *The*

Sound the Stars Make Rushing through the Sky: The Writings of Jane Johnston Schoolcraft, ed. Parker (Philadelphia: University of Pennsylvania Press, 2007); Richard G. Bremer, *Indian Agent and Wilderness Scholar: The Life of Henry Rowe Schoolcraft* (Mount Pleasant, MI: Clarke Historical Library, Central Michigan University, 1987), 55–120.

3. Henry R. Schoolcraft, *Travels in the Central Portions of the Mississippi Valley: Comprising Observations on Its Mineral Geography, Internal Resources, and Aboriginal Population (Performed under the Sanction of Government, in the Year 1821)* (New York, 1825), 76; Henry R. Schoolcraft, "The Unchangeable Character of the Indian Mind" (1826), in *The Literary Voyager or Muzzeniegun*, ed. Philip P. Mason (East Lansing: Michigan State University Press, 1962), 107. Henry R. Schoolcraft, *Schoolcraft's Expedition to Lake Itasca: The Discovery of the Source of the Mississippi*, ed. Philip P. Mason (East Lansing: Michigan State University Press, 1993), 62; Henry R. Schoolcraft, *Notes on the Iroquois; or Contributions to American History, Antiquities, and General Ethnology* (1846; Albany, 1847), 382–89, at 384–86; *Historical and Statistical Information*, 1:v. On Schoolcraft's life and his shifting views, see Bremer, *Indian Agent and Wilderness Scholar*, 215–20, 232–46; Robert E. Bieder, *Science Encounters the Indian, 1820–1880: The Early Years of American Ethnology* (Norman, OK, 1986), 155–60, 166–69, 179, 189–93.

4. Schoolcraft to Francis Lieber, May 24, 1851, copy in Schoolcraft Papers (DPL); Schoolcraft, *Personal Memoirs*, 209. See Guy Deutscher, *Through the Language Glass: Why the World Looks Different in Other Languages* (New York: Picador, 2010) for a current view on "mirror" and "lens."

5. [Lewis Cass], "Art. V," *North American Review* 22.50 (Jan. 1826): 53–119, at 65; Lewis Cass to David B. Douglass, June 7, 1821, Douglass Papers; John C. Calhoun to Cass, Feb. 11, 1822, in *The Territorial Papers of the United States*, vol. 11, *The Territory of Michigan, 1820–1829*, ed. Clarence Edwin Carter (Washington, DC: National Archives, 1943), 225. See also Cass to Secretary of War, May 15, 1823, in ibid., 363. The call for extermination is quoted in Willard Carl Klunder, *Lewis Cass and the Politics of Moderation* (Kent, OH: Kent State University Press, 1996), 10. For the pamphlet, see [Lewis Cass], *Inquiries, Respecting the History, Traditions, Languages, Manners, Customs, Religion, &c. of the Indians, Living within the United States* (Detroit, 1823), which combines a shorter edition of the same title (1821) and *Additional Inquiries* (1822). Though they understate the philological context, Ronald Gregory Miriani, "Lewis Cass and Indian Administration in the Old Northwest, 1815–1836" (Ph.D. diss., University of Michigan, 1974), 74–83; Anthony F. C. Wallace, *The Long, Bitter Trail: Andrew Jackson and the Indians* (New York: Hill and Wang, 1993), 41–48, examine Cass's project. Richard Drinnon, *White Savage: The Case of John Dunn Hunter* (New York: Schocken Books, 1972), 61–94, recognizes the context but does not examine the philology. On the creation of the BIA, see Francis Paul Prucha, *The Great Father: The United States Government and the American Indian* (Lincoln: University of Nebraska Press, 1984), 130–77.

6. Cass, *Inquiries*, [2], 24–25, 36; B. F. Stickney to Schoolcraft, Jan. 1, 1824, in Schoolcraft Papers (LC), reel 2, box 4, 650–51. Cass to Eleazer Williams, July 13, 1825, in Cass Papers, vol. 3, requests Pauw's book.

7. Alexander Wolcott, "History and Language of the Pottowattomies," in Schoolcraft, *Travels*, 381; Trowbridge to Cass, Jan. 22, 1825, Mar. 6, 1826, in "Account of the Traditions, Manners, and Customs of the Twaatwaa or Miami Indians," Trowbridge Materials, I4mi; Edwin James, "Some Account of the Menomonies with a Specimen of an Attempt to form a Dictionary of Their Language, by Edwin James, an Assistant Surgeon of the U.S. Army" (1827), APS. See also Schoolcraft, *Personal Memoirs*, 100; Jedediah Morse, *A Report to the Secretary of War of the United States on Indian Affairs* (1822; New York: Augustus M. Kelley, 1970), 140. On philology for preferment, see A. G. Ellis to Charles C. Trowbridge, Mar. 3, 1826; J. F. Polk to Trowbridge, Mar. 1827, Trowbridge Papers. On Le Gros, see Bradley J. Birzer, "Entangling Empires, Fracturing Frontiers: Jean Baptiste Richardville and the Quest for Miami Autonomy" (Ph.D. diss., Indiana University, 1998), 57.

8. Charles C. Trowbridge, "Account of the Traditions, Manners, and Customs of the Lenee Lanaupee Indians . . . and, Language of the Delawares, ca. 1825," [1], Bentley Historical Library, University of Michigan (microfilm at APS); Wolcott, "History and Language of the Pottowattomies," 381–82; Schoolcraft, *Personal Memoirs*, 184–85.

9. Schoolcraft, "Difficulties of Studying the Indian Tongues," 442; Schoolcraft, *Personal Memoirs*, 120; Schoolcraft to Cass, May 31, 1823, in Schoolcraft, *Summary Narrative*, 446–47, 445. See also Schoolcraft to Cass, Oct. 26, 1822, in Schoolcraft Papers (LC), reel 2, box 3, 560.

10. "Art. V," *Quarterly Review* (London) 31 (Dec. 1824), 76–111, esp. 94, 101; Cass to Jared Sparks, July 30, 1825, Letters to Sparks, vol. 153, Sparks MSS, Houghton Library, Harvard University, Cambridge, MA; Cass, "Art. III," 366. See also Schoolcraft, *Travels*, 382–83; Cass to Calhoun, May 15, 1823, in Carter, ed., *Territorial Papers*, 11:363. On Cass's articles, see Drinnon, *White Savage*, 61–94; Wallace, *Long, Bitter Trail*, 41–48.

11. Cass, "Art. V," 94; Cass, "Art. III," 373–75, 386–87, at 386–87. Cass Papers, vol. 18, shows that Cass had placed *HLC Trans.* as the lead title on his manuscript. Editor Jared Sparks likely deleted it because Pickering had praised it in the *North American Review* years earlier.

12. Cass, "Art. III," 395, 387; "Art. V," 54. See also Schoolcraft to Cass, May 31, 1823, in Schoolcraft, *Summary Narrative*, 446–47.

13. Cass, "Art. V," 88, 58–59; "Art. III," 374–75, 377–82, at 374–75. See also Trowbridge, "Account of the Traditions, Manners, and Customs of the Lenee Lanaupee Indians," 2; Lawrence Henry Gipson, ed., *The Moravian Indian Mission on White River: Diaries and Letters, May 5, 1799, to November 12, 1806*, trans. Harry E. Stocker, Herman T. Frueauff, and Samuel C. Zeller (Indianapolis: Indiana Historical Bureau, 1938), 516; Schoolcraft to Cass, Oct. 26, 1822, Cass to Schoolcraft, Jan. 13, 1825, in Schoolcraft Papers (LC), reel 2, box 3, 560, reel 3, box 5, 815; Cass to Calhoun, Aug. 3, 1819, in Henry R. Schoolcraft, *Narrative Journal of Travels through the Northwestern Regions of the United States, Extending from Detroit through the Great Chain of American Lakes to the Sources of the Mississippi River in the Year 1820*, ed. Mentor L. Williams (East Lansing: Michigan State College Press, 1953), 287.

14. Cass, "Art. V," 79, 77, 78; "Art. III," 376. See also Bernard Cohn, *Colonialism and Its Forms of Knowledge: The British in India* (Princeton: Princeton University Press, 1996), 4–5, 21–22; Eric Cheyfitz, *Poetics of Imperialism: Translation and Colonization from The Tempest to Tarzan*, rev. ed. (Philadelphia: University of Pennsylvania Press, 1997), xi–xii, 105, 141, 195, 204–5.

15. Cass to Schoolcraft, Feb. 6, 1826, in Carter, ed., *Territorial Papers*, 11:945; Daniel Webster to George Ticknor Curtis, Mar. 1, 1826, in Ticknor, *Life of Daniel Webster* (Boston, 1870), 1:260. See also Cass to Schoolcraft, Apr. 18, 1826, Schoolcraft Papers (LC), reel 3, box 6, 962–63; Wallace, *Long, Bitter Trail*, 41, 47.

16. Schoolcraft, *Personal Memoirs*, 237; [John Pickering], "Examination of an Article in the North American Review, for January, 1826, Respecting the Indians of America, by Kass-ti-ga-tor-skee, or The Feathered Arrow," *New York Review and Atheneum Magazine*, 2 (May 1826): 405–22, esp. 415, 409; [Henry Whiting], "Cursory Remarks upon an Article in the United States Literary Gazette," *United States Review and Literary Gazette* 2 (May 1826): 40–53, esp. 51; Schoolcraft, "Unchangeable Character of the Indian Mind"; Edwin James to Du Ponceau, May 10, 1828, Du Ponceau Papers, box 1, folder 10; Howse, *Grammar*, 7, 10. See also Schoolcraft, *Travels*, 379–434, esp. 380–86; Thomas L. McKenney, *Sketches of a Tour to the Lakes, of the Character and Customs of the Chippeway Indians, and of Incidents Connected with the Treaty of Fond du Lac* (Baltimore, 1827), 487–93; Henry Whiting, *Sannillac, a Poem; with Notes, by Lewis Cass and Henry R. Schoolcraft* (Boston, 1831), 129–32; [Edwin James], "Art. V," *American Quarterly Review* 3.6 (June 1, 1828): 391–423; John Tanner, *A Narrative of the Captivity and Adventures of John Tanner (U.S. Interpreter at the Saut Ste. Marie,) during Thirty Years Residence among the Indians in the Interior of North America*, ed. Edwin James (London, 1830), 392–426; Edwin James, "Art. II. Essay on the Chippewa Language: Read before the American Lyceum, at the Third Annual Meeting, May 3d, 1833," *American Annals of Education* 3.10 (Oct. 1833): 440–46. On accusations of charlatanism in the era's scientific debate, see George H. Daniels, *American Science in the Age of Jackson* (New York: Columbia University Press, 1968), 57.

17. Albert Gallatin to Peter S. Du Ponceau, May 9, Apr. 12, May 17, Apr. 3, 1826, Du Ponceau Papers, box 1, folder 8. See also Gallatin to Du Ponceau, Mar. 20, 1826, in ibid.; Du Ponceau to Gallatin, Apr. 2, 1826, Gallatin Papers, reel 36; Alexander von Humboldt to Gallatin, Feb. 22, 1825, in *Alexander von Humboldt und die Vereinigten Staaten von Amerika Briefwechsel*, ed. Ingo Schwarz (Berlin: Akademie Verlag, 2004), 169. The correspondence with Gallatin is in French. On Adams's call for intellectual improvement, see Jean V. Matthews, *Toward a New Society: American Thought and Culture, 1800–1830* (Boston: Twayne, 1990), 149–50.

18. Gallatin to Du Ponceau, Apr. 4, Mar. 20, 1826, Du Ponceau Papers, box 1, folder 8; John Gambold to Du Ponceau, Oct. 20, Dec. 18, 1818, HLC Vocabularies, Folder 39; "Mission among the Choctaws," *Missionary Herald* 19.9 (Sept. 1823): 283–85, esp. 285; Gallatin, "Synopsis," 113. See also Du Ponceau, "Report," xxxiii; Heckewelder, "History," 114; Cass, "Art. V," 73.

19. "Department of War," May 15, 1826, Gallatin Papers, reel 36; Gallatin to Du Ponceau, Apr. 4, 1826, Du Ponceau Papers, box 1, folder 8; Thomas L. McKenney to

James Barbour, Dec. 1, 1827, OIALS, 4:163. See also S. S. Hamilton to John Jacob Astor, June 7, 1826, ibid., 3:117.

20. Gallatin to Edward Lincoln, May 29, 1826, McKenney to Gallatin, Jan. 5, 1827, Gallatin Papers, reel 36; Du Ponceau to Gallatin, Apr. 15, 1826, HLC Letter Books, 3:46–51; McKenney, *Sketches,* title page. See also Gallatin to Du Ponceau, Apr. 12, 1826, Mar. 10, 1835, Du Ponceau Papers, box 1, folder 8, box 2, folder 6; Du Ponceau to Gallatin, May 13, Gallatin to James Rochelle, May 29; Pickering to Gallatin, June 26; Cass to Gallatin, Oct. 3, 1826, Gallatin Papers, reel 36; Samuel S. Hamilton to James F. Watson, June 22; Hamilton to Rochelle, Aug. 14; Barbour to Mrs. Mary Randolph, Oct. 17, 1826; McKenney to Barbour, Dec. 1, 1827, OIALS, 3:131–32, 147, 197, 4:163; Benjamin Pixley to James Barbour, Sec. of War, April 7, 1828, ABCFM Papers, 18.8, item 74; Gallatin, "Synopsis," 1–2, 305–6. See also Edward G. Gray, *New World Babel: Languages and Nations in Early America* (Princeton, NJ: Princeton University Press, 1999), 145–47; Andrew J. Lewis, *A Democracy of Facts: Natural History in the Early Republic* (Philadelphia: University of Pennsylvania Press, 2011), 133; John Lauritz Larson, *Internal Improvement: National Public Works and Promise of Popular Government in the Early United States* (Chapel Hill: University of North Carolina Press, 2001).

21. Cass, "Art. V," 115; "Art. III," 387; Lewis Cass, "Art. III," *North American Review* 30.66 (Jan. 1830): 62–121, esp. 71–72; Schoolcraft, *Personal Memoirs,* 321. See also Lisa Ford, *Settler Sovereignty: Jurisdiction and Indigenous People in America and Australia, 1788–1836* (Cambridge, MA: Harvard University Press, 2010); Witgen, *Infinity of Nations,* 345. On *Johnson v. M'Intosh,* see "Art. III" (1830), 78, 95–96. See also Robert A. Williams, Jr., *The American Indian in Western Legal Thought: The Discourses of Conquest* (New York: Oxford University Press, 1990), 231, 312–17. Cf. Charles F. Hobson, ed., *The Papers of John Marshall,* 12 vols. (Chapel Hill: University of North Carolina Press, 1998), 9:279–84.

22. Peter Paul Osunkhirhine to S. B. Treat, Aug. 1, 1850, ABCFM Papers, 18.6.3, vol. 4, item 21; Asa B. Smith, in *Diaries and Letters of Henry H. Spalding and Asa Bowen Smith Relating to the Nez Perce Mission, 1838–1842,* ed. Clifford Merrill Drury (Glendale, CA: Arthur H. Clark, 1958), 129, 172. On "time" and "law," see Wm. Hamilton and S. M. Irvine, *An Ioway Grammar, Illustrating the Principles of the Language Used by the Ioway, Ottoe and Missouri Indians* (Ioway and Sac Mission Press, 1848), 129; D. Lee and J. H. Frost, *Ten Years in Oregon* (New York, 1844), 313. On "sacred," see Henry Perkins, "Journal" (1843–1844), in *People of the Dalles: The Indians of Wascopam Mission: A Historical Ethnography Based on the Papers of the Methodist Missionaries,* ed. Robert Boyd (Lincoln: University of Nebraska Press, 1996), 274. P. P. Wzokhilain, *Kizitokw, Wobanaki Kimzowi Awighigan* (Boston, 1830), contains no word for "soul" or "spirit." J. Hammond Trumbull to C. A. Cutter (n.d.), pasted inside the Boston Athenaeum's copy of P. P. Wzokhilain, *Wawasi Lagidamwoganek Mdala Chowagidamwoganal Tabtagil, Onkawodokodozwal wji Pobtami Kidwogan* (Boston, 1830), identifies Wzokhilain as Osunkhirhine.

23. Frederick Baraga, *A Theoretical and Practical Grammar of the Otchipwe Language* (Detroit, 1850), 4, 95–96, at 95–96; H. F. Buckner, *A Grammar of the Maskoke or Creek*

Language, to Which Are Prefixed Lessons in Spelling, Reading, and Defining (Marion, AL, 1860), 5, 9–10, at 9–10. On Creeks and gender, see also Lee Compere, "Muskhoge Vocabulary and Grammar," v–vi, NYHS. Claudio Saunt, "'Domestick ... Quiet Being Broke': Gender Conflict among Creek Indians in the Eighteenth Century," in *Contact Points: American Frontiers from the Mohawk Valley to the Mississippi, 1750–1830*, eds. Andrew R. L. Cayton and Fredrika J. Teute (Chapel Hill: University of North Carolina Press, 1998), 157, suggests significance relating to gender roles. Peter Burke, *Languages and Communities in Early Modern Europe* (Cambridge: Cambridge University Press, 2004), 33–35, discusses the common observation of gendered sociolects. John McWhorter, *The Power of Babel: A Natural History of Language* (2001; New York: Perennial, 2003), 180, notes that "evidential markers" are common worldwide.

24. Du Ponceau to Gallatin, Mar. 26 (enclosed in Apr. 2), Apr. 18, May 19, 1826, Gallatin Papers, reel 36; Du Ponceau in Zeisberger, "Grammar," 79, 83, 77–78. See also Wilhelm von Humboldt to Du Ponceau, Sept. 21, 1827, in Du Ponceau Notebooks, 5:40–45; Wilhelm von Humboldt, "On the Verb in American Languages" (1829), trans. Daniel G. Brinton, in Brinton, *The Philosophic Grammar of American Languages, as Set Forth by Wilhelm von Humboldt* (Philadelphia, 1885).

25. Du Ponceau in Zeisberger, "Grammar," 93, 248, 95–96, 85, 249. See also Ulrich Ricken, *Linguistics, Anthropology, and Philosophy in the French Enlightenment*, trans. Robert E. Norton (London: Routledge, 1994), 213–20; Sophia Rosenfeld, *A Revolution in Language: The Problem of Signs in Late Eighteenth-Century France* (Stanford, CA: Stanford University Press, 2001), 229–31.

26. [Peter S. Du Ponceau], "Language," in *Encyclopaedia Americana*, 7:409, 412–13. See also the critique of Adelung's monogenetic evolutionary linguistic theory in Robley Dunglison, *Human Physiology*, 7th ed., 2 vols. (Philadelphia, 1856), 2:675–77, esp. 677. Schlegel's remarks are in Frederick von Schlegel, *Aesthetic and Miscellaneous Works*, trans. E. J. Millington (London, 1860), 439. See also Roger Langham Brown, *Wilhelm von Humboldt's Conception of Linguistic Relativity* (The Hague: Mouton, 1967), chap. 3; Michel Foucault, *The Order of Things: An Archaeology of the Human Sciences* (1970; New York: Vintage, 1994), 217–302; Stephen G. Alter, *Darwinism and the Linguistic Image: Language, Race, and Natural Theology in the Nineteenth Century* (Baltimore: Johns Hopkins University Press, 1999), 7–14. On Cuvier, see Toby A. Appel, *The Cuvier-Geoffroy Debate: French Biology in the Decades before Darwin* (New York: Oxford University Press, 1987), 40–52.

27. Du Ponceau, "Language," 412–14. On Dante, see Du Ponceau to Pickering, June 23, 1833, in Du Ponceau Papers, box 3, 88.

28. Du Ponceau to Pickering, Jan. 23, 1826, Du Ponceau Papers, box 3; Du Ponceau to Schoolcraft, Oct. 11, 1834, Schoolcraft Papers (LC), reel 7, box 13, 2230 Du Ponceau to Gallatin, Apr. 22, 1835, Gallatin Papers, Supplement Reel. See also Du Ponceau to Pickering, Aug. 24, 1823, July 15, 1826, July 23, Sept. 30, 1835, Du Ponceau Papers, box 3; P. -Ét. Du Ponceau, *Mémoire sur le système grammatical des langues de quelques nations indiennes de l'Amérique du Nord* (1838), 130, in *Prix Volney*. Du Ponceau's earlier "Essai

de solution du problème philologique" is in ibid. On etymology–grammar debates, see Robert Henry Robins, "Du Ponceau and General and Amerindian Linguistics," in ibid., 21.

29. Pickering to Du Ponceau, Apr. 18, July 5, May 23, 1838, Du Ponceau Papers, box 3; Eleazer Williams to the Secretary of the A.P.S., Apr. 18, 1854, APS Archives; Du Ponceau to Schoolcraft, Oct. 11, 1834, Schoolcraft Papers (LC), reel 7, box 13, 2230. On the philology lobby for the Wilkes Expedition, see also Du Ponceau, "Philology" and "Ethnography," in Edwin G. Conklin, "Connection of the American Philosophical Society with our First National Exploring Expedition," *APS Proc.* 82 (1940): 519–41, esp. 533–36; J. N. Reynolds, *Pacific and Indian Oceans: or, The South Sea Surveying and Exploring Expedition: Its Inception, Progress, and Objects* (New York, 1841), 135–47, 153–55, 433–34; Mahlon Dickerson to Pickering, Nov. 21, 1836, in Mary Orne Pickering, *The Life of John Pickering* (Boston, 1887), 441. On Schoolcraft's hopes for federal publication, see Schoolcraft to James M. Porter (Sec. of War), June 8, 1843, Schoolcraft Papers (LC), reel 10, box 20, 3445. On the APS and non-publication, see Du Ponceau to Gallatin, Mar. 22, Apr. 18, 1826, Gallatin Papers, reel 36; "Minutes of the HLC, July 10, 1840–Nov. 8, 1843," 2–4, APS. On the AAS and "Synopsis," see Gallatin to Du Ponceau, Feb. 6, 1837, Du Ponceau Papers, box 2, folder 8.

30. Edward Everett to Gallatin, June 27, 1826, Gallatin Papers, reel 36; John Russell Bartlett, "On the Indian Languages, Read Before the Franklin Society February 1836," Bartlett Papers, Box 13; James Cowles Prichard, *Researches into the Physical History of Mankind*, 2nd. ed. (London, 1826), 2:610; Jefferson to Pickering, Feb. 20, 1826, in Pickering, *Life*, 335–36. For examples of asserted grammatical similarities, see Alexander Bradford, *American Antiquities and Researches into the Origin and History of the Red Race* (New York, 1841), 311–13, 434; Howse, *Grammar*, xii; *Historical and Statistical Information*, 2:349, 4:386, 397.

31. "The Aborigines of America," *Yankee and Boston Literary Gazette*, 2.1 (July 1829): 10–21, at 18–19; "Customs and Peculiarities of the Indians," *Southern Literary Journal and Magazine of the Arts*, 4.6 (Dec. 1838): 430–37, at 433; E. G. S., "American Ethnology," *American Review, A Whig Journal Devoted to Politics and Literature* 3.4 (Apr. 1849): 385–98, at 392. See also James G. Swan, *The Northwest Coast; or, Three Years' Residence in Washington Territory* (New York, 1857), 310–13. Cf. [Robert Chambers], *Vestiges of Natural History of Creation* (London, 1844), 294; "Art. III—Unity of Mankind," *De Bow's Review and Industrial Resources* 5.4 (Apr. 1861): 407–10, at 408.

32. Kah-ge-ga-gah-boh (George Copway), *The Traditional History and Characteristic Sketches of the Ojibway Nation* (London, 1850), 126–27; Peter Jones (Kahkewaquonaby), *History of the Ojebway Indians; with Especial Reference to Their Conversion to Christianity* (London, 1861), 179, 37, 31; William W. Warren, *History of the Ojibway People* (1887; St. Paul: Minnesota Historical Society Press, 1984). Copway disputed John Summerfield, alias Sahgahjewagahbahweh, *Sketch of Grammar of the Chippeway Language, to Which Is Added a Vocabulary of Some of the Most Common Words* (Cazenovia, 1834). For the reliance upon Jones, see Howse, *Grammar*, viii. On these writers' ideas of race, ancestry, and sovereignty, see Maureen Konkle, *Writing Indian Nations: Native Intellectuals and*

the Politics of Historiography (Chapel Hill: University of North Carolina Press, 2004), 216–17; Meghan C. L. Howey, "'The Question Which Has Puzzled, and Still Puzzles': How American Indian Authors Challenged Dominant Discourse about Native American Origins in the Nineteenth Century," *AIQ* 34.4 (Fall 2010): 435–74. See also Donald B. Smith, *Sacred Feathers: The Reverend Peter Jones (Kahkewaquonaby) and the Mississauga Indians* (Lincoln: University of Nebraska Press, 1986), 161–66, 221–23; Roger L. Nichols, *Indians in the United States and Canada: A Comparative History* (Lincoln: University of Nebraska Press, 1998), 174–205.

33. On diverse venues for philology, see note 16, above, and throughout this section. On the broader ethnological context, see George W. Stocking, Jr., *Victorian Anthropology* (New York: Free Press, 1987); Bieder, *Science Encounters the Indian;* Bruce Dain, *A Hideous Monster of the Mind: American Race Theory in the Early Republic* (Cambridge, MA: Harvard University Press, 2002); Ann Fabian, *The Skull Collectors: Race, Science, and America's Unburied Dead* (Chicago: University of Chicago Press, 2010); Brian W. Dippie, *Catlin and His Contemporaries: The Politics of Patronage* (Lincoln: University of Nebraska Press, 1990); Robert Silverberg, *The Mound Builders of Ancient America: The Archaeology of a Myth* (Greenwich, CT: New York Graphic Society, 1968); Lewis, *Democracy of Facts,* 72–106. Ibid., 101–2, notes the decline of archaeology among the learned in the 1820s

34. Josiah Priest, *American Antiquities, and Discoveries in the West: Being an Exhibition of the Evidence That an Ancient Population of Partially Civilized Nations, Differing Entirely from Those of the Present Indians, Peopled America, Many Centuries before Its Discovery by Columbus. . . . Compiled from Travels, Authentic Sources, and the Researches of Antiquarian Societies,* 2nd ed. (Albany, 1833), iii–iv; Francis Parkman, *The California and Oregon Trail* (New York, 1849), 316–17, 321. See also George Bancroft, *History of the Colonization of the United States,* vol. 3 of *History of the United States, from the Discovery of the American Continent,* 7th ed. (Boston, 1841), 254–65.

35. "Indian Eloquence," *Knickerbocker* 7.4 (Apr. 1836): 385–90, at 389; Pliny Miles to Schoolcraft, June 24, 1845, Schoolcraft Papers (LC), reel 10, box 21, 3729–30; [E. G. Squier], "A Visit to the Guajiquero Indians," *Harper's New Monthly Magazine* 19.113 (Oct. 1859): 602–19, at 615. For philology's funny side, see also James, *Account,* 16:210–11, 235; John Russell Bartlett, *Personal Narrative of Explorations and Incidents in Texas, New Mexico, California, Sonora, and Chihuahua, connected with the United States and Mexican Boundary Commission, during the Years 1850, '51, '52, '53,* 2 vols. (New York, 1854), 1:451–53, 464; 2:7–8, 92; E. G. Squier, *Nicaragua: Its People, Scenery, Monuments, and the Proposed Interoceanic Canal,* 2 vols. (London, 1852), 1:283, 2:22. For diverse graphic practices, see chap. 4 note 26, above. On the cultural contexts for popular interest, see also Gordon M. Sayre, *The Indian Chief as Tragic Hero: Native Resistance and the Literatures of America, from Moctezuma to Tecumseh* (Chapel Hill: University of North Carolina Press, 2005); Scott C. Martin, "Interpreting *Metamora:* Nationalism, Theater, and Jacksonian Indian Policy," *JER* 19.1 (1999): 73–101; Carolyn Eastman, "The Indian Censures the White Man: 'Indian Eloquence' and American Reading Audiences in the Early Republic," *WMQ* 65.3 (July 2008): 535–64; Samuel Brown,

"Joseph (Smith) in Egypt: Babel, Hieroglyphs, and the Pure Language of Eden," *Church History* 78.1 (Mar. 2009): 26–65. My thanks to Brett Rushforth for that last citation.

36. C. S. Rafinesque, *The American Nations; or, Outlines of a National History; of the Ancient and Modern Nations of North and South America* (Philadelphia, 1836), 1:8–9, 122–24; C. S. Rafinesque, "The Ancient Monuments of North and South America, Compared with the Eastern Continent," *American Museum of Science, Literature, and the Arts* 1.1 (September 1838), 21; [Ephraim G. Squier], "Historical and Mythological Traditions of the Algonquins; with a Translation of the 'Walum Olum' or Bark Record of the Linni-Lenape," *American Review* 3.2 (Feb. 1849): 173–93, at 177. See also C. S. Rafinesque, "Important Historical and Philological Discovery. To Peter Duponceau," *Saturday Evening Post,* 6.285 (Jan. 13, 1827), 2; "Philology. First Letter to Mr. Champollion, on the Graphic Systems of America, and the Glyphs of Otolum or Palenque, in Central America," *Atlantic Journal, and Friend of Knowledge,* 1.1 (Spring 1832), 4–5. On Rafinesque's character, see Caleb Atwater to Isaiah Thomas, Sept. 29, 1820, Atwater Letters; Charles Caldwell to Rejoice Newton, Feb. 24, 1822; AAS Archives, 3.10. Although Du Ponceau scrupulously avoided mentioning Rafinesque in print, he did record his vocabularies. See HLC Vocabularies, Nos. 25–26; Du Ponceau Notebooks, 6:29–38. Leonard Warren, *Constantine Samuel Rafinesque: A Voice in the American Wilderness* (Lexington: University of Kentucky Press, 2007), 137, stresses Rafinesque's decision to aim at a popular audience. Daniels, *Jacksonian Science,* 53–60, addresses his marginalization. On the Walam Olum, see David M. Oestreicher, "Roots of the Walam Olum: Constantine Samuel Rafinesque and the Intellectual Heritage of the Early Nineteenth Century," in David L. Browman and Stephen Williams, ed. *New Perspectives on the Origins of Americanist Archaeology* (Tuscaloosa: University of Alabama Press, 2002); Charles Boewe, "The Other Candidate for the 1835 Volney Prize: Constantine Samuel Rafinesque," in *Prix Volney;* Andrew Newman, "The *Walam Olum:* An Indigenous Apocrypha and Its Readers," *American Literary History* 22.1 (Spring 2010): 26–56.

37. Schoolcraft, *Algic Researches,* 10; *Personal Memoirs,* 622–23; Schoolcraft to Washington Irving, Mar. 28, 1842, in Schoolcraft Papers (LC), reel 32, box 46.

38. "A Prospective American Literature, superinduced from Indian Mythology" (n.d.), in Schoolcraft Papers (LC), reel 53, box 63; Schoolcraft, *Algic Researches,* 43; *Personal Memoirs,* 515, 625, at 515; "The Algic Magazine, and Annals of Indian Affairs" (prospectus), Schoolcraft Papers (LC), reel 9, box 19, 3276; Robert H. Morris et al. to James M. Porter, May 26, 1843, ibid., 20:3442; *Historical and Statistical Information,* 1:315. See also Schoolcraft to George Johnston, Aug. 31, 1844, Schoolcraft–Johnston Correspondence; E. Dieffenbach to Schoolcraft, July 11, 1842, in Schoolcraft Papers (LC), reel 9, box 19, 3357; Schoolcraft, "Criticisms of American Literature"; "The Indian Mythology Considered as an Element in the Future Phases of American Literature" (n.d.), ibid., box 62. On Schoolcraft's texts, see Bieder, *Science Encounters the Indian,* 160–64; Bremer, *Indian Agent and Wilderness Scholar,* 109–15; Richard Bauman and Charles L. Briggs, *Voices of Modernity: Language Ideologies and the Politics*

of Inequality (Cambridge: Cambridge University Press, 2003), 197–254; Joshua David Bellin, *The Demon of the Continent: Indians and the Shaping of American Literature* (Philadelphia: University of Pennsylvania Press, 2001), 131–82.

39. "To the Honourable the Senate and House of Representatives of the United States," Nov. 30, 1846, in *Historical and Statistical Information,* 3:617; Schoolcraft to L. Lea, Commissioner of Indian Affairs, July 22, 1850, in ibid., 1:iv; W. Medill to Albert Gallatin, July 1847, "Circular," enclosed in the copy of *Inquiries Respecting the History, Present Condition, and Future Prospects of the Indian Tribes of the United States* (n.p., n.d.), transcribed from Schoolcraft to R. Wilmot Griswold, at NYHS. See also Schoolcraft, *Notes on the Iroquois,* vi, 412; "American Ethnological Society," *Literary World* 9 (Apr. 3, 1847), 205; *Historical and Statistical Information,* 4:662–67, at 662; Schoolcraft to John R. Bartlett, Apr. 3, 1856, Bartlett Papers. On the political and social context, see Thomas R. Hietala, *Manifest Design: Anxious Aggrandizement in Late Jacksonian America* (Ithaca, NY: Cornell University Press, 1985), 142–52; Yonatan Eyal, *The Young America Movement and the Transformation of the Democratic Party, 1828–1861* (New York: Cambridge University Press, 2007), 150–65; William Stanton, *The Leopard's Spots: Scientific Attitudes toward Race in America, 1815–59* (Chicago: University of Chicago Press, 1960), 93–96; Bremer, *Indian Agent and Wilderness Scholar,* 274–83, 293–97. Cf. Oz Frankel, *States of Inquiry: Social Investigations and Print Culture in Nineteenth-Century Britain and the United States* (Baltimore: Johns Hopkins University Press, 2006), 236–37, which views this project primarily as "commemoration."

40. See Robley Dunglison, *A Public Discourse in Commemoration of Peter S. Du Ponceau, LL.D., Late President of the APS* (Philadelphia, 1844), 20, 22–23, 25, 31–32; Pickering, *Life,* 506; John Russell Bartlett, *Autobiography of John Russell Bartlett,* ed. Jerry E. Mueller (Providence, RI: John Carter Brown Library, 2006), 22–26.

41. On the decline of a degenerationist framework, see Stocking, *Victorian Anthropology,* 62–77, 110–85; Bieder, *Science Encounters the Indian,* 55–145; Dain, *Hideous Monster of the Mind,* 197–226.

42. Henry R. Schoolcraft, *Oneóta, or the Red Race of America: Their History, Traditions, Customs, Poetry, Picture-Writing, &c.* (New York, 1844), 133; *Notes on the Iroquois,* 388–89; *Algic Researches,* 12, 11, 40–41; *Expedition to Lake Itasca,* 62.

43. Schoolcraft, *Algic Researches,* 39–40; "The Meda Society," in Mason, ed., *Literary Voyager,* 36; *Historical and Statistical Information,* 1:112–13, 4:120. See also Schoolcraft to George Johnston, May 16, 1848, transcript in Schoolcraft–Johnston Correspondence. On the Midewiwin, see Michael Angel, *Preserving the Sacred: Historical Perspectives on the Ojibwa Midewiwin* (Winnipeg: University of Manitoba Press, 2002), 181. On Shingwauk, see Phil Bellfy, *Three Fires Unity: The Anishnaabeg of the Lake Huron Borderlands* (Lincoln: University of Nebraska Press, 2011), 59, 66–68, 73–75; Janet Elizabeth Chute, *The Legacy of Shingwaukonse: A Century of Native Leadership* (Toronto: University of Toronto Press, 1998), esp. 35–36.

44. Schoolcraft, *Notes on the Iroquois,* 386–87; Schoolcraft to Ephraim G. Squier, Feb. 16, 1849, in C. A. Weslager, *The Delaware Indians: A History* (1972; New Brunswick,

NJ: Rutgers University Press, 1991), 471; *Historical and Statistical Information*, 1:315, 341–42; Henry R. Schoolcraft, "Article V. Mythology, Superstitions and Languages of the North American Indians," *Literary and Theological Review* 2.5 (Mar. 1835): 96–121, at 96-97. See also Schoolcraft, *Personal Memoirs*, 443; "Considerations on the Art of Picture Writing, and the System of Mnemonic Symbols of the North American Indians," in *Oneóta*, 27–35, esp. 29. On Aztec paintings, see Du Ponceau, *Dissertation*, 44–45.

45. "Wasteful Extravagance of Public Printing," *New York Herald* (Jan. 17, 1858), 5; [Francis Bowen], "Art. XI," *North American Review* 77.160 (July 1853): 245–62, at 261–62; J. Hammond Trumbull, "Indian Languages of America" (1876), *Johnson's (Revised) Universal Cyclopaedia: A Scientific and Popular Treasury of Useful Knowledge*, 8 vols. (New York, 1889–1890), 4:233–39, at 239. For the fullest discussions of the problems then facing Indian affairs, see *Historical and Statistical Information*, 2:546–60, 4:449–73, 5:459–86, 6:623–25. Bremer, *Indian Agent and Wilderness Scholar*, 333, discusses the reception. Frankel, *States of Inquiry*, 260, states Congress spent $126,711.59 on the project, two-thirds of which stemmed from printing.

46. *Historical and Statistical Information*, 6:xxvi, 671; 1:559, 71; 4:ix. See also Schoolcraft, *Notes on the Iroquois*, 382–85, 389. W. Gilmore Simms to Henry R. Schoolcraft, Mar. 18, 1851, in *An Early and Strong Sympathy: The Indian Writings of William Gilmore Simms*, eds. John Caldwell Guilds and Charles Hudson (Columbia: University of South Carolina, 2003), 114–15, assumes polygenism. My thanks to John L. Miller for alerting me to this exchange.

47. Drury ed., *Diaries and Letters*, 103–4, 138; Buckner, *Grammar of the Maskɯke or Creek Language*, 137–38. On Lawyer, see Elliott West, *The Last Indian War: The Nez Perce Story* (New York: Oxford University Press, 2009), 51, 64–73. On Herrod, see James Constantine Pilling, *Bibliography of the Muskhogean Languages* (Washington, DC, 1889), 44–45.

48. Byington to Evarts, July 30, 1825, ABCFM Papers, 18.3.4, vol. 3, item 69; Howse, *Grammar*, 13–14; Humboldt, *Personal Narrative*, 3:244–247, at 245. See also Jonathan Edwards, *Observations on the Language of the Muhhekaneew Indians* (New Haven, CT, 1788), 10, 14; S. T. Rand, *A Short Statement of Facts Relating to the History, Manners, Customs, Language, and Literature of the Micmac Tribe of Indians in Nova-Scotia and P. E. Island* (Halifax, 1850), 18–19. Cf. Lewis H. Morgan, "Systems of Consanguinity and Affinity of the Human Family," *Smithsonian Contrib.* 17 (Washington, 1871), 134. Nicholas Ostler, *Empires of the Word: A Language History of the World* (New York: HarperCollins, 2005), 554–56, suggests that "the very essence of a language, its structure" affects language adoption.

49. John Pickering, "Indian Languages of North America," *Encyclopaedia Americana*, 6: 582; Wilhelm von Humboldt to Pickering, Feb. 24, 1821, in Pickering, *Life*, 301–2, 313, at 302; Humboldt, "On the Verb in American Languages," 29; Wilhelm von Humboldt, *On Language: On the Diversity of Human Language Construction and its Influence on the Mental Development of the Human Species*, ed. Michael Losonsky, trans. Peter Heath (New York: Cambridge University Press, 1999), 229, 34, 60. See also Paul

R. Sweet, *Wilhelm von Humboldt: A Biography*, vol. 2 (Columbus: Ohio State University Press, 1980), 398–406, 466–72; Hans Aarsleff, "Introduction," in Wilhelm von Humboldt, *On Language*, ed. Hans Aarsleff, trans. Peter Heath (New York: Cambridge University Press, 1988), xxiv-xxv, lxi–lxv. Kurt Müller-Vollmer, ed., "Wilhelm von Humboldt und der Anfang der Amerikanischen Sprachwissenschaft: Die Briefe an John Pickering," *Universalismus und Wissenschaft im Werk und Wirken der Brüder Humboldt* (Frankfurt am Main: Vittorio Kolsterman, 1974), contains the correspondence in the original French and English.

50. Alfred Maury, "On the Distribution and Classification of Tongues,—Their Relation to the Geographical Distribution of Races; and on the Inductions Which May be Drawn from Their Relations," in J. C. Nott and Geo. R. Gliddon, eds., *Indigenous Races of the Earth; or, New Chapters of Ethnological Inquiry; including Monographs on Special Departments of Philology, Iconography, Cranioscopy, Palaeontology, Pathology, Archaeology, Comparative Geography, and Natural History* (Philadelphia, 1857), 25, 35, 83. See also Maurice Olender, *The Languages of Paradise: Race, Religion, and Philology in the Nineteenth Century* (1989; Cambridge, MA: Harvard University Press, 2008), 51–105; Tuska Benes, *In Babel's Shadow: Language, Philology, and the Nation in Nineteenth-Century Germany* (Detroit: Wayne State University Press, 2008), 54–60, 197–239; Thomas R. Trautmann, *Languages and Nations: The Dravidian Proof in Colonial Madras* (Berkeley: University of California Press, 2006), 220-25.

51. "Article III. Phrenological Developments and Character of the Celebrated Indian Chief and Warrior, Black Hawk; with cuts," *American Phrenological Journal* 1.2 (Nov. 1, 1838): 51–61, at 55, 60; "Article LVI. The Phrenological Character of George Copway.—With a Likeness," *American Phrenological Journal* 11.9 (Sept. 1, 1849): 280-82, at 281; Robert Knox, *The Races of Men: A Fragment* (Philadelphia, 1850), 34; Samuel F. Haven, "Archaeology of the United States. Or Sketches, Historical and Bibliographical, of the Progress of Information and Opinion Respecting Vestiges of Antiquity in the United States," *Smithsonian Contrib.* 8 (1856), 70; Horatio Hale, "The Origin of Languages, and the Antiquity of Speaking Man," *Proceedings of the American Association for the Advancement of Science, Thirty-fifth Meeting, Held at Buffalo, New York, August 1886* (Salem, MA, 1887), 310. See also George Combe, "Phrenological Remarks on the Relation between the Natural Talents and Dispositions of Nations, and the Developments of Their Brains," in Samuel G. Morton, *Crania Americana: or, a Comparative View of the Skulls of Various Aboriginal Nations of North and South America: to which is prefixed An Essay on the Varieties of the Human Species* (Philadelphia, 1836), 270, 286; George Combe, *Notes on the United States of America, during a Phrenological Visit, in 1838–9–40*, 2 vols. (Philadelphia, 1841), 2:87; "Article II. Analysis, Function, and Location of Language, Illustrated by an Engraving of the Late Indian Interpreter, Colonel Gad," *American Phrenological Journal* 8.2 (Feb. 1846): 44–48. On physiological attention to language in the 1840s–1880s, see Gray, *New World Babel*, 161; Benes, *In Babel's Shadow*, 209–11, 233–34; Francis Schiller, *Paul Broca: Founder of French Anthropology, Explorer of the Brain* (New York: Oxford University Press, 1992),

141–49, 165–211; Gregory Radick, *The Simian Tongue: The Long Debate about Animal Language* (Chicago: University of Chicago Press, 2007), 15–122, 176–81.

52. Gallatin, "Synopsis," 6, 203–8, at 6; Albert Gallatin, "Notes on the Semi-Civilized Nations of Mexico, Yucatan, and Central America," *AES Trans.* 1 (1845), 296; Gallatin to Du Ponceau, July 3, 1838, Du Ponceau Papers, box 2, folder 9; Francis Lieber, "Plan of Thought of the American Languages," in *Historical and Statistical Information,* 2:346–49, at 347; William W. Turner, "Professor Turner's Letter on Indian Philology," *Sixth ARSI 1851* (Washington, DC, 1852), 93. On ethnology, evolutionism, and the Darwinian Revolution, see Stocking, *Victorian Anthropology,* 110–85.

53. On archaeology and the "revolution in human time," see Stocking, *Victorian Anthropology,* 69–77, 102–43, at 69.

54. *Historical and Statistical Information,* 2:362; Gallatin, "Synopsis," 159; Kah-ge-ga-gah-boh (George Copway), "The American Indians," *American Review* 3.6 (June 1849): 631–37, esp. 634. See also Gray, *New World Babel,* 162.

55. Stephen R. Riggs, *Mary and I: Forty Years with the Sioux* (Boston, 1880), 130, 41, 53; "Learning Language" (May 17, 1850), in ABCFM Papers, 18.3.7, vol. 3, item 253; S. R. Riggs, "The Dakota Language," *Collections of the Minnesota Historical Society* 1 (1850), 93, 105. On Brothertown, see David J. Silverman, *Red Brethren: The Brothertown and Stockbridge Indians and the Problem of Race in Early America* (Ithaca, NY: Cornell University Press, 2010).

56. Riggs, "Dakota Language," 107, 90, 106; "Application of the Sioux Indians to become Citizens," *The Record* (Mankato, MN), June 21, 1861, enclosed in "Dakotas Applying for Citizenship," ABCFM Papers, 18.3.1, vol. 14, item 176; Samuel W. Pond, *Dakota Life in the Upper Midwest* (1908; St Paul: Minnesota Historical Society Press, 1986), 77; Gideon Pond quoted in Carrie Reber Zeman, "Historical Perspectives on *A Thrilling Narrative of Indian Captivity,*" in Mary Butler Renville, *A Thrilling Narrative of Indian Captivity: Dispatches from the Dakota War,* eds. Carrie Reber Zeman and Kathryn Zabelle Derounian-Stodola (Lincoln: University of Nebraska Press, 2012), 94. On this community, see ibid., 15–20, 31–36; Gary Clayton Anderson, *Kinsmen of Another Kind: Dakota-White Relations in the Upper Mississippi Valley, 1650–1862* (Lincoln: University of Nebraska Press, 1984), 203–16. The variety of translations are recounted in Tamakoche [Stephen R. Riggs], "Learning English," *Minnesota Weekly Times* (St. Paul), Mar. 5, 1859, in ABCFM Papers, 18.3.7, 3:47.

57. "Application of the Sioux Indians to become Citizens." See also Riggs, *Mary and I,* 133; Stephen R. Riggs, *Tah-koo Wah-kaṅ; or. The Gospel among the Dakotas* (Boston, n.d.), 384–400. On the legal context, see Deborah Rosen, *American Indians and State Law: Sovereignty, Race, and Citizenship, 1790–1880* (Lincoln: University of Nebraska Press, 2007), ix, 128–54, esp. 130, 141. On language and Native citizenship, see Silverman, *Red Brethren,* 7, 151, 192.

58. Riggs, "Learning English"; teacher quoted in Ruth Spack, *America's Second Tongue: American Indian Education and the Ownership of English, 1860–1900* (Lincoln: University of Nebraska Press, 2002), 17, 30–31, at 31; "Report of the Indian Peace

Commissioners" (Ex. Doc. no. 97), 17, in *Executive Documents Printed by Order of the House of Representatives during the Second Session of the Fortieth Congress, 1867–'68,* 20 vols. (Washington, 1868), vol. 11. See also *Historical and Statistical Information,* 2:554; Alice C. Fletcher, *Indian Education and Civilization: A Report Prepared in Answer to Senate Resolution of February 23, 1885,* 48th Congress, 2nd Session, Senate Ex. Doc. No. 95 (Washington, DC, 1888), 167–70. Spack, *America's Second Tongue,* stresses the BIA's epistemological motivation for English-only education but misses the prevalence of these ideas in the decades before the Civil War. Gray, *New World Babel,* 162, recognizes it. On the Indian Peace Commission, see also Prucha, *Great Father,* 479–500.

6. Of Blood and Language

1. William D. Whitney, "Brief Abstract of a Series of Six Lectures on the Principles of Linguistic Science, Delivered at the Smithsonian Institution in March, 1864," *ARSI 1863* (Washington, DC, 1864), 107, 98, 101.

2. Whitney, "Brief Abstract," 95, 113.

3. See Thomas R. Trautmann, *Aryans and British India* (1997; New Delhi: Yoda Press, 2004), chap. 2–3; Tuska Benes, *In Babel's Shadow: Language, Philology, and the Nation in Nineteenth-Century Germany* (Detroit: Wayne State University Press, 2008), 211–28; Joseph Errington, *Linguistics in a Colonial World: A Story of Language, Meaning and Power* (Malden, MA: Blackwell, 2008).

4. Whitney, "Brief Abstract," 96, 113; William Dwight Whitney, *The Life and Growth of Language: An Outline of Linguistic Science* (London, 1875), 269–76, at 274. See also Stephen G. Alter, *William Dwight Whitney and the Science of Language* (Baltimore: Johns Hopkins University Press, 2005), 66–68, 146–56; Curtis M. Hinsley, *The Smithsonian and the American Indian: Making a Moral Anthropology in Victorian America* (Washington, DC: Smithsonian Institution Press, 1994), 48, 55, 160–61; Julie Tetel Andresen, *Linguistics in America, 1769–1924* (London: Routledge, 1990), 135, 164–67, 175–80.

5. See Andrew J. Lewis, *Democracy of Facts: Natural History in the Early Republic* (Philadelphia: University of Pennsylvania Press, 2011), 8–9, 129–53, esp. 133; Oz Frankel, *States of Inquiry: Social Investigations and Print Culture in Nineteenth-Century Britain and the United States* (Baltimore: Johns Hopkins University Press, 2006).

6. George Gibbs, "Report of Mr. George Gibbs to Captain Mc'Clellan, on the Indian Tribes of the Territory of Washington," in I. I. Stevens, *Report of Explorations for a Route for the Pacific Railroad, Near the Forty-Seventh and Forty-Ninth Parallels of North Latitude from St. Paul to Puget Sound* (Washington, DC, n.d.), 431; Stephen Powers, "The Tribes of California," *CNAE* 3 (1877), 411, 407, 274; F. V. Hayden, "Article III. Contributions to the Ethnography and Philology of the Indian Tribes of the Missouri Valley," *APS Trans.* n.s. 12.2 (1863): 231–461, at 233–34. See also G. Gibbs, "Observations on the Languages of California," in *Historical and Statistical Information,* 3:420–23, at 420; George Gibbs, "Tribes of Western Washington and Northwestern Oregon," in *CNAE* 1 (1877), 163. On this era of surveying, see William H. Goetzmann,

Exploration and Empire: The Explorer and the Scientist in the Winning of the American West (1966; New York: History Book Club, 2006), 222–23, 303–5, 329–31, 390–91, 489–529.

7. Henry R. Schoolcraft, "Plan for American Ethnological Investigation" (1846), in *Tenth ARSI 1885,* Part I (Washington, DC, 1886), 913; Schoolcraft to R. Wilmot Griswold, Gratz Collection, case 7, box 9. See also Joseph Henry to John R. Bartlett, Nov. 4, 1847, Bartlett Papers.

8. William W. Turner, "Professor Turner's Letter on Indian Philology," *Sixth ARSI 1851* (Washington, DC, 1852), 93–97, at 96; George Gibbs, *Instructions for Research relative to the Ethnology and Philology of America, Prepared for the Smithsonian Institution* (Washington, DC, 1863), 13; Hayden, "Contributions," 457. See also William W. Turner, "Vocabularies of North American Languages," *Reports of Explorations and Surveys, to Ascertain the Most Practicable and Economical Route for a Railroad from the Mississippi River to the Pacific Ocean. Made under the Direction of the Secretary of War, 1853–4, According to Acts of Congress of March 3, 1853, May 31, 1854, and August 5, 1854,* vol. 3 (Washington, DC, 1856), 54; "Biographical Sketch," in *Catalogue of the Entire Private Library of the Late Prof. W. W. Turner of the Patent Office at Washington* (New York, 1860), ii; Joseph Henry, "Letter of the Secretary of the Smithsonian Institution," in *ARSI 1863,* 25; John Austin Stevens, "A Memorial of George Gibbs," *ARSI 1873,* 219–25, esp. 224. On Smithsonian philology, see James C. Pilling, "Catalogue of Linguistic Manuscripts in the Library of the Bureau of Ethnology," *First ARBE 1879–'80* (Washington, DC, 1881), 558, 562–77; [Père Lionnet], *Vocabulary of the Jargon or Trade Language of Oregon,* Smithsonian Bulletin no. 1 (1853); Joseph Henry, "Report of the Secretary," *ARSI 1860* (Washington, DC, 1861), 39; George Gibbs, *A Dictionary of Chinook Jargon,* Smithsonian Miscellaneous Collections, no. 161 (Washington, DC, 1863). On the Smithsonian–Shea collaboration, see "Ethnology and Philology," *ARSI 1864* (Washington, DC, 1865), 55, with a convenient list of its 13 titles in Thomas W. Field, *An Essay towards an Indian Bibliography. Being a Catalogue of Books, Relating to the History, Antiquities, Languages, Customs, Religion, Wars, Literature, and Origin of the American Indians* (New York, 1873), 357. See also Hinsley, *Smithsonian and the American Indian,* 15–40, 47–57; Stephen Dow Beckham, "George Gibbs, 1815–1873: Historian and Ethnologist" (Ph.D. diss., University of California at Los Angeles, 1969), 232–37, 248–54.

9. Stephen R. Riggs, *Mary and I: Forty Years with the Sioux* (Boston, 1880), 117–19, at 118; *Prospectus for Publishing a Dakota Lexicon, under the Patronage of the Historical Society of Minnesota* (St. Paul, 1851), in ABCFM Papers, 18.3.7, vol. 3, item 45; S. R. Riggs, ed., "Grammar and Dictionary of the Dakota Language, Collected by Members of the Dakota Mission," *Smithsonian Contrib.* vol. 4 (Washington, DC, 1852), xiii–xiv, xix. For Riggs's contribution to the Congressional project, see *Historical and Statistical Information,* 5:695–97. Cyrus Byington chronicled his frustrations in publishing a Choctaw dictionary and grammar with the Smithsonian in letters to S. B. Treat, Jan. 23, Apr. 17, June 21, Sept. 1, Sept. 25, Dec. 14, 1852, in ABCFM Papers 18.3.4, vol. 6, items 304, 317, 323, 340, 347, 359. It appeared, posthumously, in Cyrus Byington,

"Grammar of the Choctaw Language," ed. [Daniel G.] Brinton, *APS Proc.* 11.81 (Jan. 1869): 317–67.

10. *Historical and Statistical Information,* 1:15, 4:482, 479, 523. On linguistic groupings for colonial administration in Africa, see Judith T. Irvine and Susan Gal, "Language Ideology and Linguistic Differentiation," in *Regimes of Language: Ideologies, Polities, and Identities,* ed. Paul V. Kroskrity (Santa Fe, NM: School of American Research Press, 2000), 50.

11. William Clark to James Barbour, Mar. 1, 1826, in *Am. State Papers,* 2:653–54. On the context for these recommendations, see Francis Paul Prucha, *The Great Father: The United States Government and the American Indian* (Lincoln: University of Nebraska Press, 1984), 293–97; Jay H. Buckley, *William Clark: Indian Diplomat* (Norman, OK, 2008), 163–67. On the Treaty of Prairie du Chien, see ibid., 172–74; Gary Clayton Anderson, *Kinsmen of Another Kind: Dakota-White Relations in the Upper Mississippi Valley, 1650–1862* (Lincoln, NE, 1984), 121–27, 131.

12. Edwin James, *A Narrative of the Captivity and Adventures of John Tanner, (U.S. Interpreter at the Saut Ste. Marie,) during Thirty Years Residence among the Indians in the Interior of North America* (London, 1830), 18; Schoolcraft, *Personal Memoirs,* 434; Speech of Edward Everett, May 19, 1830, *Register of Debates in Congress, Comprising the Leading Debates and Incidents in of the First Session of the Twenty-first Congress* (Washington, DC, 1830), 6:1066–67; "Address to the People of the United States by the General Council of the Cherokee Nation, July 1830," in E. C. Tracy, *Memoir of the Life of Jeremiah Evarts* (Boston, 1845), 448. Ronald N. Satz, *American Indian Policy in the Jacksonian Era* (Lincoln, NE, 1975), 227, notes that attempted consolidation led to increasing hostilities by the late 1830s and early 1840s.

13. Lewis Cass to the president of the United States, Feb. 16, 1832; Cass to William Carroll, Montfort Stokes, and Roberts Vaux, July 14, 1832, OIALS, 8:267, 9:35–36. Cf. John H. Eaton to Greenwood Leflore, June 1, 1831, ibid., 7:261–64; "Art. I," *Biblical Repertory* 10.4 (Oct. 1838): 513–35, at 528, for consolidation plans not focused on language. On these consolidations, see Satz, *American Indian Policy,* 102–3, 136–37; Prucha, *Great Father,* 223–26, 248–52. On the Stokes commission, see ibid., 226–29, 297, 304–5.

14. Kah-ge-ga-gah-bouh (George Copway), *Organization of a New Indian Territory, East of the Missouri River: Arguments and Reasons submitted to the Honorable Members of the Senate and the House of Representatives of the 31st Congress of the United States* (New York, 1850), 13–15. See also "The Choctaws," *Copway's American Indian* 1.10 (Sept. 13, 1851), 2. Cf. Bernd C. Peyer, *The Tutor'd Mind: Indian Missionary-Writers in Antebellum America* (Amherst, MA, 1997), 247–48, 263–71.

15. Ethan Allen Hitchcock, *A Traveler in Indian Territory: The Journal of Ethan Allen Hitchcock, late Major-General in the United States Army,* ed. Grant Forman (1930; Norman, OK, 1996), 84–85, 172–73, at 172–73. See also Robbie Ethridge, *From Chicaza to Chickasaw: The European Invasion and the Transformation of the Mississippian World, 1540–1715* (Chapel Hill, NC, 2010), 1–5; Wendy St. Jean, *Remaining Chickasaw in Indian Territory, 1830s–1907* (Tuscaloosa, AL, 2011), 2, 8, 15–26.

16. "Remonstrance of Col. Peter Pitchlynn, Choctaw Delegate, against the Passage of the Bill to Unite under One Government the Several Indian Tribes West of the Mississippi, February 3, 1849," 30th Congress, 2nd Session, Ho. of Reps. Misc. No. 35, in *Miscellaneous Documents Printed by Order of the House of Representatives during the Second Session of the Thirtieth Congress, begun and Held at the City of Washington, December 4, 1848* (Washington, DC, 1849), 1.

17. William Medill, "Report of the Commissioner of Indian Affairs," Nov. 30, 1848, in *Annual Report of the Commissioner of Indian Affairs, Transmitted with the Message of the President at the Opening of the Second Session of the Thirtieth Congress* (Washington, DC, 1848–1849), 5, 7–8; Orlando Brown, "Annual Report of the Commissioner of Indian Affairs," Nov. 30, 1849, in *Message from the President of the United States to the Two Houses of Congress at the Commencement of the First Session of the Thirty-First Congress,* Part 2 (Washington, DC, 1849), 946. On the emergence of the reservation system, see Robert A. Trennert, *Alternative to Extinction: Federal Indian Policy and the Emergence of the Reservation System, 1846–51* (Philadelphia: Temple University Press, 1975), 3, 10–14, 25–31, 46–47, 59–60; Stephen J. Rockwell, *Indian Affairs and the Administrative State in the Nineteenth Century* (New York: Cambridge University Press, 2010), 6, 246–62. According to Prucha, *Great Father,* 562–66, at 563, consolidation became "almost an obsession."

18. Gibbs, "Report," 424–25. See also Gray H. Whaley, *Oregon and the Collapse of Illahee: U.S. Empire and the Transformation of an Indigenous World, 1792–1859* (Chapel Hill: University of North Carolina Press, 2010), 117–18, 176–89.

19. Charles Maltby to D. N. Cooley, Sept. 15, 1866; Lorenzo Labadi to J. K. Graves, Jan. 4, 1866, in *Report of the Commissioner of Indian Affairs for the Year 1866* (Washington, DC, 1866), 139, 140. See also Brendan C. Lindsay, *Murder State: California's Native American Genocide, 1846–1873* (Lincoln: University of Nebraska Press, 2012), 179–209, 288–303; C. L. Sonnichsen, *The Mescalero Apaches* (1958; Norman: University of Oklahoma Press, 1973), 99–176.

20. J. W. Powell, "Indian Linguistic Families of America North of Mexico," *Seventh ARBE* (Washington, DC, 1891), 31. On economic dependency and cultural oppression on reservations, see Jeffrey Ostler, *The Plains Sioux and U.S. Colonialism from Lewis and Clark to Wounded Knee* (New York: Cambridge University Press, 2004), 128–216. On earlier ethnic identities among Shoshones and Bannocks, and reservation ethnogenesis, see Gregory E. Smoak, *Ghost Dances and Identity: American Indian Ethnogenesis in the Nineteenth Century* (Berkeley: University of California Press, 2006), 16–21, 85–151, esp. 147. On the Ghost Dance in the Modoc War, see Lindsay, *Murder State,* 335–41. On the Powell-Ingalls Commission, see Donald Worster, *A River Running West: The Life of John Wesley Powell* (New York: Oxford University Press, 2001), 273–85; Steven J. Crum, *The Road on Which We Came [Po'i Pentun Tammen Kimmappeh]: A History of the Western Shoshone* (Salt Lake City: University of Utah Press, 1994), 34–35. On public outcry for reform, see Prucha, *Great Father,* 437–686, esp. 447–57, 536–39.

21. Gallatin, "Synopsis," 3–7, at 4; Albert Gallatin, "Hale's Indians of North-West America, and Vocabularies of North America; with an Introduction," *AES Trans.* 2

(1848), xcviii, cxiii–cxiv, cxlviii, at cxlviii. On his methods, see Gallatin to Du Ponceau, Mar. 29, 1826, Mar. 21, 1835, Mar. 14, 1837, Du Ponceau Papers, box 1, folder 8, box 2, folders, 6, 8; William W. Turner to John R. Bartlett, Nov. 9, 1849, in "1847–1850 Biographical Notes on Albert Gallatin," Bartlett Papers. For administrative and missionary uses of Gallatin's work, see "Department of War, May 15, 1826," [1–2], Gallatin Papers, reel 36; George Folsom to John Davis, July 15, 1842, David Greene to Samuel F. Haven, May 29, 1848, AAS Archives, box 7, folder 31, box 8, folder 11. For other examples of missionary interest in taxonomy, see Alfred Wright to Jeremiah Evarts, Jan. 1, 1829, Cyrus Kingsbury to David Greene, Sept. 4, 1834, Cyrus Byington to Greene, Sept. 4, 1834, ABCFM Papers, 18.3.4, vol. 3, item 105, vol. 5, items 63, 169; Asher Wright to Greene, Apr. 1840, ibid., 18.5.8, vol. 1, item 83; S. R. Riggs, "The Dakota Language," *Collections of the Minnesota Historical Society* 1 (1850), 93–95; Richard E. Jensen, ed. *The Pawnee Mission Letters, 1834–1851* (Lincoln: University of Nebraska Press, 2010), 87–88, 155–56. For European praise of Gallatin's work, see "Synopsis," 1; Adrien Balbi, *Introduction à l'atlas ethnographique du globe, ou classification des peuples anciens et modernes d'apres leur langues* (Paris, 1826), 279; James Cowles Prichard, *Researches into the Physical History of Mankind*, 3rd ed., 5 vols. (London, 1847), 3:301, 307. On the religious underpinnings of much of early 19th-century philology, see George W. Stocking Jr., *Victorian Anthropology* (New York: Free Press, 1987), 41–77.

22. Albert Gallatin, "Notes on the Semi-Civilized Nations of Mexico, Yucatan, and Central America," *AES Trans.* 1 (1845) 29, 21, 170, 174, 181; Gallatin to Gen. Winfield Scott, Nov. 2, 1847, in Gallatin *Writings*, 2:650–52. See also Gallatin to W. L. Marcy, Mar. 17, 1846, in ibid. 625–27; Gallatin to W. Medill, July 21, 1846, in *Historical and Statistical Information*, 3:397–400, esp. 399; Albert Gallatin, *Peace with Mexico* (New York, 1847), 13, 15. On multiplicity, cf. Humboldt, *Political Essay*, 137–38; John L. Stephens, *Incidents of Travel in Central America, Chiapas, and Yucatan*, 2 vols. (New York, 1841), 2:343. Stocking, *Victorian Anthropology*, 154, stresses that the possibility of "independent progress" separated evolutionists from degenerationists. Gallatin articulates this opinion outside a Darwinian framework.

23. Samuel George Morton, *Crania Americana; or, a Comparative View of the Skulls of Various Aboriginal Nations of North and South America* (Philadelphia, 1839), 4–5, 17, 63, 81–82, 260. See also Samuel G. Morton, "An Inquiry into the Distinctive Characteristics of the Aboriginal Race of America," *Boston Journal of Natural History* 4 (1843–1844), 222–23; idem, "Account of a Craniological Collection, with Remarks on the Classification of Some Families of the Human Race," *AES Trans.* 2 (1848), 219; H. Hotz, "Analytical Introduction," in *Moral and Intellectual Diversity of Races, with Particular Reference to their Respective Influence in the Civil and Political History of Mankind, from the French of Count A. de Gobineau* (Philadelphia, 1856), 37. On Morton and his milieu, see Robert E. Bieder, *Science Encounters the Indian, 1820–1880: The Early Years of American Ethnology* (Norman: University of Oklahoma Press, 1986), 55–103; Bruce Dain, *A Hideous Monster of the Mind: American Race Theory in the Early Republic* (Cambridge, MA: Harvard University Press, 2002), 197–226; Ann Fabian, *The Skull Collectors: Race, Science, and America's Unburied Dead* (Chicago: University of Chicago Press, 2010), 9–45, 79–119.

24. Gallatin, "Synopsis," 14, 142, at 142; Morton, "Inquiry," 211–14. Humboldt, *Personal Narrative* 3:294, was ambivalent about this taxonomic problem, while Prichard, *Researches*, 5:374, agreed with Du Ponceau and Gallatin.

25. Morton, "Account," 219; Bartlett to Morton, Dec. 21, 1846, Morton Papers (LCP), box 3, folder 4; Morton to Bartlett, Jan. 28, 1847, Bartlett Papers. See also Gallatin to Du Ponceau, Apr. 14, 1835, Society Collection; [John R. Bartlett?] to William W. Turner, Feb. 21, 1851, Turner Papers, Box 1. The prominent British anatomist, Robert Knox, *The Races of Men: A Fragment* (Philadelphia, 1850), 13, used "race" and "hereditary descent" interchangeably. William Stanton, *The Leopard's Spots: Scientific Attitudes toward Race in America, 1815–59* (Chicago: University of Chicago Press, 1960), 97–98, mentions this debate in passing. On Bartlett and the contingency of antebellum literary communities, see Robert L. Gunn, "The Ethnologists' Bookshop: Bartlett & Welford in 1840s New York," *Wordsworth Circle* 41.3 (Summer 2010): 159–63.

26. E. G. Squier "Observations on the Archaeology and Ethnology of Nicaragua," *AES Trans.*, 3.1 (1853), 99–119, at 119; Alfred Maury, "On the Distribution and Classification of Tongues,—Their Relation to the Geographical Distribution of Races; and on the Inductions which may be drawn from their Relations," in *Indigenous Races of the Earth; or, New Chapters of Ethnological Inquiry; including Monographs on Special Departments of Philology, Iconography, Cranioscopy, Palaeontology, Pathology, Archaeology, Comparative Geography, and Natural History*, eds. J. C. Nott and Geo R. Gliddon (Philadelphia, 1857), 30, 35; George R. Gliddon to Morton, Oct. 28 1843, Morton Papers (APS), ser. IV; Geo. R. Gliddon, "The Monogenists and the Polygenists: Being an Exposition of the Doctrines and Schools Professing to Sustain Dogmatically the Unity or the Diversity of the Human Races: With an Inquiry into the Antiquity of Mankind upon Earth, Viewed Chronologically, Historically, and Paleontologically," in *Indigenous Races*, 578, 586, 575–76. Contrast A. de Gobineau, *Essai sur l'inégalité des races humaines*, vol. 1 (Paris, 1853), 307, with Gobineau, *Moral and Intellectual Diversity of Races*, trans. Hotze. Reginald Horsman, *Josiah Nott of Mobile: Southerner, Physician, and Racial Theorist* (Baton Rouge: Louisiana State University Press, 1987), 204–7, discusses Gobineau's dissatisfaction with Nott's editing. On Squier's philology, see also E. G. S., "American Ethnology," *American Review* 3.4 (Apr. 1849): 385–98, esp. 392; E. G. Squier, *Monograph of Authors who have Written on the Languages of Central America, and collected Vocabularies or Composed Works in the Native Dialects of that Country* (London, 1861), vi. See also Terry A. Barnhart, *Ephraim George Squier and the Development of American Anthropology* (Lincoln: University of Nebraska Press, 2005). On disputes between philologists and physical ethnologists in Europe, see Trautmann, *Aryans and British India*, chap. 2–3; Benes, *In Babel's Shadow*, 211–28.

27. Eugene Vetromile, *The Abnakis and Their History, or Historical Notices on the Aborigines of Acadia, by Eugene Vetromile, missionary of the Etchemins; Corresponding Member of the Maine Historical Society, etc.* (New York: James B. Kirker, *Sold for the Benefit of the Indians*, 1866); R. G. Latham, *The Ethnology of the British Colonies and Dependencies* (London, 1851), 232, 237; idem, *Man and His Migrations* (New York, 1852),

131–32; Friedrich Max Müller, "The Last Results of the Researches Respecting the Non-Iranian and Non-Semitic Languages of Asia and Europe, or the Turanian Family of Languages," in Christian Karl Josias Bunsen, *Outlines of the Philosophy of Universal History, Applied to Language and Religion*, 2 vols. (London, 1854), 1:273. On Humboldt, see Daniel G. Brinton, *The Philosophic Grammar of the American Languages, as set forth by Wilhelm von Humboldt* (Philadelphia, 1885), 5. See also Stocking, *Victorian Anthropology*, 56–62; Benes, *In Babel's Shadow*, 211–21.

28. J. C. Nott and George R. Gliddon, *Types of Mankind: or, Ethnological Researches, Based upon Ancient Monuments, Paintings, Sculptures, and Crania of Races, and upon Their Natural, Geographical, Philological, and Biblical History* (Philadelphia, 1854), 285; Gliddon, "Monogenists and the Polygenists," 419, 568–69, 578. On religious skepticism and the American School, see Stanton, *Leopard's Spots*, 194; Dain, *Hideous Monster of the Mind*, 221–26.

29. Nott and Gliddon, *Types of Mankind*, xi, 79; William B. Hodgson to John Quincy Adams, June 29, 1829, in Du Ponceau Papers, box 1, folder 11; William B. Hodgson, *Notes on Northern Africa, the Sahara and Soudan, in relation to the Ethnography, Languages, History, Political and Social Condition, of the Nations of Those Countries* (New York, 1844), 67–68; Hodgson to Samuel G. Morton, Mar. 29, 1844, in Morton Papers (LCP), box 1, folder 27; Hodgson, "The Creek Confederacy," *Collections of the Georgia Historical Society* 3.1 (1848), 17–18. On Hodgson, see Michael O'Brien, *Conjectures of Order: Intellectual Life and the American South, 1810–1860*, 2 vols. (Chapel Hill: University of North Carolina Press, 2004), 1:172–78. For abolitionist use of philology, see Frederick Douglass, "The Claims of the Negro Ethnologically Considered, address delivered at Western Reserve College, July 12, 1854," in *Frederick Douglass: Selected Speeches and Writings*, eds. Philip S. Foner and Yuval Taylor (1950; Chicago: Lawrence Hill, 1999), 292.

30. Charles Caldwell, *Thoughts on the Original Unity of the Human Race* (New York, 1830), 166–69; Charles Pickering, *The Races of Man: and Their Geographical Distribution*, vol. 9., *United States Exploring Expedition during the Years 1838, 1839, 1840, 1841, 1842. Under the Command of Charles Wilkes, U.S.N.* (Boston, 1848), 277. See also A. Desmoulins, *Histoire naturelle des races humaines* (Paris, 1826), 345–47; Josiah C. Nott, *Two Lectures on the Natural History of the Caucasian and Negro Races* (Mobile, AL, 1844), 40; Gliddon, "Monogenists and the Polygenists," 578. On Caldwell, see Dain, *Hideous Monster of the Mind*, 72–74; Stanton, *Leopard's Spots*, 19–23, but these neglect his linguistic views. On Charles Pickering, see ibid., 93–96; Barry Alan Joyce, *The Shaping of American Ethnography: The Wilkes Exploring Expedition, 1838–1842* (Lincoln: University of Nebraska Press, 2001).

31. L. A., "Art. VIII—The Diversity of Origin of the Human Races," *Christian Examiner and Religious Miscellany* 49.1 (July 1850): 110–45, at 140; Agassiz to Nott and Gliddon, Feb. 1, 1857, in *Indigenous Races of the Earth*, xv. Cf. Daniel Wilson, *Prehistoric Man: Researches into the Origin of Civilisation in the Old and New World*, 2 vols. (Cambridge, 1862), 1:75–82. See also Alter, *Darwinism and the Linguistic Image*, 4, 40–42.

32. Nott, *Types of Mankind*, 284; Gliddon, "Monogenists and the Polygenists," 578, 586, 575–76; Maury, "Distribution and Classification of Tongues," 34–35. On hybridity, see Stanton, *Leopard's Spots*, 66–67, 113–18, 126–28, 134–39, 189–91; Robert J. C. Young, *Colonial Desire: Hybridity in Theory, Culture and Race* (London: Routledge, 1995); Dain, *Hideous Monster of the Mind*, 229–35, 254–61; Claude Blanckaert, "Of Monstrous Métis? Hybridity, Fear of Miscegenation, and Patriotism from Buffon to Paul Broca," in *The Color of Liberty*, eds. Sue Peabody and Tyler Stovall (Durham, NC: Duke University Press, 2003).

33. John R. Ridge, "The North American Indians. What They Have Been and What They Are.—Their Relations with the United States in the Existing National Crisis.—The Modifications of Their Character by the Infusion of White Blood and the Contact of Civilization.—Their Probable Destiny" (1862), in *A Trumpet of Our Own: Yellow Bird's Essays on the North American Indian; Selections from the Writings of the Noted Cherokee Author John Rollin Ridge*, eds. David Farmer and Rennard Strickland (San Francisco: Book Club of California, 1981), 69; William W. Warren, *History of the Ojibway People* (1887; St. Paul: Minnesota Historical Society Press, 1984), 60, 247, 61, 55, 135–36, 59, 62. See also Heidi Bohaker, "*Nindoodemag:* The Significance of Algonquian Kinship Networks in the Eastern Great Lakes Region, 1600–1701," *WMQ* 63.1 (Jan. 2006): 23–52; Cary Miller, *Ogimaag: Anishinaabeg Leadership, 1760–1845* (Lincoln: University of Nebraska Press, 2010), 183–226. On Ridge's California, see Lindsay, *Murder State;* Albert L. Hurtado, *Indian Survival on the California Frontier* (New Haven, CT: Yale University Press, 1988).

34. Alexander W. Bradford, *American Antiquities and Researches into the Origin and History of the Red Race* (New York, 1841), 246; Latham, *Man and His Migrations*, 87–88, at 87; Max Müller, "Last Results," 349.

35. Charles De Wolf Brownell, *The Indian Races of North and South America* (New York, 1857), 437; Schoolcraft, *Historical and Statistical Information*, 3:405, 407. For a list of vocabularies, see ibid., 4:552–53.

36. Horatio Hale, *Ethnography and Philology*, vol. 6. *United States Exploring Expedition during the Years 1838, 1839, 1840, 1841, 1842. Under the Command of Charles Wilkes, U.S.N* (Philadelphia, 1846), 223, 199, 225, 630; Catlin, *Letters and Notes*, 2:237, 234. On taxonomic problems in the West, see also Adam Johnson, "Languages of California," in *Historical and Statistical Information*, 4:407; William Carr Lane, "Letter on Affinities of Dialects in New Mexico," in ibid., 5:689; Turner, "Vocabularies of North American Languages," 93. On relations around Sutter's Fort, see Anne F. Hyde, *Empires, Nations, and Families: A New History of the American West* (New York: HarperCollins, 2011), 183–91.

37. For expressions of linguistic resistance to intermixture, especially in grammar, despite lexical borrowing, see J. Hammond Trumbull, "Words Derived from Indian Languages of North America," *APA Trans.* 3 (1872): 19–32, esp. 19–20; Max Müller, "Last Results," 1:265. Thomas R. Trautmann, *Languages and Nations: The Dravidian Proof in Colonial Madras* (Berkeley: University of California Press, 2006), 10–12, 18–38, examines philology's rejection of a model of language change that acknowledged

language mixing. Cf. Benes, *In Babel's Shadow*, 232. On Darwin and philology, see Alter, *Darwinism and the Linguistic Image*. Current linguists, including Peter Bakker, *A Language of Our Own: The Genesis of Michif, the Mixed Language of the Canadian Métis* (New York: Oxford University Press, 1997), 192–213; Emmanuel J. Dreschel, *Mobilian Jargon: Linguistic and Sociohistorical Aspects of a Native American Pidgin* (Oxford: Clarendon Press, 1997), 354–57; John McWhorter, *The Power of Babel: A Natural History of Language* (2001; New York: Perennial, 2003), 93–176, have called for greater attention to linguistic collision producing new languages.

38. Schoolcraft, *Historical and Statistical Information*, 4:552; John Scouler, "Observations on the Indigenous Tribes of the N.W. Coast of America," *Journal of the Royal Geographical Society of London* 11 (1841): 215–50, esp. 226, 229; Lieut. C. R. Collins, "Report on the Languages of the Different Tribes of Indians Inhabiting the Territory of Utah," in Captain J. H. Simpson, *Report of Explorations across the Great Basin of the Territory of Utah for a Direct Wagon-Route from Camp Floyd to Genoa, in Carson Valley, in 1859* (Washington, DC, 1876), 467; Powers, "Tribes of California," 72, 17; Catlin, *Letters and Notes*, 2:234. See also Theodore Binnema, *Common and Contested Ground: A Human and Environmental History of the Northwestern Plains* (Norman: University of Oklahoma Press, 2001), 11–17; Whaley, *Oregon and the Collapse of Illahee*, 10–11; James F. Brooks, *Captives and Cousins: Slavery, Kinship, and Community in the Southwest Borderlands* (Chapel Hill: University of North Carolina Press, 2002), 1–40; Ned Blackhawk, *Violence over the Land: Indians and Empires in the Early American West* (Cambridge, MA: Harvard University Press, 2006), 7, 51, 57–58, 71–80, 105–14, 133, 142–43, 240; Lisa Jane Conathan, "The Linguistic Ecology of Northwestern California: Contact, Functional Convergence, and Dialectology" (Ph.D. diss., University of California, Berkeley, 2004), 22–23, 105–112.

39. Hale, *Ethnography and Philology*, 635–36, 640, 643. On linguistic intermixture in the fur trade, see George Henry Loskiel, *History of the Mission of the United Brethren among the Indians in North America, in three parts*, trans. Christian Ignatius LaTrobe (London, 1794), 1:20; Washington Irving, *Astoria: Or Anecdotes of an Enterprise beyond the Rocky Mountains*, 2 vols. (Philadelphia, 1836), 1:47–48, 149. For modern scholarly discussion, see Bakker, *A Language of Our Own*, 45–77; George Lang, *Making Wawa: The Genesis of Chinook Jargon* (Vancouver: University of British Columbia Press, 2008), 85–121.

40. Hale, *Ethnography and Philology*, 635–36, 644, 184, 174. On Fiji, cf. Charles Pickering to Samuel G. Morton, Aug. 8, 1840, Morton Papers (LCP), ser. IV. Lang, *Making Wawa*, 100–3, 123–35, affirms Hale's linguistic description. On racial intermixture and expansionism, see Reginald Horsman, *Race and Manifest Destiny: The Origins of American Racial Anglo-Saxonism* (Cambridge, MA: Harvard University Press, 1981), 210–12, 222, quoted at 222. See also Whaley, *Oregon and the Collapse of Illahee*, 138–42, 169–76; Peggy Pascoe, *What Comes Naturally: Miscegenation Law and the Making of Race in America* (New York: Oxford University Press, 2009), 77–80, 94–104.

41. James G. Swan, *The Northwest Coast; or, Three Years' Residence in Washington Territory* (New York, 1857), 90; John Ball, *Autobiography of John Ball*, ed. Kate Ball

Powers, Flora Ball Hopkins, and Lucy Ball (Grand Rapids, MI: Dean-Hicks, 1925), 96; William Fraser Tolmie, *The Journals of William Fraser Tolmie: Physician and Fur Trader* (Vancouver, BC: Mitchell Press Ltd., 1963), 210; Horatio Hale, *An International Idiom: A Manual of the Oregon Trade Language, or "Chinook Jargon"* (London, 1890), 21; Horatio Hale, "Man and Language; or, the True Basis of Anthropology," *American Antiquarian and Oriental Journal* 15.1 (Jan. 1893): 15–24, at 16–17. On Chinook Wawa as a real language, see Robert Gordon Latham, *The Natural History of the Varieties of Man* (London, 1850), 319, 555–565; James Cresswell Clough, *On the Existence of Mixed Languages: Being an Examination of the Fundamental Axioms of the Foreign School of Modern Philology, More Especially as Applied to English* (London, 1876), 9, 12; Swan, *Northwest Coast*, 309, 312. On "miscegenation" in the fur trade and in Oregon, see *Miscegenation: The Theory of the Blending of the Races, applied to the American White Man and Negro* (New York, 1864), 89; George Gibbs, "The Intermixture of Races," *ARSI 1864* (Washington, DC, 1865), 375–77.

42. Gallatin, "Hale's Indians," xlv, xxxvi; Gallatin to W. H. Emory, Oct. 1, 1847, in Emory, *Notes of a Military Reconnoissance, from Fort Leavenworth, in Missouri, to San Diego, in California, Including Parts of the Arkansas, Del Norte, and Gila Rivers* (Washington, DC, 1848), 127–30, at 128. See also Josiah C. Gregg, *Commerce of the Prairies: Or the Journal of a Santa Fé Trader, during Eight Expeditions across the Great Western Prairies, and a Residence of Nearly Nine Years in Northern Mexico*, 2 vols. (New York, 1844), 1:269, 285. On Comanche and Apache raids creating the conditions for war, see Brian DeLay, *War of a Thousand Deserts: Indian Raids and the U.S.-Mexican War* (New Haven, CT: Yale University Press, 2008).

43. Gallatin, "Hale's Indians," xcvii, cviii, lxxxiii, cxlvi. On the "miniscule" print run of the Wilkes Expedition reports, see Frankel, *States of Inquiry*, 113. Bieder, *Science Encounters the Indian*, 50–53, discusses Gallatin and Pueblos. On the transformation of the region in the first half of the nineteenth century, see Andrés Reséndez, *Changing National Identities at the Frontier: Texas and New Mexico, 1800–1850* (New York: Cambridge University Press, 2005).

44. Turner, "Vocabularies of North American Languages," 83–85, at 84; William W. Turner, "The Apaches," *Literary World* 10.272 (Apr. 17, 1852): 281–82. On Buschmann's work in the 1850s, see Hubert Howe Bancroft, *The Native Races of the Pacific States*, vol. 3. *Myths and Languages* (New York, 1875), 581–82. On Athapaskans and indication of Asian origins, see Robert Gordon Latham, *Opuscula. Essays Chiefly Philological and Ethnographical* (London, 1860), 411; Franciscan Fathers, *An Ethnologic Dictionary of the Navaho Language* (St. Michaels, AZ, 1910), 26–30. For current scholarly views, see Deni J. Seymour, *From the Land of Ever Winter to the American Southwest: Athapaskan Migrations, Mobility, and Ethnogenesis* (Salt Lake City: University of Utah Press, 2012). On the Mexican Boundary Survey, see Robert Gunn, "John Russell Bartlett's Literary Borderlands.": Ethnology, War, and the United States Boundary Survey," *Western American Literature* 46.4 (Winter 2012): 349–80.

45. *Historical and Statistical Information*, 1:198; John Sibley to the Secretary of War, 1807, in OIALR, 1:41; J. C. Frémont, *Narrative of the Exploring Expedition to the Rocky*

Mountains in the Year 1842, and to Oregon and North California in the Years 1843–'44, 2nd ed. (Washington, DC, 1845), 132; Edward B. Tylor, "IX. Remarks on Buschmann's Researches in North American Philology," *Transactions of the Ethnological Society of London,* n.s. 2 (1863): 130–36, at 135, 133–34. In favor, see also Latham, *Opuscula,* 363, 399; Daniel G. Brinton, *The American Race: A Linguistic Classification and Ethnographic Description of the Indian Tribes of North and South America* (1891; Philadelphia, 1901), 44, 118. Against the connection, see Bancroft, *Native Races,* 661; J. Hammond Trumbull, "Indian Languages of America" (1876), *Johnson's (Revised) Universal Cyclopaedia: A Scientific and Popular Treasury of Useful Knowledge,* 8 vols. (New York, 1889–1890), 234–35; Powell, "Indian Linguistic Families," 28. On Numic peoples, their varied ways of life, and the social conditions they faced at midcentury, see Pekka Hämäläinen, *The Comanche Empire* (New Haven, CT: Yale University Press, 2008), 22–23, 141–238; Blackhawk, *Violence over the Land,* 119–75, esp. 135–44; Smoak, *Ghost Dances and Identity,* 15–47. For differing views on Uto-Aztecan and the spread of maize cultivation, see Jane H. Hill, "Proto-Uto-Aztecan: A Community of Cultivators in Central Mexico?," *American Anthropologist* 103.4 (Dec. 2001): 913–34; William L. Merrill, "The Historical Linguistics of Uto-Aztecan Agriculture," *Anthropological Linguistics* 54.3 (Fall 2012): 203–60.

46. Trumbull, "Indian Languages of America," 239, 236; Brinton, *American Race,* 55–56; Daniel G. Brinton, *Essays of an Americanist* (Philadelphia, 1890), 362, 305–6. See also Charles Frederic Hartt, "Notes on the Lingoa Geral or Modern Tupí of the Amazonas," *APA Trans.* 3 (1872), 58. On grammatical differences among Siouan languages, see Horatio Hale, *Indian Migrations, as Evidenced by Language: Comprising the Huron-Cherokee Stock: the Dakota Stock: the Algonkins: the Chahta-Muskoki Stock: the Moundbuilders: the Iberians. A Paper Read at a Meeting of the American Association for the Advancement of Science, Held at Montreal, in August, 1882* (Chicago, 1883), 13. On phonetic variation, see chap. 4, note 52. On discovering phonetic laws, see also Albert S. Gatschet, "The Test of Linguistic Affinity," *American Antiquarian* 2.2 (Oct.–Dec. 1879): 163–65, at 165. On comparative philology and sound changes, see Benes, *In Babel's Shadow,* 113–57, 236–39; Trautmann, *Languages and Nations,* 218–20; Andresen, *Linguistics in America,* 183–89. On U.S. knowledge production in Latin America, see Ricardo D. Salvatore, "The Enterprise of Knowledge: Representational Machines of Informal Empire," in *Close Encounters of Empire: Writing the Cultural History of U.S.-Latin American Relations,* eds. Gilbert M. Joseph et al. (Durham, NC: Duke University Press, 1998).

47. Albert Gatschet, "Linguistics. Prefaced by a Classification of Western Indian Languages," in Engineer Department, U.S. Army, *Report upon the United States Geographical Surveys West of the One Hundredth Meridian, in Charge of First Lieut. Geo. M. Wheeler,* 7 vols. (Washington, DC, 1879), 7:405. On Gatschet, see Hinsley, *Smithsonian and the American Indian,* 177–80.

48. Lewis H. Morgan, *Ancient Society; or Researches in the Lines of Human Progress from Savagery through Barbarism to Civilization* (New York, 1877), 5; Lewis H. Morgan, "Systems of Consanguinity and Affinity of the Human Family," *Smithsonian Contrib.*

17 (1871), v–ix, 10–15, 131–41, 151, 196, 494–508, at 136, 508, vi, 15. Morgan's contempo-
raries understood the philological character of his kinship studies. See Joseph Henry,
"Advertisement," in ibid., iii; Whitney, *Life and Growth of Language*, 262; W. H. Dall,
"Tribes of the Extreme Northwest," in *CNAE* 1 (1877), 117–19; Brinton, *Essays of an
Americanist* 37. Morgan's early work includes a letter in Henry R. Schoolcraft, *Notes on
the Iroquois; or Contributions to American History, Antiquities, and General Ethnology*
(Albany, 1847), 495–97; and the series "Letters on the Iroquois, by Skenandoah:
Addressed to Albert Gallatin," in *American Review* between February and December
1847. See also Bieder, *Science Encounters the Indian*, 194–246; Daniel Noah Moses, *The
Promise of Progress: The Life and Work of Lewis Henry Morgan* (Columbia: University of
Missouri Press, 2009); Philip J. Deloria, *Playing Indian* (New Haven, CT: Yale
University Press, 1998), chap. 3.

49. Trumbull, "Indian Languages of America," 236; Dall, "Tribes of the Extreme
Northwest," 95 (cf. 97); F. L. O. Roehrig, "On the Language of the Dakota or Sioux
Indians," *ARSI 1871* (Washington, 1873), 435-37. On Turanian, see also Powers, "Tribes
of California," 76; Albert S. Gatschet, "Linguistic Notes," *American Antiquarian* 2.2
(Oct.–Dec. 1879): 171–74, esp. 173–74; James Wickersham, *Major Powell's Inquiry:
'Whence Came the American Indians?' An Answer. A Study in Comparative Ethnology*
(Tacoma, WA, 1899), 10. On Basque, see Hale, *Indian Migrations*, 24–27, and, more
ambiguously, Brinton, *American Race*, 32.

50. Gibbs, "Report," 402; George Gibbs, "Prefatory Note," in James G. Swan, "The
Indians of Cape Flattery, at the Entrance to the Strait of Fuca, Washington Territory,"
Smithsonian Contrib. 16 (Washington, DC, 1870), v; Albert Samuel Gatschet, "The
Klamath Indians of Southwestern Oregon," *CNAE* 2.1 (Washington, DC, 1890), lvi;
Gatschet, "Linguistics," 409. For complaints, see Albert S. Gatschet, "Indian
Languages of the Pacific States and Territories," in *The Indian Miscellany*, ed. W. W.
Beach (Albany, NY, 1877), 417–21. Regarding "nation" and "tribe," cf. Morgan,
"Systems of Consanguinity," 139–41. On the end of the treaty system, see Prucha,
Great Father, 479–533, esp. 527–33.

51. J. W. Powell, *Introduction to the Study of Indian Languages, with Words, Phrases,
and Sentences to Be Collected*, 2nd ed. (Washington, DC, 1880), vi; J. W. Powell, *Report
on the Methods of Surveying the Public Domain, to the Secretary of the Interior, at the
Request of the National Academy of Sciences* (Washington, DC, 1878), 15.

52. Powell, *Report*, 16. See also Elliott West, *The Last Indian War: The Nez Perce
Story* (New York: Oxford University Press, 2009).

53. Powell, "Indian Linguistic Families," 8; J. W. Powell, "On Limitations to the
Use of Some Anthropological Data," *First ARBE 1879–'80* (Washington, DC, 1881),
81. E. Sapir, "Linguistic Publications of the Bureau of American Ethnology, a General
Review," *International Journal of American Linguistics* 1.1 (1917): 76–81, esp. 76–78, lists
64 BAE linguistic publications. Hinsley, *Smithsonian and the American Indian*, 264,
stresses Powell's avoidance of policy issues.

54. These addresses are described in W. H. Holmes, "The World's Fair Congress of
Anthropology," *American Anthropologist* 6 (1893): 423–35, esp. 429–30.

55. Powell, "Indian Linguistic Families," 8, 7, 141, 12; Powell, "On Limitations," 79; John W. Powell, "Whence Came the American Indians?," *Forum* 24.6 (Feb. 1896): 676–88, at 684; "Report of J. W. Powell and G. W. Ingalls," in *Annual Report of the Commissioner of Indian Affairs to the Secretary of the Interior for the Year 1873* (Washington, DC, 1874), 65. See also J. W. Powell, "On the Evolution of Language, as Exhibited in the Specialization of the Grammatic Processes, the Differentiation of the Parts of Speech, and the Integration of the Sentence; from a Study of Indian Languages," in *First ARBE*. On resistance to linguistic intermixture, see Washington Matthews, *Ethnography and Philology of the Hidatsa Indians*, United States Geological and Geographical Survey Miscellaneous Publications No. 7 (Washington, DC, 1877), 17; John C. Cremony, *Life among the Apaches* (San Francisco, 1868), 92. See also Mary R. Haas, "The Problem of Classifying American Indian Languages: From Duponceau to Powell," in *Language, Culture, History* (Stanford, CA: Stanford University Press, 1978). Hinsley, *Smithsonian and the American Indian*, 125–89, provides a thorough discussion of Powell, evolutionism, and the early BAE.

56. Otis T. Mason, "Ethnological Exhibit of the Smithsonian Institution at the World's Columbian Exhibition," in *Memoirs of the International Congress of Anthropology*, ed. C. Staniland Wake (Chicago, 1894), 211, 214; G. Brown Goode, "Report upon the Condition and Progress of the U.S. National Museum During the Year Ending June 30, 1893," in *ARSI 1893* (Washington, DC, 1895), 127, 128. See also, Holmes, "World's Fair Congress," 433. On this exhibit, see Hinsley, *Smithsonian and the American Indian*, 97–100, 109–11; Robert W. Rydell, *All the World's a Fair: Visions of Empire at American International Expositions, 1876–1916* (Chicago: University of Chicago Press, 1984), 55–60. Thanks to Ann Fabian for pushing me to consider this exhibit.

57. Powell, "Indian Linguistic Families," 30–31; J. W. Powell, "Museums of Ethnology and Their Classification," *Science* 9 (June 24, 1887): 612–14, at 613–14; Powell, "On Limitations," 81. On making empire cartographically visible, see also Matthew H. Edney, *Mapping an Empire: The Geographical Construction of British India, 1765–1843* (1990; Chicago: University of Chicago Press, 1997); Norman Etherington, ed., *Mapping Colonial Conquest: Australia and Southern Africa* (Crawley, Perth: University of Western Australia Press, 2007).

58. Franz Boas, *Handbook of American Indian Languages*, Part 1, BAE Bulletin 40 (Washington, DC, 1911), 14. See also Andresen, *Linguistics in America*, 211–20; George W. Stocking, Jr., "The Boas Plan for the Study of American Indian Languages," in *The Ethnographers Magic and Other Essays in the History of the Anthropology* (Madison: University of Wisconsin Press, 1992); Regna Darnell, *Invisible Genealogies: A History of Americanist Anthropology* (Lincoln: University of Nebraska Press, 2001), 33–67; Matthew Frye Jacobson, *Barbarian Virtues: The United States Encounters Foreign Peoples at Home and Abroad* (New York: Hill and Wang, 2000), 143–63.

Epilogue

1. J. N. B. Hewitt, "Polysynthesis in the Languages of the American Indians," *American Anthropologist* 6.4 (Oct. 1893): 381–407, at 381, 397, 400, 402.

2. J. N. B. Hewitt, "The Teaching of Ethnology in Indian Schools," *Quarterly Journal of the Society of American Indians* 1 (1913), 30–35, at 30, 31, 33, 34. Hewitt, "Polysynthesis," 383. See also Elizabeth Tooker and Barbara Graymont, "J. N. B. Hewitt," in *Histories of Anthropology Annual*, vol. 3, eds. Regna Darnell and Frederic W. Gleach (Lincoln: University of Nebraska Press, 2007); Lucy Maddox, *Citizen Indians: Native American Intellectuals, Race, and Reform* (Ithaca, NY: Cornell University Press, 2005), 89–125, esp. 119–20.

3. David Reich et al., "Reconstructing Native American Population History," *Nature* 488 (Aug. 16, 2012): 370–75. See also Joseph H. Greenberg et al., "The Settlement of the Americas: A Comparison of the Linguistic, Dental, and Genetic Evidence," *Current Anthropology* 27.5 (Dec. 1986): 477–97; Patrick Manning, "*Homo sapiens* Populates the Earth: A Provisional Synthesis, Privileging Linguistic Evidence," *Journal of World History* 17.2 (2006): 115–58, esp. 116, 133.

4. John Colopinto, "The Interpreter: Has a Remote Amazonian Tribe Upended Our Understanding of Language?," *The New Yorker* (Apr. 16, 2007), at http://www .newyorker.com/reporting/2007/04/16/070416fa_fact_colapinto, accessed 7/24/2012; Tom Bartlett, "Angry Words: Will One Researcher's Discovery Deep in the Amazon Destroy the Foundation of Modern Linguistics?," *The Chronicle of Higher Education* (Mar. 20, 2012), at http://chronicle.com/article/Researchers-Findings-in-the/131260/, accessed 3/23/2012. See also Daniel L. Everett, "Cultural Constraints on Grammar and Cognition in Pirahã: Another Look at the Design Features of Human Language," *Current Anthropology* 46.4 (Aug.–Oct. 2005): 621–34; Daniel L. Everett, *Language: The Cultural Tool* (New York: Pantheon, 2012). On Noam Chomsky and debates over universal grammar, see Randy Allen Harris, *The Linguistics Wars* (New York: Oxford University Press, 1995). On language evolution and differentiation, see John McWhorter, *The Power of Babel: A Natural History of Language* (2001; New York: Perennial, 2003); Christine Kinneally, *The First Word: The Search for the Origins of Language* (New York: Viking, 2007); "Babel or Babble? Languages All Have Their Roots in the Same Part of the World. But They Are Not as Similar to Each Other as Was Once Thought," *The Economist* (Apr. 14, 2011), at http://www.economist.com /node/18557572, accessed 4/19/2011; David Robson, "Powers of Babel," *New Scientist* (Dec. 10, 2011): 34–37. On language and thought, see Guy Deutscher, *Through the Language Glass: Why the World Looks Different in Other Languages* (New York: Picador, 2010); Lera Boroditsky, "How Language Shapes Thought: The Languages We Speak Affect Our Perceptions of the World," *Scientific American* (Feb. 2011): 63–65.

5. Terrence G. Wiley, "Language Planning, Language Policy, and the English-Only Movement," *Language in the U.S.A.: Themes for the Twenty-First Century*, eds. Edward Finegan and John R. Rickford (New York: Cambridge University Press, 2004); Jane H. Hill, "The Racializing Function of Language Panics," in *Language Ideologies: Critical Perspectives on the Official Language Movement*, 2 vols., eds. Roseann Dueñas González and Ildikó Melis (London: Routledge, 2001); Andrew Dalby, *Language in Danger: The Loss of Linguistic Diversity and the Threat to Our Future* (New York: Columbia University Press, 2003), 143–49, 158–66, 280–85; Kelsey Klug, "Native American Languages Act: Twenty Years Later, Has It Made a Difference?," at http://

www.culturalsurvival.org/news/native-american-languages-act-twenty-years-later
-has-it-made-difference, accessed 7/25/2012. Ives Goddard, "Introduction," in *Handbook,* 3, provides the estimate of 400 languages c. 1492.

6. National Museum of the American Indian website, at http://www.nmai.si.edu
/education/codetalkers/html/chapter2.html, accessed 10/29/2009. For other Native
perspectives, see Scott Richard Lyons, "There's No Translation for It: The Rhetorical
Sovereignty of Indigenous Languages," in *Cross-Language Relations in Composition,*
eds. Bruce Horner, Min-Zhan Lu, and Paul Kei Matsuda (Carbondale: Southern
Illinois University Press, 2010), 130; Paul V. Kroskrity and Margaret C. Field, eds.,
Native American Language Ideologies: Beliefs, Practices, and Struggles in Indian Country
(Tucson: University of Arizona Press, 2009). See also Marianne Mithun, *The Languages
of Native North America* (New York: Cambridge University Press, 1999), 2.

Acknowledgments

"Having now read nearly all that has been written on the Subject," philologist Peter S. Du Ponceau remarked nearly two hundred years ago, "I think something interesting may be done without extraordinary talents." I came to a similar view about this project early on. Numerous individuals and institutions must have felt the same way.

Native Tongues began in the Lyon G. Tyler Department of History at the College of William & Mary, which provided six years of funding and several additional grants for research. Fellow W&M grad students provided friendly ears, continuous encouragement, and great ideas. Thanks especially to Ellen Adams, Merit Anglin, Gordon Barker, Josh Beatty, Dave Brown, Celine Carayon, Jim David, Jack Fiorini, Sarah Grunder, Caroline Hasenyager, Dave McCarthy, Sarah McLennan, Amanda Kay McVety, John Miller, Caroline Morris, Emily Moore, Liam Paskvan, Andrew Sturtevant, and John Weber. The W&M faculty made this project better through their teaching, their scholarship, and their questions and criticism. Special thanks to Katie Bragdon, Chandos Brown, Andy Fisher, Bob Gross, Jack Martin, Paul Mapp, Charlie McGovern, Carol Sheriff, Jim Whittenburg, Karin Wulf, and the late Rhys Isaac. Omohundro Institute of Early American History and Culture colloquia inspired me time and again. James Axtell, Tuska Benes, and Dan Richter—provided expertise and suggestions for the eventual book. Chris Grasso has provided unfailingly astute edits, friendship, and a lot of good advice.

Several outside institutions provided the resources that made *Native Tongues* possible. The Robert H. Smith International Center for Jefferson Studies, the American Philosophical Society, the William H. Clements Library at the University of Michigan, the Library Company of Philadelphia, and the Historical Society of Pennsylvania supported my early research. A fellowship from the Mellon Foundation and the American Council of Learned Societies provided me the resources to finish while spending a stimulating year at the McNeil Center for Early American Studies.

The New England Regional Fellowship Consortium supported two months of research at the Boston Athenaeum, Harvard University's Houghton Library, the Massachusetts Historical Society, and the Rhode-Island Historical Society that provided a foundation for revisions. A yearlong National Endowment for the Humanities fellowship at the American Antiquarian Society, with its breathtaking collections and unparalleled scholarly environment, allowed me to read more widely, think more deeply, and write a better book. A steady stream of short-term fellows offered continuous edification, and a wonderful cohort of long-term fellows shared their ideas, their criticisms, and their own work: Elizabeth Maddock Dillon, Dan Rood, Kyle Volk, and Lisa Wilson. The staffs at all of these institutions were great, but I owe special thanks to Anna Berkes at Monticello; Roy Goodman, Charlie Greifenstein, and Earl Spamer at APS; Connie King at LCP; Conrad Wright at MHS; Lee Teverow at RIHS; and Ashley Cataldo, Paul Erickson, Lauren Hewes, and Tom Knowles at AAS. Each pointed me to sources that I would not have found on my own.

Numerous scholars elsewhere have provided sounding boards and criticism: Richard Beeman, Josh Bellin, Tim Cassedy, Brian Connolly, Matthew Crow, Bruce Dain, Kathleen Du Val, Patrick Erben, Ann Fabian, Aaron Fogleman, Edward Gray, Amy Greenberg, Hunt Howell, Kristen Huffine, John Lauritz Larson, Joan Leopold, Michael McGandy, Martin Müller, Laura Murray, Drew Newman, Steven Peach, Britt Rusert, David Samuels, Claudio Saunt, Erik Seeman, Jim Schmidt, David Silverman, Andrea Smalley, James Snead, Christina Snyder, David Spanagel, Laura Keenan Spero, Rachel Wheeler, Kariann Yokota. Robert Gunn and Sarah Rivett have been generous in exchanging ideas. Nancy Shoemaker offered trenchant criticism of the complete manuscript, as did the readers for Harvard University Press. My colleagues at Seton Hall University have been wonderful. Nathaniel Knight and Kirsten Schultz have helped me understand my project from a wider view, and Vanessa May and Thomas Rzeznik usefully shredded early drafts of the introduction. Sam Spofford and Kathleen Richards were invaluable through the copyediting process. At HUP, Kathleen McDermott showed early interest and Andrew Kinney's editorial mind and hand have made the book better. Thank you.

My family offered me love, support, and confidence (perhaps misplaced, I wondered at times) that I knew what I was doing. I would not be here if not for my mother Eileen Werner, my sister Kathleen Harvey, and my late father John Harvey. Sarah L. Grunder has listened to me ramble on about philology and ethnology at dinner, over drinks, and on hikes for many years now, offering encouragement, criticism, and love. This is for you.

Index

Abenaki, 36; language of, 1, 30, 139, 157

abolition, 13, 175, 208

Acadia, 25, 27, 37

Acosta, José de, 40, 54

Adam, language of, 83–84, 162

Adams, John, 109

Adams, John Quincy, 154

Adair, James, 37, 40, 46, 55

Adelung, Johann Christoph, 96

Africans 9; languages of, 20, 45–46, 80, 121, 183, 188, 200, 223; Native languages compared with, 52, 64, 143. *See also* specific languages

Agassiz, Louis, 143, 201–02, 210

Ahyokah (Cherokee), 124

Aitteon, Joe (Abenaki), 1

Alabama, language of, 77

Alaska, 77, 188, 204, 209, 214

Aleut, 197–199, 212

Algonquian languages, 6, 30, 39, 49–50, 65–71, 73, 74, 78, 102, 138, 139, 140, 150, 158, 171, 186, 190, 202–203, 206. *See also* specific languages

Algonquin, 19, 27

Alighieri, Dante, 159

alphabet, invention of, 42; roman, 119, 121–122; inadequacy of for Native languages, 122, 139–142. *See also* orthography

American Academy of Arts and Sciences, 105, 111, 120, 169

American Antiquarian Society, 95, 105, 106–107, 161, 176

American Bible Society, 83, 116

American Board of Commissioners for Foreign Missions, 110, 113–114, 117, 120–125, 128, 132–133, 141, 144, 154, 179–180, 189, 193

American Ethnological Society, 167, 168, 169, 186, 188, 195–198, 199, 203

American Fur Company, 155

American Oriental Society, 169, 188

American Philological Association, 210

American Philosophical Society, 5, 58, 81–82, 84, 86, 91, 121, 157, 169, 186–87, 189; Historical and Literary Committee of, 96–105, 107–110

American Revolution, and race, 12; and suspicion of missions, 80. *See also* War for Independence

American School of Ethnology, 176, 207, 215; critique of philology, 183, 196–202.

American Society for Promoting the Civilization and General Improvement of the Indian Tribes of the United States, 117

Amerind language phylum, 224

Index

anatomy, 45–46, 159, 176–177, 202. *See also* craniology

Anishnaabeg, 135, 145, 162–163, 170–171

Andover Theological Seminary, 113

Anthropological Society of Washington, 220

anthropology, 90, 142, 176, 185, 209, 215, 219, 220. *See also* ethnology

Apache, 140, 193, 208–209, 213.

Apess, William (Pequot), 93

Arapaho, 204

archaeology, and convergence with language study, 57, 77, 82, 86–88, 106, 163–66, 195, 198; and methodological competition with etymology and philology, 12, 57, 82, 90, 106–07, 163–64, 199, 219; and theories of Indians' ancestors building western mounds, 85–88; and theories about distinct race of "Mound Builders," 67, 106–07, 163, 164, 197; and overturning scriptural chronology, 10, 169, 178, 199–200, 219; and evolutionary theories, 178

Arkansas River, 77

Armenian, 121

Armstrong, Robert (Wyandot), 5

army officers, 20, 25–26, 34–35, 36, 52, 72–73, 76–77, 92, 111, 142, 153, 185, 190, 192, 196, 206, 211, 212, 219

Asia, languages of, 80, 121, 223; Native languages compared with, 52, 54, 56, 62–64, 90–95. *See also* Indo-European languages; specific languages

assimilation, debates regarding 17, 114–115, 117–119, 128, 130–132, 136–144. *See also* civilization program

Assiniboin, 73, 174

Astor, John Jacob, 155

Athapaskan languages, 77, 136, 199, 204, 206, 213, 215, 218

Atwater, Caleb, 106, 111, 140

Aulneau, Jean-Pierre, 28

Aupaumut, Hendrick (Mohican), 68–70, 74, 86

Australia, languages of, 223; compared with Native languages, 143, 204

Aztecs, 143, 171, 209

Babel, Tower of, 8, 52, 80, 82, 83–84, 92, 106, 159, 199–200. *See also* scriptural narrative

Bancroft, George, 164, 175

Banks, Joseph, 62

Bannock, 193

Bannock War, 194

barbarism. *See* stadial theory; evolution

Baraga, Frederic, 157

Barbour, James, 154

Bartlett, John Russell, 161, 197–198, 208

Barton, Benjamin Smith, likens himself to settler, 2; and vocabulary collection, 51, 57, 61–62, 69, 90; and Native knowledge, 62, 69; and views of Indian origins, 63–65, 90; and views of Native linguistic unity, 62–65, 87; and collaboration with Heckewelder, 81, 85–86, 88–89; on western mounds and previous Native cultivation, 82, 85–88, 95; and turn away from etymology, 90; loss of Lewis and Clark vocabularies, 79; scholarly support for, 90–91; scholarly criticism of, 91–92; and views of "civilization" program, 88–90, 118

Barton, Thomas, 88

Bartram, William, 62

Basque, 102–03, 175, 212

Beattie, James, 44, 127

Beatty, Charles, 52

Beecher, Catharine, 130

Beecher, Lyman, 117, 119

Berber, 103

Beresford, William, 23

Biard, Pierre, 28, 31, 32

Biddle, Nicholas, 72

Bingham, Hiram, 120

biology, 159, 169, 219. *See also* natural history

Blackburn, Gideon, 117

Blackfoot, 174, 195, 204, 206

Black Hawk (Sauk), 171, 176; Black Hawk War, 171, 203

Black Hoof (Shawnee), 75

Blair, Hugh, 43–44, 127

Blumenbach, Johann Friedrich, 9, 46, 50, 83, 94, 196, 201

boarding schools, 15, 180, 221, 225

Boas, Franz, 142, 215

Böhme, Jacob, 83

Bosque Redondo, 193

Boudinot, Elias, 93

Boudinot, Elias (Buck Watie) (Cherokee), 78, 129–30, 131–32

Bougainville, Louis Antoine de, 36

Brackenridge, Henry Marie, 61

Bradford, Alexander, 203

Brainerd, David, 32, 33

Brainerd mission, 113

Brant, Joseph (Mohawk), 70, 74

Brazil, 210, 224; languages of, 43, 45

Brebeuf, Jean de, 30, 31, 32, 37, 38

Bressani, Francesco, 30

Brinton, Daniel G., 189, 210, 215, 220

British and Foreign Bible Society, 135, 137

Broca, Paul, 176–77

Brosses, Charles de, 45, 53

Brothertown, 68, 118, 179

Brown, David (Cherokee), 102, 111, 113–114, 129, 130, 154, 162

Brown, Orlando, 193

Brownell, Charles De Wolf, 204

Bryant, William, 90

Buckner, H. F., 3, 139, 157

Buffalo Creek mission, 122–123

Buffon, George-Louis Leclerc, comte de, 45, 59, 64, 83

Bukaru, Doalu, 136

Bureau of Ethnology, 15, 185, 194, 213–219, 220–222

Bureau of Indian Affairs, 3, 131, 148, 161, 180, 214; and ethnologically informed policy, 168, 192–193. *See also* U.S. Indian agents

Buschmann, Johann, 209

Butler, Richard, 66–67

Butrick, Daniel S., 108, 113, 119, 122

Byington, Cyrus, 122, 132, 174, 189

Caddo, 73, 101

Caddoan languages, 186

Caldwell, Charles, 12, 94–95, 128, 201

Calhoun, John C., 107, 148

California, 188, 193, 202, 209, 213; languages of, 140, 143, 184–186, 204–206

Campanius, John, 23

Camper, Peter, 46

Canada, 49, 77, 101, 135, 136–138, 145, 185, 188, 209. *See also* New France

Captain Pipe (Delaware), 69–70

captives, 21, 153

Caribbean Sea, 25, 80, 184

Carib, 25; language of, 47

Carolina Algonquian, 19, 121

Carter, Kilpatrick (Chickasaw), 6

Carver, Jonathan, 26, 52

Cass, Lewis, 73; and linguistic collection, 5, 145, 148–151, 155, 164; and opposition to Du Ponceau and Heckewelder, 5, 148, 150–153, 156, 180–181; on savagery, 150–152, 156; on Cherokee syllabary, 128; and prominence through philology, 156, 169; and support for Indian removal, 128, 139, 155–156; views opposed, 153–154, 157–58; as Secretary of War, 156, 191; on linguistic consolidation, 191

Catawba, 86

Catherine II (the Great), of Russia, 56–57, 66, 81

Catlin, George, 163, 205, 206

Cayuse, language of, 193, 221; Cayuse War, 193

Central America, 164–65, 184, 194, 195

Central Eurasia, languages of. *See* Turanian languages

Chamberlain, William, 125

Champollion, Jean-François, 166, 171

Charlevoix, Pierre-François-Xavier de, 19, 53, 87

Chaumonot, Pierre Joseph Marie, 31
Chazotte, Peter S., 127
Chehalis, 140, 206
Cherokee, 75, 117, 123–33, 156, 190–91; language of, 49–50, 59, 62, 63, 77–78, 88, 102, 108, 113–15, 119, 123–33, 136, 122, 154, 162; syllabary, 15, 17, 113–15, 123–33, 136.
Cheyenne, 77–78, 204
Chickasaw 37, 114; language of, 5–6, 26, 59, 63, 102, 154, 191–192
Chimariko, 206
Chinese, 9, 19, 42, 52, 94, 103
Chinook, 140–41, 206–207
Chinook Jargon, 188, 206–208
Chipewyan, 9, 24, 174
Chippewa (see Ojibwe)
Choctaw Academy, 174, 192
Choctaw, 34, 114, 116; language of, 6, 50, 59, 63, 77, 122, 132, 133, 154, 174, 189–191
Chukchi, 102, 116
citizenship, 12, 168, 179–80
Civil War, 180, 183
civilization program, 5, 12, 13–14, 17, 66, 70, 72, 74, 82, 88–90, 107, 111–12, 114–24, 127–32, 144, 148, 170, 179–80, 223; consolidation and, 190, 192, 194; white opposition to, 128, 197, 200
Clatsop, 156
Clark, William, 72, 190. *See also* Lewis and Clark Expedition
classification, of Native languages, 17–18, 65–79, 189–194, 195, 197, 204–219, 223, 224; of non-Native languages, 8–9, 93–94, 182–183, 199–200, 212–213, 215–218, 221; of races, 9, 65, 196–198, 204–210, 213, 214, 218–219; place in eighteenth-century natural history, 58; Native views on linguistic difference or similarity of other Native peoples, 7, 21, 49–50, 69–70, 75–76, 78, 124, 191–192, 202–203
Clavigero, Francisco Xavier, 62–63, 64, 87
Clifford, John D., 106
Cockenoe (Montaukett), 31

Colbert, Martin (Ibbaryou Klittubbey) (Chickasaw), 6
Colden, Cadwallader, 37, 40, 43
Coleridge, Samuel Taylor, 125
College of William and Mary, 86
Collin, Nicholas, 91
Collins, C. R., 206
colonialism, U.S., overview of in U.S., 10, 12–14; overview of role of language study in, 2–7, 12–13, 219, 223; overview of linguistic effects of, 14–15; as basis for U.S. philology, 11, 101, 104–105, 195–196; ideology of expressed in language study, 2, 152, 202, 217. *See also* boarding schools; civilization program; classification; expansion; Indian removal; language death; missions; pacification; reservations; trade; treaties
Colton, Calvin, 139
Comanche, 204, 209
Comenius, Jan Amos, 100
Condillac, Etienne Bonnot de, 8, 42–43, 45
confusion of tongues. *See* Babel
Congo, language of, 183
Congress, and support for ethnology, 167–68, 171–73
Connecticut, 32, 80, 113, 128
Connecticut Society of Arts and Sciences, 66
conquest treaties, 66
Cooper, James Fennimore, 151
Copway, George (Ojibwe), 162–163, 166, 176, 178, 190–191
Corps of Discovery (see Lewis and Clark Expedition)
Cotton, Josiah, 30, 111
Court de Gébelin, Antoine, 45, 46, 56, 81, 96, 109
Covenant Chain alliance, 39, 67, 107
craniology, 162, 169, 196–98
Cree, 28; language of, 24, 26, 135–138, 174, 191, 206; syllabics, 135–136
Creeks, 62, 66, 74, 76, 77, 87, 114, 174, 200; Creek Civil War, 76, 89, 95, 203; language of (*see* Muskogee)

Crow, 7, 187; language of, 101
culture area, anthropological concept of, 217–218
cultural nationalism, 5, 11, 62, 84–85, 104–105, 115
Cuvier, Georges, 159
Cusick, David (Tuscarora), 69

Dakota, 122, 132, 140, 157, 179–180, 188–190; Dakota War (1862), 180
d'Alembert, Jean le Rond, 53
Dall, W. H., 212, 214
Darwin, Charles, 10, 178, 201–202, 206; Darwinian Revolution, 177–78, 183–84, 212, 219
Davis, Edwin, 163
Dearborn, Henry, 73
degeneration, theory of, 82–90, 107–109; U.S. fears about, 64–65, 83; discrediting of, 169, 178
Delaware, 39, 67–70, 74, 88–89, 107–08, 117, 119, 166, 174, 195; language of, 5, 23, 33, 63, 69, 80–82, 85, 96–99, 101–02, 108, 138, 139, 150, 151–52, 158, 166
Deluge, 42, 53; and sons of Noah, 94
Demoulins, Antonie, 201
Destutt de Tracy, Antoine Louis Claude, 100; and ideology, 158
Devangari script, 135
developmentalism (see evolution, stadial theories)
Diderot, Denis, 53
Dighton Rock, 56, 170
diplomacy, 21–22, 35–40. *See also* specific treaties
Donation Land Act (1850), 193
Drayton, John, 86
Dred Scott v. Sanford (1857), 180
Dunbar, James, 47
Dunbar, William, 92
Du Ponceau, Peter Stephen, 3, 4–6, 95–112, 144–145, 166, 201; and collaboration with John Heckewelder, 4–6, 81, 96–104; and colonialist cultural nationalism, 5, 104–105; and refutation of notion of

"savage" languages, 6, 97–100, 157–59, 181; and federal philology, 5, 101, 155, 161; and Native knowledge, 5–6, 101–102; and network for collection, 101–102, 108; and scholarly network, 104–105, 175; and philanthropy, 5, 108–110, 112, 114–115, 144; and cultural prestige, 160, 169; and common "plans of ideas" in all Native languages, 5–6, 95–104, 158–159, 195; and distinctness of American languages, 5, 102–104, 112, 158–159, 200; and fixity of grammatical organization, 158–159, 181; on Chinese, 103, 127, 158–59; on Native pronunciation, 142, 143; on social condition and writing, 127, 160, 171; response to his philology, 104–112, 145–156, 160–162, 166, 175–177, 180–181, 210, 220–221
Dunglison, Robley, 142
Dwight, Timothy, 139

Edwards, Jonathan, Jr., 34, 66–67, 93, 111
Eastman, Seth, 172–173
Eel River, 76
Egyptology, 141, 199, 200. *See also* hiero-glyphics
Eliot, John, 27–28, 29, 31, 33, 52, 56, 65, 111, 115, 117
eloquence, stereotype of Indian, 22, 35–40, 43–44, 48, 81, 97–99, 152, 164, 170
Enlightenment, 40–48
English language, 19, 110, 115, 182, 206–207, 217; as part of U.S. nationalism, 64, 116–118, 144, 224; Native views of, 117, 129, 131–132, 178; U.S. imposition of, 117, 119, 178–181, 217, 218, 219; relevance of African Americans speaking, 183–184, 201, 208; official language movement, 224
environmentalism, as theory in natural history or moral philosophy, 9, 45–48, 52, 83, 95, 142–143, 198; attacks on, 94–95, 158–59, 197–98. *See also* stadial theory
Eskimo-Aleut languages, 77, 102, 136, 197–198, 224

Eskimos (*see* Inuit; Aleut)
essentialism (see languages; philology;
    physical ethnology; race)
ethnographic maps, 77–78, 204–205, 215–218
ethnography, 12, 188, 195, 198; and impor-
    tance of linguistic knowledge for, 81,
    214, 218
ethnology: methodological competition
    within, 57, 181, 182–84, 194–204, 217–219;
    and revolution in human time, 10, 178;
    visual display of, 217–218. *See also*
    archaeology; ethnography; philology;
    physical ethnology
etymology, 51–65, 170; association with
    materialism, 92–93; methods attacked,
    91–93, 96. *See also* vocabularies
European languages, Native languages
    compared with, 30, 44, 52; Native views
    of, 19, 27–28, 36, 141–142, 162–163. *See
    also* Indo-European languages; specific
    languages
Evans, James, 135–138, 141–142
Evarts, Jeremiah, 128–129, 130
Everett, Daniel, 224
Everett, Edward, 161, 190–191
evolution, 45, 82–83, 154, 166, 183–185, 186;
    and ideas of inheritance, 10, 208–210;
    and philology, 9, 13, 18, 177, 182, 196,
    211–219, 223; increasing legitimacy of,
    169, 177–178; of language, 211, 216–17,
    220, 224; and pessimism regarding
    social change, 10, 178; Native view of,
    220–21
expansion, commercial, 101, 103, 143,
    164–165, 184, 194, 198; territorial, 71–72,
    140–143, 164–165, 168, 181, 183–189,
    192–196, 211
exploration, U.S., 51, 71–72, 185, 219. *See
    also* specific expeditions

factory system, 72; discontinued, 148
Fidler, Peter, 9
Fiji, 207
Finno-Ugric languages, 198, 212
Five Nations (see Haudenosaunee)

Florida, 76, 92
Fontaine, John, 36
Foreign Mission School, 113, 128
Fort Hall, 193
Fort Vancouver, 207
Foxes (see Sauks and Foxes)
Franklin, Benjamin, 36–37, 39, 56, 100
Franklin Society, 161
French, 5, 19, 24, 178, 206–207
French and Indian War. *See* Seven Years
    War
French Revolution, 92–93
Frost, Joseph H., 142

Gabriel's Rebellion, 116
Gallatin, Albert, and U.S. treaty practice,
    76; and expanding federal linguistic col-
    lection, 77, 154–155, 160–161; and classifi-
    cation, 77–78, 155, 195, 208, 216, 218; and
    Native knowledge, 78, 131, 195; on social
    condition and writing, 127–128; on evolu-
    tion, 154, 177, 196, 208, 212; and publish-
    ing philology, 160–161, 167; and cultural
    prestige, 169; on importance of English,
    178; on linguistic ethnology, 77–78,
    195–198, 208; on language and race, 198,
    211; and Indian origins, 195–196, 198;
    views opposed, 197–198, 202–203
Gambold, John, 154
Gatschet, Albert S., 210, 211, 213
gender, in languages, 98, 102, 150, 151, 157,
    170
Georgia, 69, 115, 118, 129–130, 200
Georgia Historical Society, 200
German, 5, 80, 121. *See also* Germanic lan-
    guages; Indo-European languages
Germanic languages, 51, 59, 174, 206
gesture, 22, 30, 37–38
Ghost Dance, 194, 214
Gibbon, Edward, 125
Gibbs, Adin (Delaware), 174
Gibbs, George, 140, 185, 188–189, 193, 213
Gila River, 208
Gliddon, George R., 199–200, 202
Gobineau, Arthur de, 176, 199

Goguet, Antoine Yves, 125, 127
Goode, G. Brown, 218
Gookin, Daniel, 115
Gothic, 71
graphic practices, Native, 42, 56, 87, 126–127, 136, 143, 164, 166–173. *See also* alphabet; Cherokee syllabary; Cree syllabics; Dighton Rock; hieroglyphics
Great Basin, 206, 209
Great Lakes, 26, 27, 135, 152
Great Plains, 20, 73, 140, 164, 186, 206, 209
Greek, 30, 51, 71, 99, 110, 121, 158
Greenberg, Joseph, 224
Greenland, 80, 95, 103
Greenleaf, Moses, 58
Guajiquero, 165

Haida, 215
Haldeman, Samuel S., 132, 141, 143
Hale, Horatio, 17–18, 204–208, 211, 219
Hamilton, William, 140
Hammer, Joseph von, 104
Harriot, Thomas, 19, 121
Harris, Thaddeus Mason, 95
Harris, T. S., 123
Harrison, William Henry, 76–77
Hartt, Charles Frederic, 213
Harvard College, 56
Haudenosaunee, 19, 35, 38–39, 49, 65–70, 87, 107, 139, 168, 199
Haven, Samuel F., 177
Hawaiian, 120, 206
Hawkins, Benjamin, 59
Hayden, F. V., 186
Hebrew, 51, 55, 66, 93, 106, 121
Heckewelder, John, 80–82; and views of Native linguistic relationships, 69–70; and collaboration with Barton, 85–88, 92, 112; and collaboration with Du Ponceau, 5, 96–104, 107–08, 112, 114, 119–120, 144, 145, 166; and views of Delaware, 80–82, 97–99; and castigation of frontier whites, 107, 156; and Delaware traditions, 69–70, 164, 166; views on orthography, 113, 139; views on

Native pronunciation, 139, 142; views opposed, 148–149, 151–152
Hennepin, Louis, 20, 23
Henry, Alexander, 38
Henry, Charles, 140
Henry, Joseph, 182, 188–189
Herder, Johann Gottfried, 47
Herrod, Goliah (Creek), 174
Hervás y Panduro, Lorenzo, 96
Hewitt, J. N. B. (Tuscarora), 15, 220–221
Hidatsa, 142, 217
hieroglyphics, Egyptian, 42, 166, 171. *See also* graphic practices
Hillis Hadjo (Josiah Francis) (Creek), 75, 89
Historical Society of Michigan, 167
Historical Society of Pennsylvania, 169
Hitchcock, Ethan Allen, 192
Hodgson, William B., 200
Honduras, 165, 198
Hopi, 209
Hopoo, Thomas, 120
Howse, Joseph, 2, 153, 174
Hudson's Bay Company, 9, 135, 153, 207
Humboldt, Alexander von, 61, 88, 91, 94, 95, 103, 106, 154, 174
Humboldt, Wilhelm von, 8, 104, 130, 158–160, 174–177, 199
Hungarian, 200
Hunter, James, 136, 138
Hupa, 206
Huron, 66, 69–70, 75; language of, 5, 19, 27, 30–32, 37–38, 45, 47, 65, 102
Hyde, Jabez, 123

Illinois country, 27, 74
immigration, 13, 183
India, 94, 117, 135, 175
Indian Civilization Act (1819), 90, 107. *See also* civilization program
Indian Peace Commission, 180
Indian removal, 13, 89–90, 114–115, 123–124, 128–132, 138, 163; justification for, 5, 14, 118, 128, 143–144, 148–156, 223; administration of, 189–192

Indian Removal Act (1830), 14

Indian Territory, 133, 138

Indo-European languages, 8–9, 11, 93–94, 95–96, 106–107, 158, 175–176, 182–183, 220

Industrial Revolution, 13, 217

Ingoldesby, Richard, 20–21

inheritance, 9–10, 47; linguistic relationship and, 191, 208–210, 222; conflation of biological and cultural, 9–10, 13, 178, 191, 211; relationship to evolution, 178, 196, 208–210, 223

Interior Department, 186, 223. *See also* U.S. Indian agents

interpreters, 14, 36–37, 39, 60, 61, 68–69; unsuitability for philology, 146, 149

Inuit, 197–199, 212

Iowas, 73, 190; language of, 140, 156, 193

Iroquoian languages, 6, 30, 39, 40, 49–50, 63, 65–71, 78, 102, 133, 221. *See also* specific languages

Iroquois. *See* Haudenosaunee

Irvin, S. M., 140

Irving, Washington, 167

Isham, James, 24

Jackson, Andrew, 131, 139, 156, 160, 191

James, Edwin, 111, 149, 153, 190

Jarvis, Samuel F., 106

Jefferson, Thomas, on language and descent, 2, 51, 57, 77; and vocabulary collection, 51, 57–61; role in expanding federal collection of linguistic information, 2, 51, 71–79; failure to compare vocabularies, 78–79; views on Native linguistic fragmentation, 59–61, 71, 103, 116; views on Indian origins, 59–61, 162; views of humanity's original savagery, 83; views of Native traditions, 84; departure from Federalist Indian policy, 74; and civilization program, 89–90, 117; importance of English to, 116–117; views opposed, 61, 64–65, 71, 92–93, 103

Jenks, William, 90

Johnson, Guy, 40

Johnson v. M'Intosh (1823), 156

Johnson, William, 36, 39, 40

Johnston, George, 170

Johnston, John (trader at Sault Ste. Marie), 145

Johnston, John (U.S. Indian agent at Piqua), 73

Johnston, Susan. *See* Ozhaguscodaywayquay

Jones, Evan, 113, 132

Jones, Peter (Ojibwe), 122, 133, 135, 142, 162–163

Jones, William, 8–9, 90, 92, 93–94, 95–96, 106, 121

Kalispel (Flathead), 101, 174

Kames, Henry Home, Lord, 55–56, 84, 92, 159

Kane, Paul, 140–141

Kansa, 77, 192–193

Kenny, James, 23

Killbuck, John (William Henry) (Delaware), 67, 69

King, Peter, 119

King Philip's War, 116

King, Titus, 21

Kingsbury, Cyrus, 88, 95

Kirkland, Samuel, 68

Klamath, 193, 213, 214

Klaproth, Julius, 104

Knapp, Samuel L., 128–129

Knox, Henry, 68

Knox, Robert, 176

Kootenai, 174

Labadi, Lorenzo, 193

La Condamine, Charles Marie, 43

Laet, Johan de, 20

Lafayette, Marie Joseph Paul, marquis de, 56, 67

Lafitau, Joseph François, 24, 34, 37, 38, 45

La Flesche, Francis (Omaha), 15

Lahontan, Louis Armond de Lom d'Arce, baron, 20, 52

Lakota, 73, 77, 192; language of, 164

Lalemant, Jerome, 30

language, classical views of, 7–8, 41, 52, 142; as subject of interest in U.S. early republic, 11–12, 64, 95–96, 116; and identity, 20–21, 74–75, 116, 217, 223–224; and genealogical theories, 2, 8–9, 10, 16, 34, 49–79, 93–94, 102–104, 158–159, 161–162, 175, 182–219, 221, 223–225; and psychological theories, 2, 5, 8–9, 10, 26–35, 40–48, 52–53, 84–85, 87–88, 89, 96–104, 136, 144, 145–181, 183, 217, 221, 223–225; and convergence of genealogical and psychological views, 33–34, 46–47, 52–54, 99–104, 158–159, 169–181, 185, 210–211, 222–223; and phonetic differences among languages, 19–20, 114, 121–122, 132–144; and theories of race, 4–6, 8–9, 17–18, 48, 93–94, 96–104, 142–144, 158–159, 169–181, 182–185, 198–199, 200, 204–211, 213, 221–222; conventionalism-naturalism debate, 1, 8, 33–34, 41, 44–47, 53, 182–184; theories of evolution of, 26, 40–48, 175–178, 211, 215–217; theories of degeneration of, 83–84, 146–147, 172; theories of fixity of, 6, 94–95, 99–100, 158–159, 169–175; as marker of alliance or hostility, 66, 73–78, 190–194, 196, 212, 213; as marker of nationhood, 72, 114–117, 213; and intermixture, 43, 64–65, 197–198, 202, 206–208, 217; Native views of origin of language, 7, 163; Native views of grammatical organization, 7, 101–102; Native views of beauty and effectiveness of Native languages, 15, 97, 114–115, 162–163. *See also* classification, etymology, orthography, philology, physiology of speech, vocabularies.
language death, 4; federal pursuit of, 15, 178–81, 221, 223; Native view of 15, 178
language revitalization, 224–225
La Peyère, Isaac, 55
Latham, Robert Gordon, 199, 203–04
Latin America, 101, 168, 181, 208, 210. *See also* Mesoamerica; specific countries
Latin, 30, 51
Lawrence, Lorenzo (Dakota), 180

Lawson, John, 24, 35, 66
Lawyer (Nez Perce), 174
learned societies, 12, 81–82, 104–111, 164, 210, 222; and place in early U.S. cultural life, 105, 169, 200, 222; and relationship with federal government, 101, 161, 186–189, 210. *See also* specific societies
Ledyard, John, 57, 92
Leibniz, Gottfried Wilhelm, 52–55, 56
LeConte, John L., 143
Le Gros (Miami), 149
Le Jeune, Paul, 24, 28, 30, 31, 32
Le Mercier, François, 30
Lenni Lenape. *See* Delaware
Le Page du Pratz, Antoine-Simone, 25–26, 34–35, 52
Lepsius, Richard, 141
Lescarbot, Marc, 25
Lewis and Clark Expedition: and linguistic observations, 72, 73–74; and vocabulary collection, 3, 77, 79
Lewis, Meriwether, 72
Liberia, 136
Lieber, Francis, 125–126, 136, 143, 177
Lincoln, Benjamin, 84
lingua franca, 20
linguistic poverty, stereotype of Indian, 22, 25–26, 32–33, 40, 43–44, 48, 85, 150–151
linguistic sovereignty, 4, 114, 117
linguistics (see language, philology)
Linneaus, Carl, 9, 45–46, 50
Little Turtle (Miami), 60, 61, 76
Locke, John, 8, 41–42, 45, 53
Long Expedition, 73, 79, 101
Long, John, 24
Long, Stephen H., 77
Longfellow, Henry Wadsworth, 167
Lost Tribes of Israel, theory of Indian origins, 40, 51, 55, 92, 93, 106, 199; Native view of, 106; compatibility with "Tartar" theory, 93
Louisiana, French colony of, 25–26
Louisiana Purchase, 72
Love, Sloan (Chickasaw), 192
Lowery, George (Cherokee), 114, 124, 129

Madison, James, 59

Maillard, Pierre, 37

Maine, 1, 58, 164.

Malay, languages of, 56, 103; theory of
Indian origins, 143, 203, 221

Maltby, Charles, 193

Mandans, 3, 77, 217

manifest destiny, ideology of, 143, 195–196,
207

Mannahoacs, 73

Maricopas, 217

Marsh, John, 140

Marshall, John, 156

Mason, Otis T., 217–219

Mason, Sophia (Cree), 135

Mason, William, 135, 138

Massachusett, 30, 33, 65; Massachusett
Bible, 29, 116, 117, 135

Massachusetts, 52, 110, 114

Massachusetts Historical Society, 84, 111,
117

materialism, philosophical theory of, 45,
92–93

Mather, Cotton, 33

Matthews, Washington, 142

Maupertuis, Pierre-Louis Moreau de, 5,
100

Maury, Alfred, 176, 198–199, 211

Max Müller, Friedrich, 199, 204

Maya, 166, 196, 198, 208, 221

Mayhew, Experience, 51

McCoy, Isaac, 122, 138

McCulloh, James H., 92, 111

McGillivray, Alexander (Creek),
59, 88

McKenney, Thomas L., 3, 131, 155

Medill, William, 168, 192–193

Meeker, Jotham, 135, 138–139

Menominee 190; language of, 149

Mesoamerica, 86, 103, 197, 208

Mesquakie, 136

metaphor (see eloquence)

métis, 146, 147, 150, 151, 156, 160, 179,
207–208

Mexican Boundary Survey, 209

Mexican Cession, 192

Mexico, 20, 52, 63, 67, 94, 101, 143, 165, 188,
194–196, 209, 215. *See also* Mesoamerica;
New Spain

Miami, 68, 70, 74, 76, 149; language of,
60, 61

Michif, 14

Michaëlius, Jonas, 25

Michigan Territory, 5, 145–46, 148–50, 156,
181, 191

Mide Society (Ojibwe), 170

Mi'kmaqs, 19; language of, 25, 37, 164

Miles, Pliny, 164

Mingo, 74

Minnesota, 179–180

Minnesota Historical Society, 179,
189

miscegenation, 207–208, 209

missions, and Native-language evangelization and education, 5, 26–35, 80–82,
113–144, 156–157, 174, 179–180; language
learning in, 21–22, 26–32, 80–81, 100,
119–121, 174, 179; dependence upon
Native tutors and translators, 22, 28–32,
174, 222; and religious translation, 3, 14,
17, 32–34, 115, 156–157, 174; and ideas of
Native psychological difference, 26–35,
174, 179; and attention to linguistic similarities among Native languages, 33–34,
51–52, 65, 71, 118, 133, 195; and place in
scholars' networks, 5, 39, 11, 12, 39, 56,
62, 67, 80–82, 85–88, 96–108, 112, 121,
151–152, 196, 222; and philological publication, 156–157, 174, 179, 189, 220; post-
1815 expansion of, 115–123, 132–144; and
English instruction in, 115–118, 132, 180;
opposition to, 80, 107, 200; and federal
linguistic collection, 149, 155; linguistic
intermixture in, 21, 133, 152, 206; Congregationalist, 27, 34; Jesuit, 27–34, 53,
63, 87, 95, 111, 122; Anglican, 27, 116,
138; Baptist, 113, 122, 132, 135, 138–139;
Methodist (British), 122, 133, 135–136;
Methodist (U.S.), 119, 120, 138, 142;
Moravian, 5, 27, 39, 56, 62, 80–82, 152,

154; Presbyterian, 27, 32, 117, 119, 140. *See also* American Board of Commissioners for Foreign Missions; New-York Missionary Society

Mississippi River, 18, 47, 59, 77; valley of, 86

Mississippian chiefdoms, 86, 154.

Missouris, 193

Missouri Valley, 72, 186

Mitchell, Samuel L., 61, 106

Mendi, 183

Mobilian Jargon, 24

Modoc, 193, 214; Modoc War, 193–194

Mohawk, 32, 36; language of, 24, 39, 49–50, 66, 93, 102, 116, 133–134

Mohegan, 69, 86–87

Mohican, 25; language of, 34, 66, 68–70, 86, 93, 117–118

Molina, Juan Ignacius, 95

Monacans, 73

Monboddo, James Burnet, Lord, 44–45, 99–100, 127

Mongolic languages, 200, 212

monogenism. *See* evolution; scriptural narrative; polygenism

Monroe, James, 107

Monotunkquanit (Nipmuck), 28

Montaigne, Michel de, 87

Montagnais, 65; language of, 27–28, 31, 33

Montesquieu, Charles Louis Secondat, baron de

Moore, Clement, 93

moral philosophy, 5, 9, 12, 40–48, 52–56, 82–84, 125–127. *See also* environmentalism; stadial theory

Morgan, Lewis Henry, 163, 211–212, 219

Morse, Jedidiah, 118

Morton, Samuel George, 163, 169, 196–198, 200, 202

Morton, Thomas, 51

mounds. *See* archaeology; Mississippian chiefdoms

museums, 186, 217–218, 225

Muskogean languages, 6, 63, 77, 102

Muskogee, 50, 62, 63, 76, 77, 139, 155, 157, 174

mythology. *See* traditions

Nadene languages, 208–209, 224

Nahuatl, 20, 63, 171, 196, 208, 209, 213

Napoleonic Wars, 95

Narragansett, 116; language of, 23, 63

Natchez, 34; language of, 154, 157

National Museum. *See* Smithsonian Institution

National Museum of the American Indian, 225

Native languages. *See* specific languages; language families

Native language texts, as means to publicize and raise support for missions, 120, 189; as means to relieve dependence upon Native tutors, 31–32; Native and white destruction of to maintain cultural purity, 116; place in philology, 111, 157–158, 189; role in language revitalization, 225

nativism, 14–15, 36, 50–51, 66, 74–76, 80, 89, 116, 124; and destroying Native-language texts, 116; and European linguistic difference, 36; and linguistic differences among Native people, 75–76; and opposition to alphabetic literacy, 125

natural history, 9, 12, 45–46, 53–54, 58, 59, 61–63, 83, 166. *See also* biology

natural selection. *See* Charles Darwin, evolution

Navajo (Dene), 7, 193, 204, 213; language of, 208–09

Naxera, Emmanuele, 103

networks, for the collection and production of scholarly knowledge, 11, 58–59, 62, 96, 101–02

Ned, a slave, 79

Nettles, John (Catawba), 86

New England, 20, 23, 24, 27–34, 69, 90, 92–93, 111

New France, 19, 27–38, 53, 66

New Mexico, 79, 193, 204

New Spain, 52. *See also* Mexico

New Stockbridge, 68, 69, 117, 118

New Sweden, 23

New York, 21, 37, 39, 61, 68, 80; ethnographic survey of, 139, 168

New-York Historical Society, 106, 169

New-York Missionary Society, 59, 123

Nez Perce, 157, 174, 193, 214; Nez Perce
War, 214

Nia-man (Colonel Louis) (Abenaki), 99

Nicaragua, 198

Niger-Congo languages, 102, 136; compared with Native languages, 102

Nipmuck, 28

Nootka, 206, 221

Nootka Jargon, 26

North Carolina, 24

Norton, John (Mohawk-Cherokee), 49–50,
69, 139

Nott, Josiah, 199–200, 202

Numic languages, 209, 213

Nuttall, Thomas, 106

Occom, Samson (Mohegan), 69, 87

Odawa, 66, 73, 191; language of, 136, 138,
149. *See also* Anishnaabeg

officials, and knowledge of Native languages, 3, 17, 35–40; and place in
scholars' knowledge networks, 11, 40,
101. *See also* U.S. Indian agents; U.S.
treaty commissioners

Ohio country, 57, 65–70, 73–76, 129

Ojibwe, 38, 68, 156, 178, 190–91, 202–203;
language of, 24, 26, 38, 73, 87, 133, 135,
138–140, 141–142, 145–146, 153, 155, 160,
170–174, 191–192. *See also* Anishnaabeg

Omaha, 192

Oneida, 68, 70; language of, 21, 133–134, 139

onomatopoeia, 206

Onondaga, 7, 36; language of, 21, 63, 69

oratory, 35–40, 81, 108, 109, 152, 164,
169–70, 222

Oregon, 74, 79, 140, 142, 193, 194, 204–08,
209; boundary settled, 168, 184, 188, 192

Oregon Trail, 164, 209

Oriental languages, 104, 189

orthography: Euro-Americans' difficulties
and experimentation with, 17, 112,
113–124, 132–144, 223; Native views of,
113–114, 122–125, 131–136, 138–139

Osage 73, 143, 190–192; language of, 77, 157

Osunkhirhine, Peter Paul. *See* Wzokhilain,
Peter Paul

Oto, 193

Otomi, 103

Ozhaguscodaywayquay (Ojibwe), 145–146,
170, 173

Pachgatgoch, 32

Pacific islands, 143, 204. *See also* Fiji;
Hawaii; Polynesia

Pacific Northwest, 23, 26, 72, 140, 164, 193,
208, 213, 215. *See also* Oregon;
Washington

Pacific Railroad Surveys, 185, 188

pacification, 214–15, 219. *See also* specific
wars

Painted Pole (Messaquakenoe), 74

Paiute, 194, 209, 214

Pallas, Peter S., 56, 62, 96

Panama, 63

Panther (Oglala Lakota), 164

Parker, Nicholson H. (Ga-I-Wah-
Go-Wah) (Seneca), 132

Parkman, Francis, 164

Parrish, Elijah, 93

Pauw, Corneille de, 46, 103, 149

Pawnee, 192; language of, 73, 101,
209

Paxton Boys, 88

Payne, John Howard, 130

Pennsylvania, 39, 54, 61–62, 75, 80, 88,
107–108, 169

Penobscot, 122

Pentecost, story of, 8

Pequot, 93

Percy, George, 19

Perez, Pedro (Quechua), 102

Perkins, Henry, 120

Persian, 9, 94

Peru, 20, 66, 90, 94, 102, 197

philanthropy, as program of cultural eradication, 4, 14; white opposition to, 200.
See also civilization program

philology, and focus on grammar, 5–7,
95–104, 145–181, 210, 215–216, 220–221;
and "philanthropy" and missions,
107–112, 113, 115, 119–124, 133–144, 156–157;
and psychological ideas, 96–104, 136,
144, 145–181, 182, 188, 210; and physiological ideas, 132–144, 159, 162, 176–177, 223;
and genealogical ideas, 77–78, 102–103,
106, 143, 161–162, 182–219, 221; and linguistic essentialism, 6, 10, 17, 99–104,
145–184, 199; and competition with other
ethnologies, 94, 163–164, 181, 182–184,
194–204, 217–219; and ideas of race, 8–10,
15, 96–104, 142–144, 158–159, 169–181,
182–185, 194–200, 222–223; and Native
participation in, 4–7, 15, 101–102, 111,
113–114, 121–122, 145–146, 149–150, 160,
162, 169–170, 173, 174, 179, 185–186,
188–189, 212, 222; and polygenesis,
103–104, 158–159, 161–163, 169; and voluntary association, 12, 81–82, 105–07, 111,
160–161, 200, 222; and phonetic differences among languages, 114, 141,
120–122, 132–144, 210, 215; and print culture in U.S., 3, 12, 17, 105–111, 119–120,
129, 136, 147, 153, 161–170, 172, 179,
185–189, 219, 222; cross-fertilization
among scholarly, missionary, and
administrative forms, 3, 17, 101, 145–147,
156, 179–181, 182–194, 204–219, 222; cross-
fertilization among European and U.S.,
10, 93–94, 104–105, 160, 161, 172, 175–176,
182–183, 198–199, 208–210, 221; differences in U.S. and European practice, 11,
182, 198, 203–208, 221; federal support
for, 12, 142, 147–148, 149, 154–156, 168,
171–174, 180–181, 182–194, 204–219; and
destabilization of ideas about race, 18,
181–184, 204–211, 213, 215–219, 222. *See also*
classification; etymology; orthography

Phoenician, 52, 56

phrenology, 176–77

physiology, 12, 159, 176, 202; of speech, 9,
45–46, 138–44, 201–02, 222

physical ethnology, 9–10, 12; convergence
with language study, 10, 84, 143–44, 162,
176–77; competition with language
study, 18, 90, 94, 169, 177, 183–84,
194–204, 219, 223

Piankeshaw, 76

Pickering, Charles, 201

Pickering, John, and dissemination of philology, 107–108, 110–11, 120, 153, 175; and
uniform orthography, 110, 113, 120–24,
141, 144, 155; and Cherokee grammar,
110, 113, 123, 154; views of Cherokee syllabary, 123, 130–31; attack on Cass, 153;
on popular indifference to philology,
160; role in federal linguistic collection,
155, 161; and cultural prestige, 169

Pickering, Timothy, 68–70

Pidgin Algonquian, 24

pidgins, 24–25, 206–08, 217

Pima, 204, 217

Pirahã, 224

Pitchlynn, Peter (Choctaw), 192

placenames, Native, 57–58

Plains Indian Sign Language, 92

Plateau Penutian languages, 213, 214

polygenesis, of languages, 55–56, 106, 159,
161–162, 212, 215–217; of races, 9–10, 18,
55–56, 63, 143, 168, 169, 196–202, 215;
after Darwinian Revolution, 178; Native
views of, 7, 36, 61, 162–163

Polynesia, 103, 221

Pontiac (Odawa), 66, 171

postcolonialism, of U.S. with respect to
Britain, 11, 62

Potawatomi, 73, 190, 191; language of, 136,
138, 150. *See also* Anishnaabeg

Pott, August Friedrich, 176

Powell, John Wesley, 194, 213–218

Powers, Stephen, 186, 206, 213

Powhatans, 73

Prairie du Chien, 140. *See also* Treaty of
Prairie du Chien (1825)

Prichard, James Cowles, 91–92, 94, 161
Priest, Josiah, 164, 166
Priestley, Joseph, 62
Prix Volney, 160, 166
pronunciation, Euro-American criticisms
    of Natives', 19–20, 44–45, 140–144; Native
    criticisms of Europeans', 19; Native
    views on importance of, 114, 119–120,
    141–142; similarity of European and
    Native, 139; missionary attention to, 30,
    112, 115, 119–120; scholarly attention to,
    44–45, 92, 139–144, 174; racial difference
    and, 139–144, 174
prophecy. *See* nativism
Protestant Reformation, 8
Pueblos, 204, 208, 209, 213, 218

Quapaws, 77, 157
Quechua, 20, 47, 102

race, as category defined differently
    regarding Indians and African
    Americans, 12; as continental grouping of
    people, 9, 46–47, 196–198; as genealogical-
    psychological category that transcended
    the body, 2, 7, 9; as identity, 7, 70; as
    legal category, 6–7, 12; as lineage, 9; as
    something heard, 1, 138–144; as unsettled
    category, 46–48, 50, 65, 78, 197–198, 218;
    ideas of "savagery" or "barbarism" and,
    12–14, 155–156, 169–180, 223; philological
    theories and, 7–8, 93–94, 96–104, 142–
    144, 158–159, 169–181, 182–184, 197–198,
    221–222, 223; as language families, 2,
    17–18, 49–50, 69, 139, 190, 198–199, 211;
    physical classification and, 9, 94, 196–198,
    201; rise of biological understanding of,
    18, 196–204, 222–223; ideas of inheri-
    tance and, 9–10, 47, 178, 208–211; fixity
    of, 10, 95, 169, 223
Rafinesque, Constantine S., 62, 165–167,
    171–172
Rask, Rasmus Christian, 199
Rasles, Sebastien, 30–31, 32, 44, 111
Raynal, Guillaume Thomas François, 46

Reconstruction, 183
Red River, 77
Red Sticks. *See* Creek Civil War; nativism
Reland, Adrian, 52
Renan, Ernest, 176
reservations, 13, 14, 183, 188–194, 214, 218,
    219, 223
Rhode-Island Historical Society, 107
Ridge, John (Cherokee), 78, 129–130, 131
Ridge, John Rollin (Cherokee), 202
Riggs, Stephen R., 119, 122, 132, 179–180,
    189
Rio Grande, 208
Robertson, William, 40, 41, 43, 46–47
Rocky Mountains, 73, 77, 204
Roehrig, F. L. O., 212
Romance languages, 51, 174. *See also* par-
    ticular languages
Romans, Bernard, 55
Rosier, James, 23
Rousseau, Jean-Jacques, 43, 44, 46
Royal Society, 40, 51

Sagard, Gabriel, 30, 31, 44
Sagourrab, Lauurance (Penobscot), 36
Sahaptian languages, 204, 214
Salish languages, 204
Sand Creek Massacre, 180
Sanskrit, 9, 94, 99, 106, 158, 184, 204
Santa Fe Trail, 190, 209
Saponi, 36
Sarcee, 20, 174
Sauks. *See* Sauks and Foxes
Sauks and Foxes, 72, 89, 140, 190, 203
Sault Ste. Marie, 135, 145–146, 150, 153
savagery. *See* stadial theory; essentialism
Say, Thomas, 73, 79
Schaffer, Frederick Christian, 109–110
Schlegel, Friedrich von, 99, 159
Schoolcraft, Henry Rowe, and interdepen-
    dence of philology and missionary work,
    3, 146; and learning Ojibwe, 145–146,
    150; on classification, 73, 189–190, 206;
    on importance of English, 130, 178; on
    orthography, 122, 135, 139–140; on

Cherokee syllabary, 130, 136; on pronunciation of Native languages, 139, 140, 147; and seemingly fixed "Indian mind," 147, 153, 169–174, 181; and degeneration, 146, 150, 172–174; and philology that included traditions and graphic practices, 87, 167–173, 181; and Lost Tribes theory, 146–147, 172–174, 199; and reaching popular audience, 147, 167–168; and informing policy, 167, 189–190; and ethnographic survey of New York, 139, 168, 212; and commission from Congress as ethnologist, 140, 147, 167–173, 189–190, 204; and Smithsonian Institution, 186, 188

Schoolcraft, Jane Johnston (Bamewawagizhikequay), 146–147, 150

Scientific Revolution, 8

Scouler, John, 206

scriptural narrative, 8, 63, 83–84, 90–94; chronology of, 10, 64, 195; challenged, 10, 169, 178, 199–200, 219. *See also* Adam; Babel; Deluge; Lost Tribes of Israel

Scythian, and Native languages, 54; as mother tongue, 55. *See also* Turanian languages

Second Great Awakening, 12

Seminole, 76, 139; Seminole Wars, 76, 139, 203

Semitic languages, 8, 40, 94, 175–176. *See also* Hebrew; Lost Tribes of Israel

Seneca, 109; language of, 122–123, 132–133

Sequoyah (Cherokee), and invention of Cherokee syllabary, 15, 17, 113, 123–133; and possible attempt at a universal Indian alphabet, 133; influence of among missionaries, 133–138

Sergeant, John, 118

Seven Years War, 21, 36, 39

Sewall, Samuel, 56

Shakespeare, William, 87

Shawnees, 70, 74–76; language of, 66–68, 138–139

Shea, John G., 189

shibboleth, story of, 8, 142

Shingwauk (Ojibwe), 170–171, 173

shorthand systems, 135

Shoshone, 193–194; language of, 101, 204, 214

Sibley, John, 73

sign language, 76. *See also* Plains Indian Sign Language

Sigourney, Lydia H., 57

Sinclair, John (Cree), 135

Siouan languages, 63, 136, 140, 186, 189, 190, 209, 220. *See also* specific languages

Sioux, 73, 199; language of, 19, 53, 77–78. *See also* Dakota; Lakota

Six Nations (see Haudenesaunee)

slavery, African American, 12, 175, 195, 200, 219

Slavic languages, 220

Smith, Adam, 43

Smith, Asa Bowen, 157, 174

Smith, Joseph, 164

Smith, Samuel Stanhope, 84

Smithsonian Institution, 141, 163, 177, 182–189, 208, 210–212, 217–219

Society of American Indians, 221

South America, 204, 215

South Carolina, 86, 162

Southwest, North America, 165, 208, 209

Spencer, Herbert, 178

Squier, Ephraim G., 13, 162, 163, 165, 166, 198

stadial theories, and notions of "savagery" or "barbarism" and, 9, 12–13, 40–48, 52, 82–85, 136, 143, 145–156; and views of former Native "civilization," 82, 85–88; Cherokee syllabary and, 115, 125–131, social bases for, 21–22, 47–48; polygenism and, 55–56; convergence with hereditarian ideas, 46–47, 169–180. *See also* evolution; race

Steinhauer, Henry B. (Cree), 135

Stephens, John L., 163

Stickney, Benjamin, 149

Stiles, Ezra, 61

Stith, William, 20

Stockbridge, 34, 66, 68. *See also* New Stockbridge

Stokes Commission, 191

Strahlenberg, Philip John von, 54

Sullivan Expedition, 116

Summerfield, John (Ojibwe), 15, 162

surveyors, and knowledge of Native languages, 3, 24, 58, 66, 140, 185, 206, 211, 213, 214, 219. *See also* specific surveys

Sutter's Fort, 204–205

Swan, Caleb, 76

Swan, James G., 140, 162

Swasen, Tahmunt (Abenaki), 1

syllabaries, 133–139, 144. *See also* Cherokee syllabary; Cree syllabics

Tanner, John, 153

Tartar, languages, 54, 103, 110; theory of Indian origins, 54, 61, 67, 103, 106, 110, 199; Native view of, 163; compatibility with Lost Tribes theory, 93. *See also* Scythian; Turanian

Tatamy, Moses Tunda (Delaware), 32

taxonomy. *See* classification

Tecumseh (Shawnee), 50, 74–76, 89

Teedyuscung (Delaware), 39

Tenino, 213

Tennessee, 129

Tenskwatawa (Shawnee), 50, 74–76, 89

Tesuque, 204

Texas, annexation of, 168, 184; languages of, 188

Thoreau, Henry David, 1

Thornton, William, 84, 121

Tlingit, 209, 215

totemic system, 203, 218

Trade and Intercourse Acts, 72

trade, Native communication strategies in, 16, 21–26; decline of fur trade, 135, 145; expansion of in upper Missouri Valley, 190. *See also* pidgins

traders, and knowledge of Native languages, 2, 3, 8, 9, 21–26, 37, 79, 145; and place in scholars' knowledge networks, 11, 92, 222; and unsuitability as linguistic tutors, 28

traditions, Native, about language, 7; about linguistic change, 49, 69, 87; about linguistic relationships, 49–50, 69–70, 75, 202–203; about writing, 125, 136; about cultural decline, 85–86; about emergence, 7, 163, 195, 209, 212, 224; about migration, 7, 195; Euro-American denigration of, 84, 170, 195; scholars seeking, 49–50, 70, 73, 85–87, 161, 164, 167–173, 188, 195, 218.

Trail of Tears, 132. *See also* Indian removal

translation: as metaphor for colonization, 4, 152; of religious terms, 3–4, 29, 32–34, 81, 89, 152, 156–157, 223; of concepts related to "civilization" and citizenship, 4, 108, 156, 223; of scripture, 28, 50; Native views of, 27–28, 32, 114, 117, 157

travel narratives, 41, 43, 47

treaty councils, 13, 16–17, 35–40, 66, 71, 81, 152, 169–170, 203; views of U.S. treaty commissioners on Native languages, 84, 111, 140, 185, 213; U.S. exploitation of diversity in, 74–76, 223; U.S. discontinuation of, 13, 213. *See also* oratory

Treaty of Doaksville (1837), 192

Treaty of Easton (1756), 39

Treaty of Fort Wayne (1807), 76

Treaty of Greenville (1795), 70

Treaty of New Echota (1835), 132

Treaty of Prairie du Chien (1825), 190, 191

Treaty with the Sioux (1858), 180

Trowbridge, Charles C., 149–150

Trumbull, James Hammond, 172, 210, 212

Tupí-Guaraní languages, 210

Turanian languages, 175, 199–200, 212–213

Turkic languages, 200, 212

Turner, William W., 177, 186–189, 208–209

Tuscarora, 68, 69, 220–221

Tylor, E. B., 209

Umfreville, Edward, 20

Union Theological Seminary, 189

universal grammar, 16, 30, 56, 98, 99, 224

universal language, 8, 32, 121

Unkechaug, 59

Ural-Altaic languages, 212

U. S. Exploring Expedition. *See* Wilkes Expedition

U.S. Indian agents, 51, 59, 73, 122, 130, 140, 190, 193, 194, 196, 207; and learning Native languages, 59, 145–146, 149–150. *See also* Bureau of Indian Affairs; War Department

U.S. Geographical and Geological Survey, 186, 213–14

U.S. Geographical Surveys West of the One Hundredth Meridian, 211

U.S.-Mexican War, 168, 184, 192, 196

U.S. Patent Office, 188

Utah, 204, 209

Uto-Aztecan languages, 209–210, 213, 218

Vai language, 136

"vanishing Indian," trope of, 10, 58

Vater, Johann Severin, 88, 91, 94, 96, 97, 102–103, 104

vernaculars, increasing legitimacy of, 8

Vetromile, Eugene, 122, 139, 199

Virginia, 19, 24, 36, 39

Virginia Algonquian, 19

vocabularies, collection of, 3, 16, 50, 56–66, 101, 154–155, 188–189, 200, 204, 208, 214; comparison of, 62–64, 195, 208–209; logic of, 54; humorous narration of, 165; Native consultants and, 23, 56, 59, 62, 81, 165; reasons for discrepancies in, 92, 141. *See also* etymology

vocal organs, 9, 17, 45–46, 48, 141–143, 147, 176, 184, 201, 211, 223. *See also* physiology of speech; pronunciation

Volney, Contantin-François, 60, 61, 91, 121

Voltaire, François Marie Arounet, 55

voluntary associations. *See* learned societies; missions; philology; specific organizations

Waban (Nipmuck), 28

Wakashan languages, 221

Waler, Isaac (Wyandot), 5

Walker, Alexander, 26

Walla Walla, 156, 193

Wallam-Olum, 166, 171–172

Wampanoag 116; language of, 51

wampum, 36–38, 43, 66, 117. *See also* graphic practices

War Department, 3, 62, 67–70, 101, 107, 117–118, 148–150, 191, 196, 223; and collection of linguistic materials, 71–79, 154–156, 160–161. *See also* U.S. Indian agents

War for Independence, U.S., 39–40, 66, 116

War of 1812, 76, 89, 104, 115, 116, 148

Warren, William W. (Ojibwe), 2, 162–63, 202–203

Washington, George, 56, 57, 66

Washington Territory, 140, 162

Wea, 76

Webster, Daniel, 153

Webster, Noah, 58, 116

Weiser, Conrad, 24, 39

Wells, William, 60, 61

Welsh, 52

West, W. Richard (Southern Cheyenne), 225

western confederacy, pan-Indian, 65–70, 74–76, 89, 90, 95

Western Shoshones, 194, 209

Western Union Telegraph Survey, 214

White, Charles, 46

White Eyes (Delaware), 69

White, John, 24

Whiting, Henry, 153

Whitman Massacre, 193

Whitney, William Dwight, 182–184, 188, 211, 219, 220

Wilde, Richard, 118

Wilkes Expedition, 161, 168, 201, 204–205, 206–207, 208

Williams, Eleazer (Mohawk), 102, 111, 133–134, 160

Williams, Loring S., 133

Williams, Roger, 20, 21, 23, 51, 119

Winnebago 73, 190; language of, 136

Wisconsin, 179

Wodziwob (Paiute), 194

Wolcott, Alexander, 149–150

Wood, William, 20

Worcester, Samuel A., 123

Worcester v. Georgia (1832), chap.4 n. 35

World's Fair Congress of Anthropology,
  215

Wright, Asher, 122, 123, 133

writing. *See* alphabet; graphic practices;
  orthography; syllabary

Wyandot. *See* Huron

Wzokhilain, Peter Paul, 157

Yale College, 61

Yellowstone Valley, 186

Yoghum (Mohican), 66

Yolof, 64

Young, James (Seneca), 133

Yoruba, 188

Yuki, 193

Yuma, 213

Zeisberger, David, and Delaware
  grammar, 5, 96, 108, 153, 157; mixing
  Native languages, 21, 152; on Native oratory, 35, 37, 39–40; on thinking in "Indian,"
  5, 33, 100; role in linguistic collection
  projects, 56, 67, 80–81; support for U.S.
  in War for Independence, 39, 69, 80;
  support for English education, 117

zoology, 53, 201–02. *See also* natural
  history; biology

Zuni, 204